The New
Walt Whitman
Handbook

1854

The New
Walt Whitman
Handbook

Gay Wilson Allen

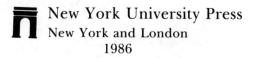
New York University Press
New York and London
1986

Library of Congress Cataloging-in-Publication Data

Allen, Gay Wilson, 1903–
    The new Walt Whitman handbook.

    Bibliography: p.
    Includes index.
    1. Whitman, Walt, 1819–1892.   2. Poets, American—
19th century—Biography.   I. Title.
PS3231.A7   1986   811'.3   85-21423
ISBN 0-8147-0556-1
ISBN 0-8147-0585-5 (pbk.)

To
Arthur Golden
II Kings 2.13

Contents

Introduction 1986

The first *Walt Whitman Handbook* was published in 1946 by Packard and Co. in Chicago, a one-man firm started by Walter Hendricks. In spite of the fact that it contained an embarrassing number of typographical errors (some the fault of the author's inept proofreading and others the failure of the printer to make corrections marked in proof), and amateurish promotion, it was well received and became a standard reference for Whitman's life and works. I had hoped for good reviews in scholarly journals but was surprised that it was prominently reviewed in leading book review magazines. Willard Thorpe said in *The Saturday Review of Literature* that it was a more important book than its modest title indicated. At that time there were no "Handbooks" for American writers, and the *Walt Whitman Handbook* was indeed more encyclopedic than the "Handbooks" for the major British poets.

Mr. Hendricks was so pleased with the reception that he announced a series of similar guides for other American authors with myself as general editor. A few years later under the name of Hendricks House he was taken into partnership by Farrar and Straus in New York. At the time this seemed like good fortune for the *Walt Whitman Handbook*. However, Mr. Hendricks, a man of many talents and ambitions, decided to found a college in Vermont while continuing to publish his books in New York. The arrangement did not work, and Farrar and Straus dissolved the partnership in a couple of years. I resigned as general editor of the projected series of "Handbooks." Attempts to buy back my contract were unsuccessful. I wanted to revise and correct the book before it was reprinted, but that request was refused, and the book was twice reprinted against my wishes.

At this point I agreed to prepare *A Reader's Guide to Walt Whitman* for the Noonday series which Farrar, Straus and Giroux had purchased from another one-man publisher. At the time I hoped this would be a substitute for the *Handbook* which I could not control. Of course much of the information in the two books had to be the same, but I tried in the *Guide* to present it in as different a style and organization as I could, to reduce the duplication. I believe the *Guide* is more literary, but the *Handbook,* in all versions, remains more encyclopedic.

When the copyright to the Packard edition ran out, New York University Press offered to publish a revised edition, which was entitled *The New Walt Whitman Handbook* to distinguish it from the 1946 edition (and the reprints of 1958 and 1962 of Hendricks House). The bibliographical definition of an "edition" is a book printed from a completely new setting of type. *The New Walt Whitman Handbook* was a true second edition—though set with computer tape rather than old-fashioned "hot lead." I found out, however, that even computer operators make errors, and the second edition was not as perfect as I had hoped, though a vast improvement over the original letterpress edition.

On p. xxiv of the 1975 Preface I explained what had been discarded (two whole chapters) and how they had been replaced. That explanation still stands for this 1986 paperback issue. And the chapter on "Literary Technique" remains completely unchanged. The only significant contribution to this subject since 1975 has been C. Carroll Hollis's *Language and Style in Leaves of Grass* (1983). Others have discussed the influence of nineteenth-century oratory on Whitman's "oral style," but Hollis has found some new sources. One of the books on rhetoric which Whitman studied used periods (. . . .) to indicate rhetorical pauses, which the poet used with great effect in his 1855 *Leaves.* This device worked so well that it is surprising Whitman did not continue using it in subsequent editions. Very important, too, was his use of what the textbooks called the *cursus,* a stress to emphasize the end of a *clause,* something like *cadence* to mark the phrase in the theory and practice of French "free verse" poets, mentioned below. Though Hollis's book is not specifically about prosody, it shows why Whitman made use of certain prosodic forms.

Some critics have complained that the "parallelism" I find in Whitman's verse does not explain his music. I do not claim that it does, but Whitman used it as a structural technique, and patterns of repetition are the foundation of any kind of rhythm. One of the strongest evidences that Whitman's verse is musical (when successful) is the attraction he has had for musicians. Well over three hundred musical compositions have been written to interpret his poems. Perhaps the only accurate way to describe Whitman's music would be to score each line, but that would be cumbersome and meaningless for music illiterates.

The Israeli poet Benjamin Krushovski found "two levels of rhythm" in the poetry of Whitman and Mayakovski, which he analyzed in his "Theory and Practice in U. Z. Grinberg's Expressionist Poetry" (see pp. 325-26). Krushovski says Whitman wrote "free verse," but this term is so ambiguous that it has little meaning. When Francis Viele-Griffin declared in his preface to *Joies* (1888–89) that *"Le vers est libre"* he gave a name to a kind of poetry being written in France at the end of the century. (For a history of this subject in English see Mathurin Dondo, *Vers Libre a Logical Development of French Verse,* 1922; in French, E. Dujardin, *Les Premiers Poètes du Vers Libre,* 1922.)

American "free verse" derived from France, as T. S. Eliot explained in the *New Statesman,* March 3, 1917 (Vol. VIII, pp. 518-19), but indirectly from Whitman, who influenced several of the French poets, including Jules Laforgue, whose influence Eliot admitted (see p. 284). The versification of William Carlos Williams, Marianne Moore, and Wallace Stevens has superficial resemblances to Whitman's, but is closer to *vers libre.* Carl Sandburg's verse has often been compared to Whitman's, and he did admire Whitman very much, but it too is closer to *vers libre.* Actually, Whitman's greatest contribution was simply his revolt against the prosodic conventions of the nineteenth century. After Whitman and the Symbolist poets of France, few poets believed that rhyme and meter were necessary, though of course they were still used. My discussion of "Whitman in France" has been enlarged and updated by Betsy Erkkila's *Walt Whitman Among the French* (1980). But when we speak of "influence" we do not mean *imitation.* In fact, Whitman's outright imitators, such as Horace Traubel in America and Edward Carpenter in England, have been dismal failures. No one anywhere has ever been able to draw Whitman's long bow—and sometimes even he was too weak to bend it.

The most important Whitman scholarship during the past decade has been in the field of editing. His major works in poetry and prose had already been edited and published in the *Collected Writings* being published by the New York University Press. In 1977 Edwin Miller added a slender volume to his monumental *Correspondence,* including letters recently discovered, and an inclusive index for all six volumes. Unfortunately, letters and post cards continue to be found, so that Miller's edition may never be absolutely finished.

Few poets have left such a tremendous pile of manuscripts as Whitman. As all students of him know by this time, he was eternally revising, emending, and jotting down thoughts for additional poems. In 1946 Stephen Spender in an essay called "The Making of a Poem" said that there were two kinds of composers of music and poems. Mozart thought out whole symphonies in his head and then transcribed them on paper. "Beethoven wrote fragments of themes in notebooks which he kept beside him, working on and developing them over years." Spender confessed that he created like Beethoven. And so did Walt Whitman. For that reason his notebooks and manuscripts take on a special significance. When the *Collected Writings* was planned, the notebook material was assigned to William White and Edward F. Grier, with the expectation that they would be able to organize it into one chronological edition. No one dreamed that there would be so much of it—nine volumes as it turned out. Finally White was permitted to edit the "Day-books" (diaries) and certain units of notebooks separately. Grier then gathered up all the remaining unpublished notebooks and manuscripts into a single edition. This huge edition, published in 1984, inevitably contains considerable trivia, but also many real gems. For scholarly use it is often difficult to decide what is important—or may be important to some researcher—and what is of no value whatsoever. At any rate, there it is, all the notes and fragments the poet saved and are now carefully preserved in libraries—and in *The Collected Writings of Walt Whitman.*

A *Variorum Edition of Leaves of Grass* is important for many of the same reasons as the poet's notebooks and what Spender called Beethoven's "fragments of themes": trial lines, emendations, cancellations, etc. The original editors of a Variorum Edition for the *Collected Writings* worked on the assumption that only "significant" variants would be recorded. Experts in bibliography scornfully rejected their method, and as a consequence the Variorum remained uncompleted for many years. But in 1979 it was found that, with the help of Arthur Golden, the published variants (that is, printed in the various editions of *Leaves of Grass*) could be put into proper order for publication. Thus the first half of the *Variorum* was published in three volumes in 1980. The "Manuscript Variants" should be ready in another year or two.

Publication of manuscript variants of Whitman's poems will essentially complete the *Collected Writings,* originally planned for an estimated fifteen volumes, but now running to more than twenty. A definitive bibliography is needed, and may eventually be added. Also a scholarly edition of Whitman's Journalism is needed, but is not at present planned for *The Collected Writings.* Meanwhile the various Holloway editions of the journalistic writings will have to serve.

In biography there have been only two significant contributions since 1975: Justin Kaplan's *Walt Whitman: A Life* (1980), a competent and well-written book, containing no new discoveries; and Paul Zweig's *Walt Whitman: The Making of a Poet* (1984). Actually Zweig was more interested in criticism than biography, but he did try—and fail, as others have done—to explain the "miracle" of the mediocre journalist's metamorphosis into the great poet. Nevertheless, this is a book with many critical insights of one poet studying another. Aside from these books, new light on Whitman's family has been revealed in editions of letters written to him by his sister-in-law, Mrs. Jefferson Whitman (*Mattie: Martha Mitchell Whitman,* edited by Randall H. Waldron, 1978), and "Jeff's" letters to Walt, in *Dear Brother Walt: Letters of Thomas Jefferson Whitman,* edited by Dennis Berthold and Kenneth Price (1985). Though these do not change Walt Whitman's own biography, or even his relations with his favorite brother and most loved sister-in-law, they do fill out the biographies of these two important persons in his life.

Critics of Whitman have been active during the past decade, even if they have not produced an epoch-making book. But it is difficult to see a major trend, perhaps because the views are so varied: psychoanalytical, existentialist, structuralist, deconstructionalist—every new fad and old represented, including old-fashioned philological and historical. A glance at the entries for Whitman in the *MLA International Bibliography* for the past five years will reveal that a preponderant amount of the criticism has been devoted to interpreting individual poems. I take this to be a healthy sign of Whitman's continued importance to students of American literature.

In 1975 I ended the chapter on "Walt Whitman and World Literature" with a brief mention of Whitman in the People's Republic of China, and wondered if he had a future there. In perspective, it is not surprising that information on this subject was almost nonexistent, for he had been banned in China for a decade. Even today information in English is scarce, but Mr. Xilao Li, who in 1985–86 is on leave from Peking (or Beijing) University to study American literature in the United States has given me some details, which he will soon publish in two articles.

Modern Chinese literature began in 1919 with the May Fourth Movement, which happened also to be the centennial of Walt Whitman's birth. In the July number of the *Young China* Tian Han published an enthusiastic article on Whitman, whom he called a "common man" whose poems inculcated Democracy and humanism. He advised young Chinese poets to study his poetic expression. Although Wen Yidua was a strong nationalist, he became an admirer of Whitman while studying in the United States, as Guo Morou had done also while studying in Japan, where Whitman was admired, especially by a well-known novelist, Arishima Takeo. Others were also translating and writing about Whitman in the 1920s, including Xu Zhimo, who translated "Song of Myself." Zheng Zhenduo in *The General Outline of Literature* called Whitman a world poet, not just American.

During Japan's attack on China in 1957 Mu Mutian called for poets to save their country, as Du Fu, Milton, Whitman, Hugo, and Shelley had done in time of crisis. In the early '40s several more poets continued translating Whitman, the most important being Ch'u Tunan, who began his translation in jail. Another poet, Ai Qing, became acquainted with Whitman in France, and praised him highly after returning to China. All saw him as "the poet of democracy." Ku Chi compared Whitman and Lincoln as parallels to Mayakovsky and Lenin. (This was before China and Russia began to drift apart ideologically.)

With the founding of the People's Republic in 1949 Chinese writers turned against the United States because it had supported the Nationalist Government. However, Whitman and the "realistic" writers such as Theodore Dreiser, Jack London, Howard Fast, and

Langston Hughes were still accepted. In 1955 China joined the So-viet Union in grandly celebrating the 100th anniversary of *Leaves of Grass*. Whitman was still admired because, it was said, he exposed the hypocrisy of American Democracy. Of course in *Democratic Vistas* he did lament the failure of his country to achieve the ideals of a true democracy, but he was still hopeful for the future.

During the "Cultural Revolution" (1966–1976) all foreign liter-ature was officially banned, including Whitman, but as soon as the ban was lifted in 1978 Ch'u Tanan's *Selections* from Whitman was again republished. Professor Zhao Luorui of Peking University made a trip to the United States to study Whitman, and published a new trans-lation on his return home. Now, under the present modernization program of the Chinese government, Mr. Li says that millions of Chinese are reading Whitman, and a complete translation of *Leaves of Grass* has been announced.

I'm afraid millions do not read Whitman in his own country, un-less we count every school child who reads "O Captain! My Captain!" in a school text. And yet his place in American literature has never been more secure, or his influence on writers more strongly felt. This fact is abundantly evident in *Walt Whitman: The Measure of His Song*, edited by Jim Perlman, Ed Folsom & Dan Campion, a collection of tributes to and criticism of Whitman. As Ed Folsom (co-editor of the *Walt Whitman Quarterly Review*) says in his Introduction, "So palpable is Whitman's presence that it's difficult for an American poet to de-fine himself or herself without direct reference to him." They "argue with him, agree with him, revise, question, reject and accept him. . ." They still feel his presence as he prophesied they would in "Crossing Brooklyn Ferry" over a century ago. If this trend continues, a new edition of this *Handbook* (revised and reset) may be needed in 1995.

This *issue* of *The New Walt Whitman Handbook* is not a new edition, as defined in paragraph four above. Some reviewers of the 1975 edi-tion complained of the price, and the publisher's main purpose in printing this paperback issue is to make it available at a lower price—though printing costs have continued to soar since 1975. Unfortu-nately, this could not be accomplished if the book were completely reset. So as a substitute for a new edition I am using this "Introduc-tion 1986" and the appended "Selected Bibliography 1975–1985" to up-date the 1975 edition. However, even with the reprinting of the book by photo-offset, I am able to correct typographical and other errors. They are mainly in Chapter V, and especially in foreign titles and quotations. Professor Roger Asselineau kindly marked misspellings and misplaced accents for me. Edwin H. Miller, Jerome Loving, William White, Arthur Golden, and Ed Folsom have also reported misprints and suggested improvements in wording. To all of them, and the editor of the NYU Press, Despina P. Gimbel, I am grateful for their expert help.

G. W. A.
Oradell, N. J.
February 1986

Selected Bibliography   1975–1985

EDITIONS

The Collected Writings of Walt Whitman, New York University Press. General Eds. Gay Wilson Allen and Sculley Bradley, 1965–, 22 Vols.

————. *The Correspondence: A Supplement with a Composite Index.* Ed. Edwin H. Miller. (Vol. 6 of *Correspondence*) 1977.

————. *Day-books and Notebooks.* Ed. William White. 3 Vols. 1978.

————. *Leaves of Grass: A Textual Variorum of the Printed Poems, 1855–1892.* Eds. Sculley Bradley, Harold W. Blodgett, Arthur Golden, William White. 3 Vols. 1980.

————. *Unpublished Notebooks and Prose Manuscripts.* Ed. Edward F. Grier. 6 Vols. 1984.

Note: William White edits a quarterly bibliography of Walt Whitman publications in the *Walt Whitman Quarterly Review* as he did previously in the *Walt Whitman Review.*

Leaves of Grass: Facsimile of 1856 Edition. With Introduction by Gay Wilson Allen. Norwood, Pa.: Norwood Editions. 1976.

Walt Whitman: Complete Poetry and Collected Prose. Including *Leaves of Grass* (1955); *Leaves of Grass* (1981–92); *Complete Prose Works* (1892); Supplementary Prose. Ed. Justin Kaplan. The Library of America. New York Literary Classics of the United States, Inc. 1982. 1380 pp.

BIBLIOGRAPHY: CRITICISM

BOSWELL, JEANETTA. *Walt Whitman and His Critics: A Checklist of Criticism, 1900–1975.* Metuchen, N.J.: Scarecrow Press. 1980.

GIANTVALLEY, SCOTT. *Walt Whitman, 1858–1939: A Reference Guide.* Boston: G. K. Hall. 1981.

KUMMINGS, DONALD D. *Walt Whitman, 1940–1975: A Reference Guide.* Boston: G. K. Hall. 1982.

TRANSLATIONS

Ts 'ao Chi Hsuan [Selections from *Leaves of Grass*]. Trans. by Ch'u T'u-nan. Peking: Jen-min wen-hsuch ch'u-pan she [People's Literary Society]. 1955, 1978.

Walt Whitman: Hojas de Hierba. [Selections from *Leaves of Grass*]. Trans. with notes by Leandro Wolfson. Buenos Aires: Ediciones Librarias Fausto. 1976.

CRITICISM: BOOKS (AND CHAPS. IN)

ALLEN, GAY WILSON, "Walt Whitman and Stoicism." In *The Stoic Strain in American Literature: Essays in Honour of Marston La France.* Ed. Duane J. MacMillan. Toronto: University of Toronto Press. 1979. Pp. 43-60.

———. "How Emerson, Thoreau, and Whitman Viewed the Frontier." In *Toward a New American Literary History.* Eds. Louis J. Budd, Edwin H. Cady, and Carl L. Anderson. Durham, N.C.: Duke University Press. 1980. Pp. 111-28.

———. *The Solitary Singer: A Critical Biography of Walt Whitman.* With Preface, 1984. Chicago: University of Chicago Press. 1985. (Paperback edition).

ASPIZ, HAROLD. *Walt Whitman and the Body Beautiful.* Urbana: University of Illinois Press. 1980. [Sources in physiology and health.]

ASSELINEAU, ROGER M. *The Transcendentalist Constant in American Literature.* New York: New York University Press. 1980.

BABIC, LJILJANA. "Walt Whitman in Jugoslavia." *Acta Neophilogica* (Ljubljana), 9 (1976), 9–58. [Translations and criticism in Serbo-Croatian].

BERTHOLD, DENNIS and PRICE, KENNETH, Eds. *Dear Brother Walt: Letters of Thomas Jefferson Whitman*. Kent, Ohio: Kent State University Press. 1985.

BONETTI PARO and MARIA CLARA. *A Recepção Literária de Walt Whitman No Brasil Prīmeiro Tempo Modernista (1919–1929)*. São Paulo: Dissertação de Mistrado área de Teoria Literaria de Lingüistrea e Lingua Orientais da Faculdade de Filosofia Letras e Caências Humanas da U. S. P. 1979.

EITNER, WALTER H. *Walt Whitman's Western Jaunt*. Lawrence, Ks.: University of Kansas Press. 1981.

ERKKILA, BETSY. *Walt Whitman Among the French*. Princeton: Princeton University Press. 1980.

FRANCIS, GLORIA and LOZYNSKY, ARTEM. *Whitman at Auction 1889–1972*. Introduction by Charles E. Feinberg. Detroit: Gale Research. 1978.

FREEDMAN, FLORENCE BERNSTEIN. *William Douglas O'Connor: Whitman's Chosen Knight*. Athens, Ohio: Ohio University Press. 1985.

FRENCH, ROBERT W. "Whitman and the Poetics of Lawrence." In *D. H. Lawrence and Tradition*. Ed. Jeffry Meyers. Amherst: University of Massachusetts Press. 1985. Pp. 91–114.

HARKINS, WILLIAM E. "Walt Whitman and Jaroslav Vrchlicky." In *Xenia Slavica:* Papers Presented to Gojka Ruzičič on the Occasion of his Seventy-Fifth Birthday, 2 Feb. 1969. (SPR 279.) Hague, Holland: Mouton. 1975.

HOLLIS, C. CARROLL. *Language and Style in Leaves of Grass*. Baton Rouge, La.: Louisiana State University Press. 1983.

KAPLAN, JUSTIN. *Walt Whitman: A Life*. New York: Simon & Schuster. 1980. Bantam. 1982.

KRIEG, JOANN P. Ed. *Walt Whitman: Here and Now*. [Papers delivered at the 125th commemoration of *Leaves of Grass* at Hofstra University]. Westport, Conn.: Greenwood Press. 1985.

LOVING, JEROME. *Emerson, Whitman and the American Muse*. Chapel Hill: University of North Carolina Press. 1984.

———. *Walt Whitman's Champion: William Douglas O'Connor*. College Station, Tx.: Texas A&M University Press. 1977.

LOZYNSKY, ARTEM, Ed. *The Letters of Dr. Richard Maurice Bucke to Walt Whitman*. Detroit: Wayne State University Press. 1977.

MARKI, IVAN. *The Trial of the Poet: An Interpretation of the First Edition of "Leaves of Grass."* New York: Columbia University Press. 1976.

MARTIN, BICKMAN. *The Unsounded Centre: Jungian Studies in American Romanticism.* Chapel Hill: University of North Carolina Press. 1980. [Discusses Whitman].

MARTIN, ROBERT K. *The Homosexual Tradition in American Poetry.* Austin: University of Texas Press. 1979.

MENDELSON, MAURICE. *Life and Work of Walt Whitman: A Soviet View.* Trans. by Andrew Bromfield. Moscow: Progress Publications. 1976.

MILLER, JAMES E. *The American Quest for a Supreme Fiction: Whitman's Legacy in the Personal Epic.* Chicago: University of Chicago Press. 1979.

NAMBIAR, O. K. *Mahayogi Walt Whitman: New Light on Yoga.* Bombay: Jeevan Publications. 1978.

PEARLMAN, JIM, FOLSOM, ED, and CAMPION, DAN, Eds. *Walt Whitman: The Measure of His Song.* Minneapolis: Holy Cow Press. 1981. [Tributes and critical comments on Whitman].

PALLIKUNNEN, A. G. *Eastern Influence on Whitman's Mysticism, and Other Essays in Literature.* Alwar, India: Pontifical Institute Publications. 1975.

RENNER, D. K. "Tradition for a time of Crisis: Whitman's Poetic Stance." In *Poetic Prophecy in Western Literature,* Ed. Jan Wojcèk and Raymond-Jean Frontain. Madison, N.J.: Fairleigh Dickinson University Press. 1984. Pp. 119-30.

SALSKA, AGNIESZKA. *Walt Whitman and Emily Dickinson.* Philadelphia: University of Pennsylvania Press. 1985.

SHIMIZU, HARUO. *Whitman no Shin-sho Kenkyu.* Tokyo: Shinazaki. 1984. [A study of Whitman's imagery—text in Japanese].

WALDRON, RANDALL H., Ed. *Mattie: Letters of Martha Mitchell Whitman.* New York: New York University Press. 1978.

WARREN, JAMES PERRIN. " 'The Free Growth of Metrical Laws': Syntactic Parallelism in 'Song of Myself.' " *Style* 18 (Winter 1984), 27-42.

WHITE, WILLIAM, Ed. *The Bicentennial of Walt Whitman: Essays from the Long-Islander* [annual Whitman numbers]. Detroit: Wayne State University Press. 1976.

―――. *1980: Leaves of Grass at 125: Eight Essays.* Detroit: Wayne State University Press. 1980.

WOODRESS, JAMES, Ed. *Critical Essays on Walt Whitman.* [Fifty-nine essays from Emerson (1955) to present; written for this volume: Jerome Loving, "Emerson, Whitman, and the Paradox of Self-Reliance," pp. 306-19; Roger Asselineau, "Nationalism vs. Internationalism in *Leaves of Grass*," pp. 320-29.] Boston: G. K. Hall. 1983.

Preface

When I proposed a "Handbook" for Walt Whitman to a major textbook publisher in 1944, I was told that such works for major British authors were needed, but not yet for an American poet. However, when I suggested the idea to Professor Walter Hendricks, who had recently started the venturesome Packard and Company in Chicago (later Hendricks House in New York), he offered me a contract without hesitation. Except for his faith and foresight, the *Walt Whitman Handbook* might not have been written; but his confidence was justified, for the time had indeed arrived for such a reference and critical guide to Whitman. To my great surprise, the book was favorably reviewed in the *New York Times Book Review, Saturday Review of Literature*, and the *New York Herald Tribune Book Review*. Of course I expected reviews in scholarly journals, but they were better than I had dared hope. And the book sold well enough to justify two reprintings—unfortunately without corrections or revisions.

It is now possible, nearly a generation later, to publish a complete and thorough revision. Every page of this edition has received at least minor emendations, and every chapter except IV (formerly V) has been greatly augmented or entirely rewritten. Chapter I has been brought up to date and extended. Major biographies were published in the 1950s, and important biographical interpretations since then, such as Edwin H. Miller's *Whitman's Poetry: A Psychological Journey*. Chapter II needed considerable rewriting because important texts have been edited in recent years. Scholars also now count *six* editions of *Leaves of Grass* instead of nine or ten as formerly.

I have discarded former chapters III and IV and combined the subject matter in a new approach. The social and political ideas of former Chapter III have been used to introduce the new Chapter III on Whitman's intellectual world; and in the new Chapter I eliminated the pedantic definitions and discussions of the "Great Chain of Being" and "Pantheism." Though "Chain of Being" concepts are certainly in Whitman's poems, the poet never used the term and may have been unaware of the concept. As for "Pantheism," that term is too handy and familiar in Whitman criticism to be avoided altogether, but I have tried to approach his cosmic and theistic assumptions and metaphors through the contemporary science he knew (Joseph Beaver's *Walt Whitman, Poet of Science* should be better known), through his familiarity with French rationalistic theism, and concepts of cosmic evolution (partly original) for which there seem to be illuminating parallels in the writings of the late Pierre Teilhard de Chardin. Hindu scholars have also discovered Vedantic parallels in *Leaves of Grass*, and I have made some use of these, though I personally find Whitman's "mysticism" more like Teilhard's cosmotheism.

The chapter on Whitman's literary techniques (now Chapter IV) I have let stand. Recently in a dissertation at the University of California (at Davis) Charles T. Kollerer used modern linguistic analysis and musical notation in a new approach to Whitman's prosody. He very kindly loaned me his unpublished manuscript, and I admit that his method may lead to subtler ways of analyzing and explaining Whitman's poetic techniques. But the basic Hebraic "thought-rhythm" will, I believe, remain, though Dr. Kollerer, or others, may supplement it. Until these new approaches are published my old chapter may still be useful, key portions of which have been reprinted in anthologies of poetic theory and Whitman criticism and are widely used.

But for Chapter V (former Chapter VI) there was no question of the new information needed. Whitman was already a major world poet in 1946, and since then there have been many new translations in almost every country in the world (except the new nations), and important criticism in several languages. Some of this information was given in 1955 in my edition of *Walt Whitman Abroad*, but the celebration of the Centennial of *Leaves of Grass* that very year outdated parts of that book. Chapter V will be found to be greatly enlarged and, I hope, enriched. To a considerable extent the state of the world is reflected in foreign criticism of Whitman—cf. Pablo Neruda's. Of course all bibliographies have been updated, and the notes extended. To eliminate some notes I have placed page numbers in square brackets [thus] for consecutive analysis of a single title.

In addition to the many friends and scholars who made the first edition possible, I am indebted to many new ones for this revised edition, including my colleague Edwin H. Miller; all editors of the new *Collected Writings of Walt Whitman* (Thomas L. Brasher, Floyd Stovall, Harold W. Blodgett, Sculley Bradley, Edwin Miller, Edward Grier, Herbert Bergman, and William White); Arthur Golden, editor of the *Blue Book*; Fredson Bowers, editor of *Whitman's Manuscripts (1860)*; Malcolm Cowley, for provocative and stimulating criticism; Charles S. Grippi, for his dissertation on Whitman in Italy; Roger Asselineau, for all his excellent Whitman publications, including his recent edition of *Walt Whitman in Europe Today* (and to the contributors); Sholom Kahn in Jerusalem for his critical ideas and invaluable information about Whitman in Hebrew; the late Kornei Chukovsky in Russia; Juliusz Zuławski in Poland; Ladislas Orszagh in Hungary; Om Prakesh Sharme, T. R. Rajasekharaiah in India; in Japan William Moore, Shigetaka Naganuma, Iwao Matsuhara, Norihiro Nabeshima, and Shigenobu Sadoya; Fernando Alegría at Stanford; V. K. Chari in Canada (formerly India); Peter Mitilineos, translator of Jannaccone; Stephen Stepanchev for information about Whitman in Slavic countries; and Charles E. Feinberg, the perennial friend of Whitman scholars. My wife, Evie Allison Allen, has translated, given bibliographical assistance, and read proof. The Managing Editor of the New York University Press, Robert Bull, and his able associate Editor, Despina Papazoglou, have aided the project at all stages, with patience, kindness, and technical skill. I am particularly grateful to Arthur Golden for sharing his bibliographical expertise and his assistance in reading proof.

For permission to quote several lines from Pessoa's "Saudação a Walt Whitman" I am indebted to Edwin Honig, the translator, and the Swallow Press. My gratitude for the "Carybé" drawing reproduced on the jacket and a second pen-sketch goes to the Brazilian painter Hector Júlio Páride Bernabó, and to Simona and Frederic Tuten for locating this famous artist in Bahĭa, Brazil, and securing his written consent for me.

G. W. A.
ORADELL, N. J.
February 1975

Chronological Table

Significant Events in Whitman's Life

1819   Born May 31 at West Hills, Huntington Township, Long Island. (Now 246 Walt Whitman Rd., Huntington Station, N.Y. 11746.)

1823   Family moved to Brooklyn.

1825   Lafayette visited Brooklyn, July 4—one of the poet's most cherished memories.

1825-30   Attended public school in Brooklyn. Family frequently shifted residence in city.

1830-31   Office boy in lawyer's office, then doctor's; probably quit school at this time.

1831-32   Worked in printing offices, began to learn the trade. Printer's apprentice on *Long Island Patriot*.

1832   Summer. Worked at Worthington's printing establishment.

1832   Fall—to May 12, 1835. Worked as compositor on *Long Island Star*.

1833   The Whitman family moved back to the country.

1835   May 12th—till May, 1836. Worked in printing offices in New York City.

1836-38 Taught in various schools on Long Island. Participated in debating societies.

1838   Spring—Spring, 1839. Edited *Long-Islander* in Huntington.

1839-41 Returned to teaching on Long Island.

1840   Fall. Campaigned for Van Buren.

1841   May. Went to New York and worked as compositor for *The New World*.

1842   Edited for a few months *The Aurora* and *The Tattler*.

1843   Spring. Edited *The Statesman*.

1844   Summer. Edited *The New York Democrat*.

1844   October. Worked on *The New York Mirror*.

1841-48 Contributed to several prominent New York journals: *Democratic Review, Broadway Journal, American Review, New York Sun, Columbian Magazine*.

1846-47 Edited the Brooklyn *Daily Eagle*.

1848   Quit (or was discharged from) editorship of *Eagle* in January. February 11 left, with brother Jeff, for New Orleans to take up editorial position on the *Crescent*. First number of *Crescent*, published March 5, contained Whitman's poem "Sailing the Mississippi at Midnight." May 24 resigned position, sailed to St. Louis May 27. Arrived home June 15. Back in Brooklyn, became editor of the *Brooklyn Freeman*, first number issued Sept. 9, 1848, office burned that night.

1849   In spring the *Freeman* became a daily. In April Whitman was also conducting a printing office and bookstore on Myrtle Avenue—still listed in the *Brooklyn Directory* for 1851. Resigned editorship Sept. 11, Free-Soilers having joined regular party.

1851-54   Built houses in Brooklyn. Addressed Brooklyn Art Museum, March 31, 1851.

1855   First edition of *Leaves of Grass* published by the author, on or near July 4; Father died July 11. Fowler and Wells were agents for the book. Conway first to visit the poet. Emerson wrote his "greetings" July 21.

1856   Second edition of *Leaves of Grass*, published sometime between Aug. 16 and Sept. 12, Fowler and Wells unacknowledged publisher. In November Alcott and Thoreau visited the poet—Emerson the following year.

1857-59   Edited Brooklyn *Times*; unemployed by summer of 1859. Frequented Pfaff's Restaurant, a Bohemian gathering place.

1860   Third edition of *Leaves of Grass* published in Boston by Thayer and Eldridge; rejected Emerson's advice to omit "Children of Adam" poems.

1861   Thayer and Eldridge failed and the plates for the third edition were secured by a dishonest publisher, who printed and sold pirated copies for a number of years. Soon after the bombardment of Fort Sumter, April 18, Whitman recorded in his diary a moral and physical dedication. About this time deserted Pfaff's and Bohemian friends.

1862   Dec. 14 read brother George's name in list of wounded and went immediately to the war front in Virginia to find him. In Washington began daily visits to soldiers in hospitals.

1863-64   Worked in field and army hospitals. Beginning of friend-

ship with O'Connor and Burroughs.
Health broke down in mid-summer of '64 and he returned
to his mother's home in Brooklyn for six months.

1865-66   In January 1865 appointed clerk in Indian Bureau of the
Department of the Interior, discharged by James Harlan on
June 30, but in July became clerk in Attorney General's
office. *Drum-Taps* issued in 1865; *Drum-Taps* with annex
called *Sequel to Drum-Taps* published in fall, containing
"When Lilacs Last in the Dooryard Bloom'd and Other
Pieces." After Whitman's discharge from clerkship,
O'Connor began writing his "vindication," published in
1866 as *The Good Gray Poet.*

1867   Fourth edition of *Leaves of Grass.* Reviewed by William
Rossetti. Burroughs published first biography, *Notes on
Walt Whitman as Poet and Person.*

1868   Rossetti edited selections from *Leaves of Grass*; well received in England. O'Connor published *The Carpenter,*
presenting in thin disguise Whitman as a modern Christ.

1869   Mrs. Anne Gilchrist became acquainted with Whitman's
poetry.

1870   Mrs. Gilchrist published "An English-woman's Estimate of
Walt Whitman" in the Boston *Radical Review.* First edition of *Democratic Vistas,* incorporating essays published
in the *Galaxy* during 1867-68.

1871   Fifth edition of *Leaves of Grass.* First edition of *Demo-
cratic Vistas,* incorporating essays published in the *Galaxy*
during 1867-68; *Passage to India* pamphlet.
Delivered "After All, Not to Create Only" ["Song of the
Exposition"] at opening of the American Institute of New
York.
Swinburne greeted Whitman in *Songs Before Sunrise;*
Tennyson wrote fraternal letters; Rudolf Schmidt trans-
lated *Democratic Vistas* into Danish.
Mrs. Gilchrist wrote a proposal of marriage and Whitman
diplomatically declined in letter of November 3.

1872 Delivered "As a Strong Bird on Pinions Free" ["Thou Mother with thy Equal Brood" in 1881 ed.] at Dartmouth College commencement. Thérèse Bentzon (Mme. Blanc) published critical article in *Revue des Deux Mondes*, June 1.
Quarrel with O'Connor over Negro suffrage, and perhaps personal matters.

1873 Paralysis in February after preliminary spells of dizziness for over a year. Began living with brother George in Camden, New Jersey. Mother died May 23.

1874 "The Song of the Universal" read at Tufts College commencement by proxy.
Discharged during midsummer from position in Washington, which had been filled by a substitute since Feb. 1873. In "Prayer of Columbus" the poet identified himself with the "battered, wrecked old man."

1876 Wrangle in United States over Whitman's neglect started by article published in Jan. 26 *West Jersey Press*, which Robert Buchanan quoted in London *Daily News*, March 13.
Spring to autumn spent at Timber Creek.
Celebrates 1876 Centennial with publication of poems and prose in two volumes: *Leaves of Grass* (I), *Two Rivulets* (II), with "Passage to India" annex. Rossetti and Mrs. Gilchrist sold many copies in England; the money and recognition aided poet's recovery.
In September Mrs. Gilchrist arrived in Philadelphia and rented a house, which Whitman visited frequently.

1877 January, spoke in Philadelphia on Tom Paine's anniversary. February, New York friends gave a reception and lionized the poet. Visited Burroughs on the Hudson. In May, Edward Carpenter arrived from England. Dr. R. M. Bucke, recently appointed head of asylum at London, Ontario, visited Whitman and became close friend.
Burroughs published "The Flight of the Eagle" in *Birds and Poets*.

1878 Health better. Repeated excursion up Hudson.

1879   April 14 gave Lincoln lecture in New York (given each
         year for thirteen years).
         Sept. 10 started trip West—visited St. Louis (where favorite
         brother, Jeff, lived), Topeka, Rockies, Denver.

1880   Returned from western trip in January.
         April, delivered the Lincoln Memorial Address in Boston.
         June, went to Canada to visit Dr. Bucke. Took boat trip up
         St. Lawrence.

1881   Sixth edition of *Leaves of Grass*, published in Boston by
         Osgood (title-page bears 1881–82).

1882   February, the Society for the Suppression of Vice claimed
         the Osgood edition immoral. May 17 Osgood ceased publi-
         cation, gave plates to Whitman. After his own "Author's
         Edition" in Camden, Whitman found a new publisher in
         Rees Welsh and Company, Philadelphia (soon succeeded
         by David McKay). Edition of 3,000 copies sold in one day.
         Leaves of Grass now practically complete, subsequent
         editions being reprints with annexes.
         Pearsall Smith, wealthy Philadephia glass merchant and
         prominent Quaker, became friend.
         Specimen Days and Collect published in autumn.

1883   Dr. Bucke published his biography with Whitman's
         collaboration.

1884   Sale of the Philadelphia issue enabled Whitman to buy a
         house in Mickle Street, Camden, New Jersey; March 26
         moved in, remained until his death.
         June, Edward Carpenter made a second visit.
         New friends: Traubel, Harned, Talcott Williams, Donald-
         son, Ingersoll, others.

1885   Sun stroke in July. Walking became difficult and many
         friends, headed by Donaldson, bought a horse and phaeton
         for Whitman.

1886   Royalties from 1881 edition dwindled. *Pall Mall Gazette* promoted fund which resulted in a New Year's present of eighty pounds. Boston friends made up a purse of $800 for a cottage on Timber Creek (never built).

887   The Lincoln lecture at Madison Square Theatre attended by many notables—took in $600. Poet sculptured by Sidney Morse and painted by Herbert Gilchrist and Thomas Eakins.

888   Another paralytic stroke, early in June.
       Managed to finish *November Boughs*.

889   "House-tied."

891   Last birthday dinner in Mickle Street home. Dec. 17, chilled, took pneumonia.

892   Managed to publish "authorized" issue of *Leaves of Grass*, which the literary executors (Traubel, Harned, Bucke) were commanded to perpetuate.
       Died March 26, buried in prepared tomb in Harleigh Cemetery, Camden, N.J.

Illustrations[*]

Chapter I

The Growth of Walt Whitman Biography

When I read the book, the biography famous,
And is this then (said I) what the author calls a man's life?
And so will some one when I am dead and gone write my life?

—"When I Read the Book"

INTRODUCTION

Leaves of Grass is one of the most personal, and in many ways the most naively frank, collections of poetry ever written. From 1855 to 1892, Walt Whitman himself did everything in his power to foster the literary illusion that the poet and the book were identical.

I celebrate myself, and sing myself,

he announced in his song of himself, adding later in "So Long,"

Camerado, this is no book,
Who touches this touches a man.

It is hardly an exaggeration to say that after the 1855 edition, Whitman's every act, gesture, manner of dress, and creative expression was calculated to achieve this literary purpose. The poetic theory which he enunciated in the '55 Preface was his own personal ambition. The bard who was "to be commensurate with a people," to "incarnate" its geography and life, and to span his country from east to west, was of course himself. The poet who believed that "All beauty comes from beautiful blood and a beautiful brain" was confessing a personal ambition—even a dedication of himself to an ideal—to live and to record a beautiful life.

1

So devoutly did Walt Whitman desire to live the ideal life en visioned in *Leaves of Grass*—and so sincerely did he believe in his success—that in the first biographies, which he helped to write, the illusion of the complete identity between the man and his book was further strengthened and developed (we might say the thesis documented), thus postponing, almost thwarting, a critical biography for many years. It was inevitable, therefore, that most biographers would search for the details of the poet's life in the confessions of his poems—and this is the secret of his perennial fascination. But *Leaves of Grass*, however autobiographical it may be, is also a work of art, which is to say the product of a creative imagination, and to search for biographical fact in its pages is to write literary criticism rather than the history of a man's life. Yet, it is not possible, even less so than with most poets, to separate the criticism of his work from the biography of his life.

Walt Whitman biography has grown, therefore, not by the simple accumulation of newly discovered and more exact information concerning his daily goings and comings, but by new and fresh insight into his motives, wider knowledge of the intellectual world in which he lived and moved, clearer understanding of the meanings which his poetry and prose have had for himself and for the many critics who have interpreted him. Moreover, his biography is no longer simply the story of Walt Whitman, or of a remarkable book which he wrote. He has become a legend, a national symbol, even a pivotal figure in an international literary movement. To tell the story of his biographical growth is also to tell much of the story of the growth of modern literature and thought. For this reason, what critics and biographers have thought of Walt Whitman and the theories on which they have based their interpretations of him, is fully as important as the literal facts of his life. After discovering when and why the various interpretations arose, however, the student of Whitman should be better able to sift fact from legend. Furthermore, if definite trends are discovered in the evolution of these biographies, perhaps future stages of Whitman scholarship may be anticipated—even aided and hastened.

THE TESTIMONY OF FRIENDS:
O'CONNOR, BURROUGHS, BUCKE

The circumstances under which Walt Whitman's friends began to write about his life profoundly affected the course and development of his biography. On June 30, 1865, he was dismissed from his government clerkship by the Secretary of the Interior, Mr. James Harlan, who had discovered that his employee was the author of *Leaves of Grass*, a book which Mr. Harlan thought to be "full of indecent passages," meaning of course the sex poems ("Enfans d'Adam" and "Calamus" in the 1860 edition). One of the poet's devoted friends, William Douglas O'Connor, a government clerk, several months later published a bitter denunciation of Harlan and "a vindiction" of Whitman which he called *The Good Gray Poet.*[1]

Though hardly to be called a biography, this pamphlet laid the foundation for the first legends in Whitman biography and influenced many succeeding interpretations in Europe as well as America. The personality described by O'Connor sprang from the poet's avowed purposes in *Leaves of Grass* fully as much as from O'Connor's personal love and admiration. This personality, familiar to "thousands of people in New York, in Brooklyn, in Boston, in New Orleans, and latterly in Washington [is] . . . a man of striking masculine beauty—a poet—powerful and venerable in appearance; large, calm, superbly formed; oftenest clad in the careless, rough, and always picturesque costume of the common people."[3] There is something almost mythical in the description of the "head, majestic, large, Homeric, and set upon his strong shoulders with the grandeur of ancient sculpture." Reverently O'Connor continues:

I marked the countenance, serene, proud, cheerful, florid, grave; the brow seamed with noble wrinkles; the features, massive and handsome, with firm blue eyes; the eyebrows and eyelids especially showing that fulness of arch seldom seen save in the antique busts; the flowing hair and fleecy beard, both very gray, and tempering with a look of age the youthful aspect of one who is but forty-five; the simplicity and purity of his dress, cheap and plain, but spotless, from snowy falling collar to burnished boot, and exhaling faint fragrance; the whole form surrounded with manliness, as with a nimbus, and breathing, in its perfect health and vigor, the august charm of the strong.[4]

Almost everyone who knew Walt Whitman intimately was conquered by his magnetic presence, and there is no reason whatever to doubt the sincerity of O'Connor's enthusiatic description; nevertheless, we have here the first of the superman legends. "We who have looked upon this figure, or listened to that clear, cheerful, vibrating

voice, might thrill to think, could we but transcend our age, that we
had been thus near to one of the greatest of the sons of men."

O'Connor is also the first source for some of the typical anec-
dotes. "I hold it the surest proof of Thoreau's insight, that after a
conversation, seeing how he incarnated the immense and new spirit
of the age, and was the compend of America, he came away to speak
the electric sentence, 'He is Democracy!' " The names of Whitman
and Lincoln are linked by the story of the President's seeing the poet
walk by the White House, inquiring who he was, and remarking
thoughtfully, "Well, *he* looks like a MAN!" The anecdote of
Lafayette's passing through Brooklyn and by chance holding the
future poet in his arms sounds like an omen of his future destiny.
And at the time he wrote the essay, O'Connor could say of Whitman,
as of a Modern Christ:

He has been a visitor of prisons; a protector of fugitive slaves; a
constant voluntary nurse, night and day, at the hospitals, from the
beginning of the war to the present time; a brother and friend
through life to the neglected and the forgotten, the poor, the degraded, the criminal, the outcast; turning away from no man for his
guilt, nor woman for her vileness.[7]

On the theory that Whitman's poems grew out of the "great
goodness, the great chastity of spiritual strength and sanity" of this
saintly life, no vileness can possibly be found even in the frankest of
them, though O'Connor admits that in all some eighty lines in the
entire book might be objectionable to the ultra-prudish and
squeamish. But he maintains that if these were expurgated, far
greater portions of the Bible, the *Iliad* and the *Odyssey*, Shakespeare,
Dante, and other masterpieces in world literature would also have to
be rejected.

On the one hand *Leaves of Grass* is elevated to an eminent
position in the greatest literature of all time, and on the other hand it
is praised as "a work purely and entirely American, autochthonic,
sprung from our own soil; no savor of Europe nor of the past, nor of
any other literature in it."[26] Such of course was the poet's own
ideal, and we have here the first glorified confirmation of Walt
Whitman's literary fame on his own grounds.

John Burroughs, a friend of the same period, no less ardent but with more reserved emotions and intellect, published his first book on Whitman two years later, 1867. *Notes on Walt Whitman as Poet and Person* was a collaboration, for parts of it were actually written by Whitman himself and he freely edited the whole manuscript.[2] Both Burroughs and Whitman have been severely blamed by some commentators for this fact, but John Burroughs was then a young man taking his first steps in writing, more or less under Whitman's tutelage, and he doubtless thought that the poet's help made the book more accurate and authoritative. Nevertheless, Burroughs's *Notes* presented interpretations which must have been thoroughly congenial to Whitman himself and should be considered, like Burroughs's later studies and Bucke's more systematic account, as semi-autobiography.

The *Notes* is divided into two parts: the first a study and interpretation of *Leaves of Grass*, including a defense of the author's theory and expression of Beauty and Personality; and the second, a personal biographical sketch, followed by a criticism of *Drum-Taps*. The book is, therefore, mainly an exegesis, more or less "official," although the manner in which the author exploits his own country origin gives it an informal, personal tone which sounds completely original. But considering the origin of the *Notes*, it is significant that Burroughs confesses: "I am not able, nor is it necessary, to give the particulars of the poet's youthful life."[79] In fact, he is convinced that the "long foreground" mentioned in Emerson's famous "greeting" letter of 1855, "that vast previous, ante-dating requirement of physical, moral, and emotional experiences, will forever remain untold."[83] However, the Lafayette episode is given, and we are also told that "From the immediate mother of the poet come, I think, his chief traits."[79] Here is the basis, but not yet the elaboration, of the theory soon to be developed by Bucke and Whitman himself that the poet's genius was a product of his ancestry and environment.

The mythical account given of his travels may have been due either to Whitman's vagueness concerning his New Orleans period or to Burroughs's drawing erroneous factual conclusions from the literary theory that the poet must first absorb his country, sounding every experience, before expressing it in verse. At any rate, the reader is told that in 1849 Whitman began traveling, and is given the impression that he spent one year in New Orleans (actually only a little over two months) and another wandering around in the West. "He saw Western and Northwestern nature and character in all their phases, and probably took there and then the decided inspiration of his future poetry. After some two years, returning to Brooklyn. . . ."[82] It is an ironical commentary that when Whitman actually did visit the West in 1879—exactly thirty years later!—he reannounced in *Specimen Days:* "I have found the law of my own poems." Already in Burroughs's *Notes* biographical fact and poetic imagination have become almost inseparably intergrown, perhaps for the very reason that the poet, "Like Egypt's lord he builds against his form's annihilation. . . . Strange immortality! For in this book Walt Whitman, even in his habit as he lived, and ever gathering hearts of young and old, is to surely walk, untouched by death, down through the long succession of all the future ages of America."[73]

The *Notes* contains also the theory on which all the early friends of *Leaves of Grass* were to justify and explain the style which most of the first readers found obscure: "The poet, like Nature, seems best pleased when his meaning is well folded up, put away, and surrounded by a curious array of diverting attributes and objects."[43]

The first complete life of the author of *Leaves of Grass* was Dr. Richard Maurice Bucke's *Walt Whitman*, 1883. Whitman told Edward Carpenter that he himself "wrote the account of my birthplace and antecedents which occupies the first twenty-four pages of the book."[3] So highly did he think of this collaborated biography that in 1888 he asked Bucke not to revise it but to *"let it stand just as it is,"*[4] and on his seventy-second birthday he defended this work as the final word on his life: "I thoroughly accept Dr. Bucke's book."[311]

The poet who had announced at thirty-seven:

My tongue, every atom of my blood, form'd from this soil, this air,
Born here of parents born here from parents the same, and their
    parents the same.["Song of Myself," Sec. 1]

and who prided himself that,

Before I was born out of my mother generations guided me,
My embryo has never been torpid, nothing could overlay it.[Sec. 44]

has now had time to investigate his genealogy and to draw definite conclusions regarding his ancestry. With the aid of Savage's *Genealogical Dictionary* he thought he could trace his lineage back to Abijah Whitman in seventeenth-century England, whose son, the Rev. Zechariah Whitman, came to America on the *True-Love* in 1640, or "soon after."[5]

Though the ancestry is presented as sound on both sides, the Whitmans as "a solid, tall, strong-framed, long-lived race of men" and the Van Velsors as "a warm-hearted and sympathetic" people, we read that

There is no doubt that both Walt Whitman's personality and writings are to be credited very largely to their Holland origin through his mother's side. A faithful and subtle investigation (and a very curious one it would be) might trace far back many of the elements of *Leaves of Grass*, long before their author was born. From his mother also he derived his extraordinary affective nature, spirituality and human sympathy. From his father chiefly must have come his passion for freedom, and the firmness of character which has enabled him to persevere for a lifetime in what he has called "carrying out his own ideal."[17]

But to Louisa Van Velsor is given chief credit: "Walt Whitman could say with perhaps a better right than almost any man for such a boast, that he was 'Well-begotten and rais'd by a perfect mother.' "[18]

The environment, however, is found to be no less perfect: "Perhaps, indeed, there are few regions on the face of the earth better fitted for the concrete background of such a book as *Leaves of Grass*."[18] The poems have achieved the purpose announced in the '55 Preface, for it is now said that, "In their amplitude, richness, unflagging movement and gay color, *Leaves of Grass* . . . are but the putting in poetic statements of the Manhattan Island and Brooklyn of those years [poet's youth], and of today."[20]

The mythical travels encountered in Burroughs's *Notes* are continued:

The fifteen years from 1840 to 1855 were the gestation or formative periods of *Leaves of Grass*, not only in Brooklyn and New

York, but from several extensive jaunts through the States. . . . Large parts of the poems, and several of them wholly, were incarnated on those jaunts or amid these scenes. Out of such experiences came the physiology of *Leaves of Grass*, in my opinion the main part. The psychology of the book is a deeper problem; it is doubtful whether the latter element can be traced. It is, perhaps, only to be studied out in the poems themselves, and is a hard study there.[136]

These "extensive jaunts through the States" are puzzling not only because later biographers have found no record of them, but also because in *Specimen Days*, published one year before Bucke's biography, Whitman gives an accurate, though general, account of his New Orleans trip. In a newspaper article, reprinted in *Specimen Days*, he does make a statement which, for lack of punctuation, could have been misunderstood by Bucke: "I enjoy'd my journey and Louisiana life much. Returning to Brooklyn [,] a year or two afterward I started the 'Freeman'. . . ."[6] But surely in his close cooperation—or collaboration—with Dr. Bucke on the biography Whitman would have corrected the mistaken belief that he returned to Brooklyn *a year or two after* the New Orleans trip. One must conclude that the poet had no objection to such imaginative interpretations of the origin of his poems.

The point is that Dr. Bucke accepted in the most literal sense Whitman's literary claim that his poems were the expression of the life which he had absorbed. On such grounds the admirer of *Leaves of Grass* feels himself compelled to idealize the poet's whole life and background. Thus his education in printing offices, contact with people, and private study were not only adequate but "the most comprehensive equipment ever attained by a human being."[19] One wonders whether Taine's theory of "race, surroundings, epoch"[7] could have influenced both the poet and the biographer in their belief that the creator of literature must be the product of perfect ancestry, perfect environment, and perfect training or experience. On the romantic doctrine of "absorbing" and "expressing" the life of a nation, they thought the poet's meager formal education was more than compensated by his contact with "things" and "humanity"; hence that "reading did not go for so very much" in his education.[21]

Bucke's *Walt Whitman* does not attempt to solve one of the greatest problems in the biography of the poet, the almost miraculous contrast between Whitman's writings before and after 1855. But it was the personal contact with Whitman and the study of his writings that later led Dr. Bucke, the alienist, to study the phenomenon of mysticism, which the doctor called "cosmic consciousness."[8] The double nature of the poet, a profound spirituality mingled with an exuberant animality, remains a paradox in the biography—though it is not treated as such. But Dr. Bucke's later book helps to explain this puzzle, for it is a familiar paradox among mystics. In defense of the animal side of Whitman's disposition, Bucke claims in his biography that the "Children of Adam" poems have established "the purity, holiness and perfect sanity of the sexual relation,"[166] while "Calamus" presents "an exalted friendship, a love into which sex does not enter as an element." Not the slightest taint of abnormality is seen in either of these groups. And as for Whitman's illness in the summer of 1864 and his paralysis in 1873, these are attributed simply to the contraction of "hospital malaria" and overwork as a war-nurse.

O'Connor's interpretation of Whitman as a modern prophet is strongly confirmed by Bucke: *Leaves of Grass* belongs to a religious era not yet reached, of which it is the revealer and herald. . . . What the Vedas were to Brahmanism, the Law and the Prophets to Judaism . . . the Gospels and Pauline writings to Christianity . . . will *Leaves of Grass* be to the future of American civilization." It is "the bible of Democracy."[183-85]

The great value of Dr. Bucke's biography is that it conveys the remarkable personality of Walt Whitman. And others have confirmed the testimony which he gave after the poet's death: "To the last [his face] had no lines of care or worry—he lived in an upper spiritual stratum—above all mean thoughts, sordid feelings, earthly harassments."[9] Such observations led this devoted friend to study the lives of other mystics and to write a forerunner of William James's analysis of the psychology of mysticism in *The Varieties of Religious Experience*.

FIRST BRITISH INTERPRETATIONS:
ROSSETTI TO SYMONDS

Before continuing the story of Whitman biography in America, we need to observe his reception and growing reputation abroad—especially in England—for what the foreign critics said about him had, sooner or later, considerable influence on American evaluations. Professor Harold Blodgett has already ably told the story of Walt Whitman in England[10] and it need not be repeated here in detail, but it is important to know that the first edition of *Leaves of Grass* reached the British several months after its appearance in America, and that by the 1860s Whitman had many prominent admirers there, including William Michael Rossetti, John A. Symonds, Moncure Conway, Mrs. Anne Gilchrist, Swinburne (who later renounced Whitman), and others.

In 1866 Conway published an account[11] —later denounced by Whitman as fanciful[12] —of a visit to the poet in which he found him lying on his back on the parched earth in a blazing sun of nearly 100°, "one of his favorite places and attitudes for composing 'poems.'"[13] The following year William Michael Rossetti published a sane and discriminating article on Whitman in the London *Chronicle*.[14] This led, Rossetti says, to an opportunity to edit the poems, and the edition was published in 1868.

This edition, called *Poems by Walt Whitman*,[15] was both a selection and an expurgation, for the only reason for not reprinting the complete fourth edition of *Leaves of Grass* was the desire of Rossetti and the publisher to eliminate the "objectionable" poems, and Whitman would not agree to outright expurgation of the complete collection.[16] Rossetti's "Prefatory Notice"—mainly the *Chronicle* article—is reserved and admits the poet's faults (as Rossetti saw them) as freely as his virtues. The faults: "he speaks on occasion of gross things in gross, crude, and plain terms"; he uses "absurd or ill-constructed" words; his style is sometimes "obscure, fragmentary, and agglomerative"; and "his self-assertion is boundless"[17]—though partly forgivable as being vicarious. But these are balanced by the poet's great distinctions, "his absolute and entire originality," and his comprehension and intensity in both subject matter and expression, which Rossetti thinks great enough to enlarge the canon of poetic art. The volume contains about half the poems of the 1867 edition of the *Leaves* and the original preface. The selections are well chosen and proved a fortunate introduction of Walt Whitman to England. But it is significant to observe that the British were spared the poems which had so shocked America and that even Whitman's friendly editor found objectionable crudities in the style of *Leaves of Grass*, as have most British critics since then.

As a result of Rossetti's edition, one of the most remarkable episodes in Whitman's life and literary influence took place. Mrs. Anne Gilchrist, the brilliant widow of the great biographer of Blake, read Rossetti's *Selections*, then the complete *Leaves of Grass*, and came to feel that the American poet's message was a personal plea for love which she could answer. The strange story of this one-sided and pathetic courtship is well known and has been sympathetically told by Holloway.[18] Whitman fully appreciated her tender feeling for his poems but was unable to return a personal emotion, even after she had come to America and he had been hospitably received in her Philadelphia home. Of special interest to the growth of his reputation, however, is the essay, "An Englishwoman's Estimate of Walt Whitman," published in the Boston *Radical Review*, May, 1870.[19] Here for the first time a woman, and one widely known in artistic and literary circles, defended in print the sanity and purity of the infamous sex poems. The article was doubly reassuring to Whitman after Rossetti's reserved critical introduction.

After Rossetti and Mrs. Gilchrist's championship of Whitman came Edward Dowden. In his essay on "The Poetry of Democracy: Walt Whitman"[20] he shows considerably more enthusiasm than Rossetti. Like Burroughs and Bucke he interprets Whitman as the product and representative of American environment and life. He thinks that the American poet is "not shaped out of old-world clay ... and [is] hard to name by any old-world name." As the spokesman for "a great democratic world, as yet but half-fashioned"[473] he is not terrified by the fear of vulgarity, and selection seems forbidden to him; all words are eligible for his poetry, and he does not have to sacrifice directness and vividness to propriety. Here we have a new twist to Whitman's own theory, an application not possible for his American biographers, and yet given with admiring approval, just as the sex poems are declared to the product of "a robust, vigorous, clean man, enamored of living, unashamed of body as he is unashamed of soul, absolutely free from pruriency of imagination, absolutely inexperienced in the artifical excitements and enchancements of jaded lusts."[505]

In 1886 Ernest Rhys edited a new selection of *Leaves of Grass*.[21] The complete work was still too strong for British tastes, despite the fact that the book was far more widely appreciated in England than in America. Rhys's introduction adds nothing new to Whitman's biography or criticism, merely echoing the poet's old-age conclusion that his function is initiative, rather than a consummation in poetry and that his "poetic vision [is] fearlessly equal to the far range of later science,"[xi] a claim later amplified by an Australian scientist, William Gay.[22]

One of the keenest and most competent students of Whitman's life and art in the nineteenth century was the brilliant classical scholar, John Addington Symonds. Admitting that at the age of twenty-five *Leaves of Grass* was a revelation to him, influencing him more than any other book except possibly the Bible, and that, "It is impossible for me to speak critically of what has so deeply entered into the fibre and marrow of my being,"[23] he nevertheless was actually the first critic to raise certain embarrassing questions which have agitated biographers ever since.

In the strictly biographical part of his book Symonds agrees with Bucke and Burroughs that, "Walt inherited on both sides a sound constitution, untainted blood, comeliness of person, well-balanced emotions, and excellent moral principles,"[11-12] and gives a sketch of the biographical facts which differs from the previous accounts only in the more restrained and discriminating language. But in the "Study" of *Leaves of Grass* we encounter the first attack on O'Connor's "modern Christ" interpretation: "the ways [Whitman] chose for pushing his gospel and advertising his philosophy, put a severe strain on patience. Were Buddha, Socrates, Christ, so interested in the dust stirred up around them by second-rate persons, in third-rate cities, and in more than fifth-rate literature?"[38]

As a student of "Greek friendship" and Renaissance homosexuality among artists, Symonds recognized in the "Calamus" poems symptoms of emotional abnormality in the poet. Finally he wrote Whitman a frank letter asking for information. The reply, dated August 19, 1890, has become famous:

My life, young manhood, mid-age, times South, &c., have been jolly bodily, and doubtless open to criticism. Though unmarried I have had six children—two are dead—one living Southern grandchild, fine boy, writes to me occasionally—circumstances (connected with their fortune and benefit) have separated me from intimate relations.[24]

Symonds did not publish this letter, and it was not made public until Edward Carpenter quoted it in 1906, but it had an important influence on Symonds's own thinking. In fact, he seems to have been so convinced by it that he was reassured about "Calamus." He decided that what the poet called "the 'adhesiveness' of comradeship is meant to have no interblending with the 'amativeness' of sexual love ... it is undeniable that·Whitman possessed a specially keen sense of the fine restraint and continence, the cleanliness and chastity, that are inseparable from the perfectly virile and physically complete nature of healthy manhood."[25] And yet he must admit that "those unenviable mortals who are the inheritors of sexual anomalies, will recognize their own emotion in Whitman's 'superb friendship ... latent in all men.' " Symonds is still "not certain whether [Whitman's] own feelings upon this delicate topic may not have altered since the time when 'Calamus' was first composed."

Like all the English critics, Symonds is bothered by Whitman's "form," or rather lack of conventional form. "Speaking about him," he says, "is like speaking about the universe ... Not merely because he is large and comprehensive, but because he is intangible, elusive, at first sight self-contradictory, and in some sense formless, does Whitman resemble the universe and defy critical analysis." Such a justification would, of course, have pleased the poet who declared,

I am large, I contain multitudes.

Despite all his misgivings and reservations, however, Symonds renders homage to the man who helped him to strip his own soul of social prejudices, and he gratefully recommends *Leaves of Grass* to others.

THE AMERICAN APOTHEOSIS: TRAUBEL, KENNEDY, DONALDSON, BURROUGHS

Whitman's death in 1892 stimulated his personal friends in America to renewed activity in spreading his fame, an activity which long ago had become a "cause," an almost religious as well as a literary crusade. One of the first acts of his literary executors, Horace L. Traubel, Dr. R. M. Bucke, and Thomas B. Harned, was to publish a memorial volume called *In Re Walt Whitman*.[26] In addition to the tributes of friends and admirers, this book contains translations of the most important criticisms which had appeared in France, Germany, and Denmark. Here we find abundant proof that the American poet had already attained considerable international reputation and influence (a subject to be treated later in this *Handbook*).[27]

In Re is also the first of the Boswellian publications of the inner circle. Traubel, especially, had long been recording indiscriminately the poet's old-age garrulity and had now begun to question his family and acquaintances. His record of conversations with Walt's brother George [33-40], however, opens up new biographical possibilities. Here we get a glimpse of the Whitman family. It is revealing to see their literary ignorance, their indifference and even antagonism to the young poet's ambitions because he showed so little desire for making money; we are not surprised that Walt was never known to fall in love, in fact, seemed completely indifferent to girls, and they to him. Whether or not Walt was as "clean in his habits" as George thought he was, we nevertheless get in these notes a convincing picture of uneventful, commonplace, though not uncongenial family background. Walt Whitman's family did not lack affection for him, but it was as unaware of his genius as were his literary enemies. George's testimony helps to explain the loneliness, discouragement and despair so evident in the third edition of *Leaves of Grass*.

Another contributor to the *In Re* volume was William Sloane Kennedy, a devoted friend of the poet in his Camden period, who in two essays discussed the "Dutch" and the "Quaker Traits of Walt Whitman."[195-99; 213-14] These interpretations Kennedy amplified in his *Reminiscences of Walt Whitman*, published in 1896. There was nothing new in emphasizing these traits in which the poet himself took considerable pride, but Kennedy contributed to the subject a richer fund of information and a more vigorous gusto than previous biographers had displayed. Kennedy himself could be Quixotic as any of the "hot little prophets," to use Bliss Perry's phrase, but he brought to his Whitman idolatry an alert and cultivated mind. Reporting a conversation with the poet in 1880, Kennedy remarks, "I can't tell how it was, but the large personality of the man so vivified the few words he spoke that all the majesty of Greece— especially her sculpturesque art-idea—seemed to loom up before me as never before in my life, although the study of Greek literature had been a specialty of my collegiate and post-collegiate years."[1]

Reminiscences includes a good deal of biographical material, "Memories, Letters, Etc.," and some valuable sympathetic criticism of *Leaves of Grass*. The second part of the book, "Drift and Cumulus," is still useful to a Whitman student for its analyses of the meaning of individual poems; and the third part, "The Styles of Leaves of Grass," contains the first adequate explanation of the "organic principle" which Whitman had borrowed or inherited indirectly from German romanticism. The poet himself had insisted that the analogy of his rhythm was to be found in Nature, but Kennedy made the first real start in rationalizing his prosodic theory and practice. His *Fight of a Book for the World*, 1926, which might be called the first Whitman handbook, continues the interpretations of Kennedy's earlier publication and is of considerable value to the Whitman bibliographer.

The year 1896 also saw the publication of a second book by one of Walt Whitman's personal friends, Thomas Donaldson.[28] His *Walt Whitman, the Man* was based on first-hand knowledge of the poet during two periods, Washington from 1862-73 and Camden 1873-1892, but it contains meager biographical details. "No man tells the public the whole story of his life," says Mr. Donaldson. "Mr. Whitman never told the public the story of his life. . . . I do not now propose to tell it for him."[17] Perhaps this is negative evidence that Whitman told his friends little about his early life. But Donaldson's book made one positive contribution which was later to be extensively amplified. He indicated plainly that Whitman's poems celebrating "love of comrades" were written not out of actual experience but as a compensation for his own loneliness. He put into his poems the "passionate love of comrades" for which he found no human recipient. If Donaldson had developed this interpretation he would have been the first psychological biographer of Whitman. The book remains best known, however, for its testimony to the way the poet affected his intimate associates. "I never met a man of such standing who possessed as little personal egotism, or rather who made it less manifest in contact with him."[77]

The third friend to publish a book in 1896 was John Burroughs, who called his new biography *Walt Whitman, A Study*. He pled guilty to the same sort of "one-sided enthusiasm" found in all the publications of the personal friends: Bucke, Kennedy, Traubel, and Donaldson. When Burroughs met Whitman in the fall of 1863 "he was so sound and sweet and gentle and attractive as a man, and withal so wise and tolerant" that Burroughs soon trusted the book as he trusted the man, for he "saw that the work and the man were one, and that the former must be good as the latter was good."[29] If Whitman could have had the same hand in this book that he had had in the *Notes*, the work could not have been more favorable.

Although John Burroughs knew Whitman over a longer period

than most of the friends who wrote about him, the theory which he held—following the author's own clues—of the origin of *Leaves of Grass* was not likely to lead him to question, examine, or discover new biographical information. "What apprenticeship he served, or with whom he served it, we get no hint,"[72] he is content to say. Of course the apprenticeship and the days of doubt and uncertainty were nearly or entirely over by the time Burroughs made Whitman's acquaintance in Washington; hence he can truthfully testify: "We never see him doubtful or hesitating; we never see him battling for his territory, and uncertain whether or not he is upon his own ground." All these interpretations are based on the theory that Whitman himself cultivated: " 'Leaves of Grass' is an utterance out of the depths of primordial, aboriginal human nature. It embodies and exploits a character not rendered anaemic by civilization, but preserving a sweet and sane savagery, indebted to culture only as a means to escape culture, reaching back always, through books, art, civilization, to fresh, unsophisticated nature, and drawing his strength from thence."[76] This theory would not encourage Burroughs to undertake biographical research.

He made another interpretation, however, which might have—and in recent years has—led to literary investigation. "We must look for the origins of Whitman," he says, " ... in the deep world-currents that have been shaping the destinies of the race for the past hundred years or more; in the universal loosening, freeing, and removing obstructions; in the emancipation of the people ...; in the triumph of democracy and of science: ... the sentiment of realism and positivism, the religious hunger that flees the churches ... etc."[231]

Although Burroughs finally became impatient with Whitman's senile pleasure in the fawning of the Camden and Philadelphia claque, he never modified the conviction which he expressed in "The Flight of the Eagle," published in *Birds and Poets*, 1877: "to tell me that Whitman is not a large, fine, fresh, magnetic personality, making you love him, and want always to be with him, were to tell me that my whole past life is a deception, and all the impression of my perceptives a fraud."[30] Clara Barrus's valuable book, *Whitman and Burroughs, Comrades,* was later (1931) to document this friendship with the publication of many interesting letters, which reveal Burroughs as a more intelligent partisan than most of the inner circle, but one who, until the end of his life, was unwavering in his loyalty and devotion to Whitman. This record of one of the most important friendships in the poet's life is itself a distinguished contribution to scholarship, containing much new material on Whitman's reputation at home and abroad, and sound, intelligent critical judgments. The publication of the ten-volume deluxe edition of Whitman's works in 1902[31] may be taken as a convenient termination of the first stage of his biography. Two intimate admirers (Trowbridge and Edward Carpenter—to be discussed presently) were to publish important testimony after this date, but the first cycle had practically run its course. The biographical "Introduction" to the Camden Edition, written by the literary executors Bucke, Harned, and Traubel, adds only a few meager details. But since this Introduction is based on the publications of Burroughs, Bucke, Donaldson, Kennedy and the favorable criticism of friends and admirers in Europe, a précis of the essay will serve to emphasize the state of Whitman biography in 1902.

The sketch begins by stressing the antiquity and typical Americanism of the poet's ancestry. These "working people, possessed of little or no formal culture, and with no marked artistic tastes in any direction," had large families, were long-lived, and passed on to Walt their virile moral and physical energy. "There was no positive trace of degeneracy anywhere in the breed."[I, xviii] Little seems to be known about Walter Whitman, Senior; the brothers are vaguely described as of "solid, strong frame, fond of animals, and addicted to the wholesome labors and pleasures of the open air";[xxi] but the simple, almost illiterate, mother is represented as sweet, spiritual, ideal, and the poet's most important ancestor.[xxi]

Whitman's "long foreground" is interpreted as mainly his boyhood environment, the outdoor scenes and activities on Long Island and his contact with all sorts of people, especially unlettered folk. This "study of life" is said to have provided a better education for the future poet than the schools could possibly have done. Although his reading of Shakespeare, Homer, and the Bible is emphasized, these biographers agree that books were less important in his "apprenticeship" than outdoor experiences, urban life, and such amusements as the opera, concerts, theatrical performances, and fairs and museums.[xxvi–xxviii]

The New Orleans trip is thought to have been significant in the poet's development, but "There was an atmosphere of mysteriousness unconsciously thrown about the episode."[xxxv] The only known reason for Whitman's leaving was Jeff's poor health. No

precise information is given for his inability to hold any job more
than a few weeks or months.

In the publication of the first edition of *Leaves of Grass* the
"hidden purpose of his life was suddenly revealed."[xxxvii] The
gestation, experimentation—in short, the sources—of this work are
unknown to these biographers. Since they believe that the book is
"cosmic and baffles all adequate account," they are not predisposed
to exert much effort to find the "hidden purpose." From this time
on they make the story of the book the story of Walt Whitman.
Everything is grist for the mill; any effort to spread the "new gospel"
is laudable, even writing anonymous reviews and self-advertizing; the
poet's life and personality are observed to grow more Christ-like each
day. The sex poems express the divine order of paternal and fraternal
love; the poet sacrificed his health in his overly-zealous hospital
ministrations; all persecutors and depreciators of the man or his book
are properly condemned. But through all suffering, disappointments,
and misunderstanding Walt Whitman grows daily more serene,
lovable, and triumphant over the world and the flesh. Such was the
apotheosis of Walt Whitman in 1902, ten years after his calm death
in Camden.

FIRST STEPS IN A RE-EVALUATION:
TROWBRIDGE, EDWARD CARPENTER

The process of re-evaluation had already begun in 1903. Although John Townsend Trowbridge was one of Walt Whitman's
Boston friends, his autobiography, *My Own Story: with Recollec-
tions of Noted Persons*, shows plainly the new epoch dawning in
Whitman's biographical and critical interpretation. Ever since
O'Connor's partisan defence of the "Good Gray Poet," Whitman's
indebtedness to Emerson had become a problem in criticism and
biography. After addressing Emerson as "Master" in the impulsive
open-letter of the second edition of *Leaves of Grass*, Whitman finally
in a letter to Kennedy in 1887 denied flatly that he had read the
master before beginning his own book.[32] Burroughs, whose youthful
enthusiasm for Emerson first led him to read Whitman, was always
divided on the question. The Camden circle tried to deny any influence whatever. Of considerable value, therefore, is Trowbridge's testimony that when the poet visited Boston in 1860 to see his ill-fated
third edition through the press he confessed to having read Emer-

son's *Essays* in 1854. "He freely admitted that he could never have written his poems if he had not first 'come to himself,' and that Emerson helped him to 'find himself' . . . 'I was simmering, simmering, simmering; Emerson brought me to a boil.' "[33]

Traubel, Harned, and Bucke, were always inclined to accept every utterance of the poet as gospel truth, but Trowbridge expresses the opinion that Whitman's long invalidism affected his memory.[34] For example, it is obviously not true that without the Civil War years "and the experience they gave, *Leaves of Grass* would not now be existing,"[398] for the third edition was published in 1860. Furthermore, Trowbridge is convinced that "in matters of taste and judgment he was extremely fallible, and capable of doing unwise and wayward things for the sake of a theory or a caprice."[397] He can foresee the time when "some future tilter at windmills will attempt to prove that the man we know as Walt Whitman was an uncultured impostor," but Trowbridge sensibly concludes that "after all deductions it remains to be unequivocally affirmed that Whitman stands as a great original force in our literature."[400]

At this point we might note the corroborating evidence and opinion of the British disciple, Edward Carpenter—though at the moment we are violating strict chronology, for *Days with Walt Whitman* appeared in 1906, after important books by Binns, Perry, and Bertz. Edward Carpenter was a young, impressionable English poet who visited Whitman for the first time in 1877 and thereafter joined the band of followers, even to the extent of trying to adopt the thought and style of *Leaves of Grass* in his own poetry. But when he came to write his book, Carpenter perceived clearly that the inner circle of American friends was "more concerned to present an ideal personality than a real portrait."[52] Without in the least minimizing his admiration or personal indebtedness, Carpenter tried to give a "real portrait," and thereby succeeded in making a valuable contribution to the growth of Whitman biography.

Carpenter's most sensational revelation is Whitman's letter to Symonds in 1890 regarding the illegitimate children.[142-43] As we have already seen, this letter seems to have allayed Symonds's worst suspicions about the origin of the "Calamus" emotions, but Carpenter can see that there is more to the subject than has yet been revealed. Remembering Doyle's testimony that he had never known "a case of Walt's being bothered up by a woman,"[35] George's word that Walt had always been indifferent to girls,[36] and Burroughs's statement that the poet's "intimacies with men were much more numerous and close than with women,"[37] Carpenter concluded that there must have been "a great tragic element in his nature"[47] which prevented happiness in love affairs. And yet he knows that love ruled Whitman's life, "that he gave his life for love." The implications are plain that the poems are a sublimation of this love.

Walt Whitman's "double nature" had been hinted before, but Carpenter offers fresh evidence of this paradoxical disposition. He records his impression of the poet's "contradictory, self-willed, tenacious, obstinate character, strong and even extreme moods, united with infinite tenderness, wistful love, and studied tolerance ..."[38] Carpenter reports a most revealing confession that Whitman made to him: "There is something in my nature *furtive* like an old hen! ... That is how I felt in writing 'Leaves of Grass.' Sloane Kennedy calls me 'artful'—which about hits the mark."[43] And then Whitman added a sentence which deserves to be italicized: *"I think there are truths which it is necessary to envelop or wrap up."* Carpenter left for later biographers the pastime of guessing what these "truths" were, but he fully appreciated the importance of the confessed "furtive" sensation which the poet experienced in writing *Leaves of Grass* (meaning how many editions?). In the summer of 1886 Whitman demonstrated his own understanding of the psychological significance of these revelations in a self-analysis for Carpenter: "The *Democratic Review* essays and tales came from the surface of the mind, and had no connection with what lay below—a great deal of which indeed was below consciousness. At last came the time when the concealed growth had to come to light ..."[73]

Carpenter no less than Bucke thought Whitman's cosmic consciousness his strongest faculty. For this reason both believed he was a new type of man. But Carpenter did not see him with the distorted perspective of the "hot little prophets" who would like to worship at the shrine of a new Messiah: "while [Whitman] does not claim to deliver a new Gospel, he seems to claim to take his place in the line of those who have handed down a world-old treasure of redemption for mankind."[75] In "To Him that was Crucified" we have not a successor of Christ but a continuer of a world-wide and age-long tradition.[76] In an appendix called "Whitman as Prophet" Carpenter cites parallels to *Leaves of Grass* from the Upanishads. This emphasis on religious tradition and literary analogies for *Leaves of Grass* links Edward Carpenter with the first of the critical biographers, though his first-hand information and his literary discipleship classify him as one of the apostles—even if at times a doubting Thomas.

CRITICAL BIOGRAPHY: BINNS, BERTZ

We have already seen how arbitrary classifications of the biographers can be. Although on the whole Burroughs wrote as much under the spell of Whitman's personal influence as anyone, at times he could be acutely objective and critical. And both Symonds and Edward Carpenter, who eagerly confessed their profound indebtedness to the American poet, did much to bring about a complete re-evaluation of Walt Whitman in biography; while Henry Bryan Binns, an Englishman whose *Life of Walt Whitman* (1905) is the first complete, factual, and exhaustive biography, was as tenderly sympathetic with the poet as his most intimate friends had been.

Binns did his job so thoroughly that his book is still, seventy years later, one of the most reliable accounts of Walt Whitman's life. Not content with reading all available Whitman literature, Mr. Binns came to the United States and observed the scenes which had exerted the greatest influence on the life of his subject. For example, when Sculley Bradley visited Timber Creek and made an exhaustive study of the place where Whitman one summer regained the use of his limbs after a spell of invalidism, he found that only Binns had given an accurate description of the place.[38] Such accuracy was certainly new in Whitman biography, though in his Preface Binns disclaims any intention of writing a "critical" or "definitive" life.

Nevertheless, after a factual account of Whitman's youth and early manhood, Binns originates the most colorful of all the conjectures about the poet's mysterious New Orleans period. In the attempt to account for the marked change which seems to have come over Whitman after this trip, he creates a New Orleans romance.

It seems that about this time Walt formed an intimate relationship with some woman of higher social rank than his own—a lady of the South where social rank is of the first consideration—that she became the mother of his child, perhaps, in after years, of his children; and that he was prevented by some obstacle, presumably of family prejudice, from marriage or the acknowledgment of his paternity.[39]

As evidence for this conjecture Binns cites the letter to Symonds, Whitman's old-age remarks to Traubel, and the emotional awakening and poetic power which is evident in *Leaves of Grass* a few years after this trip. The awakening and the power are acknowledged by all the biographers, but Binns was the first to create so bold a theory: "Who emancipated him? May we not suppose it was a passionate and noble woman who opened the gates for him and showed him himself in the divine mirror of her love?"[52] Future biographers were slow to relinquish so romantic a picture as the warm-blooded, dark-skinned Southern lady of high-born Creole caste.

This theory works best for the "Children of Adam" poems. The "Calamus" group is explained by Binns as not the product of experience but of frustrated love: "he who knew and loved so many men and women, seems to have carried forward with him no equal friendship from the years of his youth. ... He longed for Great Companions, but he did not meet them at this time upon the open road of daily intercourse."[163]

Despite Binns's avowed purpose not to indulge in critical interpretations, he was the first biographer or critic to attempt a close reading of the subjective meaning of Whitman's poems as they developed through the many editions. For example, *Drum-Taps* "is a Song of the Broad-Axe, not a scream of the war-eagle."[209] The poet who had formerly expressed his awakened sensibility and his frustrated longing for human companionship learned, through the War and the hospital, social solidarity and a "sense of citizenship."

Binns also uses effectively the comparative method to clarify Whitman's relations to his age and to other writers. Like Triggs,[40] he finds revealing parallels in the thought of Whitman and Browning. Tolstoi, with his "Oriental tendency toward pessimism and asceticism,"[295] serves mainly as a contrast. Whitman's mysticism is thought to be indirectly indebted to George Fox, and his individualism directly influenced by Mill's *Principles of Economy*.[298, 308] A very interesting parallel is Proudhon, "the peasant, who ... looked forward to voluntarism as the final form of society."[309]

In a calm, reasonable manner Binns accepts Whitman as a modern prophet. "To be an American prophet-poet, to make the American people a book which should be like the Bible in spiritual appeal and moral fervour, but a book of the New World and of the new spirit—such seems to have been the first and the last of Whitman's daydreams."[55] But whereas, "Other men have given them-selves out to be a Christ, or a John the Baptist, or an Elijah; Whit-man, without their fanaticism, but with a profound knowledge of himself, recognized in a peasant-born son of Manhattan, an average American artisan, the incarnation of America herself."[335]

The story of the rise and growth of the Whitman cult in Ger-many belongs to the history of *Leaves of Grass* in world literature more than to the growth of biography, and will therefore be treated in Chapter V. But the publicaton of Eduard Bertz's *Der Yankee-Heiland* in 1905 marks an important turn in Whitman biography because this was the first outright attempt to destroy completely the "Yankee-Saint" legend. Whitman's works were discussed in Germany as early as 1868 by Ferdinand Freiligrath. And soon after Knortz-Rolleston's translation in 1889 the American poet was practically worshiped in the Rhineland,[41] much as Shakespeare had been in the eighteenth century. But most German critics merely elaborated the "official" portrait created by Whitman and his acolytes, though more fanatically than even the most ardent American friends. Especially is this true in the writings of Johannes Schlaf.[42]

Bertz first read *Leaves of Grass* in 1882 while he was living in his "woodland retreat" in Tennessee. After returning to Germany he sent Whitman in 1889 an appreciative article which he had published in the *Deutsche Press* to celebrate the poet's seventieth birthday. In response Whitman showered Bertz with favorable reviews and self-advertising, and the German admirer could not reconcile this action with his idealization of the saintly prophet. Bertz, still and always, regarded Whitman as one of the major lyric poets of the world,[43] but from this time on he became suspicious and critical of Whitman's life and character.

These suspicions led to a study of Walt Whitman's sex pathol-ogy, published as "Walt Whitman, ein Charakterbild" in the *Jahrbuch für sexuelle Zwischenstufen*, 1906. Here Bertz argued that Whitman belonged to the "intermediate sex", to use Edward Carpenter's term, or "Uranians".[44] This psychopathic interpretation dominates Bertz's attempt to unmask the poet in *Der Yankee-Heiland*.

The feminine and even hysterical *Grundton* of his being is obvi-ous to any observant reader, in the emotional, impassioned character of his world-outlook. No one familiar with modern psychology and sex-pathology is in the slightest doubt that the erotic friendship, which is found in the poetry and life of our wonderful prophet, is to be explained in any other way than by his constitutional deviation from the masculine norm.[228-29]

This interpretation casts a new light on many phases of Whitman's life. His love for the young soldiers suffering in the hospitals was "fundamentally sexual,"[205] though sublimated and ennobled. His "abundant joy" was another myth; actually "his life was filled with the intense agony of a confused soul. His love was unrequited; it was a renunciation and so he placed it beyond the grave."[212] Even his "supposedly universal sympathy . . . [was] rooted not so much in his heart as in his phantasy" and turns out to be only a "formal, artistic theory."[203] In the same manner, Whitman's paralysis is thought to have been the result of some hereditary taint; the breakdown due to the hospital strain was a myth, like the similar myth about Nietzsche's hospital work.[30]

Bertz's attempt to destroy the "prophet myth" results also in an attack upon Whitman's pretensions as a thinker and a philosopher. Though he claimed to be the poet of science and progress, he was "at heart opposed to Darwinism but afraid to say so openly."[127] His "new religion" actually came far more from the Hebrew prophets than from scientific thought, though he fooled himself into thinking that he had reconciled the two through some sort of Hegelian sophistry. His chiliasm and theodicy[45] were intuitive and romantic and irreconcilable with empirical rationalism.

. . . if he had wished to be nothing except a lyricist his poetic greatness would certainly be uncontested. But unfortunately he wanted above all to be a prophet and . . . the founder of a tenable scientific religion with a definitely philosophic world outlook, and this point of view conflicted with his spiritual nature; his purely lyrical talent was not sufficient for that. [100]

SCHOLARLY BIOGRAPHY IN AMERICA:
PERRY AND GEORGE RICE CARPENTER

The beginnings of Whitman scholarship—the attempt to discover and tell the whole truth—might be dated from Binns. But before Bliss Perry's *Whitman* in 1906 at least no one in America had even attempted to tell the poet's life completely and impartially. Perry did not have access to many of the private notebooks and unpublished manuscripts which have since been collected and edited by Holloway and Furness, but he made the most of the sources available. In his biography Perry traces down the known facts of Whitman's ancestry, which he finds to be undistinguished but respectable. The events of his youth and early manhood are recited calmly and without bias. Not even the New Orleans trip provokes any fanciful guesses or romantic interpretations. Where the facts are inadequate or missing altogether, Perry freely admits the lacunae. He rejects the pathological interpretations of the "Calamus" poems, though agreeing with Burroughs that there was a good deal of the woman as well as the man in Walt Whitman. He agrees also with Burroughs that there is "abundant evidence that from 1862 onward his life was stainless so far as sexual relations were concerned,"[46] yet frankly admits that the evidence for earlier years is scanty. The first *Leaves of Grass* was "a child of passion" and "sexual emotion" helped to generate it. "Its roots are deep down in a young man's body and soul," but it is "a clean, sensuous body and a soul untroubled as yet by the darker mysteries."[47] In the poems of joy Perry finds "the spirit of blissful vagrancy which dominated his early manhood."[21] Perry travels a road separate from that of the later psychological biographers.

Without denying or minimizing Walt Whitman's affectations of dress and manner, a sympathetic interpretation is placed on them by the observation that "the flannel shirt and slouch hat are as clearly symbolical as George Fox's leathern breeches, or the peasant dress of Count Tolstoi."[74] Whitman's letters to his mother and friends give the reader a clear, eye-witness account of the War and the hospital experiences. With kindly detachment Perry chronicles the poet's dismissal from his clerkship in Washington and O'Connor's feud not only with the puritanical Harlan but also with all British literature and European influences. Even the Camden period—with "its *vates sacer*, ... the band of disciples, the travel-stained pilgrims and ultimately the famous tomb"[214]—is neither satirized nor sentimentalized.

But probably Perry's greatest service for Whitman biography and criticism, and for American literature, was his interpretation of *Leaves of Grass* in terms of international literary and artistic developments. "A generation trained to the enjoyment of Monet's landscapes, Rodin's sculptures, and the music of Richard Strauss will not be repelled from Whitman merely because he wrote in an unfamiliar form."[282-83] Perry also helped to lessen the shock for readers by calling attention to the parallels between *Leaves of Grass* and Oriental poetry (so much admired by the American Transcendentalists) and the familiar English version of the poetry of the Bible.[276]

Whitman's faults and literary lapses are also freely admitted. In a left-handed manner the "physiological passages" are defended as usually bearing "the mark, not so much of his imaginative energy as of his automatic describing-machine."[289] Perry finds absent in Whitman love of man for woman and a sense of family, home, and social cooperation. "Beyond the unit he knows nothing more definite than his vague 'divine average' until he comes to 'these States' and finds himself on sure ground again."[293] But most objectionable to the Camden disciples was such a criticism as this: "Monist as he was in philosophy, he was polytheist in practice: he dropped on his knees anywhere, before stick or stone, flesh or spirit, and swore that each in turn was divine."[294] Nevertheless, Walt Whitman, "in spite of the alloy which lessens the purely poetic quality and hence the permanence of his verse, is sure . . . to be somewhere among the immortals."[307]

The condition in which Perry left Whitman biography after the publication of his book may be summed up in his own conclusion:

No Whitman myth, favorable or unfavorable, can forever withstand the accumulated evidence as to Whitman's actual character. . . . The 'wild buffalo strength' myth, which he himself loved to cultivate, has gone; the Sir Galahad myth, so touchingly cherished by O'Connor, has gone, too; and Dr. Bucke's 'Superman' myth is fast going. We have in their place something very much better; a man earthy, incoherent, arrogant, but elemental and alive.[291]

It is not in the least surprising that Perry's biography should have, as Kennedy put it, "excited . . . much protest from Whitmanites."[46] And he, himself, was no exception. The Whitmanites could not bear any qualification of their hero and were quick to attribute any reservations either to prudery or the stultifying influence of "culture." Kennedy thought the book was "written with an eye on Mrs. Grundy," by an author who lived in the stuffy air of libraries and the class-room. "He is a spokesman of the genteel, conforming, half-baked middle-class. . . ."[94]

A work more to the taste of the "Whitmanites" was Horace Traubel's *With Walt Whitman in Camden*, the first volume of which appeared in 1906. Three more volumes were published, the fifth in 1964.[47] From March 28, 1888, Traubel kept daily notes of his conversations with Whitman, and in these books he reports them with a fullness that puts Boswell to shame—though unfortunately Traubel had Boswell's industry without his genius. Because the books do provide many minute details of the poet's last years that would not otherwise have survived, they have some value for the student of his ideas; but they also do Whitman a disservice by embalming his trivial, garrulous, and often foggy thoughts in the final years of pain, failing memory, and perhaps at times of outright delusion.[48] Only limitless veneration and uncritical judgment could have enabled anyone to accumulate such a mass of commonplace manuscript— though Traubel did preserve valuable letters.

The new epoch of scholarly biographies in America was continued, however, with George Rice Carpenter's *Walt Whitman*, published in the "English Men of Letters" series in 1909. This book, like others in the series, is not particularly original or distinguished, though it summarizes the facts accurately and coherently. It might be described as a concise version of Bucke (for facts) and Perry (for interpretation). Bucke's account of Whitman's sound ancestry is retained in chastened rhetoric, Binns's New Orleans romance is passed over in silence, and the story of the illegitimate children is unquestioningly accepted. "We know (and wish to know) nothing more than that he had at times been lured by the pleasures of the flesh, like many a poet before him, and that he had known the deep and abiding love of woman."[49] (Later biographers were to lack such well-bred reticence.) In the next to the last paragraph of the biography Carpenter mentions literary relationships but quickly asserts that these are "not of great importance in Whitman's case. He was little influenced by books,"[171] and apparently was thought not to have influenced others—as of course he had not in America before 1906, though he had in Europe.

FRENCH AND BRITISH CRITICS: BAZALGETTE, DE SELINCOURT, LAWRENCE, BULLETT

In 1908 Léon Bazalgette, in his *Walt Whitman: L'Homme et son Oeuvre*—still known in the United States mainly in a bowdlerized translation[50]—revived the idealized interpretations of Burroughs and Bucke with a critical enthusiasm and lack of reserve possible only to a master of the French language. Like the earliest biographers, he believes that the man cannot be separated from the book, and therefore frequently "evoke[s] the work to explain the man."[5] As a matter of fact, he deliberately carries on the work of the Bucke school, for he announces in the preface the intention of building, "to the measure of my strength, a French dwelling for the American bard."[xvii] And his sources are Whitman's personal friends, rather than later biographies: "I efface myself as much as possible, in the humility of a compiler, behind those who were in personal contact with him and caught him on the spot."[4]

Once more the poet's ancestry shines in resplendent glory. From the Whitmans, "the most vigorous British element in one section" of the isle, and the Van Velsors, "typical representatives of the old Americanized Dutch," Walt Whitman inherited, from the one, "firmness of character verging almost upon hardness," and from the other, "abundant vitality and joviality."[12, 13] Little Walt "found in his cradle the enormous strength and health accumulated by his family, nowise diminished like the family fortune, but increased each generation."[23] The "centuries of silent labour close to the earth and to the sea, centuries of robustness and open air"[94] had prepared the way for him.

Bazalgette idealizes Whitman's youth and apprenticeship years with a more vivid imagination than either Burroughs or Bucke possessed. "The memory of this happy period remained dear as ever to the poet, past the period of his virility . . . What animal strength and what largeness these intervals of life, wild, exultant, diffusive of unconscious joy, near the sea and on it, were preparing for the individual!"[35] And then when he comes to the young man's sexual awakening, which again is believed to have been the New Orleans period, Bazalgette displays an exuberance which evidently shocked the American translator, for she thought it necessary to leave whole paragraphs unrevealed in sober English.

It is not easy in a few words to explain Bazalgette's exact interpretations of the New Orleans period, for it is both subtle and sophisticated. He is quite aware that Walt Whitman did not conduct himself like a typical Anglo-Saxon young man in love. But Bazalgette is sure that he was not abnormal. Whitman merely appeared to be cold because he did not abandon himself to flirtations and pretty speeches. And he may not have been sexually aroused until his brief sojourn in the South:

Il est possible, toutefois, que, jusqu'à son séjour à La Nouvelle-Orléans, l'amour n'ait été pour lui qu'une expérience concrète parmi mille autres expériences et qu'il n'ait pas eu encore la révélation totale de la femme, âme et corps, la sensation despotique et toute-puissante de son être entier, aimant et aimé.[51]

But the hypothetical romance first created by Binns, "dans son livre si nourri, si pieux, si chaleureux,"[52] seems to Bazalgette to exaggerate the importance of this education in love. The future poet tore himself away and returned to his home in the North because "he could not endure that a woman should hold a place in his life which might fatally lessen the domain of his liberty."[84] Still, "Walt had plunged into the heart of the continent and, undoubtedly, into the heart of woman."[86]

Although other biographers admit the scarcity of exact information concerning Whitman's life between the New Orleans trip and the first edition of *Leaves of Grass*, Bazalgette asserts confidently that at thirty "the perfect concordance between the interior Walt and his physical appearance is a genuine subject of astonishment." In fact, "however magnificent, however eternal may be for us his book, Walt, the man in the flesh who is about to put it forth, is at least its peer at ths moment."[91] Perhaps such enthusiastic statements were intended to be understood in a symbolical manner, for Bazalgette goes on to say that Walt Whitman "was more a Whitman man than his father or his brother George, more a Van Velsor than his mother or his brother Jeff...."[97] When so little is known about either family, this superinheritance must be mystical rather than biological. And the same is true in Bazalgette's treatment of the "Calamus" motif in *Leaves of Grass*. He admits the "impassioned character" of some of Whitman's "attachments of man to man,"[220] but thinks Schlaf[53] has successfully replied to the psychopaths who had seen in these friendships "a sexual anomaly":

In any case, it is not the searchers for anomalies who will ever find the key. Perhaps he who shall describe the exact nature of the attachment which united the Apostle of Galilee [*sic*] to his diciple John will be able to clear the mystery of love which is concealed in the tender comradeships of the Good Gray Poet.[220-221]

After this point, to summarize the rest of Bazalgette's book would be an anticlimax in this account of the growth of Whitman biography, not because the French biographer falters or weakens, but because from here on the point of view is thoroughly familiar to us. With gusto Bazalgette dilates on "Walt Whitman, a Cosmos," with vicarious pleasure he exults in O'Connor's avenging the Harlan "insult," shares the pride of the intimate friends over the poet's victories in the British Isles, and finally with loving tenderness describes the calm death "while the rain gently fell," and the "pagan funeral" which intrusted the last remains to the elements. No biographer has written Walt Whitman's life with more genuine emotion.

Basil De Selincourt's English biography shares a good deal in spirit and point of view with the French biography of Bazalgette and was no doubt influenced by it. Both are, strictly speaking, critics rather than biographers, for they are interested less in discovering facts and establishing new evidences for their interpretations than in reading the text sympathetically; and at times their reading is so sympathetic that they too become mythmakers.

De Selincourt does, however, give a new twist to the New Orleans hypothesis started by Binns: "There can be no doubt that his trip South was taken with conscious intention, that his new job attracted him because of the new contexts it would afford to his daily dreams and meditations."[54] Not even Burroughs and Bucke assumed that the poet thus consciously planned and controlled his destiny. Accepting Binn's theory completely that Whitman first experienced love in the romantic South, De Selincourt discovers a pregnant symbolism: "This visit to the South, always associated in his mind with the ecstatic and desolating history of his loves, became typical to him of the fusion of the Northern and Southern States into a nation, and seemed to give him the right to speak as representative of the whole."[18-19]

Although he insists that Whitman "was not the type to sow wild oats," De Selincourt nevertheless accepts completely the story of the six illegitimate children and the romance with the New Orleans lady of "gentle birth," but

his six children were not all the offspring of one mother, their father convincing himself, under the influence partly of his feelings, partly of confused theory, that, as an exceptional man, loved now by this woman and now by that, he could find and give an adequate conjuga ove in more than one relationship . . . pledged already to transcendental union with his country, [he] may have felt that the serene confiding joys of domesticity and its complete personal surrender must not be his.[20-22]

Such promiscuity on principle certainly reaches a new high, or a new ow, of some sort in Whitman biography! De Selincourt asserts that 'Out of the Cradle Endlessly Rocking," which he conveniently dates back to "one of the all but earliest *Leaves*," is "the song virtually of a husband mourning for the death of one who was in all but name his wife,"[23-24] *i.e.*, the New Orleans woman of gentle birth, while "Once I Pass'd through a Populous City" may refer to a "humble woman."

De Selincourt admits an inconsistency in Whitman's pretending to despise culture yet trying to write poetry. "He was without the discipline of education and underrated or ignored its value."[31] And another paradox is found in the war poems: although Whitman "regarded himself and we regard him as peculiarly the poet of the war; yet . . . the bulk of his most characteristic expression preceded it,"[42-43] for much of *Drum-Taps* had already been completed when Walt went to Virginia to look for George. But in Whitman's letters to his mother and to Peter Doyle, De Selincourt thinks that we observe for the first time "his actual personality by the side of the assumed personality of the hero of *Leaves of Grass*, and find to our astonishment that the man is greater than the book and different from it; in fact, that he is its complement."[45]

Bucke and Whitman himself would have approved this interpretation of the poet's spontaneous unconventionality:

His own wild music, ravishing, unseizable, like the song of a bird, came to him, as by his own principles it should have come, when he was not searching for it. And his greatness as a poet, when we regard his poetry on its formal side, is that conventional echoes damaged him so little, that in spite of unavoidable elements of wilfulness and reaction in his poetry, he was able to achieve so real an independence.[73]

Perhaps only a European critic could have declared finally that Walt Whitman "epitomised his people so perfectly that he could make no impression upon them."[241]

Four years later, in 1918, a French critic, Valéry Larbaud,

voiced a revolt from the Bazalgette interpretation which was to be
heard in ever-increasing volume in the next two decades. He rejected
three Whitman legends, those of the prophet, the laborer, and the
philosopher, and we might add a fourth, that of the American:

Oui, il est Américan; mais c'est parce que nous flairons dans la partie
vivante de son oeuvre une certaine odeur (indéfinissable) que nous
trouvons aussi dans Hawthorne, Thoreau, un roman de H. K. Viélé et
trois nouvelles de G.W. Cable. Mais il n'est pas Américain parce qu'il
s'est proclamé le poète de l'Amérique. Encore le démenti immédiat:
il a été aussi méconnu aux Etats-Unis que Stendhal à Grenoble ou
Cézanne à Aix. Sa doctrine est allemande, et ses maîtres sont anglais
par toute sa vie purement intellectuelle il fut un Européen habitant
l'Amérique. Mais, surtout la plupart de "the happy few" vivent en
Europe. C'est donc en Europe seulement qu'il pouvait être reconnu
et qu'il l'a été.[55]

In his chapter on Whitman in *Studies in Classic American Literature* (1918) D.H. Lawrence attacked savagely a mystical doctrine and
a personal characteristic of the poet in a manner wholly new in
biography and criticism of him. When Whitman looks at the slave,
says Lawrence, he *merges* with him, vicariously shares his wounds—
"is it not myself who am also bleeding with wounds?" But, "This
was not *sympathy*. It was merging and self-sacrifice."[56] The merging
theme is morbid and disintegrating. Whitman starts out boldly on the
open road—explorer, adventurer, pioneer—but then he wants to
merge with everything, all people, nature, the womb, finally with
Death. He confounds sympathy (which would help the slave to free
himself or the prostitute to secure medical and economic aid) with
sentimental Christianity.

But the prophet and carpenter legend died hard. As late as 1921
Will Hayes, one of the last fundamentalists, published in London a
book called *Walt Whitman: the Prophet of the New Era,* with chapters on "The Christ of Our Age," "The Carpenter of Brooklyn," and
"A Sermon on the Mount." The book is too trivial to mention
except as an example that the old faith still lingered on.

The extent to which Rossetti's attitudes toward Whitman had
survived in Great Britain is evidenced in Gerald Bullett's *Walt Whitman: A Study and a Selection,* 1924. "If we regard a poet as an
infallible seer," says Bullett, "we are at once saved the trouble of
reading his work intelligently, with critical faculty alert," and this, he

thinks, is exactly what some of Whitman's countrymen have done, they "who regard every word that he wrote, every comma that he omitted, as so infinitely precious that they reprint even his juvenile metrical verse, his temperance novel, and his newspaper reports."[57] "Apart from the defect in taste that blemished his literary expression, he possessed personal idiosyncrasies that were due largely to an excess of qualities admirable in themselves. His occasional mawkishess, the endearments and kisses bestowed on the men who were his dearest friends: this, I feel, was but the odious superflux of a generous affection."[30] Like most of the British critics, Bullett censures Whitman for blabbing about intimate details of life that should be kept secret and accuses him of utter lack of artistic sense and taste. "Why make bones about it that Whitman at thirty-five was a satyr, and some of the first *Leaves of Grass* the natural expression of a satyr?"[3] He knew nothing of selection. But he was not lacking in poetic power. He was best when he was cosmic. And when by "sheer strength of thought or depth of passion" his work escapes from graphic journalism it rises to the realm of great literature.[45]

John Bailey's *Walt Whitman* (1926) stands in about the same relation to the English biographies as G. R. Carpenter's book to the American biographies. It is reliable, complete, and always reasonable and conservative in interpretations, without adding anything new or especially significant. Bailey has great respect for those men fortunate enough to have known the poet personally and yet is always suspicious of their unrestrained enthusiasm. "In a man's lifetime lucky or unlucky personal characteristics often lead to his receiving more praise, or less, than his achievement deserved. But the function of later criticism is to take the book, or other work, and judge it as it is, apart from all prejudices of personal liking or disliking."[58] These words adequately summarize the state of Whitman biography and criticism in 1926. The influence of the "hot little prophets" had almost faded out completely and sober criticism both of the man's life and his work were becoming well established. As the living personality of Walt Whitman faded from the memory of men, the scholar and the critic began to turn a concentrated light upon the poetry itself and to read it with increasing depth of understanding and appreciation. After all, the man and the book were not exactly one and the same, even in a mystical sense, for the man had passed on but the book remained.

RESEARCH AND TEXTUAL STUDY:
HOLLOWAY, CATEL, SCHYBERG

Emory Holloway laid the foundation for a new era in Whitman studies when he published in 1921 the *Uncollected Poetry and Prose of Walt Whitman,* containing the poet's private notebooks, early journalistic writings, and other juvenilia in poetry and prose.[59] Later Professor Holloway and his assistants continued to salvage and edit practically every journalistic scrap that can be assigned to Whitman, along with some that can be credited to him only hypothetically. Consequently, when Holloway was ready to publish his biography, *Whitman, An Interpretation in Narrative* (1926), he was undoubtedly familiar with more of the poet's total life output of writing than anyone else. His greatest achievement, therefore, was the first full account of Walt Whitman's life as journalist and editor. And on the natural assumption that the child is father to the man, he attempted to explain the mature poet in terms of his early life and intellectual development.

Holloway's book begins, therefore, not with the poet's ancestors—about which, after all, little can ever be known except names, dates, places of residence, and occupations—but with the journalistic years in Brooklyn, a subject on which the author had already become a recognized authority. Perhaps, as Holloway remarks, Whitman could hardly have become the poet of Democracy without his training and experience in the newspaper office. But the astonishing thing is that the more we learn of the mediocre mind and expression of Walt Whitman the journalist, the greater seems the miracle of his becoming, in the short space of four or five years, a genuine poet. Some of the relaxed, undisciplined habits of thought and expression were carried over into *Leaves of Grass,* but in his more inspired moments he does seem literally a new man.

No one has ever been more aware of this miracle than Professor Holloway himself. In fact, so conscious is he of it, and so inadequately do the journalistic writings provide any satisfactory clues, that once more the biographer must fall back upon two of the earlier hypotheses, *viz.,* Dr. Bucke's mysticism and Binns's New Orleans romance. Practically all the biographers are unanimous on Whitman's mystical experiences, but Holloway's acceptance of the New Orleans conjecture shows the ironical dilemma he is in, for he himself had convincingly demolished the whole "romance"-school in an earlier article.[60] One of the supposed bits of evidence nearly always cited to support the New Orleans theory is the poem, "Once I Pass'd through a Populous City," but Professor Holloway discovered that in the manuscript the poem was addressed to a man rather than a woman and belonged, therefore, to the "Calamus" group. Perhaps one poem does not prove or disprove the theory, but so great is Holloway's dilemma that he now cites the same poem once more to substantiate the love-affair which he had once rejected on the basis of this poem. "I am convinced," he explains, "by many years of study and investigation that the gossip which linked the young journalist with the peculiar *demi monde* of New Orleans was substantially true."[61] No new and conclusive evidence, however, is brought forth.

The reader has the feeling that the biographer knows more than he dares to tell. Commenting on the first edition of *Leaves of Grass*, Holloway says, "Indeed, had [Whitman] known as much about psychology as we do to-day, he might not have had the temerity to publish such a book."[123] In discussing the "Calamus" poems Holloway says of Whitman, "he did not carefully distinguish between . . . the sort of affection which most men have for particular women and that which they experience toward members of their own sex." [169] And he adds that these poems were born of "an unhealthy mood."[173]

Perhaps the basis for these paradoxes is the fact that, as Holloway accurately points out, *Leaves of Grass* contains several kinds of sex poems: (1) the "sentimental lyrics born of an ideal romance" (*i.e.*, hetero-sexual love), (2) celebrations of procreation (philosophical), (3) "emotions which accompany the initial act of paternity," (physiological); and to these the biographer at least implies a fourth type, the poems celebrating what the poet called "manly attachment."[169-70] Which of these types represents Whitman's real nature? Or is it possible for one man to experience all of these different sexual emotions? These questions are not answered, though perhaps Holloway inclines to a belief in the poet's sexual versatility, for he regards as pathetic and almost tragic the craving for manly affection in the third edition. "The emotion here venting itself was so great as to carry with it, for a time, Walt's every ambition. The book was published when his craving for affection was at its height." [172] Later he succeeded in spiritualizing the passion. On the strength of Mrs. O'Connor's testimony Holloway accepts the story of Whitman's being in love with a married woman in Washington, apparently believing that soon after the third edition he recovered from his "unhealthy mood."

Perhaps in line with this interpretation, Holloway finds a great
change in Whitman after 1870. He now "makes rendezvous, not with
the Great Companions, but with the Comrade perfect."[245] He
who declared in 1856, "Divine am I inside and out," now has ideals
for his gods. "He sings, not the 'average man,' but the 'Ideal Man'
..." The meaning of the poems written in former periods now takes
on a new significance for the poet himself. Concerning the "Children
of Adam" poems, for example. "It was characteristic of his type of
mind that he should himself have read into these poems, not merely
the youthful impulses out of which they were born, but the religious
aspirations which succeeded."[260]

In making these illuminating interpretations, Holloway went
considerably beyond any previous biographer and opened the way
for further searches for the poet's psyche in his unconscious
betrayals in *Leaves of Grass*.

And Whitman biography did not have long to wait. In Jean
Catel's *Walt Whitman: La Naissance du Poète* the soul of the poet
was exhumed for a psychoanalytical autopsy. With clinical thoroughness this critic searches, like Holloway, through every fragment of
juvenilia, through diaries, letters, and finally *Leaves of Grass* for the
key to Whitman's genius, and there in the first edition he believes he
finds the answer.

In *Leaves of Grass* we discover what escapes us in his real life
and emotion. And of *Leaves of Grass*, it is the first edition which
retains in its music the secret that Whitman consecrated his life to
disguise. If it is not there, it is nowhere. It is not in his public life,
nor his journalistic articles, nor in his relations with a group of
friends as ardent as they were blind. It is not in the biographical
notes which he wrote himself, nor in those which he asked Horace
Traubel to transmit to posterity. So much concern on his part lest he
be misunderstood must arouse our suspicion.[11]

Thus for what he hid Whitman substituted the soul of a poet
ready to receive the habiliments of glory. To his real self he preferred
a legend. He forgot only one thing—for one can not remember
everything—: that first edition, all aquiver in a revolt which maturity
and old age were to repudiate. After that edition is pruned, recast,
and diluted into the later editions of *Leaves of Grass*, it lacks the air
of reality of that first long, revealing cry."[11]

Once more biography has returned to the identification of the poet and his work, but a vast gulf of psychology separates Catel from Bucke. Dr. Bucke believed that the poet was able to tap the sources of intellectual power of a "cosmic consciousness" but he scarcely thought of searching in the subconscious for the hidden motives of daily action.

The first illusion which Catel attempts to dispel is Walt Whitman's sound ancestry. He finds it impossible "to agree with the optimism of Mr. Bazalgette . . . [that] 'The union of the two races [English and Dutch] was the extraordinary promise of a completer human type, one profiting by all the power of a new soil.' On the contrary, everything tended to create a type of mediocre humanity, harassed by anxiety."[22, n.2] In short, the marriage of the discontented and austere Walter Whitman with the loving, sunny Louisa Van Velsor was an unfortunate union. "Some would say that it was a fortunate mis-mating, since it produced a poet. Undoubtedly true, but this poet was not the product of a perfect equilibrium of physical and moral forces, as he and his devoted friends thought and said."[22]

Believing from the study of other writers, such as Dickens and Chateaubriand, that the adolescent impressions registered on the memory are the ones that reappear in the images and imaginative scenes of the creative mind of an author, Catel searches Whitman's writings for clues to his youth. What he discovers is a boy who felt himself from all sides "pushed out of doors, for at the time when the home is the most solid reality to the average child, it did not exist for him. At fifteen he felt himself to have no part in the house which his father had built and was living in temporarily."[38] Therefore, "young Whitman, having only the loosest home ties, roamed the streets of Brooklyn and they received him with affection; they were like a home to him."[39] Thus does Catel account for the vividness with which the mature poet describes moving crowds, trips on the ferry, and the pleasure of merging his own ego with the mass of humanity.

Catel's thorough examination of Whitman's journalistic writings before he began *Leaves of Grass* reveals a maladjusted young man, unsuccessful in the economic world, unsure of himself, unable to make social adjustments. In New Orleans, far from having "found himself" as some biographers believed, he was faced by the same necessities as in Brooklyn and New York, and once again failed miserably to meet them, having to return home after a row with his employer. But by this time one of the chief causes of his difficulties becomes apparent. There is some peculiarity in his sexual nature. Catel finds strong indications that Whitman had had experiences with "professional love" in New York or Brooklyn,[62] but this sauntering, dreaming, introspective young man did not find satisfaction in these relationships, for he was naturally "auto-erotic."[435] And it is this peculiarity which accounts for his maladjustment to life.[63]

After returning to Brooklyn, and unsuccessfully trying journalism again, he abandoned so far as possible the physical struggle for adjustment to the world of reality and began to create a compensating inner world of fantasy and imagination, which found expression through his poems. Thus does Catel explain Whitman's almost miraculous acquisition of literary power without recourse either to mysticism or a sexual awakening in the romantic city of the South. Furthermore, the explanation gives a revealing significance to the style, the egoism, and the motifs of *Leaves of Grass*.

The myself that Whitman 'celebrates' on each page . . . is the projection of the unconscious. If in reading Whitman's work, the reader will replace mentally the *I* or the *myself* by 'my unconscious', while giving to this word the dynamic sense which we have indicated, then he will understand better: first, the origin, the profound reason for the first edition of *Leaves of Grass*; second, the end, what certain critics have called the messianic in Whitman. [400-01]

His conscious mind agitated by a sense of failure, frustration, and loneliness. Whitman's poetic imagination returns to an idealized childhood of peace, innocence, and purity, and it is then that he feels in his soul that he is the equal of God.

Books became a powerful force in Whitman's attempt to find happiness through artistic creation. The subjective philosophy of the post-Kantians in America, and of Emerson especially, provided both a framework and a rationalization for the psychological adjustments which his inner nature compelled him to make. Perhaps he was only dimly aware of his great debt to Emerson, but Transcendentalism, like a religion, opened up a new life to Walt Whitman. Like many a man who has experienced a religious conversion, from this time forth Whitman's whole life, outer as well as inner, became harmonized and tranquilized. He had found a pattern and a purpose.

As the years passed and the adjustment became more settled and habitual, perhaps the poet himself forgot, or may never fully have understood, the emotions which he first conquered in *Leaves of Grass*. Certainly he was inclined more and more to interpret those first naïve confessions with a disingenuousness that has baffled many a biographer. A study of the successive editions reveals the life-long effort which he gave to revising, deleting, and disguising those first outpourings of his subconscious in his attempt to spiritualize and sublimate the record of his inner life. But there in the 1855 edition is the secret of the whole life and the completed book—the key to Whitman's poetic stimulus, his literary expression, his symbolism, and his unceasing efforts to perpetuate an "official portrait" of himself.

The prodigious researches of Holloway and the Freudian interpretations of Catel culminated in 1933 in the most extensive study of the editions and of Walt Whitman's place in world literature so far accomplished, Frederik Schyberg's *Walt Whitman*.[64] Although Schyberg's language predetermined a small audience for his book, his nationality and geographical location gave him advantages not possessed by American or English biographers. Like most Danish scholars, possessing a knowledge of several languages, including English, and being thoroughly familiar with the history of European literature, Schyberg was able to interpret and judge Whitman in terms of the international currents of thought and poetic theory to which he was unconsciously indebted.

Schyberg's first chapter, an attempt to orient Whitman with respect to the national history and the culture of the poet's land, is superficial and has little value for the American student. His second chapter, a strictly biographical sketch, is of interest mainly because it indicates the author's sources and attitudes. Here we see that Schyberg is fully aware of his debt to Catel, though he does not accept Catel's whole thesis and eventually goes far beyond him. He calls the publication of the journalistic writings "negative research"; they contributed to destroy the myths, but offered nothing to fill the gap. We can see Schyberg's indebtedness to Catel in his belief that the myths which Whitman invented to conceal the uneventful periods in his life—or to shield some innate weakness of character—, he thought concerned himself and himself alone.[6] Thus, the Danish biographer believes with Catel that there were truths and secrets which the poet concealed, either consciously or unconsciously, but he makes less use of Freud than the French biographer did. He is equally sure, however, that the New Orleans romance never existed except in the brain of Bazalgette and his followers, but he disagrees with Catel on the auto-eroticism; he thinks that Whitman was simply abnormally slow in his biological development, and that he always retained some feminine characteristics (as even John Burroughs had observed.)[65]

On one fundamental point Schyberg agrees with Bertz: "At one time Whitman's followers wanted to make him more than a poet; they wanted to make him a philosopher and a prophet. Both rôles were impossible ... Whitman was a lyricist, not a logician; he was a mystic, not a philosopher."[8] Schyberg acknowledges that he was a religious prophet in the same sense and degree that Nietzsche and Carlyle were, but no more. In his lyric forms and his treatment of sex Walt Whitman created a new epoch and became a major figure in world literature, and these were superlative achievements, but Schyberg sweeps aside all other claims for the American poet.

Although the earliest biographers often quoted the poet's idealization of himself, his ancestry, and his conception of his own mission in *Leaves of Grass*, no one before Schyberg had examined all the editions to discover Whitman's biography in the *changes* and *growth* of the editions.

Schyberg's long and intricate analysis of the first edition belongs rather to the subject of textual criticism than biographical interpretation, but significant here is the fact that he also finds "the joy, confidence, and optimism" of the first volume a literary rather than a biographical reality.[44, 83] And in the comparison of the wording and the feeling of Whitman's cosmic visions and pantheistic sentiments with the works of many European romanticists, we see that they were not unique and that they need not, therefore, have been the product of distinctly abnormal psychology.

The second edition of *Leaves of Grass*, coming only one year after the first, was similar to the '55 version. It was the third edition, in Schyberg's opinion, not the first, that recorded the poet's psychological crisis. If Whitman did experience a tragic romance, it must have been between 1855 and '60, for in this 1860 edition traces of some sort of defeat are plainly visible. Since some of the private notebooks for this period are missing (possibly destroyed by the poet himself), Schyberg wonders whether he might not have led a disgraceful and dissolute saloon life[143] until the war broke out in 1861, when he recorded his dedication of himself to inaugurating a new regime which would give him "a purged, cleansed, spiritualized, invigorated body."[66] Soon he walked out of Pfaff's restaurant and turned his back on the New York Bohemians. But whatever the secret of this period may be, Whitman guarded it well—except for the emotional tone of that third edition. The key poems express personal grief and discouragement.

"The unspoken word, 'the word' which Whitman sought so zealously and so arrogantly in Section 50 of 'Song of Myself,' and of which he said:

> It is not chaos or death—it is form, union, plan—
> it is eternal life—it is happiness.

that word Whitman found in the years between 1856-1860, and it was both death and chaos—but primarily death."[147] What loved one had died we do not know, but the real theme of "Out of the Cradle" is "Two together," and the fact that in later revisions the poet generalized and partly disguised the extremely personal tone of the first version lends credence to the suspicion that the original poem gave expression to some deep and genuine experience between the second and third editions. Schyberg notes also a sense of frustration and despair in "As I Ebb'd with the Ocean of Life."[149] The "ship-wreck motif" is prominent in this edition. And it is highly significant that *Leaves of Grass* has become "a few dead leaves." Certainly, "The arrogant pantheism of the earlier editions had become a hopeless pantheism."[150]

The only clue to the morbidity of the 1860 *Leaves* is probably the "Calamus" poems of that edition. In future revisions the poet gradually blurred the original impulses, even eliminating some poems altogether (despite his refusal to expurgate a single line for Thayer and Eldridge). On the basis of the later versions, Binns and Bazalgette tried to interpret these poems as a social program, but Schyberg thinks they are just as unmistakably love poems as Sappho's are, and the only love poems that Whitman ever wrote[159]—for the "Children of Adam" group is philosophical rather than personal. "In Paths Untrodden," which gives the "program" of this group, suggests that there is something different and rather daring in this love. And it is significant that two of the most revealing poems were later deleted: "Long I Thought that Knowledge Alone Would Suffice" expresses the poet's willingness to give up his songs because his lover is jealous, and in "Hours Continuing Long,

Sore and Heavy-Hearted" we find him in utter dejection because he
has lost his lover: "Hours sleepless . . . discouraged, distracted . . .
Hours when I am forgotten . . ."

> Sullen and suffering hours! (I am ashamed—but it is useless—
>   I am what I am;)
> Hours of my torment—I wonder if other men ever have the like,
>   out of the like feelings?

Schyberg thinks that this poem, and the experience it reveals,
rather than a tragic New Orleans romance, gives the real origin of
"Out of the Cradle Endlessly Rocking." However, he adds that,
"Whitman probably wrote these verses quite innocently and published them without considering how he exposed himself—because
they spring from unrequited love . . . ."[160] D. H. Lawrence and
Whitman released their erotic impulses in their work, not in their
lives.[67] Furthermore, the puberal and effeminate character of Whitman's erotic mentality[162] is paralleled in the writings of other
mystics, such as the medieval Heinrich Suso and the Persian Rumi. It
is not an isolated phenomenon in *Leaves of Grass* but is common in
the history of religious and poetic mystics. Furthermore, after the
first impulse of the poems had passed, "Calamus" became for Whitman a "city of friends," and in *Democratic Vistas* (1871) he was able
to give it a genuine social interpretation.

The 1860 edition contains not only the record of the great
spiritual crisis of Whitman's life—in which he seems to have con-
templated suicide—but it also reveals the means by which he saved
himself. This is a discovery of vast importance both to Whitman
biography and the critical interpretation of *Leaves of Grass*. Though
torn and racked by conflicts within, he was struggling for both a
personal and a literary unity. (The "Poem of Many in One"—later
"By Blue Ontario's Shore"—is characteristic.) Conflicts within himself would be conquered because they were found collected in one
body as the many poems were collected in one book.[154] And by a
kind of unconscious ironical symbolism, the nation was becoming
divided as Walt Whitman had been. Thus he proclaimed the Union
when the states were on the verge of a break; he hailed adhesiveness,
though he had not found it. In "To a President," "To the States,"
and other poems we find "spontaneous confession of the real situation." Thus it was not entirely accidental that, "For Whitman the

great democratic fiasco of these years came to correspond to the fateful character of his love in the 'Calamus' poems, and thus confirmed the duality of the book's proclamation of 'evil as well as good!' "[172] But presently he turned his attention to America's future greatness, and thus regained his faith and confidence. "On the Beach at Night" in the 1871 edition answers the despairing question of "As I Ebb'd with the Ocean of Life" in the 1860 edition. By this time Whitman's spiritual crisis was completely over.

What saved him, above all else, was the unifying effect of the Civil War—not only through his own patriotic and devoted services in the army hospitals, but also because the war gave Whitman and the nation Abraham Lincoln.

Lincoln and Whitman complemented each other. Lincoln saved the union and he probably saved Whitman spiritually and practically, and it is also interesting that he appreciated *Leaves of Grass*. In Lincoln Whitman found his great Camerado, and the funeral hymn speaks of him as "my departing comrade." At any rate, at that time a revolution took place in Whitman's inner life, a recovery from "the 1860 psychosis."[181] Because the "Wound-Dresser" became a man who personally did what he had celebrated as an ideal, Schyberg finds *Drum-Taps* (1865) "an important and remarkable advance" in Whitman's art. The poet's sex emotions have become completely sublimated in his hospital work and in his poetry. "The Washington period was a peak in Whitman's life, a great strain, but also a great release and relief."[186] After *Drum-Taps* Whitman's works really became a unity, though gradually, step by step.

Discouragements returned to the poet after the Washington period, as in his "Prayer of Columbus" (written 1874), in which the mood of the "batter'd, wreck'd old man" is that of the paralyzed and dependent poet himself;[232] but the progress toward personal and literary unity continued until, in "A Backward Glance" (*November Boughs*, 1888), he could relax the struggle and look back upon his work as an evolution, a growth.[246] The links in the stages of development, however, had been obscured by the earlier efforts for unity, and the 1892 edition remained a record of the life Whitman wanted remembered, not entirely the one he had actually lived.

In his final chapter Schyberg says:

To discuss Whitman in world literature is to discuss those he resembled and those who resemble him. If we limit the problem to

include only his imitators and followers in modern literature, we rob
it of the greater share of its interest. In the relationships of literary
history the influence of one author on another is only half the story,
and often the least interesting; on the other hand, the problem of
types, of parallel intellectual development of authors who may never
have heard of each other, is a genuine and truly interesting
one.[248]

Since Whitman's place in world literature is the subject of the
final chapter in this *Handbook* it is sufficient here to point out that
Schyberg's study has an important bearing on Whitman biography,
for it reveals the American poet as less of a unique phenomenon and
an anomaly than his friends and most of the biographers have
thought. His temperament, conduct, and characteristic expression
link him with the lives and writings of the great mystics of all ages
and all lands. And in his typical thought and poetic form he was
preceded and followed by similar poets in the current of European
romanticism. This interpretation not only makes Walt Whitman personally less abnormal but it also helps to explain his astounding
world-fame and influence.

MASTERS AND SHEPHARD TO
FURNESS AND CANBY

Edgar Lee Masters' poorly-organized *Whitman* (1937), the first
full-length life in the United States after Catel's and Schyberg's
books in France and Denmark, made no significant contribution to
Walt Whitman scholarship or biography, but it did plainly indicate
changing attitudes toward the life of the American poet. Here we
find a frank discussion of Whitman as one of those "sports" in nature
which sex pathologists call "Uranians." Masters applies to Whitman
de Joux's definition: "They are enthusiastic for poetry and music,
are often eminently skilful in the fine arts, and are overcome with
emotion and sympathy at the least sad occurrence. Their sensitive-
ness, their endless tenderness for children, their love of flowers, their
great pity for beggers and crippled folk are truly womanly."[68] The
same authority on the conduct of this type of man: "As nature and
social law are so cruel as to impose a severe celibacy on him his
whole being is consequently of astonishing freshness and superb
purity, and his manners of life as modest as those of a saint."[143]
Thus on the basis of modern psychology Whitman's character is now
defended with a new tolerance and veneration.

The poet of Spoon River thinks Whitman's "poems of nakedness" not a "survival of youthful exhibitionism," but the result of
"his free and barbaric innocent days in the country, by the sea ...
and of his own wonderful health and vitality."[44] And of "Calamus": "Whitman took America for his love and his wife, in somewhat the same way as Vachel Lindsay did later."[45] Masters admits
that there was unusual warmth in the poet's affection for Doyle but
does not think there was anything shameful about it. "Foreigners
have remarked that men in America are not really friends, and that
love is not so passionate, so tender, among Americans as among the
Latin races, or the Germans."[132]

In the opinion of Masters, Whitman's greatest achievements were
his literary pioneering and his breaking the bonds of narrow conventionalism. "He was a great influence in inaugurating this better
respect for the body which we know today. He stood for sanity in
matters of sex and for the outspoken championship of sexual delight
as one of the blessings of human life."[323] As poet "he felled to
some extent the encumbering forest and let later eyes see in part
what the lay of the land was ..."[327]

In the following year (1938) the bitterest attack on Whitman
since Bertz's *Yankee-Heiland* was published in the United States by
Esther Shephard as *Walt Whitman's Pose*. Mrs. Shephard would deny
that it was an attack, but so disillusioned was she by her "discoveries" that she branded Whitman's whole literary career as a "pose"
and a calculated attempt to deceive the public. She found such
striking parallels between *Leaves of Grass* and the epilogue of George
Sand's *Countess of Rudolstadt* that she concluded the American poet
got the first conception of his literary rôle from George Sand's "vagabond poet, dressed in laborer's garb, who goes into a trance and
composes what is described as 'the most magnificent poem that can
be conceived.' "[69] Likewise Sand's *Journeyman Joiner* which Whitman reviewed in 1847, gave him ideas for this pose:

It is a story of a beautiful, Christ-like young carpenter, a proletary
philosopher, who dresses in a mechanic's costume but is scrupulously
clean and neat. He works at carpentering with his father but patiently takes time off whenever he wants to in order to read, or give
advice on art, or share a friend's affection. In short, he is very much
the kind of carpenter that Walt Whitman became in the time of the
long foreground ... [201]

There can be no doubt that Whitman read George Sand before writing the first edition of *Leaves of Grass*, and he was also certainly influenced by the French novelist. Mrs. Shephard admits that, "If *Leaves of Grass* is a great book, it does not matter that Walt Whitman was a sly person and a poseur."[237] But in her whole discussion she makes him sound like a fraud and seems to cast suspicion not only on his honesty but also on the value of his literary creation.[70] Undoubtedly her discovery did have some influence on later Whitman biography, for she had at least proven that books had had a great deal more importance in his life than most of the biographers had yet realized. But there were other writers aside from George Sand whom he could—and certainly did draw upon too.[71] Nearly every critic who reviewed Mrs. Shephard's book agreed that she had exaggerated the importance of this one source. And anyway, like the "Happy Hypocrite" of Max Beerbohm's delightful little allegory, Whitman wore his mask with such sincere intention that underneath he too became, no less than Beerbohm's reformed rake, an exact and genuine facsimile of the former disguise. At the beginning of his career as the poet of *Leaves of Grass*, Walt Whitman may have assumed a pose in his life and his book, but all eye-witnesses of his conduct and personality confirm the belief of most biographers that to a remarkable degree he actually became the person and poet he wished to be.

By a lucky coincidence, Haniel Long's *Walt Whitman and the Springs of Courage* (1938) answered the skepticism of Mrs. Shephard's "pose theory," though unfortunately the book was published by an obscure press[72] and is not yet well known. "Wars and pestilence and pestilential literary fashions come and go," says Long, "but literature remains the picture of man adapting himself to the new-old necessities of intimacy with the universe and himself."[142-43] This book is not, properly speaking, a biography but it is a critical interpretation which reveals Whitmans's biography in a new light. As the author says, "To examine Whitman's life with an eye to observing what his springs of courage were, is simply to respond to our need of outwitting and defying those forces in society today which would rob us of the last shred of self-confidence."[3] Or to put it a little differently:

Now I will begin writing what I can discern of the things that gave Whitman trouble, and the things that gave him no trouble; and how, in spite of troubles which were his fault, or the fault of others, or merely the result in any age of being born, he was able to grow into a tremendous oak, root himself well in the soil, and extend wide branches for any who for centuries to come might be needing shade.[7]

Since this book is not, as stated above, a conventional biography, Whitman's faults and troubles are not treated specifically, but anyone familiar with the story of his life knows in general what they were. Starting then, with a recognition that Walt Whitman's life was haunted by doubts, uncertainties, and human frailty, what was the secret of the healing courage which he attained and all men desire? "First of all is the diverting fact that Whitman, like Rilke's Fraülein Brahe, lived in wonderland—though his sojourn there was brief."[9] This wonderland was phrenology. Every student of Whitman's life knows that at one time he took stock in this pseudo-science and cherished for years the flattering interpretation that had been made of his own cranial bumps. One scholar, Edward Hungerford, even reached the conclusion that the phrenologist's extremely favorable reading of Whitman's "chart of bumps" first gave him the serious ambition of trying to be a poet[73]—a theory perhaps as oversimplified as Mrs. Shephard's. Long does not know whether "phrenology told Whitman correctly where he was strong and where he was weak," but, "We need to be praised, we need also to be alarmed, about ourselves,"[14] and phrenology temporarily served this purpose.

That pseudo-science furnished Whitman a picture of a balanced harmonious life, from which if one were sensible nothing human need be excluded: which makes it an important factor in his growth. Its terminology has not stuck, its names seem fantastic. Yet it achieved an enviable simplification, and above all it heartened one with its moral blessings and warnings. American life was neither balanced nor harmonious, nor was Whitman's own life. By including all aspects of his being, and by indicating certain aspects of himself he might well guard against, phrenology left him with a vigorous hope for himself, and for his native land. It was part and parcel of the gospel of the 'healthy-mindedness,' and Whitman became its poet.[15]

Thus phrenology met the pragmatic test for Walt Whitman, as

religion and all sorts of rag-tags of philosophy do for other men.

The second spring of courage for Whitman was Emerson.[16ff] First of all his essays, his poems, and his transcendentalism; and second, that generous, impulsive greeting of the 1855 *Leaves of Grass*. The letter went to Whitman's head for a while and made him do some silly things, but it gave him courage at a time when he most needed it and ultimately strengthened his self-reliance until he had less need for Emerson. The arrogant tone of the first two editions is misleading; actually, "Whitman exceeded the rest of the brotherhood of writers in his anxiety to make sure of bouquets."[26] He needed more, not less, than most men to find "springs of courage."

This need was intensified by the hostile opposition which he encountered on almost every side: prudish conventionalism, the Bostonians' belief that American culture should "stay close to the mother culture of England,"[40] and ignorant blindness of readers unconditioned to a new poetic art. Much of Long's book is taken up with the courage the poet derived from his contact with common people, personal friends, Mrs. Gilchrist, Peter Doyle, and from the philosophy and religion which he painfully worked out for himself. This book might be called *an intellectual biography*. It attempts to lay bare the organic pattern of ideas and faiths, and the expression of them which integrated one man's life and gave it the strength of an oak tree with shade for future generations of men.

Newton Arvin's *Whitman* is even less biography than Long's book, for it is mainly a study of Whitman's social thinking, but it deserves to be mentioned among the memorable publications of 1938 which future biographers must take into consideration in their re-evaluation of *Leaves of Grass* and its author. Arvin finds two powerful and opposing intellectual currents in the life and thought of Whitman. "He was so powerfully worked upon by the romantic mood of his generation that it has largely been forgotten or ignored how much he had been affected, in boyhood and earliest youth, by an older and tougher way of thought ... he was the grandchild of the Age of Reason."[74] Arvin makes out Whitman's father to have been a sort of intellectual rebel himself, a subscriber to the "freethought" journal edited by Frances Wright and Robert Dale Owen, a follower of the unorthodox Hicksite Quakers, and a democrat of the Jefferson and Paine tradition. No other critic or biographer had given Walter Whitman credit for so much intellectual curiosity and vitality.

Although he raises in the mind of the reader the possibility of an intellectual antithesis in the Whitman home, the father leaning toward eighteenth-century rationalism and the mother toward romantic mysticism, Arvin is careful to point out that this contradiction was actually characteristic of the age in which the poet grew up. Even the leading scientists, "almost to a man ... succeeded in 'reconciling' their inherited Calvinism or Arminianism with their Newtonian or their Darwinian knowledge."[170-71]

Nevertheless, the Quaker influence which Whitman derived in part at least through his family was unfortunate because the "inner light" doctrine encouraged him "in a flaccid irrationalism,"[174] and "For the poet whose book was allegedly to be pervaded by the conclusions of the great scientists, this was hardly the wisest habit to form." Arvin thinks that Whitman's anti-intellectualism and obscurantism grew with age. In the first edition he found the earth sufficient, but as he became older he found it less and less sufficient and he sought assurance in "world-weary and compensatory mysticisms."[229]

On the vexing question of Whitman's sex "anomaly," Arvin is unequivocal. "There was a core of abnormality in Whitman's emotional life," but it was not the whole of his nature; "he remained to the end, in almost every real and visible sense, a sweet and sane human being ... who had proved himself capable of easy and genial friendship with hundreds of ordinary people."[277] Arvin expresses the opinion that "it would not be incredible if even the most personal poems in 'Calamus' should come to be cherished, as Shakespeare's sonnets have been, by thousands of normal men and women,"[278] and adds the information that André Malraux and Thomas Mann have accepted Whitman's "virile fraternity" and "a patriotism of humanity" as social and political slogans.[282]

The duality which Arvin finds in Whitman's age and in the poet's own life and conduct gives this critic himself a divided attitude toward his subject. Though he bitterly denounces Whitman's refusal to take an active part in the Abolitionist movement—believing to the last that the Civil War was only a struggle to preserve the Union[75] — and deplores his indifference to socialism and trade unionism, Arvin nevertheless concluded that *Leaves of Grass* is a full and brave "anticipatory statement of a democratic and fraternal humanism."[290]

Whether or not Long's and Arvin's books would occupy a permanent place in Whitman scholarship, they did at least contribute intelligent discussions of fundamental critical and biographical problems. But the old schools were not dead. In 1941 Frances Winwar published *American Giant: Walt Whitman and His Times*, an inaccurate, sentimental and journalistic rehash of the worst features of nearly all the previous biographies, though it was audaciously advertised as a "definitive life." Here we find the dust brushed from the hoary New Orleans romance, even the Washington romance revived from Holloway, and the most dogmatic denial of any taint of homosexual psychology in the "Calamus" poems. Despite her fanciful idealization of her hero, she perpetuates the inaccurate story of the "thousands of dollars" which the supposedly indigent poet spent in the building of his tomb. The whole Whitman family is sentimentalized, but especially is this true of "Mother Whitman," who is made into an ideal mother and housekeeper and a sort of moral saint.

Clifton Furness, the editor of the *Workshop*,[76] corrected the worst of Winwar's errors in a long review in *American Literature*.[77] From unpublished manuscripts he quoted passages to show the real emotions back of one of the poems which she used to support her belief in a normal love-affair in New Orleans, and he quoted from Mother Whitman's illiterate letters to show the confusion, squalor, bickering, and complaining in her household.

Meanwhile, Mrs. Katharine Molinoff had already published a monograph, *Some Notes on Whitman's Family* (1941)[78] which revealed sufficient reason for Mother Whitman's dejection and her whining letters. Her daughter Mary was capricious and headstrong.[79] Her youngest son, Edward, was a life-long cripple and imbecile, a constant care and worry to Walt and his mother. The oldest son, Jesse, died in the lunatic asylum. Andrew, an habitual drunkard, married a disreputable woman, who after her husband's death of tuberculosis of the throat, "became a social outcast and set her children to beg on the streets." Hannah married a mean, improvident artist who starved and beat her—not without "ample cause"—until she became psychopathic.

The whole picture is almost incredibly sordid, and yet there are only the vaguest hints in the biographies before 1941 of these conditions. Furness and Mrs. Molinoff, in these brief and pathetic glimpses into Walt Whitman's family relationships, gave a better understanding of "that baffling reluctance to mention any member of his family which is so puzzling to biographers."[5] Furthermore, Walt's letters to his mother, his constant financial help for her and

Eddie, and his worrying and planning for them, reveal his devotion, unselfishness, and gentleness as no biographer has done. In these relationships he is truly and incontrovertably heroic.

Furness's review of Winwar and Mrs. Molinoff's sordid revelations increased the Whitman scholar's dissatisfaction with all the published biographies. Furness had let it be known that he was working on a life of Whitman based on all existing sources, especially unpublished letters and manuscripts, and his biography was impatiently awaited. In 1942 Hugh I'Anson Fausset published *Walt Whitman: Poet of Democracy*, but it was not the kind of book Furness had promised, and even the title was misleading, for the author was less concerned with the poet's democratic ideas than Arvin had been—and more superficial in his treatment. He presented "the poet of democracy" in the manner of Rossetti and Dowden, and more or less Symonds and Bailey, *i.e.*, as the true representative of a raw, undeveloped, undiscriminating American culture.

The thesis of Fausset's book is that Whitman was a split personality, never able to achieve poise, serenity, and unity in either art or life. This thesis leads Fausset into a dilemma familiar to the reader of Whitman biography. The man he reveals is mentally indolent, uncritical, almost sloven; as a personality, by turns affectionate and secretive, egotistical and shrinking; as a poet, undisciplined, unsure of his technique, a "true poet" only on rare and lucky occasions. Yet Fausset wrote the book because he was convinced of the importance of Walt Whitman as a poet, a man whose heart was in the right place but head always undependable. The biographer, in short, finds himself unable to explain the literary power and world-wide fame of the man he attempts to analyze.

A year later (1943) one of the major literary editors and critics of the period, Henry Seidel Canby, almost produced the biography so eagerly awaited. His *Walt Whitman: An American* epitomizes the best of recent Whitman scholarship, resolves many of the biographical cruxes with plausible and sensible conclusions, and leaves the reader with the conviction that Walt Whitman, both as man and poet, deserves the reputation and influence which he has attained throughout the modern world.

Canby has not presumed to write a "final book on Whitman," or to assemble, "for the benefit of scholars, . . . all known information about his friends, his family, and his daily doings"—information "much needed, and . . . soon to be made readily accessible in a book by my friend, Mr. Furness"[v]; his book is frankly an interpretation, an attempt to "make intelligible Whitman himself and his 'Leaves'."[vi] Canby's success is due in part to his basic assumption that, "Walt Whitman's America was not a real America, though the real America was his background and a source of his inspiration. It was a symbolic America, existing in his own mind, and always pointed toward a future of which he was prophetic." He agrees with Catel and confirms Schyberg (whose book had been translated orally to him) that "a satisfactory biography of Whitman must be essentially a biography of an inner life and the mysterious creative processes of poetry."[2] But he does not psychoanalyze or draw sensational contrasts between fiction and reality:

This biographer and that, using hints or boastings, or the dubious evidence of poems, has endeavored to spice this daily life with hypothetical journeys, unverified quadroon lovers, illegitimate children, and dark suggestions of vice and degeneracy. Yet even if all these stories about Whitman's hidden activities were true, they would not account for a passionate fervor that has deeper and more burning sources.[3]

For despite the fact that he was "a poseur sometimes, and often a careless carpenter of words," Whitman "made articulate and gave an enduring life in the imagination to the American dream of a continent where the people should escape from the injustices of the past and establish a new and better life in which everyone would share."

Most biographers have attempted to explain the mystery of this ordinary youth who suddenly revealed himself as a poetic genius. Some thought he was aroused by a "dark lady," others by psychological frustration, but most were inclined to believe that a mystical experience "made him a prophet and a poet." Canby finds no mystery at all—except in so far as poetic genius is always something of a miracle. During Whitman's childhood in Brooklyn and his youthful contact with the country and village people of Long Island, he was storing up experiences and impressions which enabled him to become a "representative" poet of nineteenth-century America. Small towns, printing offices, country schools, political newspapers, all these were important during the formative years when the future poet's "imagination was like a battery charging."[29] Canby thus makes little of Whitman's boasted heredity, much of his environment.

This approach enables Canby to avoid some of the pitfalls of other biographers, for he is content to describe Whitman's social and intellectual milieu instead of attempting to create or reconstruct his inner life before he became articulate. "He was a happy familiar of streets and market-places, and a spokesman for society [through his editorials], before he began to be egoist, rebel, and prophet."[72] After 1847, when Whitman began to record in his notebooks his poetic ambitions and his intimate thoughts, subjective biography is possible, and with these as the primary source this critic-biographer began the "inner life" of his subject.

When the young journalist turns poet and mystic, the biographer meets his first real test. To Whitman's contemporaries, and even to many later critics, "This self-assumed apostleship, this mantle of a prophet put on at the age of twenty-eight, seems a little strong."[92] Canby shows that, "This new Walt Whitman proposes to inspire because he is inspired. Greatness is growth, he says, and his soul has become great because in mystical, imaginative experiences it has grown until it identifies itself with the power of the universe." He was neither his own ego nor the editorial "we," "but 'my soul,' by which he meant an identification of himself with the power for greatness which he felt intuitively to be entering his own spirit." The poet thus began the long career of dramatizing this "soul," presenting "a 'Walt Whitman' who was symbolic, yet in his knowledge of men and cities and scenes and emotions of the common man was also representative of the merely human Walt who had been absorbing the life of America so passionately for many years."[93] No previous biographer had so convincingly reconciled the "symbolic" Whitman with the objective Whitman.

This reconciliation, however, does not eliminate the "problems" which have harassed the biographers for half a century; nor does it necessarily "solve" them, but what it does do above all else is to undermine their former importance. No doubt in some cases, too, it is too facile. For example, Canby, like Schyberg, recognizes in the 1860 edition the evidences of spiritual "crisis", and he readily admits that during the later 1850s the poet was troubled by "deep perturbations of sexual passion,"[162] but Canby's thesis leads him to attribute Whitman's crisis to national rather than personal causes— "this was a decade of rising hate," and hate was the antithesis of the poet's dream of an "ideal democracy."

Canby does not, however, attempt to deny or disguise the sex problem in Whitman's life and writing; he refuses to conjecture or theorize where there is no evidence. "There may of course have been, as his later biographers think, other journeys, other residences in the South before 1860—perhaps lovers, perhaps a mother of his alleged children. We do not know, and there is no real evidence."[168] Discussing "Children of Adam," Canby says, "This man's greatness is in some respects a function of his excessive sexuality. Whole sections of the 'Leaves' are either sheer rhetorical fantasy or the articulation and sublimation of experience." But, he adds, "Of that experience we know actually very little . . . [186] Unfortunately, much has to be omitted because we simply have no facts and in all probability never will have."[187]

Like Catel, Schyberg, and Masters, Canby recognizes in Whitman a kind of extraordinary sexual versatility which is at least in part responsible for his universal love and cosmic imagination. Canby calls this characteristic "auto-eroticism," but thinks it was psychological rather than physical:

He could feel like a woman. He could feel like a man. He could love a woman—though one suspects that it was difficult for him to love women physically, unless they were simple and primitive types. He could love a man with a kind of father-mother love, mingled, as such love often is, with obscure sexuality. Because all reference was back to his own body, he seemed to himself to be a microcosm of humanity. There are, I think no truly objective love poems in the 'Leaves of Grass.'[204-05]

Schyberg thought that Whitman's "turmoils" were calmed by his active participation in the war through his hospital work, and Canby added more weight to the argument, extending the influence from the personal to the intellectual realm. The poet "becomes less interested in himself as a religion incarnate, less rhetorical about democracy, more certain of his confidence that democracy has firm ground in human nature."[230] Fully aware of the "corruption, degeneracy, pettiness, both physical and spiritual,"[263] in his postwar America, Whitman attempted to counteract these evils by preaching respect for the individual personality and the dangers of selfishness. No other biographer or critic has succeeded so well in combatting the superficial belief that Whitman's democratic teachings were impractically visionary and optimistic. "His vision of democracy as the guardian of personality, the nurse of individual growth, seems overconfident until one discovers how much more he knew of the danger and diseases of democracy than even the ablest of his critics."[268] Not only, therefore, does Canby regard Walt Whitman as a true prophet of American democracy, who is "intelligible and dynamic" for this generation, but he succeeds in unifying the poet's personality, his literary creations, and his message into a new symbolical expression of the ideals which Americans profess—and may some day apply: "it is impossible today to escape his voice." Therefore, "Intent upon a task not yet amenable to fact and reason, he was like the Hebrew prophets who had no private life that mattered."[354] With all its admirable insights, Canby's book is unsatisfactory because he concludes, finally, that intimate details of Whitman's physical life are far less important than his life of imagination and artistic creation. But by mid-century biographers were becoming more acutely aware that the psychic and physical life feed on each other—a doctrine, in fact, which Walt Whitman himself emphasized in the first edition of *Leaves of Grass*:

> I have said that the soul is not more than the body,
> And I have said that the body is not more than the soul, . . .
> "Song of Myself," sec. 48.

ASSELINEAU, ALLEN, AND CHASE

The first biographer following Canby to attempt a deeper exploration of Whitman's psyche and the source of his art was Roger Asselineau in France. After two years of intensive research in the United States, he wrote a doctoral dissertation for the Sorbonne entitled *L'Evolution de Walt Whitman après la Première Edition des Feuilles d'Herbe,* which received the highest mark of approval by the Université de Paris and was published by Didier in 1954. Asselineau began his study with the first edition because Catel had already traced Whitman's development from his childhood through 1855—though Asselineau did draw upon details of the poet's early life when they were needed in his interpretation. Since this book was originally a thesis, it conformed to the French academic tradition of "L'Homme et l'Oeuvre."

In his translation, which the Harvard University Press published in 1960 and 1962 in two volumes, Asselineau called the first volume *The Evolution of Walt Whitman: The Creation of a Personality* and the second . . . *The Creation of a Book.* The division had both ad-

vantages and disadvantages, but Asselineau handled it with such skill
and grace that one easily forgives the artificiality of the dichotomy,
and it does emphasize the two great ambitions of Walt Whitman: to
achieve his own idea of a perfect personality and to express it in a
poetic masterpiece.

Whitman himself said that his childhood was unhappy, and
Asselineau traces his vain searchings, continuing into early manhood,
in a series of frustrated attempts to find friends and "lovers" to
satisfy his emotional hungers. He was by nature homosexual, and he
did not know how to come to terms with society or himself. He
longed to be an example of joyous, healthy, masculinity, but he
knew where he was "most weak," and as a consequence was lonely
even in the midst of crowds. He sought compensation, therefore, in
the creation of a lyrical "I" corresponding to his dreams of love,
power, and happiness. Like Schyberg, Asselineau thinks that if
Whitman had found relief in sexual relations, he would not have
become a poet—or at least not the kind he did become. His poems
were not only a substitute for physical satisfactions, but also a
therapy, and the marvel is how nearly he succeeded in healing himself. In his final years he appeared to be the wise, serene, heroic
personality he had longed to become when he began that first edition
of *Leaves of Grass*.

In *The Creation of a Book* Asselineau, like Schyberg, gives adequate attention to the poet's stages of evolution through the various
editions of *Leaves of Grass*, but his method is less historical and
bibliographical than philosophical. In separate chapters he defines
and illustrates Whitman's "physical mysticism," his "implicit metaphysics," his ethics, his aesthetics, his sex life, his egocentrism and
patriotism, social thought, etc.; and in Part Two Whitman's style,
language, prosody. At the heart of Asselineau's interpretation is the
inter-relationship of the poet's sensations and philosophical-artistic
intuitions. Whitman started always with his body, but "his sensuality, instead of remaining exclusively carnal, opens out and is
sublimated."[4] He broke the strongest social taboos of his time by
transposing "the center of sensibility" from the heart to the genitals:
"On this point he prefigures Freud."[p.5] This was not a completely
new observation, but no one had ever before seen its importance so
clearly in Whitman biography and criticism, or made such effective
use of it. For example, Whitman's spiritual solution to evil: "the soul
is always good and beautiful, but the flesh is sometimes rotten; in

other words, matter is the obstacle which provisionally prevents the soul from blossoming out ... there are no wicked, but only sick people (he prefigures the psychoanalysts in this respect). ..."[54]

In his conclusions Asselineau extends the insight of all previous psychological biographers of Whitman:

Poetry was for him a means of purification which, if it did not make him normal, at least permitted him to retain his balance in spite of his anomaly. In this sense, ... his *Leaves of Grass* are "fleurs du mal". ... His poetry is not the song of a demigod or a superman, as some of his admirers would have it, but the sad chant of a sick soul seeking passionately to understand and to save itself. ... His anomaly, which in all likelihood was what drove him to write *Leaves of Grass*, also explains certain of his limitations, and notably his inability to renew himself as he grew older—unlike Goethe. He lived too much alone, too much wrapped up in himself. ... he is, despite appearances, the poet of anguish. ...

Whitman had thus, at the very core of himself, a sense of defeat and frustation. He had had the ambition to create two masterpieces: a book of immortal poems and a life, the nobility and greatness of which would become legendary. He succeeded in one respect only, but his failure was, perhaps, the condition of that success.[II, 259-60]

My own biography, *The Solitary Singer: A Critical Biography of Walt Whitman*, was published a year later than Asselineau's *L'Evolution de Walt Whitman*, but was written almost simultaneously with it.[80] M. Asselineau and I had exchanged views in conversations and correspondence and found that we agreed on major questions. Furthermore, we were both influenced by the interpretations of Catel and Schyberg. Consequently, the reader will find that our biographies differ less in basic answers than in methods of presenting them. We agree that Whitman was more erotically aroused by men than women, but that clear evidence of his homosexual life is lacking. For this reason I label his sexual emotions as *homoerotic*, whereas Asselineau uses the unequivocal term *homosexual*, which is commonly interpreted to imply pederasty or other aberrant sexual practices. Perhaps today these distinctions are less important than they seemed in the decade of the 1950s.

Celebrated poets now flaunt their homosexuality and identify with Whitman as a man of their own kind. But whether or not homosexuality is *abnormal*, as most people thought in the 1950s, including psychiatrists, the evidence is overwhelming that a century earlier Whitman's erotic impulses made him feel alienated, and this caused him to rebel against the sexual taboos of his society, though he openly fought for sexual freedom in general, not for the preferences of a minority, and opposed all censorship in literature. But he did not stop with condemning prudery: he fantasized solutions to his personal problems; hence his cult of "Calamus" (or "manly love"), which he sublimated into universal brotherhood, and his rôle as "the poet of democracy." Either by coincidence or logical choice, both Asselineau and I made thematic use of Whitman's characterization of himself as "the solitary singer."

I had not intended to attempt a biography of Whitman until Clifton Furness died without having produced the book Canby had confidently predicted.[81] It then seemed to me that someone should make use of the new information about the poet's family which Furness and Molinoff had begun to reveal, and to extend the search for such material for the whole of Whitman's life. In addition to finding letters and unpublished manuscripts containing personal information hitherto not known, or suppressed by the poet and his biographers, I also examined intensively Whitman's whole social and intellectual background, not only for "sources" and "influences," but also for the purpose of orienting his life and writings in his contemporary world. Asselineau's French view of the American setting enabled him to make some refreshing observations, but his scheme did not permit him the space to treat this background in depth. However, the reader of *The Solitary Singer* will find familiar resemblances to Asselineau's portrait in my narrative, perhaps especially of the pain-wracked old man in Camden, courageously cultivating resignation, charming his many foreign visitors by his rambling garrulities. For its thoroughness some critics called my book the "definitive" biography, but it is doubtful that there ever can be a completely definitive biography of so complicated and paradoxical a man as Walt Whitman.

Instead of tracing the poet's chronological growth and decline in massive detail, Asselineau was more interested in an overview of Whitman's psychology, philosophy, and aesthetics, which he presented in highly successful critical essays in his second volume. I gave considerable attention to the influence of space on Whitman, both geographical and astronomical, but Asselineau showed how both psychologically and aesthetically the dimensions of space shrank with the poet's decline of physical vigor. In "Song of Myself" he inventoried ecstatically the sights of the earth and the worlds beyond.

He needed no less than the whole earth at the beginning of his career; in his old age, he was satisfied with a flower, a bird, a street, a printer's case—and a few lines. And yet, these humble vignettes still imply and suggest the rest of the world in the manner of the Japanese hokkus of the best period. "The first dandelion" reminds us of the everlastingness of life, the canary in its cage celebrates the "joie de vivre" in its own way; all mankind walks up and down Broadway and the "font of type" contains in latent form all the passions of men. His imagination has lost its former vigor, but his glance has remained as piercing as ever and his sight still carries to the utmost confines of the universe. [II, 101]

As Oscar Wilde said to Whistler, "I wish I had said that," and now by endorsement I do. It is exactly right, written by one poet of another.

In 1955, the first centennial of *Leaves of Grass*, Richard Chase published another biographical study entitled *Walt Whitman Reconsidered*. The first chapter, called "Beginnings," is superficial and inaccurate in a considerable number of minor facts carelessly summarized from other biographies. But Chase's book should not be dismissed as unimportant. He agreed with Schyberg (whose Danish book was now available in English)[82] and Asselineau that Whitman was not the happy extrovert of robust health and heroic personality the poet created for himself, but a troubled man torn by discordant elements in his mind and character. Yet this discord enabled him to write his masterpiece, "Song of Myself," which Chase calls "the profound and lovely comic drama of the self . . ."[48]

No one had ever before called "Song of Myself" a *comic* poem, and Chase's so labeling it gave a new direction both to biography and criticism of Whitman. Since the poet himself tried to play the role of moral leader in his poem, calling it "comic" implies that he failed on his own—or Emersonian—terms. Here Chase agrees with D. H. Lawrence, who called this Whitmanian role "tricksy-tricksy." And "as in all true, or high, comedy, the sententious, the too overtly insisted-on morality (if any) plays a losing game with ironical realism."[59] Whitman says he resists anything better than his own diversity, yet his subject is the diversity of the self celebrated in his poem. Chase thinks that Whitman himself saw the comic aspects of his incongruous diversity and deliberately assumed the tone of American humor—a point Constance Rourke had made in her *American Humor*.[83]

There is also a striking similarity, Chase says, between the "self" in "Song of Myself" and Christopher Newman in Henry James's *The American,* whom James describes as having the "look of being committed to nothing in particular, of standing in an attitude of general hospitality to the chances of life." To James, Newman was the archetypical American, whom Chase calls "the fluid, unformed personality exulting alternately in its provisional attempts to define itself and in its sense that it has no definition."[60] Chase cannot take seriously "the imagined world" of Whitman's poem, "a fantastic world in which it is presumed that the self can become identical with all other selves in the universe, regardless of time and space," as in Hindu poetry.[63] Nevertheless, this "idiosyncratic and illusory . . . relation of the self to the rest of the universe is a successful aesthetic or compositional device,"[64] enabling the poet to make of his paradoxes a comic "drama of identity." Later he lost the sense of paradox, forgetting "that self and en-masse are in dialectic opposition," and then he wrote such mechanical and vaguely abstract poems as "Passage to India."[65] This tendency finally ruined Whitman as a poet.

To the extent that Chase finds Whitman's literary successes and failures the consequence of character and personality, he is in agreement with Catel, Schyberg, and Asselineau, but as a critic he stands alone—with the possible exception of D. H. Lawrence[84] and Leslie Fiedler.[85] Malcolm Cowley also shares with him a preference for Whitman's concrete and realistic imagery and diction, but at the same time admires "Song of Myself" as an American kind of Hindu poem.[86]

Chase does not say that all of Whitman's poems after "Song of Myself" were failures, but only those, in whole or in part, in which he became vague and mechanical. The "saving grace" of "Crossing Brooklyn Ferry" is the confessional voice of "weakness and uncertainty."[108] Whitman became a great poet "under the pressure of his extraordinary capacity to imagine his own destruction."[125] He had a remarkable "sensibility of annihilation." In "Out of the Cradle" this sensibility gives meaning to "chaos and death," and " 'As I Ebb'd with the Ocean of Life' expresses the final helplessness of man before the mystery of the universe."[124] In these poems

Whitman's healthy irony saves him from self-pity, and makes him a great elegiac poet.

Whitman's strongest "personal impulses" were away from reality, reinforced by "Quaker mysticism and transcendental idealism."[134] But the excitement of the Civil War overwhelmed his introspective tendencies and enabled him to achieve a "new realism" in his *Drum-taps*. However, his "war experiences did not find a satisfactory expression in his poetry, although some of them did in *Specimen Days*. . . . The truth is that Whitman's career of hospital visiting became a substitute for poetry and not the inspiration of it."[136] In *Drum-Taps* it is obvious that his "visionary grasp of things is weakening," and he never recovered it. Some of his later poems have "valuable qualities," but most of them reveal "a mind in which productive tensions have been relaxed, conflicts dissipated, particulars generalized, inequities equalized." Dionysius had become "not Apollonian but positively Hellenistic—prematurely old, nerveless, sooth-saying, spiritually universalized."[148]

The "Hellenistic" Whitman was the Whitman Dr. Bucke knew. The poet told his first biographer (if we except Burroughs's *Notes* as a biography) that, "the character you give me is not the true one in the main—I am by no means the benevolent, equable, good happy creature you portray."[87] [174] Chase thinks he told the truth, and that he resembled the Carlyle he described in his memorial essay,[88] a person torn between "two conflicting agonistic elements."[175] Whitman called Carlyle a man whose heart was "often at odds with his scornful brain," the heart demanding reform and the brain denouncing it because his mind was haunted by "the spectre of world-destruction." To Chase the "agonistic Whitman" was the true Whitman, though it was obscured by "the bland, emasculate, pseudo-messianic ideal imposed upon him by his admirers and on the whole acquiesced in by himself."[89] [175]

SUMMARY AND CONCLUSION

Walt Whitman biography began with the hagiography of William D. O'Connor, John Burroughs, and Dr. R. M. Bucke, who adored Whitman personally and wanted to do something to overcome what they regarded as public misunderstanding and neglect of a great poet. Whitman appreciated their efforts and encouraged them. Aware that his first edition of *Leaves of Grass* was an affront to the leading poets and literary critics of mid-nineteenth-century America, Whitman himself began as early as 1855 to "promote" himself by writing anonymous reviews of his poems and cultivating the sympathy of friendly editors. Other poets have been guilty of such breaches of decorum and good taste, but few so impulsively as Walt Whitman. Even though his true greatness was not generally recognized until long after his death in 1892, he did receive some favorable reviews even for his first edition (as well as that flattering "greeting" from Emerson), and successive editions increased his audience. Whether the hagiography did any good at all is questionable. Certainly the idolatry and sentimentalism of O'Connor and Bucke (Burroughs was somewhat more discriminating) offended many possible friends, and may have delayed rather than hastened his winning the fame he deserved.

But there was at least one notable exception. At Cambridge University in England a young man from South Africa named Jan Christian Smuts (future Prime Minister of his country) read these hagiographies and decided three years after Whitman's death that his life showed "that rarest flowering of humanity—a true personality, strong, original . . . a whole and sound piece of manhood such as appears but seldom, even in the course of centuries."[90] Whitman seemed to Smuts to represent the ideal personality for an "organic" philosophy which was evolving in his mind. Of course Smuts also believed that the most perfect expression of this personality was *Leaves of Grass*, the poet's cherished conviction, too, but it is significant that the *man* was more interesting to Smuts than the poems themselves, though he presumed the "I" in the poems to be Walt Whitman. He had not heard of Yeats's *persona*, later developed in psychology by Jung, which distinguishes the *person* (the author) from his creative image (or *persona*). In fact, knowledge of the relations between the author's personal self and his *persona* would have to wait for the development of the "depth psychology" of Freud, Jung, and other psychoanalysts. Not only for Smuts, but for all of Whitman's early biographers, he literally celebrated and sang himself: ". . . this is no book,/ Who touches this touches a man."

Gradually Whitman biographies became more critical, though they were still, for the most part, by intimate friends and admirers who valued *Leaves of Grass* because the man they adored wrote it. John T. Trowbridge, however, thought that Whitman's long invalidism affected his memory, causing him to delude some of his biographers by making erroneous statements. To Edward Carpenter, the young English socialist, discovering *Leaves of Grass* had been a revelation, almost a religious experience, but in visiting Whitman in Camden he found the poet in person to be a bundle of contradictions, willful, obstinate, furtive, yet also tender and loving. Although himself homoerotic, Carpenter was puzzled by Whitman's letter in 1890 to Symonds angrily denying the interpretation of the "Calamus" poems as homosexual.[91] Carpenter decided that there was "a great tragic element in his nature"—thus anticipating Schyberg a generation later. The previous year (1905) Eduard Bertz had attacked the official "Yankee Saint" portrait of Whitman and detailed his charges of homosexuality. This was now a problem not easily ignored, but Carpenter concealed his doubts and insisted that he could believe the love in "Calamus" to be fraternal and democratic.

Another English admirer of Whitman, Henry Bryan Binns, came to the United States to gather material for the first fully detailed life of Whitman (1905), but he hypothicated a "romance" in New Orleans with a "southern lady," resulting in the birth of at least one child. This "romance" would haunt Whitman biography for decades, but otherwise Binns did write a reliable and informative life of the American poet.

The following year Bliss Perry made an even greater effort to dispel the myths and present the true Whitman, a man more human, "elemental and alive." Perry was not happy with the nakedness of Whitman's sex themes and motifs, but he regarded them more as literary subjects than autobiography. This was both a retreat and an advance in comprehension. A quarter century later Emory Holloway came no nearer than Perry in reaching a compromise between myth and truth (he still clung to the "New Orleans romance"), but he had done a vast amount of documentary research, especially for Whitman's years in journalism, and gave the fullest account until Rubin in 1973[92] of Whitman's activities to 1855. Scholarly biography had now replaced the glorified, sentimental accounts of Whitman's personal friends. In fact, meanwhile fashions in English biography had changed, and the goal in biography now most respected was *truth*. This new type of biography continued with Canby (1943), Asselineau (1954), and Allen (1955), who made the fullest use of new information about the poet's sordid family background, his relations with the Civil War soldiers, and his invalidism.

Before mid-century, however, literary criticism based on twentieth-century psychology had caught up with Walt Whitman. The first to use it was Jean Catel, who found the poet's most carefully-guarded secrets revealed in the first edition of *Leaves of Grass*—his unappeased erotic hungers, his latent homosexuality, and his fantasy compensations. Schyberg in 1933 extended this search through all editions of *Leaves of Grass*, paying special attention to the poet's revisions and editorial suppressions for clues to his psychic tensions and crises. The pursuit of biographical truth through close textual study was a new road for biographers of Whitman to take. Asselineau also traveled this route to still further discoveries of Whitman's psychological problems and resolution of them. He was particularly successful in showing the effects of the poet's state of health on his imagination and artistic grasp—another application of the "wound and the bow" myth of Philoctetes.

I also picked up some useful information and *aperçus* on the borders of these psychological paths, as in Whitman's annotations in the margins of his large collection of magazine clippings, his revisions of the "program" poem "Starting from Paumanok" (in one version Whitman expressed the desire to give up his role as poet for the nation and become the exclusive poet of his male lover), his correspondence with soldiers (in which erotic emotions mingled with sublimated paternity), and in the alteration of his literary plans at different periods of his life.

All of Whitman's recent biographers agree that in his poems he sought compensations for his physical, sexual, and social failures, and found, usually, beneficial therapy both for himself and his readers. In examining the contradictions in the drama of Whitman's identity of the self, Chase also joined the procession of these psychological biographers: ". . . Whitman achieved the remarkable feat of being an eccentric by taking more literally and mythicizing more simply and directly than anyone else the expressed intentions and ideals of democracy."[81] His "comic vision" became "a great releasing and regenerative force" for himself and American literature.

It is possible that some future biographer may yet find a letter or a diary giving evidence of some disgrace or moral perversion in Whitman's life, though the search has been so intensive during the past half century that it is unlikely. But the biographers and critics have found so much strength growing out of this poet's overcoming his weaknesses and misfortunes that scarcely anything could now be found to endanger his secure reputation. It also appears at the present time that factual biography has gone about as far as it can, though critical interpretation of the facts and the literary texts may flourish indefinitely. One of the latest examples is Edwin Miller's *Walt Whitman's Poetry: A Psychological Journey* (1968). Rejecting Whitman both as a "prophet" and a "philosopher," he finds that "when he orders his feelings in his great poems, our response is visceral. For as the lonely poet of monologue, of the inner frontier, of love and death—of our anxieties—he refreshes our spirits, and our lives at least for a moment do not seem fractured and chaotic."[223] Thus have Whitman's critics, sharing the knowledge of the biographers, found, like Sampson, honey in the carcass of the lion.

10

The wild gander leads his flock through the cool night,
Ya-honk! he says, and sounds it down to me like
an invitation;
The pert suppose it ~~meaningless~~, but I listen closer
I find ~~its~~ its place and sign up there toward
~~metaphored~~ the November sky,—
The ~~moose~~ moose of the north, the cat on the housesill, the Chickadee,
~~The out of the forest, the deer,~~ the prairie-dog,
The litter of the grunting sow as they tug at her teats,
The brood of the turkey-hen, and she with her
half-spread wings,
I see in them and myself the same old law.

The press of my foot to the earth springs a hundred
affections,
They scorn the best I can do to relate them.—

MANUSCRIPT FRAGMENT OF "SONG OF MYSELF"

This is an early version, canceled by the poet (notice the strike through the whole stanza). The manuscript for the 1855 edition was destroyed. This sheet is owned by Charles E. Feinberg and is reproduced by his kind permission.

Chapter II

The Growth of Leaves of Grass
and the Prose Works

I myself make the only growth by which I can be appreciated,
I reject none, accept all, then reproduce all in my own forms.
— "By Blue Ontario's Shore"

"ORGANIC GROWTH" OF *LEAVES OF GRASS*

Every reader acquainted with *Leaves of Grass* and the circumstances under which it was written knows that the title designates not a single work, a book, like the *Faerie Queene* or one of Shakespeare's plays, but the whole *corpus* of Walt Whitman's verse published between 1855 and 1892. During these years not one but nine books bore the title *Leaves of Grass*, six of these quite different in organization and even content, though each edition after the first contained most of the poems of its predecessor in revised form, and often under new titles.[1]

If the final edition were simply an unabridged accumulation of the poems of all former publications, the earlier editions would be of interest only to scholars or readers curious about the genesis of the poet's style or his artistic growth, and a scholarly edition of *Leaves of Grass* similar to the *Variorum Spenser* would be sufficient for these final purposes. But the 1892 *Leaves* is more than an accumulation. The metaphor "growth" has often been applied to the work,[2] and is perhaps the best descriptive term to use, but even assuming that many branches have died, atrophied, been pruned away, and new ones grafted on, the metaphor is still not entirely accurate — unless we think of a magical tree that bears different fruit in different seasons, now oranges, now lemons, occasionally a fragrant pomegranate. Not only by indefatigable revising, deleting, expanding,

67

but also by constant re-sorting and rearranging the poems through six editions did Whitman indicate his shifting poetic intentions. Thus each of the editions and issues has its own distinctive form, aroma, import, though nourished by the same sap.

Why does the critic fall so easily into these biological metaphors in discussing the "growth" of the editions of *Leaves of Grass*? The nature of the work, the manner of its publication, and the theory by which the poet composed and interpreted his poems indicate the answer. In the first place, the seminal conception of the first edition was a new sort of allegory—we might even say an attempt, extending over nearly half a century, to make a life into a poetic allegory. In a novel and daringly literal application of the "organic" theory of literary composition, Walt Whitman began his first edition with the attempt to "incarnate"[3] in his own person the whole range of life, geography, and national consciousness of nineteenth-century America.

Simultaneously the poet of *Leaves of Grass* tries to express: (1) his own ego, (2) the spirit of his age and country, (3) the spiritual unity of all human experience, (4) and all of these in a justification of the ways of God to man.[4] Thus he can call the United States themselves "essentially the greatest poem" and without inconsistency attempt to span his country from coast to coast, while "On him rise solid growths that offset [*i.e.*, tally or symbolize] the growths of pine and cedar and hemlock and liveoak," etc.[5] Also he can transcend time and space, for "The prescient poet projects himself centuries ahead and judges performer or performance after the changes of time."[6]

The symbolical nature of these poetic ambitions explains why Walt Whitman did not plan, write, and finish one book but continued for the remainder of his life to labor away at the same book. He was writing not an autobiography in the ordinary sense, nor a creative history of an age like Dos Passos's *U.S.A.*—tasks which can be definitely completed—but was attempting to express the inexpressible. Writing intuitively, he could give only "hints," "indirections," symbols. Hence, so long as the afflatus moved him, he could not finish his life-work or feel satisfied with the tangible words, pages, bound volumes. On his birthday in 1861, and again in 1870, Whitman declared of his book, "The paths to the house are made—but where is the house? . . . I have not done the work and cannot do it. But you [the reader] must do the work and make what is within the following song [*i.e., Leaves of Grass*]."[7] And not long before the end of his life he could still refer to his decades of effort as, "Those toils and struggles of baffled impeded articulation."[8] None of these statements, however, were published. Although Whitman always insisted that the real poem was what the reader made out of the printed words themselves, he nevertheless found it expedient in his prefaces and public utterances about *Leaves of Grass* to make the most of what unity he could find in the work.

Furthermore, the "organic" theory helped not only to explain the poet's fundamental intentions but also rationalized the form at any given stage. After the fifth edition he believed with Burroughs that the whole volume was best understood when viewed "as 'a series of growths, or strata, rising or starting out from a settled foundation or centre and expanding in successive accumulations,' "[9] and a similar statement is found in Dr. Bucke's biography, which Whitman co-authored.[10] Of the 1881–82 edition, Bucke declared: "Now it appears before us, perfected, like some grand cathedral that through many years or intervals has grown and grown until the original conception and full design of the architect stand forth."[155] The influence of this self-inspired explanation is interestingly echoed by the poet's friend. E. C. Stedman, in a letter to Burroughs, in which he declared after Whitman's death: "Before he died . . . he rose to synthesis, and his final arrangement of his life-book is as beauteously logical and interrelated as a cathedral."[11] This authorized interpretation was officially repeated and emphasized by Dr. Oscar L. Triggs in 1902 in the essay, "The Growth of 'Leaves of Grass,' " published in the *Complete Writings*.[12] Though ostensibly the first critical study of the editions, this essay is of value mainly for its bibliographical information, with some comments on textual changes. The initial assumption on which it was based prevented genuine critical analysis:

Leaves of Grass has a marked tectonic quality. The author, like an architect, drew his plans, and the poem, like a cathedral long in building, slowly advanced to fulfillment. Each poem was designed and written with reference to its place in an ideal edifice.[101]

The accuracy and truth of this "organic" defense of the unity of *Leaves of Grass* can only be determined by examining all the editions, but the important point here is that for many years the biological and architectural metaphors prevented readers and critics from going back of the final, "authorized," edition of *Leaves of Grass*. Both the rejected passages of the manuscript of "A Backward Glance"[13] and the published preface (1888) show plainly that the poet was still conscious of the imperfect realization of his original intentions; but having in 1881 achieved the most satisfying unity so far accomplished, and being conscious of his waning physical strength and poetic energy, Whitman began to say with increasing conviction that he had accomplished his purpose. He continued to add poems until the year of his death, but attempted no major revision or rearrangement after 1881.

Finally convinced that he had done his best to express and "put on record" his life and his age, he authorized his literary executors to publish only the 1892 issue (with the inclusion of the posthumous "Old Age Echoes") and practically anathematized anyone who might dare to disturb the bones of the earlier versions of his work.[14] So sympathetically has this wish been obeyed that to this day no other text for a complete edition of *Leaves of Grass* has ever been published.[15] In fact, not until De Selincourt, did any biographer or scholarly critic question the full truth of the claim that the final *Leaves of Grass* is a perfect organism or logical structure. Concerning the organizaton of the book, De Selincourt declared in 1914: "... being a poor critic of his own writings, [Whitman] finally arranged them without regard for their poetic value, considering merely in what order the thought of each would be most effective in its contribution to the thought of all."[16] And of the additions after 1881: "The whole of the latter part of *Leaves of Grass* ... exists only as a sketch."[180]

This admirable beginning, however, was not immediately followed by other investigations of the editions. The next contribution was William Sloane Kennedy's chapter, "The Growth of 'Leaves of Grass' as a Work of Art (Excisions, Additions, Verbal Changes)," in *The Fight of a Book for the World*; but this, like Dr. Triggs's essay, is superficial, being concerned mainly with a few verbal improvements in the text. The first biographer to become skeptical of the cathedral analogy was Jean Catel, who found the 1855 edition interesting for its unconscious psychological revelations,[17] and he deserves credit for stimulating research on the growth of the final text.

A few years after the publication of Catel's biography Floyd Stovall made a study of Whitman's emotional and intellectual growth as revealed in the key-poems of the various editions, which he called

"Main Drifts in Whitman's Poetry."[18] This was the first really significant critical contribution to the subject. It was followed two years later by Killis Campbell's "The Evolution of Whitman as Artist,"[19] based on a more extensive examination of verbal changes than Kennedy's study, but agreeing in the main with the conclusions of Triggs and Kennedy that Whitman's revisions improved the style and thought of his poems.

Meanwhile Frederik Schyberg in Denmark had made the most extensive of all attempts to unravel the difficult pattern, to present *Leaves of Grass* in its gradual evolution through the six editions from 1855 to the final edition[20] in 1881,[21] but his book was known to few Whitman scholars in America until Evie Allison Allen's translation in 1951—so little, in fact, that in 1941 Irving C. Story could declare, "no detailed comparative study that considers the several editions as units, and as successive stages in an evolution toward a final product has yet been made."[22] Story was the first scholar in the United States to attempt "a complete picture of the relations of the successive editions"[23] and to point out the necessity of a variorum edition of *Leaves of Grass* for a complete understanding of Whitman's message and artistic achievement.

The need for a variorum edition was further emphasized in 1941 by Sculley Bradley in a paper read at the English Institute,[24] in which he discussed the problems that must be solved in preparing such an edition. He concluded that the text must be based on the last edition, because Whitman's purposes are apparent only in his final grouping of the poems. Here, as in Schyberg's study, we see that one of the major problems for the critic is understanding the poet's intentions as indicated by the continued experiments in grouping his poems. "The Structural Pattern of *Leaves of Grass*"[25] further corroborated this conclusion. It is significant that three scholars, widely separated and working independently, reached virtually the same judgment.

In 1958 Sculley Bradley, with the collaboration of Harold W. Blodgett, undertook the preparation of a *Variorum Leaves of Grass* as a major unit in the *Collected Writings of Walt Whitman* to be published by the New York University Press. One of their first decisions was to publish the text of *Leaves of Grass* in two editions, one using the 1892 "authorized" text purged of errors, and the other, using the same text but with the poems arranged in the order of their book publication. The first, called *Comprehensive Reader's Edition*

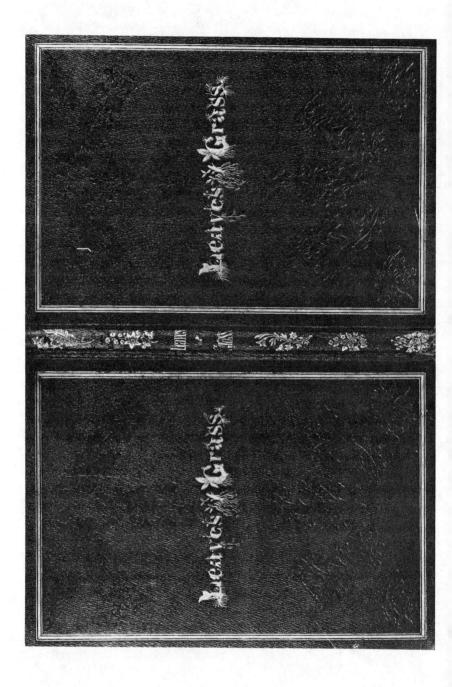

of Leaves of Grass (see note 1 above) has been published, and the
Variorum is in process of publicaton. This will provide a workshop
for the study of the growth of *Leaves of Grass* from any angle,
textual, esthetic, structural, ideational, or other.

FIRST EDITION, 1855

Although Walt Whitman published a number of poems in various
journals during the 1840s and early '50s, his poetic début took place
with the publication of the 1855 *Leaves of Grass*, printed for him by
the Rome Brothers in Brooklyn. It was a thin quarto of ninety-five
pages bound in green cloth stamped with an elaborate rococo design
of flowers and foliage. The title, printed in gold, sprouted roots,
leaves, and branches from all sides, perhaps intended to symbolize
the "organic" theory on which the poems were written. Especially
symbolical is the portrait inside facing the title page and taking the
place of the author's name, which is found only in the copyright
notice and on page 29 of the poem later called "Song of Myself,"
"Walt Whitman, an American, one of the roughs, a kosmos . . ." The
portrait shows the poet in the characteristic rôle of this poem, in
shirt sleeves, the top of his colored undershirt showing, standing in a
slouch posture, wearing a large black hat and a scraggly beard—"one
of the roughs."

The book contains a prefatory essay in prose (though parts were
later arranged as verse in "By Blue Ontario's Shore") and twelve
poems, none of which have separate titles. Though the Preface is well
known, the importance of the first edition cannot be accurately
indicated without a summary. Whitman's first avowed purpose is to
give expression to his own national life and age. America, he realizes,
is still in the formative state—"the slough still sticks to opinions and
manners and literature while the life which served its requirements
has passed into the new life of the new forms." This national self-
reliance leads to the theory that the poet must "incarnate" his country, since "The United States themselves are essentially the greatest
poem." And the expression must be "transcendent and new."

Accepting Emerson's doctrine that "the poet is representative"
and "stands among partial men for the complete man,"[26] Whitman
defines his poet as a "seer" and an individual who "is complete in
himself . . . the others are as good as he, only he sees it, and they do

not." He is a "kosmos," a leader and an encourager of other poets. He will show men and women "the path between reality and their souls."

Whitman anticipates "Pragmatism" and much of the realistic literary theory of the twentieth century in his belief that the poet shall be enamored of *facts* and *things*; that with "perfect candor" and sound health he shall represent nature, the human form, and life accurately—empirically. Hence he will strive for art without artificial ornamentation. But this must not be at the expense of spirituality. "The largeness of nature or the nation were monstrous without a corresponding largeness and generosity of the spirit of the citizen." He "does not moralize or make application of morals; . . . he knows the soul."

In a similar duality, the poet shall flood himself "with the immediate age as with vast oceanic tides" and at the same time he shall be universal: to him shall be "opened the eternity which gives similitude to all periods and locations and processes and animate and inanimate forms." Like Shelley and Emerson, Whitman thinks "There will soon be no more priests"; a new breed of poet-prophets shall take their place, and "every man shall be his own priest." But the final "proof of the poet is that his country absorbs him as affectionately as he has absorbed it."

Nearly half of the volume is taken up with the first poem, here untitled, later called "Walt Whitman," and finally in 1881 "Song of Myself." It is undoubtedly, as the title indicates, his most personal poem, and it appropriately dominates the first edition, which is certainly the most personal of all the editions, the most naïve and rudimentary. Without a guiding title, without section numbers, and covering forty-three quarto pages—no wonder the first readers could make little sense out of it. In fact, Carl F. Strauch was the first critic ever to print a defense of its logic.[27] His outline of the structure deserves to be quoted:

1. Paragraphs 1-18, the Self; mystical interpenetration of the Self with all life and experience

2. Paragraphs 19-25, definition of the Self; identification with the degraded, and transfiguration of it; final merit of Self withheld; silence; end of the first half

3. Paragraphs 26-38, life flowing in upon Self, then evolutionary interpenetration of life

4. Paragraphs 39-41, the Superman

5. Paragraphs 42-52, larger questions of life—religion, faith, God, death; immortality and happiness mystically affirmed.[599]

Since Strauch's outline, various critics have attempted other summaries—including the present author in the first edition of this *Handbook*, Malcolm Cowley in his Introduction to an edition of the 1855 *Leaves of Grass*,[28] and James E. Miller in *A Critical Guide to Leaves of Grass*.[29] They all agree in principle, but offer different interpretations of the order, the message, and the "mystical experience."

Cowley finds nine *sequences* [xvii–xx]. He calls the sections (unnumbered in 1855) "chants," and groups them as follows:

Chants 1-4: "the poet or hero introduced to his audience."
Chant 5: "the ecstasy."
Chants 6-19: "the grass."
Chants 20-25: "the poet in person."
Chants 26-29: "ecstasy through the senses."
Chants 30-38: "the power of identification."
Chants 39-41: "the superman."
Chants 42-50: "the sermon."
Chants 51-52: "the poet's farewell."

James E. Miller calls "Song of Myself" an "Inverted Mystical Experience," by which he means that it is "not necessarily a transcript of an actual mystical experience," as described, for example, by Evelyn Underhill,[30] but a work of art "conceived in the imagination" and presented dramatically with "the author assuming the main role." Thus in sections 1 and 5 the "I" of the poem enters "into the mystical state"; the self awakes in 6-16; is purified in 17-32; experiences "Illumination and the dark night of the soul," in 33-37; "union (faith and love)" in 38-43; "union (perception)" in 44-49; and "Emerges from the mystical state" in 50-52.

V. K. Chari[31] agrees with Miller that "Song of Myself" is a "dramatic representation of a mystical experience,"[122] but he thinks that Miller's dividing the poem into seven phases forces the poem into an arbitrary mould. There is, says Chari, no "clear progression" from entry to emergence from the "mystical state," nor is the poem "arranged in the narrative order of a 'moment of ecstasy' followed by a 'sequel,' as has been suggested by Cowley."[123] To Chari "the underlying principle of organization" in "Song of Myself" is the "paradox of identity,"[121] though he uses the phrase in a different sense from Chase, who meant the poet's attempt to achieve unity out of the deep-seated diversity of his own personal identity (see Chap. I); whereas Chari means the paradox of the simultaneous centrifugal and centripetal movements of the "I" of the poem, or the relating of the subjective "self" to the world of experience. This *relating* gives the order of the poem, which the poet draws from his stream of consciousness.

Cowley speaks of a "wave-like flow"[xvi] and Allen and Davis of "a spatial" rather than a logical form.[32] Chari also stresses the "static situation," his "paradox of identity,"[33] and agrees with Roy Harvey Pearce that, "There is a movement here, but not a form."[34] The movement "derives from the motion of the protagonist's sensibility . . ."[73] Some critics have compared this semblance of "motion" to stream-of-consciousness or association of ideas, but Pearce calls it "hypnagogic meditation, controlled not by rules or method but by the intensely personal pulsations and periodicities of the meditative act."[77]

Students of Whitman may have as much difficulty in understanding the subtleties of some of these terms as the poem itself, but there is general critical agreement that, (1) "Song of Myself" has a structure and an order of development, but the order is not logical or temporal; rather (2) it is the order of perception of the nature of the self (the "I" of the poem) and its relations to the world, as experienced in the mind of the poet as he composed the poem. He also developed it thematically in the musical sense (like "movements" in a symphony), with the "grass" serving both as major theme and symbol.

From the grass, "sprouting alike in broad zones and narrow zones," the protagonist miraculously soars across the continent, observing and participating vicariously in the multiple phases of its life, returning as in a trance to the first, faint beginnings of life and finding "tokens" of himself at every stage of the evolutionary journey (secs. 31-32, and 43, lines 1149-1168). In this life of "perpetual transfers and promotions" (sec. 49), sex (fecundity) is the divine, propelling energy, and the motion is circular, from birth to death to rebirth. As the protagonist flies "the flight of the swallowing soul," he transcends time and space—a theme illustrated by the esthetic structure and order of the contents of the poem, which dispenses with Aristotelian time and space. Time in the poem is an all-embracing present.

Critics like Chase who look for autobiography in "Song of Myself" find a poet (or man) searching for unity in his own divided—or even fragmented—identity. Those who read it as a literary performance, as Chari does, find intuitive revelations of the nature of *the self*, and an appreciation of its dynamic possibilities: "It is an epic of the self set in the framework of heroic and cosmic concepts, comparable in its expansive quality to *Paradise Lost*, or better yet, the heroic Song of Krishna in the Bhagavad-Gita."[127]

Which is it, then? Psychological autobiography (it is certainly not literally autobiographical) or cosmic truth? The poem can be read either way. And they need not be mutually exclusive. But this very fact—and it does seem to be a fact—also means that no two critics, or readers, are ever likely to end with complete agreement. Whether accidental or intentional, the omission of the final period appropriately indicates the open-endedness of the poem, as the poet's last words do also:

> Failing to fetch me at first keep encouraged,
> Missing me one place search another,
> I stop some where waiting for you

Critics now agree that "Song of Myself" is an extremely subtle poem, and they no longer regard it as the "barbaric yawp" of a literary barbarian. Not the least remarkable feature of the poem is its capacity for yielding surprises after many rereadings. It is now generally acknowledged to be Walt Whitman's masterpiece, especially in the version of the first edition, and one of the most provocative and stimulating poems in world literature.

The second poem in the first edition ["A Song for Occupations"], is a further development of the occupations-theme in sec. 15 of "Song of Myself." It is like a sermon continued from the first poem on the "drift" of the message—the impulse to preach dominated Whitman in 1855. The poem has poor unity and coherence, even in the final version. The extremely intimate appeal to his readers in the first seven lines—"Come closer to me,/ Push close my lovers and take the best I possess"—was dropped in later editions, drastically changing the motivation. Here it is a forerunner of the search for companions and anticipates the "Calamus" group—though after it was revised and shifted to a position in the midst of the later "Songs," the reader could scarcely guess its origin.

The third poem, ["To Think of Time"], is also a further treatment of a major theme in "Song of Myself," an animistic interpretation of death. There is no death. Everything has a soul: in cosmic processes are "promotion" and "transformation" but no death: "there is nothing but immortality! ... all preparation is for it ... and identity is for it ... and life and death are for it."

This poem is most remarkable, however, for personalizing the subject of death: what it is like to *think* of one's ceasing to exist in the physical world:

> To think that the rivers will come to flow, and the snow fall,
>   and fruits ripen ... and act upon others as upon us now
>   .... yet not act upon us; ...

It is difficult to say whether this is pathos or irony, but it is both in sec. 4, which realistically images the burial of an omnibus driver in December, under "A gray discouraged sky" with "half-frozen mud in the streets." The bleak but hurried decency of the funeral is effectively pathetic, but the presence of the corpse in the midst of the living drivers in whom he (or it) takes "no interest" is subtly ironic—so physically close yet so infinitely remote.

The fourth poem, ["The Sleepers"], is the most successfully motivated, and the most interesting psychologically, of any in the first edition. Though again taking his theme from the universal sympathy motif of "Song of Myself," Whitman achieves both poetic and mystic unity by projecting himself like a spirit among the sleepers of all lands, visiting, healing, and soothing each in turn. Dr. Bucke made one of his most acute observations when he called this poem "a representation of the mind during sleep," made of "connected, half-connected, and disconnected thoughts and feelings as they occur in dreams, some commonplace, some weird, some voluptuous, and all given with the true and strange emotional accompaniments that belong to them."[35] Malcolm Cowley calls the poem more concisely "that fantasia of the unconscious."[x]

All modern critics agree that "The Sleepers" intimately reveals the poet's sex psychology. Schyberg sees in it his "adolescent ... eroticism," and Edwin H. Miller "a re-enactment of ancient puberty rites."[36] But Miller thinks "the drama of Whitman's poem, of necessity, is played out in the protagonist's consciousness, and that the conclusion is sublimation."

As in "Song of Myself," the symbols can be interpreted in various ways, as is the nature of literary symbols. "Night," the time of dreams, also symbolizes death. "Mother" is nature, the origin of life, the unconscious to which the protagonist wishes to return (to Freud "the womb"), or in the Emersonian-Hindu sense, the "Over-Soul" or *At-man*. Thus, in the latter sense, the emergence, return, and rebirth of the soul is a process of *migration*, but unlike the Hindu doctrine, there is no transmigration. In this interpretation, *day* is the life of the body and *night* is death, which, like sleep, reinvigorates the soul and prepares it for a new *dawn*. Actually, both the psychology of eroticism in the subconscious and the philosophy of the "Over-Soul" seem to be implicit in both the imagery and the symbolism of the poem, which also succeeds esthetically.

The next poem ["I Sing the Body Electric"] also gains in meaning when read after "The Sleepers." In the "Children of Adam" group it seems generic rather than personal. Here, minus the somewhat mechanical descriptions of the parts of the body added in 1856 (and thereafter retained as sec. 9), the doctrine that the body and soul are inseparable seems to have intimate connotations for the poet.

The sixth poem ["Faces"] gives vivid expression to a variety of transmigration first encountered in "Song of Myself." As the poet looks at faces, especially those of the wicked, the deformed, the diseased, he is consoled by the thought that this is but a temporary abode for the soul; he will "look again in a score or two of ages" and will "meet the real landlord perfect and unharmed."

> Off the word I have spoken I except not one .... red white
>   or black, all are deific,
> In each house is the ovum .... it comes forth after a
>   thousand years.
>
> Spots or cracks at the windows do not disturb me,
>
> .   .   .   .   .
>
> I read the promise and patiently wait.

Since the biographical revelations of Molinoff and Furness, this doctrine has acquired a new pathos and yields greater insight into the poetic mind of Walt Whitman. The poem underwent few changes and was finally placed near the end of the *Leaves* in a group called "From Noon to Starry Night."

One poem, the eighth ["Europe"] had been published before as "Resurgemus" in the New York *Daily Tribune,* June 21, 1850, the only poem in the volume not appearing for the first time. The thought is undistinguished—that the spirits of men murdered by tyrants will live on to fight for Liberty, but Schyberg has found the poem important for a psychological reason:

It describes defeat, but the mood is optimistic and full of faith. It thus lays a foundation for all Whitman's lyricism. Just as his love poems grew out of the conflict between what he dreamed and what he actually attained, so his political lyric emerged out of the discrepancy between the America he saw and the America he wished for. That is the background of Whitman's whole paradoxical political position throughout all the editions of *Leaves of Grass* . . . Optimism of defiance—that is the formula of Whitman's lyricism.[37]

The ninth poem ["A Boston Ballad"] was probably written in 1854, for the subject is the seizure of a fugitive slave, Anthony Burns, in Boston and his return by the Court to his Virginia owner in June, 1854. It is therefore chronologically close to the other poems in the 1855 edition, but in manner it is unlike anything else in *Leaves of Grass,* for it is a satire, and Whitman did not later find this sarcastic tone congenial. In a jig tune the poet declares that King George's coffin should be exhumed and the king shipped back to Boston. Since it was Whitman's intention to use no explanatory notes in *Leaves of Grass,* he later intended to delete this poem, but Trowbridge persuaded him to let it stand.

The tenth poem ["There Was a Child Went Forth"] was much edited in later editions. The subject is the influence of natural objects on the life of a child (a Wordsworthian theme, but probably autobiographical here). The loving portrait of the mother and the description of the father as "mean, angered, unjust" give further evidence of the personal nature of this first edition, for nearly all biographers accept this poem as self-revealing in spite of Whitman's later denials. Of minor interest is the fact that the months are conventionally named, not yet called "Fourth-month" and "Fifth-month" after the Quaker custom.

The last two poems ["Who Learns My Lesson Complete" and "Great are the Myths"] are probably the weakest in the volume. The former merely asserts again that immortality is wonderful and miraculous. It was probably written hastily and carelessly. The ideas were to be much better expressed later in "Salut au Monde!," "Song of the Rolling Earth," and elsewhere. The final poem, eventually rejected, exclaims, even less effectively, that everything is great. Possibly it does serve as a general summary of the themes in the edition, though in no systematic manner, and it contains nothing to suggest new interpretations. Worst of all, it is anticlimactic.

Long regarded as more of a bibliographical curiosity and a collectors' item than a literary masterpiece, the first edition of *Leaves of Grass* has gained in reputation in recent years. In 1959 Malcolm Cowley called it "the buried masterpiece of American writing" (buried because of its small circulation), "a unified work, unlike any other edition, ... [giving] us a different picture of Whitman's achievement. ..." He pronounced the 1855 text of "Song of Myself" the "purest text ... since many of the later corrections were also corruptions of the style and concealments of the original meaning."[38] This opinion has become widely accepted by other Whitman critics, and the '55 text of "Song of Myself" is now the text most often printed in anthologies. This is not true of "The Sleepers," but the first text of this poem is equally superior to it also; and the same might be said for the other ten poems of the 1855 edition.

SECOND EDITION, 1856

Fowler & Wells, the phrenological firm, were agents for the first edition of *Leaves of Grass*, and they were the secret publishers of the second edition in 1856. Presumably they were too apprehensive of the poet's reputation, after the critical buffeting he had received for his "immoral" first edition, to give the book their official imprint.[39]

The new book was a small volume, 16 mo, of 384 pages, with a green cloth binding stamped with floral designs not quite so ornate as those of the first edition. On the backstrip, in gold letters, appeared "I Greet You at the/ Beginning of A/ Great Career/ R. W. Emerson," which Whitman had quoted from Emerson's spontaneous letter without bothering to ask permission. So great was the influence of this

letter upon the second edition of *Leaves of Grass*, and probably upon
Whitman's whole subsequent career as a poet, that it deserves to be
quoted in full. In thanks for his complimentary copy of the first
edition Emerson wrote:

Concord 21 July

Dear Sir,   Massts.   1855

    I am not blind to the worth of the wonderful gift of "Leaves of
Grass." I find it the most extraordinary piece of wit & wisdom that
America has yet contributed. I am very happy in reading it, as great
power makes us happy. It meets the demand I am always making of
what seemed the sterile & stingy nature, as if too much handiwork or
too much lymph in the temperament were making our western wits
fat & mean.

    I give you joy of your free & brave thought. I have great joy in
it. I find incomparable things said incomparably well, as they must
be. I find the courage of *treatment*, which so delights us, & which
large perception only can inspire.

    I greet you at the beginning of a great career, which yet must
have had a long foreground somewhere, for such a start. I rubbed my
eyes a little to see if this sunbeam were no illusion; but the solid
sense of the book is a sober certainty. It has the best merits, namely,
of fortifying & encouraging.

    I did not know until I, last night, saw the book advertised in a
newspaper, that I could trust the name as real & available for a
post-office. I wish to see my benefactor, & have felt much like
striking my tasks, & visiting New York to pay you my respects.

R. W. EMERSON[40]

Mr Walter Whitman

    The controversy stirred up by the publication of this letter with-
out asking Emerson's permission has scarcely died down even yet;
but whether or not Whitman was justified in using it as he did, its
importance in the preparation of the second edition of his poems can
scarcely be overestimated. Whitman's friends report that he was tremendously "set up" by it, and during the summer of 1855 he carried
the letter around with him in his pocket. It may even have encouraged him to go on writing and printing his poems despite his recent
fiasco. Certainly the exuberant confidence of the second edition is
remarkable.

    Not content with printing the letter in an appendix to the new volume, Whitman wrote a boastful and garrulous reply in which he addressed Emerson as "Master." The reply begins, "Here are thirty-two Poems, which I send you, dear Friend and Master, not having found how I could satisfy myself with sending any usual acknowledgment of your letter."[346] Then without regard to the true circumstances, he claims that the thousand-copy edition of the first volume readily sold and that he is printing several thousand copies of the second. He expects in a few years a sale of ten or twenty thousand copies. Then he launches into a theoretical discussion which is especially revealing and shows plainly that Whitman himself was not unaware of the paradox mentioned by Schyberg, the incongruity between his dream and reality. In the spirit of the literary nationalism of his day, he complains that the genius of America is still unexpressed in art. His evaluation of American life and character is almost as heroic as Paul Bunyan folklore, but the magnificence is *latent*, not actual. "Up to the present . . . the people, like a lot of large boys, have no determined tastes, are quite unaware of the grandeur of themselves, and of their destiny, and of their immense strides . . ."[352] At present America is only "a divine true sketch."[354]

In addition to helping complete the "sketch," Whitman recognizes another responsibility in the development and recording of American culture: it is the honest, truthful expression of sex:

the body of a man or woman . . . is so far quite unexpressed in poems . . . Of bards for These States, if it come to a question, it is whether they shall celebrate in poems the eternal decency of the amativeness of Nature, the motherhood of all, or whether they shall be the bards of the fashionable delusion of the inherent nastiness of sex, and of the feeble and querulous modesty of deprivation.[356]

Much sex imagery is to be found in the first edition, especially in "Song of Myself" and "The Sleepers," but beginning with the second edition it is now to be a program, a "cause," a campaign against both asceticism and puritanism.

In the twenty new poems which Whitman added in the second edition to the twelve of the former collection, his faith in himself, his sanguinary hopes, and the crystallization of his "program" are clearly discernible. The poems now have titles and their arrangement is the poet's first experiment in working out a dramatic-allegorical sequence. Omitting the '55 Preface, which was gradually being transferred to new compositions in verse, he begins the volume with the poem which in all editions will continue to be a good theme-catalog, here called "Poem of Walt Whitman, an American" (finally in 1881 "Song of Myself"), and progresses through the gamut of personal identity, sex, friendship, evolution, cosmic sympathy, to eternity and immortality. Neither here nor later do the poems treat the perpetual journey of the soul from the germ to the grave in a narrative or logical manner, but already they are falling into a kind of abstract allegory resembling Carlyle's "out of eternity, into eternity."

In 1856 Whitman's "sex program" was still so intimately a part of his whole inspiration that the new sex poems are scattered throughout the whole book. Following "Song of Myself" comes "Poem of Women" (later "Unfolded out of the Folds"). The theme is both maternity and self-reliance: "First the man is shaped in the woman, he can then be shaped in himself." The treatment is abstract, ethical, and ideal; only physically and morally strong women can produce a strong race. It is one aspect of Whitman's dream of the future glory of America.

The next sex poem is No. 7, now called "Poem of the Body" ("I Sing the Body Electric"), taken over from the first edition but considerably revised. Number 13, "Poem of Procreation" ("A Woman Waits for Me"), further extends the theme that "sex contains all." Number 28, "Bunch Poem" ("Spontaneous Me"), is the least abstract and most bizarre of the group. The "bunch" is a seminal figure, like "herbage" in "Scented Herbage of My Breast" (1860), which, however, is a "Calamus" poem, and hence not procreative. "Bunch Poem" is definitely auto-erotic, for the poet is conscious of his own body rather than the body of his lover. It celebrates the life impulse latent in him, but it is not in imagery, feeling, or thought a love poem, and may be indicative of ambiguous emotions in Whitman himself at this period.

The "Poem of the Propositions of Nakedness" is not, as the title might indicate, a sex poem, except indirectly. It is composed of a long list of satirical paradoxes for those who distrust nakedness, sex, truth, democracy, love, nature, themselves—note the relation of sex to the whole "program." After his ironical mood had passed (Cf. "Boston Ballad" in the first edition), Whitman apparently did not know exactly what to do with this poem. It was included in "Chants Democratic" (1860) as poem No. 5, later called "Respondez" and finally in 1881 rejected except for the six lines of "Reversals" and three of "Transpositions."

Though the second edition contained no poem equal in power to "Song of Myself" in 1855, it did include four or five of his most successful compositions. The first of these (No. 3) is "Poem of Salutation" ("Salut au Monde!"), in which the national "incarnation" ambition of the '55 Preface has expanded into a lyric embrace of the whole world:

My spirit has passed in compassion and determination around the
    whole earth,
I have looked for brothers, sisters, lovers, and found them ready for
    me in all lands.

This poem contradicts the theory of many critics that after failing to gain acceptance in his own country, Whitman developed an international sentiment as a compensation. And as within him "latitude widens, longitude lengthens," Walt Whitman gains tremendously in poetic power. World sentiment invigorated and stimulated his lyric growth and came in the flush of his inspiration, not afterwards.

"Broad-Axe Poem" ("Song of the Broad-Axe") contains a good deal of Whitman's earlier nationalism, perhaps imperialism, but this is due in part to the spirit of "arrogant, masculine, naïve, rowdyish" perfect health in which the broad-axe symbolizes the human activity of all lands. "Muscle and pluck forever! What invigorates life, invigorates death." The prophecy of one hundred Free States, "begetting another hundred north and south," is less imperialistic in its context than out of it, for the vision of "the shapes of fullsized men" and of vigorous women to be their equals includes all lands and peoples, "Shapes bracing the whole earth, and braced with the whole earth."

"Sun-Down Poem" (1860: "Crossing Brooklyn Ferry") is usually regarded as the best of the new poems in the second edition. In it Whitman attained a more subtle use of symbols and an allegorical structure which marked a new departure in his art.[41] As Chari observes, the basic symbolism is the paradox of "fixity in motion."[42] The protagonist commands time to stand still that he may prolong his moment of enjoyment, but only the poem, the work of art, achieves stasis—the motif of Keats's "Ode on a Grecian Urn." However, Edwin H. Miller suggests a better comparison in Wallace Stevens's "Sunday Morning," in which the lady "welcomes flux, for

'Death is the mother of beauty.' " Like Stevens's poem, Whitman's is also "a hedonistic statement of faith."[43] Although Chase is more interested in the "confession of weakness and uncertainty" (the "dark patches" in sec. 6) in this poem, he also says that here Whitman "brings a new lyric austerity and control to his capacity for pathos and musing reflection."[44]

In the carefree, light-hearted "Poem of the Road" ("Song of the Open Road"), the poetic vision expands over the whole world—and finally the universe: "Afoot and lighthearted I take to the open road! Healthy, free, the world before me! . . . The earth expanding . . . I will scatter myself among men and women as I go." The themes of travel, physical joy, and companionship are happily blended. Phrenological "adhesiveness,"[45] which was building for the poet a "city of friends" where "manly affection" would reign, is defined by the question: "Do you know what it is as you pass to be loved by strangers?" The poet travels always toward the "great companions." His poem is a new *Pilgrim's Progress*:

To know the universe itself as a road—as many roads—as roads for
    traveling souls! . . .
All parts away for the progress of souls,
All religion, all solid things, arts, governments—all that was or is
    apparent upon this globe or any globe, falls into niches and
    corners before the processions of souls along the grand roads of
    the universe, . . .

He probably knew little about Hegelianism at this time, but he could declare,

Now understand me well—it is provided in the essence of things, that
    from any fruition of success, no matter what, shall come forth
    something to make a greater struggle necessary.

My call is the call of battle—I nourish active rebellion,

thus preparing the way for his justification of evil in "Chanting the Squre Deific" a decade later.

Even the religious concept of individualism, first formulated in the '55 Preface, takes on new depth and breadth when whole passages of the Preface are transferred to "Poem of Many in One" (later "By Blue Ontario's Shore")[46] and are motivated with cosmic significance. In addition to singing a new nation, which is to build on the past and henceforth lead the world, the poet has taken on a philosophical search for the meaning of the universe.

I match my spirit against yours, you orbs, growths, mountains,
    brutes,
I will learn why the earth is gross, tantalizing, wicked,
I take you to be mine, you beautiful, terrible, rude forms.

This search for the meaning of life and existence also has considerable bearing on the poet's theory of language. In the Preface he had declared that "The English language befriends the grand American expression . . . it is brawny enough and limber and full enough," and concluded that, "It is the medium that shall well night express the inexpressible." The more mystic his poems become, the more Whitman strives to "express the inexpressible," and this leads to a fuller development of his theory of words. As a consequence of the esthetic doctrine in the Preface that "All beauty comes from beautiful blood and a beautiful brain," Whitman explains in "Poem of Many in One" that to use the language the poet must "prepare himself, body and mind." Linguistic expression is thus the product of character. In "Poem of the Sayers of the Words of the Earth" ("Song of the Rolling Earth"), Whitman gives this idea an Emersonian interpretation; in fact, he is probably indebted to the Transcendentalist belief that "Words are signs of natural facts."[47] *Words* are not sounds or marks on paper, says Whitman, but reality; the words of the poem are "the words of the eloquent dumb great mother."

I swear I begin to see little or nothing in audible words!
I swear I think all merges toward the presentation of the unspoken
    meanings of the earth!
Toward him who sings the songs of the body, and of the truths of
    the earth,
Toward him who makes the dictionaries of the words that print
    cannot touch.

Hence the need for symbols, for "indirections"—"This is a poem for the sayers of the earth—these are hints of meanings," which echo the tones and phrases of souls.

Perhaps the greatest importance of the second edition is the testimony it bears to the courage and fortitude of Walt Whitman in the face of literary failure. Nearly every new poem in the book radiates his faith in himself, in his ideas, and in his newly invented technique. And despite the brashness and bad taste of the open-letter to Emerson, this edition shows unmistakable growth in lyric power, especially when the cosmic emotion or universal sympathy carries his Muse on a vicarious journey into all lands and ages, as in "Salut au Monde!," "Crossing Brooklyn Ferry," or "Song of the Rolling Earth." Even in his most personal sex lyrics, which seem to reflect some inner struggle or irrepressible urge, he is already striving to sublimate the emotion. He has, in short, not yet attained the poise and tranquility which grew upon him after his service in the army hospitals; but as the first edition reveals his lyrical power, so does the second map out the paths which he is to follow through succeeding editions of *Leaves of Grass*.

THIRD EDITION, 1860

Soon after Fowler & Wells printed the second edition of *Leaves of Grass* (possibly even before[48]), Whitman began planning a third edition. At first his plan was to add 68 new poems to the 32 of the 1856 edition, to make a round hundred. In his notes he referred to the augmented collection as "the New Bible," meaning, apparently, a "Bible" for American Democracy, and in June 1857 he predicted, "It ought to be ready in 1859."[49]

In 1858 or early '59 the Rome Brothers, who had printed the first *Leaves of Grass*, began setting up the new poems, mainly for the purpose of giving Whitman printed versions to correct—he liked to revise in proof. Whitman may also have intended to have the Romes print the new edition, for on June 20, 1857,[50] he planned to recover the plates from Fowler & Wells and re-use them in printing a new edition. These simple details show that Whitman was planning a third edition similar to his second, with new poems simply added on to the old ones: technically, a new *issue* instead of a new edition because the 32 poems would not be reset.

The manuscripts set up by the Rome Brothers have been edited by Fredson Bowers,[51] and they are of more than bibliographical interest. For one thing, Whitman was planning a "Proem" to explain his poetic program. He first called it "Premonition," and then "Proto-Leaf" (finally "Starting from Paumanok"). The second title suggests its introductory function, which would not have been appropriate for a poem appended to the 1856 collection, and this fact shows that Whitman was considering organizing his third edition on a thematic plan, to be introduced by a program poem.

More important, the manuscript versions of "Proto-Leaf" reveal more clearly than the final version the crises and vacillations of the poet during the gestation of the third edition. Whitman's first ambition was to tally and vocalize his native land: "Solitary, singing in the west, I strike up for a new world."[52]

> Take my leaves, America!
> Make welcome for them everywhere, for
> they are your own offspring;...[7]

This motif leads easily to the theme of "companionship, ... what alone can compact The States, ..."[12] But later in the manuscript the companions are reduced to a single "comrade," a young man "kissing me so long with his daily kiss ..."[18] After more experimental songs to his native land, the poet seeks a "rendezvous at last" with his comrade, "us two only!"[34]

That some personal experience motivated this switching from the role of national bard to personal lover is indicated further by a group of poems which Whitman at first called "Live Oak with Moss," which could be called the "proto-leaf" of the 1860 "Calamus" cluster.[53] This group consisted of twelve numbered poems, in theme and form resembling an Elizabethan sonnet-sequence, probably Whitman's literary model. The poet is so emotionally attached to this male lover that he becomes indifferent to his songs celebrating "the grandeur of The States, and the examples of heroes." Now "It is to be enough for each of us that we are together...."[54] One of the most lyrical of these (free-verse) sonnets describes the poet's happiness in the anticipation and arrival of his lover.[55] Other poems, however, are concerned with loneliness, pensive longing, and a sense of guilt: "it is useless—I am what I am."[56]

These embryonic "Calamus" poems, which "tell the secret of my night and days,"[57] seem at times to describe a very real love-relationship, but more often the poet seeks compensation in a fantasy "City of Friends,"[58] and in this dream-world the themes of national bard and lover combine. The poet is consoled by the thought that "a century hence"[59] his readers will love and understand him. In an 1876 preface Whitman confessed that he had "sent out *Leaves of Grass* to arouse and set flowing in men's and women's hearts, young and old, (my present and future readers,) endless streams of living, pulsating love and friendship, directly from them to myself, now and ever."[60] This "terrible, irrepressible yearning" deep in his soul was never more intense than in the year or so preceding the publication of his 1860 edition, when he was writing the early versions of the "Calamus" poems.

The manuscripts which the Rome Brothers set up also contain five of the "Enfans d'Adam" cluster in the 1860 edition, but they do not go very far toward carrying out the intention Whitman recorded in his notes, to write "A string of Poems, (short etc.) embodying the amative love of woman—the same as *Live Oak Leaves* do the passion of friendship for man,"[61] and in a later note, after he had changed "Live Oak" to "Calamus": "Theory of a Cluster of Poems the same *to the passion of Woman-Love* as the *Calamus-Leaves* are to adhesiveness, manly love. Full of animal-fire, tender, burning. . . ."[62] Thus in addition to forecasting the conflicting motifs of national bard and "tender lover" of one person (eventually sublimated into "you" the reader), and the literary strategy of balancing homosexual and heterosexual love in two "clusters" of poems, these preliminary drafts also show the poet in the process of reorganizing and rearticulating the sequence of his poems in his next edition.

A major cluster in the third edition, "Chants Democratic," is also well represented in the Bowers edition (forty-five pages), but the unifying theme of "A nation announcing itself, (many in one,)" ("Chant" No. 1 in the 1860 edition) is still elusive, and the miscellaneous fragments are still incoherent (not individually but as an embryonic cluster). However, some of the motifs of the group appear, such as the national pride in "America always! . . . Always our own feuillage!"[63] And "How can I but invite you for yourself to collect bouquets of the incomparable feuillage of These States?"[64] Also the theme of the poet as "time-binder":

O strain musical, flowing through ages and continents—now reaching me and America!
I take your strong chords—I intersperse them, and cheerfully pass them forward.[65]

Realizing that the democratic nation he celebrates is still more dream than reality, and that he himself has not yet fulfilled his bardic announcements, the poet becomes prophetic, and addresses

Poets to come!
Not to-day is to justify me, and Democracy, and what we are for,
But you, a new brood, native, athletic, continental, greater than
    before known,
You must justify me.[66]

In the manuscript cluster for "Leaves of Grass" (a very ambiguous group-title) the poet seems to feel a compulsion to confess and to "give fair warning," calling himself "culpable" and a "traitor."[67]

Inside these breast-bones I lie smutch'd and choked,
Beneath this face that appears so impassive, hell's tides continually
    run,
Lusts and wickedness are acceptable to me,
I walk with delinquents with passionate love,
I feel I am of them—I belong to those convicts and prostitutes
    myself,
And henceforth I will not deny them—for how can I deny myself?

Whether this identification with the wicked is Christ-like compassion or a crushing sense of personal guilt, the psychological effect is clear in the versions of the next cluster to be called "Messenger Leaves" in the 1860 edition: the poet has derived positive benefit from his impassioned confession. Now, in fact, he assumes a priestly rôle for himself. In "To One Shortly to Die"

I absolve you from all except yourself, spiritual, bodily—
    that is eternal,
(The corpse you will leave will be but excrementitous.)
        .   .   .   .   .
I do not commiserate you—I congratulate you.[68]

In several short poems "To You" (the reader) the poet continues to solicit confessions: "Tell me the whole story—Tell me what you would not tell your brother, wife, husband, or physician."[69] Then as if purged of his own guilt, he writes seventeen pages (in the Bowers edition) of experimental verses for a "Poem of Joys." Among the many joys is "the beautiful touch of Death, . . . discharging my excrementitous body, . . . My voided body, nothing more to me, returning to the purifications, further offices, eternal uses of the earth."[70]

The exact date of composition of these lines has not been determined, though they were written between 1857 and 1859. The mood
suggests the latter year, during which Whitman wrote two poems in
the same state of mind. One was "Bardic Symbols" (title used for the
version published in the *Atlantic Monthly*, April, 1860—later "As I
Ebb'd with the Ocean of Life"), in which the poet, walking the
shores of Paumanok, identified with the debris cast up by the waves.
He felt "balked,/ Bent to the very earth," mocked for his "insolent
poems," without "the least idea who or what I am. . . ."[71]
    In this poem Whitman used two major symbols which he would
develop in subsequent poems: the *shore*, physical reality (also addressed as "father"); and the *ocean*, "the measureless float" (he had
used "float" once before in "Sun-Down Poem"), the source and the
dissolver of life (also "mother"). The poet envisioned his drowning in
two lines which James Russell Lowell, the editor of the *Atlantic
Monthly*, found too realistic and deleted (Whitman restored them in
his 1860 edition):

> (See! from my dead lips the ooze exuding at last!
> See—the prismatic colors, glistening and rolling!)

    Whitman wrote this poem during an ebb-tide of his life. One of
his personal discouragements may have been the loss of the "lover"
in the early versions of the "Calamus" poems, and he was doubtless
also disappointed in not having been able to find a means of publishing his planned third edition of *Leaves of Grass*. But more important, here is the dramatic rôle of the sea, the "fierce old mother"
who endlessly cries for her "castaways," singing "that dirge of
Nature."
    Another poem written at this time (probably the autumn of
1859) is linked to "Bardic Symbols" by theme, symbols, and the
pathos of death; or, more specifically, the poem treats the relations
of love, death, and poetry. This poem is "A Child's Reminiscence"
(retitled "A Word Out of the Sea" in 1860 and "Out of the Cradle
Endlessly Rocking" in 1871), published on December 24, 1859, in
the New York *Saturday Press*. It tells a story which the poet presents
as an experience rememberd from his childhood on the shore of
Paumanok, the story of a male mockingbird calling melodiously,
from early spring to autumn, for his lost mate. (How the boy knew
the singing bird was male is not part of the poem, but the assumption

is another subjective aspect of the poem.) Hearing the song at night, in the moonlight, the waves hissing on the sand, the boy felt that the bird sang to him of love and death.

> The dusky demon aroused—the fire, the sweet hell within,
> The unknown want—the destiny of me.

In remembering these "thousand warbling echoes" the boy became a man—and a poet—whose fate also was to be "a solitary singer," singing of lost love and searching for the meaning of the loss.

A passage in this poem omitted after 1860 (except for the first two lines) shows its intimate connection with the poet's despair in "Bardic Symbols":

> O give me some clew!
> O if I am to have so much, let me have more!
> O a word! O what is my destination?
> O I fear it is henceforth chaos!
> O how joys, dreads, convolutions, human shapes, and all shapes,
>   spring as from graves around me!
> O phantoms! you cover all the land, and all the sea!
> O I cannot see in the dimness whether you smile or frown upon me!
> O vapor, a look, a word! O well-beloved![72]
> O you dear women's and men's phantoms!

In "Bardic Symbols" the only answer the sea, "the old mother," gave the poet was that "the flow will return," but in "A Child's Reminiscence" it is the "delicious word Death," the key to these poems on love and death.

About six weeks after the publication of "A Child's Reminiscence" Whitman received a letter which unexpectedly made possible a third edition of *Leaves of Grass*. On February 10, 1860, Thayer & Eldridge, a young but reputable firm in Boston, wrote him: "We want to be the publishers of Walt Whitman's Poems—Leaves of Grass."[73] They offered to buy the stereotype plates of the second edition, but also inquired whether he had new poems to add to the book. When they learned that he had over one hundred unpublished poems and a plan for a greatly expanded book, they offered him a free hand in designing and supervising the printing of a new edition of *Leaves of Grass*, on a standard ten percent royalty basis.

In March, 1860, Whitman went to Boston and stayed until the
book was finished in mid-May,[74] with a first printing of one thousand copies, which was sold out in July[75] and reprinted (probably
another thousand copies). The book was a fat volume, 8vo, bound in
heavy cloth, blind stamped,[76] with 456 pages. It was well printed in
ten-point type on heavy white paper, with extensive decorative devices on the binding and throughout the book as head- and tail-
pieces. Three of the tail-pieces (line drawings) seem to be symbolic: a
butterfly poised on forefinger[77] (also blind-stamped on the spine
over the poet's name), a globe in space revealing the western hemi-
sphere (stamped on the front cover between *Leaves* and *Grass*), and a
sunset [78] at sea (likewise stamped on the back cover between *Leaves*
and *Grass*). Perhaps these emblems signified the poet's global and
cosmic inspiration and his intimacy with all living creatures.[79] But
they give no intimation of the personal pathos in some sections of
this intricately organized book.

Printer's copy for the 1860 *Leaves of Grass* has not survived, but it
could not have been the proofs of the poems set up by the Rome
Brothers because of the wide differences between the published versions and the manuscripts edited by Bowers. Probably Whitman took
a set of these proof sheets (now lost) with him to Boston, which he
had already substantially emended and amplified. The 1860 *Leaves*
contains 146 poems new to the collection, extensive revisions of the
old poems, and many new titles, some of them final. The order of
the poems is Whitman's first attempt at a thematic pattern, only
partly successful. The following table will show how he attempted to
integrate the new and old poems:

"Proto-Leaf"
"Walt Whitman" [first untitled poem in 1855 edition; "Song of
    Myself," 1881]
"CHANTS DEMOCRATIC and Native American" [poems numbered
    from 1 to 21, without titles; some new, some old] [80]
"Leaves of Grass" [numbered from 1 to 24, without title, some new,
    some old]
"Salut au Monde" ["Poem of Salutation," 1856]
"Poem of Joys"
"A Word Out of the Sea" ["A Child's Reminiscence," 1859]
"A Leaf of Faces" [sixth untitled poem in 1855; "Poem of Faces,"
    1856]

"Europe the 72d and 73d Years of These States" [untitled in 1855;
   "Poem of the Dead Young Men of Europe," 1856]
"ENFANS D'ADAM" [poems numbered from 1 to 15, without
   title]
"Poem of the Road" [1856; "Song of the Open Road," 1881]
"To the Sayers of Words" ["Poem of Sayers of The Words of The
   Earth," 1856]
"A Boston Ballad, the 78th Year of These States" [untitled in 1855;
   "Poem of Apparitions in Boston, the 78th Year of These
   States," 1856]
"CALAMUS" [45 numbered poems, without title]
"Crossing Brooklyn Ferry"
"Longings for Home"
"MESSENGER LEAVES" [fifteen short poems with titles "To . . ."
   various persons, including three to the reader]
"Mannahatta"
"France, the 18th Year of These States"
"THOUGHTS" [without title, numbered 1 to 7—epigrammatic]
"Unnamed Lands"
"Kosmos"
"A Hand-Mirror"
"Beginners"
"Tests"
"Savantism"
"Perfections"
"SAYS" [strophes numbered from 1 to 8 as if short poems, but six
   begin "I say," and they seem to be parts of one poem]
"Debris" [epigrams, without separate titles]
"Sleep-Chasings" [fourth untitled poem in 1855; "Night Poem,"
   1856; "The Sleepers," 1871]
"Burial" [third untitled poem in 1855; "Burial Poem," 1856; "To
   Think of Time," 1871]
"To My Soul"
"So long!"

It would take too much space to give either a bibliographical
description of the revised poems or a detailed analysis of the contents of all the 146 new poems, but a few observations can be made
on the *schema*. It was apparent even in the manuscript versions of
"Proto-Leaf" that it was to be a "program" poem. In 1860 it still
shows the poet trying to ride two horses—spokesman for democracy

and the pathos of "two together" (love and death), but Whitman has made some progress in resolving the contradictions. The poem ends with the poet triumphantly joining hands with his reader, hastening toward the companionship which shall compact These States. But "Proto-Leaf" suffers from its juxtaposition to "Walt Whitman" ("Song of Myself"). The new title fits in with the 1860 "program," but it lacks the overwhelming lyric power of "Song of Myself," which with less contrivance introduced the first edition (not counting the Preface in prose).

"Chants Democratic," the cluster most copiously represented in the manuscripts set up by the Rome Brothers, discussed above, is a collection of twenty-one numbered poems without titles, sixteen of which were new.[81] The group is introduced by the exclamatory poem, "Apostroph" (not in the Rome proof sheets and perhaps composed in Boston during the typesetting of the third edition). It enumerates, often in phrases later repeated in this group of poems, the various themes and intentions of the "Chants." "Apostroph" was rejected in all subsequent editions, probably not only because of its hysterical style but also because when this group was broken up in the next edition and the contents redistributed, its purpose vanished. It is interesting here only because it shows Whitman's growing tendency to use prologue poems to introduce his "clusters."

The first numbered poem in the "Chants Democratic" group is the 1856 version of the 1855 Preface, called in 1856 "Poem of Many in One" and finally in 1881 "By Blue Ontario's Shore." It proclaims Whitman's theory of the "nation announcing itself," and appropriately precedes the 1856 "Song of the Broad-Axe" and the 1855 (later title) "Song for Occupations." As Schyberg has remarked, it is ironical that just before the outbreak of the Civil War Whitman should sing the unity of The States, which he declares in poem No. 4 (later called "Our Old Feuillage") to be as united in "one identity" as the parts of his own body.[82] But it is a theoretical identity, transcending political borders, uniting the poet and his countrymen with the "antecedents" of all lands (cf. No. 7, later called "With Antecedents"), and prophesying "the ideal man, the American of the future" (No. 10, "To a Historian"). These "Chants" are less a celebration of national achievement than a search for the foundations of an ethical Democracy, which the poet finds at last (No. 19) not in history, nor in fables or legends, but in a culmination of the existence in the average life of the day, in things, inventions, customs, people. Therefore he proclaims as the most solid of all realities, Liberty, Freedom, and the "divine average" (No. 21),

> And our visions, the visions of poets . . .
> Democracy rests finally upon us . . .
> And our visions sweep through eternity.

If "Leaves of Grass," the next cluster, has a central theme it is, perhaps, the poet's own crisis of identity. L. G. No. 1 (untitled) is the *Atlantic Monthly* poem "Bardic Symbols" ("As I Ebb'd with . . ."), discussed above. But the poems of this cluster do not follow autobiographical chronology, or even a logical sequence of vicarious experiences. No. 2 returns to the 1855 confidence in the greatness of myth, truth, law, man, earth, etc. [twelfth 1855 poem, later "Great are the Myths"]. And No. 3 is the 1856 "Faith Poem."

As if recording a resolution, No. 10 begins, "It is ended—I dally no more," and proclaims that henceforth the poet will endure hardships of every kind, but he ends by asserting his independence of all restraints and charges his followers to "leave all free, as I left all free." The moods of the remaining poems in the group are so various that they seem to be a miscellany, though some are memorable, such as No. 17, in which the poet looks out upon "all the sorrows of the world" while he remains silent and inert. No. 24 is one of Whitman's cherished "farewell" poems, which partly characterize the third edition, as if he suspected it might be his last. The poet fancies that whoever is holding his book is affectionately embracing him, and to that unknown person he gives a parting kiss—a preliminary sketch of his epilogue poem, "So long!"

After the "Leaves of Grass" section in the third edition, and the miscellaneous poems which have already been discussed, we find the notorious "Enfans d'Adam" (called "Children of Adam" in 1867 and thereafter). Although twelve of these fifteen poems are new, the theme had been announced in sec. 40 of "Song of Myself":

> On women fit for conception I start bigger and nimbler
> babes,
> This day I am jetting the stuff of far more arrogant
> republics.

Indeed, these poems may have been a conscious attempt to develop this earlier theme. Thoreau believed that in the group Whitman "does not celebrate love at all. It is as if the beasts spoke."[83] D. H. Lawrence's comment was: ". . . what is Woman to Walt Whitman? Not much. She is a great function—no more."[84] The "Calamus" poems sound like genuine love poems; but the expression of "Children of Adam" is theoretical and philosophical. In No. 1 ("To the Garden the World") *love* is presented as the means of pantheistic transmigration: ". . . here behold my resurrection, after slumber,/ The revolving cycles, in their wide sweep, having brought me again . . ." Even in the second poem, which later had such a suggestive title as "From Pent-up Aching Rivers," the poet sings "something yet unfound, though I have diligently sought it, ten thousand years." He later changed this line to "sought it many a year," thus eliminating the connotation of transmigration. It is interesting that he attempted to make these poems more rather than less personal, as in his usual revisions, such as we have noticed in "Out of the Cradle." But it is perhaps still more remarkable that in this poem on the theme of birth and procreation he also sings "the song of prostitutes." This sexual attraction he declares to be "the true song of the Soul."

No. 3 in this group is less polemical and more lyrical, showing an artist's delight in the contours of the human form, especially of the body in motion. But in No. 4 we find one of the first crude attempts to give this sex program a social meaning: "I shall demand perfect men and women out of my love-spendings . . ." No. 5 ("Spontaneous Me") was first published in the second edition. Despite the careful descriptions of both male and female erotic sensations, it is vividly personal in the sense of touch, but it is autoerotic. It contains the fantastic figure "bunch" for seminal seed, which suggests the botanical imagery characteristic of the "Calamus" poems.

The central procreative theme is by no means uniformly or consistently maintained in the "Children of Adam" group. In No. 6 ("One Hour to Madness and Joy") the emotion is promiscuous, "O to be yielded to you, whoever you are," and the free love doctrine blends into the literary program of reckless abandon to impulse. In No. 7 ("We Two How Long We Were Fool'd") the "two" were apparently fooled by abstinence, by artificial repression; and there is a suggestion again of transmigration in, "We have circled and circled till we have arrived home again—we two have . . ." No. 8 ("Native Moments") is a paean of "libidinous joys only."

> I am for those who believe in loose delights—I share
> the midnight orgies of young men, . . .

and No. 9 ("Once I Pass'd through a Populous City") was originally, as Holloway discovered,[85] a "Calamus" poem. No. 10 ("Facing West from California's Shores") is connected with the procreation theme only in a vague pantheistic manner, being an anticipation of the "Passage to India" motif: "I, a child, very old, over waves, toward the house of maternity, the land of migrations, look afar . . ." No. 15 ("As Adam Early in the Morning") serves as an epilogue for the group and returns to the Garden of Eden allegory, closing the section with lyric praise of the human body, especially the sense of touch. Thus the "Children of Adam" poems contain several mingled themes and motifs carried over from the first two editions and overlap the purposes of several other poems in the third edition. The central thought is a pantheistic interpretation of procreation, but some of the poems are personal in the revolt against conventional attitudes toward sex and in the author's abnormally acute sensitivity to touch. They are in no sense love poems. The ones which are not abstract and philosophical are autoerotic or hedonistic. The poet reveals a love only for his own sensibility, and accepts indiscriminately all stimuli. Although his reverence for the origins of humanity is almost religious, he gives scarcely a hint of any social control of the sexual emotions.

"Calamus" is the most unified group in the third edition. All forty-five poems are new, and though the "great companions" motif had appeared in "Proto-Leaf" and was a part of Whitman's earliest poetic program, the tender feeling and shy expression in "Calamus" was entirely absent in "Children of Adam" and was never again duplicated in *Leaves of Grass*. In short, "Calamus" contains Whitman's love poems. As Schyberg puts it: "Whitman first celebrated the emotion of love in all its nuances in 'Calamus.' In 'Children of Adam' he was self-confident and supercilious, in 'Calamus,' shy, hesitant, wistfully stuttering."[86]

The kind of love which these poems reveal will perhaps always be debated among Anglo-Saxon critics, who cannot enjoy the lyrics of Sappho without first assessing her morality. It is like the controversy over the "Book of Canticles," whether it is erotic or a veiled allegory of church history. Let those who wish interpret "Calamus"

as an allegory of democratic brotherhood.[87] The fact remains that
the expression is the poetry of love, and sometimes almost as tender
and beautiful as the expression of affection and friendship in Shakespeare's sonnets, which these poems parallel in a number of ways,
except for being in free verse.

The first poem in the group gives the setting: a secluded spot
beside a pond "in paths untrodden." The theme is "manly attachment"; the mood is shy, secretive, utterly unlike the boastful, erotic
display in "Children of Adam." In this damp retreat, the "Scented
Herbage of my Breast" imagery in the second poem becomes
morbidly symbolical:

> Scented herbage of my breast,
> Leaves from you I yield, I write, to be perused best
>   afterwards,
> Tomb-leaves, body-leaves, growing up above me, above
>   death.

In "Song of Myself" and "This Compost" *leaves* grow out of death
and corruption but symbolize resurrection and the eternal cycles of
life. Here they seem to be a private confession of some hidden secret,
and remembering the "bunch" metaphor of "Spontaneous Me," we
guess that the leaves also have a sexual symbolism. But they and the
fragrant calamus root likewise suggest Death:

> Yet you are very beautiful to me, you faint-tinged roots—you make
>   me think of Death,
> Death is beautiful from you—(what indeed is beautiful, except Death
>   and Love?)

What is the connection between this association of Death and Love
and the tragic tone of "Out of the Cradle" and "As I Ebb'd with the
Ocean of Life"? This association is the outstanding characteristic of
the third edition of *Leaves of Grass*. The poet who doted on himself
in 1855 and declared in "Song of Myself" (sec. 24), "The scent of
these arm-pits is aroma finer than prayer," now writes like this:

> Do not fold yourselves so in your pink-tinged roots, timid leaves!
> Do not remain down there so ashamed, herbage of my breast!

Come, I am determined to unbare this broad breast of mine—I have
long enough stifled and choked . . .

Something of the psychological origin of these poems is indicated in No. 3 (addressed to "Whoever You Are"): the poet writes to
solicit love, and like a lover he is jealous and all-demanding; furthermore, he gives "fair warning" that he is "not what you supposed . . .
The way is suspicious" (Cf. also No. 12). In No. 4 ("These I Singing
in Spring") he gives tokens to all, but the calamus root "only to
them that love, as I myself am capable of loving." These select lovers
are obviously a minority; they seem to be in some way different
from the mass. However, in No. 5 ("For you O Democracy") the
poet makes an attempt to evolve from these calamus roots and leaves
a general democratic symbolism. His kind of "new friendship" shall
compact the States.

Affection shall solve every one of the problems of
freedom,
Those who love each other shall be invincible . . .

As in Shakespeare's sonnets, however, it is difficult to trace a
consecutive story of an experience in these poems. They are not
arranged either in the chronology of the experience or in the order of
a psychological drama. The social application of the love emotion in
No. 5 may be the culmination of the "Calamus" experience, but in
the group it is followed by several poems which reveal a crisis that
must surely have preceded the solution and the catharsis. No. 7, for
example, presents "The Terrible Doubt of Appearances." For a while
all existence seems a dream and a delusion, but then all doubts "are
curiously answered by my lovers, my dear friends." Whether these
were real friends or vicarious lovers created by poetic fancy, the
poem does not reveal.

More revealing is No. 8 ("Long I Thought that Knowledge Alone
would Suffice"), and one wonders why it was never again printed.
Had the sentiment passed or was it too personal? Whitman must have
known himself that it was a good poem, and several admirers protested its rejection. John Addington Symonds confessed it was this
poem which first aroused his interest in *Leaves of Grass* and was one
of the great experiences of his life. [88] The story that the poem tells is
the following: the poet believed at one time that knowledge alone

would suffice, and he aspired to be the orator of his country; then, "to enclose all, it came to me to strike up the songs of the New World," but now the lands must find another singer:

> For I can be your singer of songs no longer—One who loves me is jealous of me, and withdraws me from all but love,
> With the rest I dispense—I sever from what I thought would suffice me, for it does not—it is now empty and tasteless to me,
> I heed knowledge, and the grandeur of The States, and the example of heroes, no more,
> I am indifferent to my own songs—I will go with him I love,
> It is to be enough for us that we are together—We never separate again.

The very next poem, No. 9 ("Hours Continuing Long, Sore and Heavy-Hearted") was also published only once. It is the most painful of the group, and one of the most deeply moving in *Leaves of Grass*. The poet feels himself to be so tormented and lonely that he wonders if he is not an anomaly.

> Hours sleepless ... discouraged, distracted ... when I am forgotten ...
> Hours of my torment—I wonder if other men ever have the like, out of the like feelings?
> Is there even one other like me—distracted—his friend, his lover, lost to him?

No. 16 ("Who is Now Reading This") was likewise rejected in 1867, possibly because it was also too personal, too revealing. The poet confesses that he is puzzled at himself:

> As if I were not puzzled at myself!
> Or as if I never deride myself! (O conscience-struck! O self-convicted!)
> Or as if I do not secretly love strangers! (O tenderly, a long time, and never avow it;)
> Or as if I did not see, perfectly well, interior in myself, the stuff of wrong-doing,
> Or as if it could cease transpiring from me until it must cease.

The mood of loneliness and discouragement returns again (or

perhaps was the same occasion as in No. 9) in No. 20, "I Saw in Louisiana a Live-Oak Growing."

... I wondered how it could utter joyous leaves, standing alone there, without its friend, its lover near—for I knew I could not ...

Here we have also another, though similar, clue to the "leaves" symbolism. The word "utter" especially suggests that Whitman's *leaves* were his poems, and between the jealousy of the lover who will permit no rival distraction and the dejection of the poet when he feels his love to be unreturned, the *Leaves of Grass* experiment seems near an end.

Paradoxically, however, both of these frustrations drive the poet to a vicarious release in verse. In fact, he now has a new poetic ambition (No. 10); he wants to be known not so much for his poems as for the "measureless oceans of love within him,"

Nor speak of me that I prophesied of The States, and led them the way of their glories; ... [but]
Publish my name and hang up my picture as that of the tenderest lover ...

This poem is followed by the most ecstatic in the group (No. 11), and perhaps the most beautiful. It would be difficult to find in the whole literature of love a more tender and convincing description of the joyous day when the lover returns. Also tender, but a great deal more obscure, is No. 17, the poet's dream of his lover's death. Curiously the dream seems to reconcile the poet to death, which he henceforth finds everywhere. This experience is obviously connected in some way with the theme of "Out of the Cradle" and Whitman's philosophy of death.

Poem No. 23 shows that the "Calamus" emotions underlie Whitman's universal sympathy and his international sentiments. The poet's yearning for love leads him to think of men of other lands who might also be yearning and he decides that they could all "be brethren and lovers" together. In the next poem he would establish "The institution of the dear love of comrades." In No. 26, however, he returns to the theme of "two together." This poem, like "Song of the Open Road," probably describes an ideal rather than an actu-

ality. Two boys roam the lands, enjoying all activities, "One the
other never leaving." But the general application of the "Calamus"
emotion revives again in No. 34, which describes how the poet
"dreamed in a dream" of a "new City of Friends," and in No. 35 he
believes that the germ of exalted friendship is "latent in all men."

In the brief, three-line poem numbered 39, the steps of the
process of sublimation are clearly indicated:

Sometimes with one I love, I fill myself with rage, for fear I effuse
unreturned love;
But now I think there is no unreturned love—the pay is certain, one
way or another,
Doubtless I could not have perceived the universe, or written one of
my poems, if I had not freely given myself to comrades, to love.

And this explanation is amplified in poems No. 41 and 42, in which
we can plainly see Whitman's rôle as prophet and teacher, seeking
followers and pupils, originating in the emotions of "Calamus."

This interpretation is still further strengthened by No. 44, which
repeats and emphasizes the confessional introductory poems.
"Here," says the poet, are "the frailest leaves of me, and yet my
strongest lasting." In these "leaves" he hides his thoughts, and "yet
they expose me more than all my other poems." Could anything say
more plainly that the *secret* of Walt Whitman's poetic inspiration is
recorded in the "Calamus" poems? Out of these emotions grew his
Christ-like love for humanity, his St. Francis-like sympathy for all
living things, and the psychic turmoil for which he could find expression and release only in his life-book. In these poems we can
understand Walt Whitman better than in any other section of *Leaves
of Grass*. Their relationship to the whole book is appropriately indicated by Whitman himself in the final poem of this group, No. 45, in
which he speaks to his readers of a century or more hence, and
invites the reader of the future to be his lover. In the 1860 edition
this poem provided a transition to "Crossing Brooklyn Ferry," which
immediately followed the "Calamus" group. This sequence is so fortunate and meaningful that it is difficult to understand why Whitman
used it only in this one edition—though it is not the only example
that the 1860 edition *Leaves of Grass* is the most personal of all
editions.

A poem in the third edition which some biographers have used to support their theories of a New Orleans romance[89] is "Longing for Home" (later "O Magnet South"). Such lines as

> O Magnet-South! O glistening, perfumed South!
>   My South!
> O quick mettle, rich blood, impulse, and love!
> Good and evil! O all dear to me!

lend themselves to these romantic speculations, but as a whole the diction is trite and sentimental, in the "Carry me back to Old Virginny" tradition. The poet sings of the "trees where I was born" and the rivers in Florida, Georgia, and Carolina—which he never saw, so far as we know—and ends like a popular song-writer with, "O I will go back to old Tennessee, and never wander more!"

The remainder of the third edition is fragmentary, though it contains one more large group, "Messenger Leaves," and several smaller and even less-developed groups, such as "Thoughts" and "Says." "Messenger Leaves" has no well-defined theme, though the Messiah-rôle is prominent in several poems, such as "To Him That was Crucified," "To One Shortly to Die," "To a Common Prostitute," and "To Rich Givers."

The final poems in the book show that Whitman was working toward an arrangement to suggest an allegory of his life as a poet. Near the end we find "To Think of Time" (1855), now renamed "Burial," and this is followed by "To My Soul" (in the 1871 edition renamed "As the Time Draws Nigh" and used to introduce a new section called "Songs of Parting"). In this poem a premonition of death seems to be tremendously strong, thus emphasizing the themes of both the sea-side and "Calamus" poems of 1860. The final poem, "So long!," which was hereafter to remain the valedictory of all editions through the final arrangement in 1881, has a double farewell meaning, serving both as an *au revoir* and an *adieu*. The poet concludes his message, anticipates the end of his life, and prophesies his influence on the "plentiful athletic bards" and the "superb persons" which *Leaves of Grass* is intended to generate. With a parting kiss and a "so long!" he writes his final lines:

> Remember my words—I love you—I depart from
>   materials,
> I am as one disembodied, triumphant, dead.

The first edition of this *Handbook* stated in 1946: "Of all editions of *Leaves of Grass* before the final arrangement of the poems in 1881, the third gives us the clearest insight into Walt Whitman's growth as a poet." In making this statement, the author was influenced by Frederik Schyberg, who was the first to discover (1933) the importance of the third edition. Since then Schyberg's view has been confirmed in American scholarship, aided considerably by the edition of the transitional manuscripts by Bowers, and by a facsimile of the third edition by Roy Harvey Pearce.[90] In his Introduction Pearce says that "the 1860 *Leaves of Grass* is an articulated whole, with an argument. The argument is that of the poet's life as it furnishes a beginning, middle, and end to an account of his vocation." [xxv-xxvi]

The bulk of the new poems shows that this volume is the product of Whitman's most creative period, which included "Out of the Cradle Endlessly Rocking," admired by most critics, but not all.[91] Stephen E. Whicher, one of the admirers, says it shows that "the outsetting bard of love will be the bard of unsatisfied love because there is no other kind [for him]."[92] Pearce regards it as "a turning point" in Whitman's development as a poet; moreover "the earlier version, set in its earlier context [the third edition], is even greater than the later [1871]."[93]

The two most prominent themes of the third edition, love and death, appeared in the first and second editions, but in the third they take on such overwhelmingly tragic significance that we perceive Walt Whitman, in his tormented struggle to reconcile them, becoming a major poet—Pearce says inventing "modern poetry," discovering "the poet's vocation in the modern world."[94]

Yet at times in the third edition Whitman seems almost ready to give up the struggle and renounce his ambition to be the poet of his age and country. In his final invocation in "So long!" he has a premonition either that death is near or that this may be the last act of his poetic drama. This mood of tragic foreboding gives to the 1860 edition an intensity, a sincerity, and a tenderness lacking in the 1855 and 1856 editions. Indeed, in spite of the evidence that Whitman was growing in creative imagination and lyric skill, this might have been the last publication of his poems had not the national crisis in 1861 rescued him from his morbid obsession with his own inner problems. He was destined, like Faust in Goethe's fable, to find happiness in service to his country—in extroverted, but compassionate, activity.

ABORTED EDITIONS

In the summer of 1860 Whitman's publishing prospects seemed the brightest they had ever been. Thayer & Eldridge wrote him highly enthusiastic letters. Edwin Miller says, "On July 29, the partners conjectured that the second edition [meaning the second printing] would be exhausted within a month, and proposed a cheaper ($1) edition for the next printing as well as a slightly more expensive volume."[95] With this encouragement, Whitman began preparation of another volume of poems, and Thayer & Eldridge announced it in an advertisement in the abolitionist newspaper the *Liberator* early in November.[96] The title was to be *Banner at Day-Break*, and would contain, besides the title poem, "Washington's First Battle," "Errand Bearers," "Pictures," "Quadrel" ("Chanting the Square Deific"), "The Ox-Tamer," "Poemet," "Mannahatta," "Sonnets," and enough poems to make a book of about one hundred and fifty pages.

This book was never published because Thayer & Eldridge began to fail in the autumn of 1860, and went bankrupt in December. Apparently the new issue of *Leaves of Grass* (paperback and deluxe) was aborted also. Several of the announced poems were later published in *Drum-Taps*,[97] which would be annexed to the 1867 edition of *Leaves of Grass*. But only two of these poems are of significance. "The Errand-Bearers" was published in the New York *Times* on June 27, 1860, in commemoration of a parade on Broadway June 16, in honor of the Japanese ambassadors who had come to the United States to negotiate a treaty. Though not one of Whitman's best poems, it envisions a cultural marriage of Orient and Occident, and anticipates the 1871 "Passage to India." "Quadrel" became "Chanting the Square Deific" in *Drum-Taps*, though it was written (or begun) in 1860, and had no connection with the Civil War (see discussion below under *Drum-Taps*).

In preparation for a new edition of *Leaves of Grass* Whitman wrote rough drafts of a prose introduction and began revising the 1860 edition. One introduction, dated May 31, 1861, his forty-second birthday (he liked to reassess and rededicate his life as a poet on his anniversaries), declared: "So far, so well, but the most and the best of the Poem [*Leave of Grass*] I perceive remains unwritten, and is the work of my life yet to be done."[98] Going even further, he confessed, "The paths to the house are made—but where is the house itself?" This was partly a plea to the reader to help him finish his task, and partly the acceptance of a theory which was growing on him that all a poem could do, anyway, was to suggest—an anticipation of the later movement call "Symbolism."[99]

Dear friend! not here for you, melodious narratives, no pictures here, for you to con at leisure, as bright creations all outside yourself. But of SUGGESTIVENESS, with new centripetal reference out of the miracles of every day, this is the song—naught made complete by me for you, but only hinted to be made by you by robust exercise. I have not done the work and cannot do it. But you must do the work and make what is within the following song.[100]

In another introduction he claims to have "felt every thing from an American point of view," but insists that "America to me, includes humanity and is the universal."[101] He is trying, apparently, to generalize and universalize his book, "giving up all my private interior musings, yearnings, extasies and contradictory moods . . . "[102] He now sees his basic themes as "sacredness of the individual," Love fusing and combining "the whole," and the "idea" of "Religion." In another manuscript in this packet Whitman attempted an "Inscription/ To the Reader/ at the Entrance of Leaves of Grass" in prose,[103] a preliminary and prolix version of the poem "Inscription" eventually used to introduce the 1867 edition. By the time Whitman was finally able to get out a fourth edition, he wisely abandoned all these didactic and confusing introductions, except for the "Inscription" in verse form. Their literary value is low, but their biographical value is considerable, for they show Whitman unaware of his great achievement in his 1860 edition and now trying to impersonalize and universalize it. The poems are to depict an archetypal *great person*, "a large, sane, perfect Human Being or character for an American man and for woman."[104] Even in the third edition, as in "Proto-Leaf" and the "Calamus" poems, the lyric poet began to wage a losing battle with the didactic poet, but in 1860, as Pearce has observed, Whitman definitely "moved away from the mode of archetypal autobiography toward that of prophecy."[105] Fortunately for Whitman (as a poet) the Civil War diverted him for a few years from the plans glimpsed in these manuscript introductions.

During the Civil War period, however, Whitman did not forget his ambition to publish a revised and enlarged *Leaves of Grass*. In a copy of the 1860 edition, which he called his "Blue Book" because he had bound it in a blue wrapper, he studiously made emendations, outlines, and plans for his next edition.[106] It has now been definitively edited by Arthur Golden in two volumes, one a facsimile (so faithful that even the paste-ins have been reproduced and inserted exactly where Whitman attached them), and another volume of textual analysis, with an informative Introduction.[107]

Only a few of Whitman's revisions in the Blue Book are dated, and these are labeled 1864, 1865, and one 1866. It is known, however, that he began these revisions before he went to Washington in late 1862, leaving the Blue Book and other manuscripts (including his earliest *Drum-Taps* poems) with his mother in Brooklyn. In November he recovered these items on a visit to Brooklyn. In December 1864 and the following January he went through the poems again, marking some for deletion and others to be retained in revised form. For example, for "Chant Democratic" No. 3, after having previously written "? take this out and alter it and verify for future volume," he decided on Dec. 7, 1864, "This is satisfactory as it now is." He had changed the title to "Song of Occupations" (retained in subsequent editions). In January 1865 (no day of month given) he also found "A Word Out of the Sea" satisfactory, except for changing "A" to "The," which he changed back to "A" in 1867. He had made extensive revisions in the text, but had not yet discovered the symbolic rhythm of his first line simply by changing it from "Out of the rocked cradle," to "Out of the cradle endlessly rocking . . ."

The Blue Book has special significance in Whitman's biography because this was the copy of *Leaves of Grass* which Secretary James Harlan surreptitiously examined and decided that its disreputable author should be discharged from his clerkship in the Department of the Interior. This sequence of events caused some biographers to deduce that Whitman's "toning down" some of his grosser sex references had called Harlan's attention to them. However, the present author decided in *The Solitary Singer* that Whitman was not eliminating such passages, but simply attempting literary improvements, which sometimes resulted in stronger emphasis on sex rather than less, and Arthur Golden has authoritatively confirmed this observation. [108] One example of this kind (though not exclusively sexual) is "Calamus" No. 18, which began innocuously in 1860, "City of my walks and joys!" Whitman revised the line to read, "City of orgies . . . !"

What Whitman did de-emphasize in his Blue Book revisions was the personal despair in some of his 1860 poems. He cancelled, or marked "Out for revision," the "Calamus" poems numbered 8, 9, 12, 16, and 44, though retaining No. 7, "Of the Terrible Doubt of Appearances." Nos. 8 and 9, "Long I Thought that Knowledge Alone Would Suffice" and "Hours Continuing Long . . ." would be dropped in 1867, but No. 12, a warning to the new person drawn to him ("Are You . . ."), which Whitman marked in the Blue Book "Out without fail" would actually be retained in '67. The relation of the Blue Book to the 1867 edition is similar, therefore, to the relation of the manuscripts edited by Bowers to the 1860 edition.

Most of Whitman's Blue Book revisions were improvements in diction, rhythm, and the elimination of repetition. "Apostroph," which introduced the 1860 "Chants Democratic," was eliminated completely, and finally. The inept first line of "Chants Democratic" No. 20, "American mouth-songs" became the melodious "I hear America singing, the varied songs I hear, . . ." The imagery and rhythm of this line-title would cause this poem to be set to music by several composers in the twentieth century, be sung often in concerts, and recorded on discs and tapes.

But not all of Whitman's brilliant improvements would be used in 1867. A curious example is "Elemental Drifts" (No. 1 in the 1860 "Leaves of Grass" cluster), in which in the Blue Book he cancelled the first line and started with "As I walked where the sea-ripples wash you, Paumanok," and shifted his best line, "As I ebb'd with the ocean of life" to follow his third verse. Not until 1881 would Whitman discover his lucky first line and title in "As I ebb'd . . ." "Sleep Chasings" would also have to wait until 1871 to become "The Sleepers."

In revising the Blue Book at the time of his emotional experiences during the war, Whitman inserted references to them, even in the 1855 "Song of Myself" (still called "Walt Whitman"). In stanza 19 (1860 text) after "The sickness of one of my folks, or of myself, or ill-doing, or loss of money, or depressions or exaltations," he interpolated "Battles, the horrors of fratricidal war, the fever of doubtful news, the fitful events, . . ." As Golden has observed, the addition was inappropriate, but another three-line insertion added to stanza 341, depicting "a variety of closely personal experiences,"[109] does harmonize with the tone of the passage:

The soldier camp'd, or in battle, on the march is mine;

On the night ere the pending battle many seek me, & I do not fail
them
On that solemn night, (it may be the last,) those that know me seek
me. . . .

Thus the Blue Book gives insights into both the emotional life of
Walt Whitman during his composition of *Drum-Taps* and the preparation of the fourth edition of *Leaves of Grass*. In his Introduction
Golden points out the progression from Whitman's extreme nationalism during the war years to his more characteristic tolerance in the
later editions of *Leaves of Grass*.

DRUM-TAPS, 1865

In "A Backward Glance O'er Travel'd Roads," the preface to
November Boughs (1888), Walt Whitman estimated the influence of
the Civil War on his life and works:

I went down to the war fields in Virginia (end of 1862), lived thence-
forward in camp—saw great battles and the days and nights
afterward—partook of all the fluctuations, gloom, despair, hopes
again arous'd, courage evoked—death readily risk'd—*the cause*, too—
along and filling those agonistic and lurid following years, 1863-'64-
'65—the real parturition years (more than 1776-'83) of this henceforth homogeneous Union. Without those three or four years and the
experiences they gave, "Leaves of Grass" would not now be
existing.[14]

Precisely what Whitman meant by the last sentence it is difficult
to say, though if he referred to *Leaves of Grass* in the 1881 or 1888
editions, he was no doubt speaking accurately. As we have already
noticed, he closed the 1860 edition as if he expected it to be his last,
and the tone of the poems of that period supports this conclusion.
Furthermore, all biographers agree that Whitman's war experiences
were of great importance. Charles I. Glicksberg states that, "The
influence of the Civil War on his work can . . . hardly be exaggerated.
It was for Whitman a national crisis, a living epic, a creative
force."[110] Schyberg adds that the poet who declared in 1855,

Behold I do not give lectures or a little charity,
What I give I give out of myself.

was through his wound-dressing services successful in actually realizing his ideal.[111]

After the war finally ended, and the Union had been preserved, Whitman published in New York in 1865 a seventy-two page pamphlet of a collection of poems entitled *Drum-Taps*, to which he presently added a *Sequel: When Lilacs Last in the Door-Yard Bloom'd and Other Poems*, Washington, 1865–6, of twenty-four more pages. These two publications, usually known as *Drum-Taps* and *Sequel to Drum-Taps*, were added to the 1867 edition of *Leaves of Grass* as annexes, but in 1871–2 were incorporated into the main body of the *Leaves*.

Drum-Taps contains 53 poems, all new.[112] The emotions generated by the out-break of the war, the horrifying shock of the Confederate victory at Bull Run, and later Whitman's first-hand observations at the front in Virginia and in the war hospitals of Washington—all these experiences found expression in these poems, and gave them a greater unity and coherence than is to be found in his works of any other period. Not all of *Drum-Taps*, however, was written in the same place or near the same time. A large number seem to have been composed in Brooklyn between the attack on Fort Sumter in April 1861 and Whitman's leaving home in December 1862 to search for his wounded brother in Virginia. Walt left the manuscript with his mother and he mentions it in his letters to her, cautioning her to take good care of it.[113]

We have no way of knowing precisely which were the poems in this manuscript, but a number of the poems obviously reflect the "shock electric" felt in the metropolis at the first war news and the surge of patriotic fervor which followed. In the initial poem, untitled but beginning, "First, O songs, for a prelude!" we feel this nervous enthusiasm: "It's O for a manly life in the camp!" "Beat! Beat! Drums!" and "City of Ships" catch the excitement of parades and marching feet. The poem called "1861" states that the poet for the "arm'd year . . . of struggle" must be "a strong man, erect, clothed in blue clothes, advancing, carrying a rifle on your shoulder." Perhaps Whitman is thinking of enlisting. At any rate, the war is still adventurous—and remote.

Then there are other poems which, whether or not they were written after Whitman's visit to the front, at least show a sympathetic understanding of the life of camp and battle field. Among these are "By the Bivouac's Fitful Flame"—solemn, thoughtful, a little homesick—,"Vigil Strange I Kept on the Field One Night," "A Sight in Camp in the Day-Break Dim and Grey," and "A March in the Ranks Hard-Prest, and the Road Unknown." They sound authentic. They do not glorify war or the cause. In fact, they are forerunners of realism and give us the impression that the poet is not writing from theory or standing aloof from the conflict.

Not all poems in *Drum-Taps* are directly about the war, though even when Whitman treats other themes we can see the impact of the national crisis upon his thinking and feeling. For example, "Shut Not Your Doors to Me Proud Libraries" is an obvious war poem in *Drum-Taps* but later Whitman revised and transferred it to "Inscriptions," where it is a general plea for acceptance of *Leaves of Grass*; but in the 1867 version of the poem the poet thinks he has a patriotic service to render through his songs. In "From Paumanok Starting I Fly Like a Bird" we have an interesting example of the patriotic application of an idea from the program-poem "Proto-Leaf" ("Starting From Paumanok"); the preservation of the Union fits easily into Whitman's whole poetic program since 1855.

Apparently this grave period left its imprint upon every subject that Whitman attempted to handle during this time. In 1861 he was engaged in writing a series of antiquarian articles about Brooklyn. But as he wrote about the past, he kept finding reminders of the present emergency. For example, Washington Park in Brooklyn inspires "The Centenarian's Story." And his pleasant rambles on Long Island must be given up for "the duration." In "Give Me the Splendid Silent Sun" he renounces the sun, the woods, and Nature for people who are aroused by the passions of war. Similarly, in "Rise O Days from Your Fathomless Deeps" he has "lived to behold man burst forth, and warlike America Rise:"

Hence I will seek no more the food of the northern
    solitary wilds,
No more on the mountains roam, or sail the stormy sea.

In subject-matter and imagery "Pioneers! O Pioneers!" seems remote enough from the fratricidal war of the 60s. The theme is somewhat patriotic, since it celebrates "pioneers," and of course the word suggests the great American migration; but Whitman uses it especially for the marching army of civilization—a theme that always fascinated him. What specifically distinguishes this composition as originally a *Drum-Taps* poem (it was later shifted to "Birds of Passage") is the trochaic meter and almost conventional stanza pattern. It is a marching poem. Under the strong emotional stress of a country engaged in deadly combat, Whitman's rhythms become more regular. That is true of nearly all the poems in this collection. The fact that they are less philosophical and introspective, more concerned with some definite experience or exact spot, and with the simple emotions of courage, loyalty, or pity may account to some extent for their being briefer, more unified, and nearer conventional patterns. Perhaps they were written more hastily, "on the spot," than the earlier poems. Some critics have thought them artistically inferior to the earlier work, and no doubt the greater regularity of form is inconsistent with Whitman's literary theory; but it is also interesting to find him so absorbed in external events, and so dedicating himself to a worthy cause that for the time he can forget himself and his theory.

One of the most puzzling poems in the original *Drum-Taps* is "Out of the Rolling Ocean, the Crowd," which seems to be a perfect description of Whitman's meeting his English adorer, Mrs. Gilchrist—but the poem was published several years before he even knew of her existence, and long before her visit to America. [114] At any rate, except for the date of composition the poem does not belong in *Drum-Taps* (unless some unknown love affair in the poet's life took place during the war, and there is no other evidence in *Drum-Taps*); in the next edition it was shifted to "Children of Adam"—though the sentiment and imagery are nearer "Calamus."

Death is no less prominent in *Drum-Taps* than in the third edition of *Leaves of Grass* but the treatment is neither morbid nor romantic, as in the Novalis-like blend in "Out of the Cradle." "Come up from the Fields, Father" cannot be autobiographical, but it accurately conveys the meaning of a soldier's death to his family back home. And toward the end of the collection we get a close-up view of death, as Whitman himself finally observed it, in "Camps of Green" (later shifted to "Songs of Parting"), "As Toilsome I Wander'd Virginia's Woods," "Hymn of Dead Soldiers," and others.

Though no poet could be more deeply moved by the sight of a fallen comrade or the grave of an unknown soldier than Walt Whitman, these experiences did not embitter or disillusion him but aroused his great motherly compassion, which embraced the stricken of both armies and found a prophetic reconciliation in his poems. His

"Calamus" love found an outlet in his activities as a "wound-dresser"
(Cf. "The Dresser," later renamed "The Wound-Dresser").

The hurt and the wounded I pacify with soothing hand,
I sit by the restless all the dark night—some are so young;
Some suffer so much—I recall the experience sweet and sad;
(Many a soldier's loving arms about this neck have cross'd and rested,
Many a soldier's kiss dwells on these bearded lips.)

In 1881 Whitman added three lines to this poem which significantly
interpret the *Drum-Taps* collection:

(Arous'd and angry, I'd thought to beat the alarum, and urge relent-
    less war,
But soon my fingers fail'd me, my face droop'd and I resign'd myself,
To sit by the wounded and soothe them, or silently watch the
    dead;) . . .

This all-embracing sympathy enabled Whitman to affirm in
"Over the Carnage Rose Prophetic a Voice" that "Affection shall
solve the problems of Freedom yet." This is a new and sublimated
"Calamus" poem. In "Years of the Unperform'd" ("Years of the
Modern") he envisions, in the spirit of his earliest poems, "the solidarity of races," and in "Weave in, Weave in, My Hardy Life" (later
shifted to "From Noon to Starry Night") he uses the imagery of war
to describe "the campaigns of peace." But the complete catharsis for
the war-tragedy is Nature's dirge, "Pensive on Her Dead Gazing, I
Heard the Mother of All."

Pensive, on her dead gazing, I heard the Mother of All,
Desperate, on the torn bodies, on the forms covering the battle-fields
    gazing;
As she call'd to her earth with mournful voice while she stalk'd;
Absorb them well, O my earth, she cried—I charge you, lose not my
    sons! lose not an atom;

                .   .   .   .   .   .

Exhale me them centuries hence—breathe me their breath—let not an
    atom be lost;
O years and graves! O air and soil! O my dead, an aroma sweet!
Exhale them perennial, sweet death, years, centuries hence.

The poet has now covered the whole gamut of his own and his country's war emotions, from beating the drums for the first volunteers to burying the dead, and he ends with an epilogue in which he states his final claim for these poems ("Not Youth Pertains to Me"):

I have nourish'd the wounded, and sooth'd many a
    dying soldier;
And at intervals I have strung together a few songs,
Fit for war, and the life of the camp.

Although *Drum-Taps* was issued as a separate publication, the *Sequel* may be thought of as part of the same work. In the first place, it was soon combined in a second issue of *Drum-Taps*. Wells and Goldsmith state in their *Concise Bibliography of Walt Whitman* that, "A few copies were issued containing 'Drum Taps' only. On the death of Lincoln, Whitman held up the edition and added 'When Lilacs Last in the Dooryard Bloom'd,' with separate title-page and pagination."[115] Moreover, the *Sequel* is a continuation of *Drum-Taps* in other and more intrinsic ways. For one thing, many poems were shifted from the *Sequel* to the final (1881) text of *Drum-Taps*, such as "Spirit Whose Work is Done," "As I Lay with my Head in Your Lap, Camerado," "Dirge for Two Veterans," "Lo! Victress on the Peaks!," and "Reconciliation." The first of these is an invocation to the spirit of war to inspire the poet's martial songs; the second is a remotivated "Calamus" sentiment, though not a love poem; and the last continues the theme of reconciliation begun in *Drum-Taps*—". . . my enemy is dead, a man divine as myself is dead."

If "Chanting the Square Deific" has any special significance in this collection, it is difficult to perceive. As an epitome of Whitman's eclectic religion, clearly announced in "Song of Myself" and "Proto-Leaf" and alluded to elsewhere, it is a poem of considerable importance; but in tone it has much of the arrogance of the second edition, and as Sixbey has shown,[116] the ideas had been crystalizing for ten years. Possibly, as Sixbey has also mentioned, Whitman's deification of the spirit of rebelliousness may have been influenced by the rebellion against the Union.[117] At any rate, Whitman's earlier indignation had now given way to conciliating sympathy and forgiveness. Possibly also this spirit may have influenced the expression of the side of the "Consolator most mild," especially the following one line deleted in 1881:

(Conquerer yet—for before me all the armies and soldiers of the earth
    shall yet bow—and all the weapons of war become impotent:)
    . . .

But the main poems in the *Sequel*, for which Whitman stopped
the press, were the Lincoln elegies, later grouped as "Memories of
President Lincoln." The first of these, "When Lilacs Last in the
Dooryard Bloom'd," is widely admitted to be a masterpiece. In
structure it resembles the other great poem on death, "Out of the
Cradle Endlessly Rocking," especially in the use of the bird song. But
his use of symbols, the "Lilac blooming perennial and the drooping
star in the west," and the song of the thrush, are handled with a skill
found nowhere else in *Leaves of Grass*. The lilac with the "heart-
shaped leaves" of love, the hermit thrush singing his "song of the
bleeding heart," the resurrection of the "yellow-spear'd wheat" in
the spring, the coffin journeying night and day through the Union
that Lincoln had preseved—these are interwoven in a mighty symphony of imagery and sound, each theme briefly advanced, then
developed in turn, finally summarized in a climax (first part of sec.
16) and then repeated gently once more in a coda as the "sweetest,
wisest soul of all my days and lands" comes to rest,

    There in the fragrant pines, and the cedars dusk and
    dim.

Not since the third edition, in which love and death were so
inseparably intertwined, had Whitman used sea imagery in any striking manner. Perhaps this may have been because he had, as he said,
renounced his pleasant contacts with nature for the duration of the
war, or it may have been because in Washington he had little time for
the seashore. A better explanation, however, is that *Drum-Taps* is less
subjective and introspective than "Calamus" or "Out of the Cradle"
and "As I Ebb'd with the Ocean of Life." Whatever spiritual and
emotional crisis Whitman had passed through, the wound-dressing
preoccupations had been psychologically beneficial. Now once more,
when he is stirred to the depths of his being by the tragic death of
Lincoln, sea imagery comes back to him, and the word that the
ocean whispers is the same: "lovely and soothing Death" undulating
"round the world." But the "Dark Mother, always gliding near, with
soft feet," brings redemption and delivery, not chaos and despair.

Approach, encompassing death—strong Deliveress!
When it is so—when thou hast taken them, I joyously sing the dead,
Lost in the loving, floating ocean of thee,
Laved in the flood of thy bliss, O Death.[sec. 14]

In this great elegy Walt Whitman attained a spiritual poise and emotional tranquility that was never again wholly to leave him—except possibly for one brief period (see "Prayer of Columbus," 1874).

After the lilac poem, the other verses in the *Sequel to Drum-Taps* are an anti-climax. "O Captain! My Captain!," in syncopated iambic metre and regular stanzaic pattern, is similar to the beating of the drums in *Drum-Taps*. The music is more like Poe than Whitman, and Whitman himself later became sick of it. True, it has been his most popular poem, but it is almost impossible to appreciate it soon after reading the lilac symphony.

The original *Sequel* ends with a prophecy in "To the Leaven'd Soil They Trod," which remained largely unfulfilled,

The Northern ice and rain, that began me, nourish me to the end;
But the hot sun of the South is to ripen my songs.

The poet felt deeply this wish to reconcile the North and the South through his songs, and it is an appropriate application of his earliest poetic program, but except in a remote symbolical sense the wish was never realized. Walt Whitman was, however, soon to become a more truly *national* poet.

FOURTH EDITION, 1867

The 1867 *Leaves of Grass* might be called "The Workshop Edition," for the revisions indicate great critical activity, although in organization it is the most chaotic of all the editions. Exclusive of the annexes (two of which have been discussed above under *Drum-Taps*), this edition contains only six new poems,[118] all short and of minor significance. What makes it important is Whitman's great exertion to rework the book by deletion, emendation, and rearrangement of the poems. The confused state of the published work, therefore, bears testimony to the poet's literary and spiritual life during the War.

The manner of publication is no less confused than the contents.

The book was printed for Whitman (whose name appears only in the copyright date, 1866),[119] by a New York printer, William E. Chapin, and was bound and distributed during the year in at least four different forms: (1) *Leaves of Grass* 338 pp.; (2) *Leaves of Grass* with *Drum-Taps* (72 pp.) and *Sequel to Drum-Taps* (24 pp.); (3) *Leaves of Grass* with *Drum-Taps*, *Sequel to Drum-Taps*, and *Songs Before Parting* (36 pp.). Wells and Goldsmith say: "This edition was crude and poorly put together. [The copies] were probably bound up in small lots as sold. This may account for the many variations."[120]

The first poem in this edition, one of the new compositions, is "Inscription" ("One's-Self I Sing"), which was henceforth to stand as the opening poem in all subsequent editions. "Inscription" outlines the main subjects of the collection of the *Leaves* and gives a suggestion of their order. These subjects are: (1) "one's-self," or individualism; (2) "Man's physiology complete from top to toe"; (3) "the word of the modern . . . En-Masse";[121] (4) "My days I sing, and the Lands—with interstice I knew of hapless war"; (5) finally a personal appeal to the reader to journey with the poet. These subjects correspond roughly to (1) the personal poems, "Starting from Paumanok" and "Walt Whitman" ("Song of Myself"); (2) the physiological "Children of Adam" poems, which now follow "Walt Whitman"; (3) the consciousness of social-solidarity and world-citizenship of all humanity found both in "Calamus" and the succeeding major poems, such as "Salut au Monde!" and "Song of the Broad-Axe"; (4) the war-experiences in the annex *Drum-Taps*; and (5) the final appeal to the reader in "So long!," which now stands at the end of the last annex, "Songs Before Parting," where it would remain. So well did Whitman like the scheme outlined in this prologue that he finally expanded it to twenty-four "Inscriptions"—though few of the poems were written specifically for this purpose, most of them having been used first in various other groups. But in the 1867 "Inscription" we have a skeleton plan of the final *Leaves of Grass*, a revelation of the emerging purposes and the congealing form.

The extent to which Whitman revised his work for the fourth edition is obvious in the first poem after the "Inscription," which is now called "Starting from Paumanok"—originally "Proto-Leaf" in the third edition, where it also served as an introduction. Nearly every section contains some revisions, but the first illustrates the nature, general purpose, and extent of the changes. "Proto-Leaf" began:

Free, fresh, savage,
Fluent, luxuriant, self-content, fond of persons and
    places,
Fond of fish-shape Paumanok, where I was born,
Fond of the sea—lusty-begotten and various,
Boy of the Mannahatta, the city of ships, my city,
Or raised inland, or of the south savannas,
Or full-breath'd on Californian air, or Texan or Cuban air,
Tallying, vocalizing all—resounding Niagara—resounding Missouri,
Or rude in my home in Kanuck woods,
Or wandering and hunting, my drink water, my diet
    meat,

            .   .   .   .   .

Aware of the mocking-bird of the wilds at daybreak,
Solitary, singing in the west, I strike up for a new
    world.

This becomes:

Starting from fish-shape Paumanok, where I was born,
Well-begotten, and rais'd by a perfect mother;
After roaming many lands—lover of populous pavements;
Dweller in Mannahatta, city of ships, my city—or on southern
    savannas;
Or a soldier camp'd, or carrying my knapsack and gun—or a miner in
    California;
Or rude in my home in Dakotah's woods, my diet meat, my drink
    from the spring;

            .   .   .   .   .

Having studied the mocking-bird's tones, and the mountain hawk's,
And heard at dusk the unrival'd one, the hermit thrush from the
    swamp-cedars,
Solitary, singing in the West, I strike up for a New World.

Aside from the improvements in diction and rhythm, and the
beginning of the mannerism of writing past participles with 'd, in the
new version the poet attempts to give the impression that he has now
experienced what he expressed as poetic theory in 1860. The "Boy
of Mannahatta . . . raised inland, or of the south savannas . . ., Tallying, vocalizing all" on the basis of the '55 program, now extends his

rôle to "roaming many lands . . . Or a soldier camp'd . . . Or rude in my home in Dakotah's woods . . ." It is not a new rôle, rather the application of the "incarnating" doctrine of the first Preface, incorporating the poet's *Drum-Taps* experiences, his contact with frontiersmen (*i.e.*, soldiers from Dakota and other remote places), and his wider knowledge of America. The 1867 edition is thus an attempt to bring the poetic record up to date.

In this interim of revision Whitman tears apart most of the groups which he had started in 1860 but he has not yet had sufficient time to construct new groups. He demolishes "Chants Democratic," one of the major groups in the third edition, and redistributes the poems. The group previously called "Leaves of Grass" with twenty-four numbered poems, disappears as a unit, although five miscellaneous clusters (including one in the annex, *Songs Before Parting*) are given this ambiguous title. The only two clusters to remain more or less intact are "Children of Adam" (formerly called "Enfans d'Adam") and "Calamus." Of these two, the former has been changed least, though it is shifted from the center of the book toward the front—in accordance with the plan of the "Inscription."

"Calamus," however, needed considerable revision to bring it into line with Whitman's newest intentions. Perhaps the most disturbing reminder which he found of his 1860 mood was the three poems which he felt compelled to delete entirely, "Long I Thought that Knowledge Alone Would Suffice" (No. 8), "Hours Continuing Long, Sore, and Heavy-Hearted" (No. 9), and "Who is Now Reading This?" (No. 16). In 1867, having watched and even participated in the tragedies of the national struggle and found healing catharsis in the *Drum-Taps* experiences, Whitman blotted from the record these morbid confessions of the third edition.

"Calamus" poem No. 5 of 1860 provides another interesting example of the effect of Whitman's war experiences on his original "Calamus" program. In 1860 he had already socialized this program:

States!
Were you looking to be held together by the lawyers?
By an agreement on a paper? Or by arms?

Away!
I arrive, bringing these, beyond all the forces of courts and arms,
These! to hold you together as firmly as the earth itself is held
    together.

But he brashly wished to make his "manly affection" an evangelism associated with his own name:

There shall from me be a new friendship—It shall be called after my
     name,

.   .   .   .   .

Affection shall solve every one of the problems of freedom,
Those who love each other shall be invincible,
They shall finally make America completely victorious, in my name.

Whitman never ceased believing that affection could solve all problems, but his personal desire for recognition became sublimated in his
enlarged patriotism. In the 1867 edition a large part of this poem is
rejected and the remainder is divided into two compositions, the first
being one of the most musical of the new "Calamus" group, called
"A Song," ("For You O Democracy"), with a stanzaic pattern and a
repetend, and the second being a *Drum-Taps* poem, "Over the Carnage Rose Prophetic A Voice." Thus without renouncing his earlier
doctrines of comradeship, Whitman now blends them with his new
nationalism.
     It would be a mistake, however, to conclude that the revised
"Calamus" group is depersonalized. No. 10, called in '67 "Recorders
Ages Hence," is a good illustration. In 1860 it began:

You bards of ages hence! when you refer to me, mind not so much
     my poems,
Nor speak of me that I prophesied of The States, and led them the
     way of their glories;
But come, I will take you down underneath this impassive exterior—I
     will tell you what to say of me:
Publish my name and hang up my picture as that of the tenderest
     lover, . . .

This becomes:

Recorders ages hence!
Come, I will take you down underneath this impassive exterior—I
     will tell you what to say of me;
Publish my name and hang up my picture as that of the tenderest
     lover, . . .

The poet believes in his Calamus-program as strongly as ever, but he is acutely aware that his prophecies of The States have not "led them the way of their glories."

Some of the revised "Calamus" poems are considerably more personal than the earlier versions, like No. 39, "Sometimes with One I Love," which originally ended:

Doubtless I could not have perceived the universe, or written one of
    my poems, if I had not freely given myself to comrades, to love.

This becomes:

(I loved a certain person ardently, and my love was not return'd;
Yet out of that, I have written these songs.)

The chief difference, therefore, between these two versions of "Calamus" is not a change in motive or conviction, but in tone and emphasis. The poet has carefully erased most of the record of morbidity and discouragement of 1860, along with the temporary whim to abandon his poet-prophet rôle for the rôle of tender lover.

Perhaps the only safe conclusion to draw from the five groups (counting the third annex) called "Leaves of Grass" in the fourth edition is that Whitman had evidently not decided yet what to do with these poems. Most of the poems appeared in the 1855, 1856, and 1860 editions and have merely been reshuffled. They are drawn from several previous groups and were later placed in various other groups. It is of some importance, however, that No. 20 ("So Far and So Far, and on Toward the End") of the third edition was dropped permanently in '67. In 1860 Whitman confessed in this poem that his poetic powers had "not yet fully risen," and that

Whether I shall attain my own height, to justify these [songs], yet
    unfinished,
Whether I shall make THE POEM OF THE NEW WORLD, trans-
    cending all others—depends, rich persons, upon you,

            .   .   .   .   .

And you, contemporary America.

In 1867 Whitman was almost as unrecognized by "contemporary

America" as in the depth of his discouragement seven years previous; but the poet of *Drum-Taps* and the *Sequel* had inner resources of courage and strength which he had not had before the War.

Some of the revised "Leaves" also reveal the poet's growth, both in art and mental poise. One of these is "On the Beach at Night Alone" ("Clef Poem" in 1856; "Leaves of Grass," No. 12, in 1860). The fifteen verses of the '67 version have a far greater unity than the thirty-four of 1856-60, and this is sufficient justification for the revision. But in the original version the emphasis is on the poet's personal and physical satisfaction with this life:

> This night I am happy;
>
> .　　.　　.　　.　　.　　.
>
> What can the future bring me more than I have?

whereas in the 1867 text the central theme is the mystic intuition which comes to the poet "On the beach at night alone," that "A vast similitude interlocks all." The "similitude" section was also in the original composition, but it was preceded by seven stanzas of personal conviction that nothing in eternity can improve upon the goodness and completeness of the poet's present existence. This is not a doctrine which Whitman ever rejected, but in various periods he expressed it with different emphasis.

Since we have already discussed two of the annexes to this volume, *Drum-Taps* and the *Sequel*, which were attached to the fourth edition without revision, they need not be mentioned further here. But the third annex, *Songs Before Parting*, is a major attempt in reorientation and is, therefore, one of the most important sections of the book.

In this annex we have the beginning of a new and permanent group, *Songs of Parting*. But none of the poems were new in 1867, two of them being from 1856, "As I Sat Alone by Blue Ontario's Shore" and "Assurances," and eleven from 1860, of which five were from "Leaves of Grass" (Nos. 18, 19, 21, 22, and 23). In the fifth edition this group became the final section of *Leaves of Grass* where it remained (exclusive of annexes) throughout all future editions. But in 1871 the number of poems was pared to eight, of which only three were retained from 1867, and in the final version the number was increased to seventeen, including only four of the original group.

Thus about all that finally remained of *Songs Before Parting* was the symbolical name and the use of *So long!* as a half-personal, half-prophetic benediction.

The introductory and concluding poems in *Songs Before Parting* were extensively revised for this annex, and these changes probably reveal not only Walt Whitman's intentions in 1867 for the group but his broader purposes also. "As I Sat Alone by Blue Ontario's Shore" appeared first in the 1856 edition as "Poem of Many in One," in 1860 as No. 1 of "Chants Democratic" (the longest and perhaps the most ambitious group of the third edition), and was finally called "By Blue Ontario's Shore" in the last (1881) arrangement of the *Leaves*, where it is still one of the major poems.

The 1856-60 version of this poem is merely a poetic arrangement of the 1855 Preface, even retaining many of the same phrases and clauses. It begins with the motif of "A nation announcing itself," but the central theme is that of "the bard [who] walks in advance, the leader of leaders," teaching "the idea of perfect and free individuals, the idea of These States." In the 1867 version the whole composition has been greatly improved both in coherence and dramatic effect by the addition of an introduction, with the present shore motif, and a conclusion, changing the "Many in One" motif to the expanded vision of "the free Soul of poets," and of the "Bards" capable of singing "the great Idea" of Democracy, "the wondrous inventions . . . the marching armies," the times, the land, and the life of The States.

In 1867 Whitman developed one of the subordinated ideas of the 1856-60 poem,

Others take finish, but the Republic is ever constructive, and ever keeps vista,[sec. 8]

as the major theme—the throes of Democracy—now symbolized by the apostrophes to the "Mother" figure. To show how Whitman has amplified the call for "Bards" in "Poem of Many in One" into the new theme of Democracy in travail, the whole first section (all new) needs to be quoted:

As I sat alone, by blue Ontario's shore,
As I mused of these mighty days, and of peace return'd, and the dead that return no more,

A Phantom, gigantic, superb, with stern visage, accost'd me;
Chant me a poem, it said, *of the range of the high Soul of Poets,*
And chant of the welcome bards that breathe but my native air—
    invoke those bards;
And chant me, before you go, the Song of the throes of Democracy.

(Democracy—the   destined   conqueror—yet   treacherous   lip-smiles
    everywhere,
And Death and infidelity at every step.)

These parenthetical interpolations run like a contrapuntal theme
throughout the poem, exposing the danger to Mother-Democracy
and the Sister-States—as later in *Democratic Vistas—*, but also
indicating the hope and the means of political salvation:

(O mother! O Sisters dear!
If we are lost, no victor else has destroy'd us;
It is by ourselves we go down to eternal night.) [sec. 2]

.   .   .   .   .

(Soul of love, and tongue of fire!
Eye to pierce the deepest deeps, and sweep the world!
—Ah, mother! prolific and full in all besides—yet how long barren,
    barren?) [sec. 9]

.   .   .   .   .

(Mother! with subtle sense—with the naked sword in your hand,
I saw you at last refuse to treat but directly with individuals.) [sec.
    15]

.   .   .   .   .

(Mother! bend down, bend close to me your face!
I know not what these plots and deferments are for;
I know not fruition's success—but I know that through war and
    peace your work goes on, and must yet go on.) [sec. 20;18 in
    1881]

The tragic war has been fought and the honor of the national
flag preserved ("Angry cloth I saw there leaping!"), [sec. 11] but it is
not to celebrate the past that the poet invokes the Muse:

O my rapt song, my charm—mock me not!

Not for the bards of the past—not to invoke them have I launch'd
     you forth, . . .
But, O strong soul of Poets,
Bards for my own land, ere I go, I invoke.[sec. 22]

   One of the unconscious ironies of this poem is that Whitman's
new call for native bards leads him into an excessive nationalism—
which he dropped when he revised the composition again for the
1881 edition. For example, the characteristic robust-health motif of
1856,

How dare a sick man, or an obedient man, write poems?
Which is the theory or book that is not diseased?

became in 1867:

America isolated I sing;
I say that works made here in the spirit of other lands, are so much
     poison to These States.

How dare these insects assume to write poems for America?
For our armies, and the offspring following the armies.[122] [sec.4]

If the "great Idea" was still largely unachieved in These States, why
would "works made . . . in the spirit of other lands" be worse poison
than the sinister forces already working here against Democracy?
Furthermore, these "isolationist" sentiments are oddly at variance
with the universal sympathy and cosmic themes of the poet's earlier
works, as he himself no doubt later realized. Possibly this inconsistency arose from the fact that in "As I Sat Alone by Blue Ontario's
Shore" Whitman was still groping his way toward the theory of
Democratic Vistas.
   In the final poem of "Songs Before Parting," the revised "So
long!" of the third edition, we find eliminated the tentative, discouraged tone of 1860, when the poet evidently despaired of
accomplishing his ambitious program of 1855. For example, in 1860
strophe 2 read:

I remember I said to myself at the winter-close, before my leaves
     sprang at all, that I would become a candid and unloosed
     summer-poet.

I said I would raise my voice jocund and strong, with reference to
  consummations.

In 1867 this reads:

I remember I said, before my leaves sprang at all,
I would raise my voice jocund and strong, with reference to
  consummations.

A number of lines have been dropped in which Whitman had claimed
to be not the Messiah but a John the Baptist preparing the way:

Yet not me, after all—let none be content with me,
I myself seek a man better than I am, or a woman better than I am,
I invite defiance, and to make myself superseded,
All I have done, I would cheerfully give to be trod under foot, if it
  might only be the soil of superior poems.[1860, sec. 4]
I have established nothing for good,
I have but established these things, till things farther onward shall be
  prepared to be established,
And I am myself the preparer of things farther onward.[1860, sec.
  5.]

In 1867 Walt Whitman no longer regards his poems either as failures
or as tentative experiments for which he must apologize. Through the
Drum-Taps years he had gained tremendously in poise and self-
confidence (real confidence instead of the bravado of 1855–1856),
and he now begins in earnest to prepare his book for posterity.

DEMOCRATIC VISTAS, 1871

Although in his youthful and journalistic days Walt Whitman
published a great deal more prose than poetry, it was not until 1871,
with the publication of *Democratic Vistas*,[123] that he made a serious
contribution to prose literature. Financially the book was no more
successful than the editions of *Leaves of Grass* had been, and even to
the present day Whitman has gained only a few admirers for his
prose, which always remained extremely loose, mannered, and improvised; but nothing else he ever wrote so clarifies and rounds out
both his literary and democratic theory as this essay.

Many of the ideas in *Democratic Vistas* were first expressed in the 1855 Preface, and touched upon in many poems, such as "Song of Myself," "Salut au Monde!," "Song for Occupations," and "Starting from Paumanok"—as indicated in the discussion of the fourth edition of *Leaves of Grass*—; but the immediate starting point of the essay seems to have been some short papers which Whitman published in *The Galaxy* in 1867 and 1868. The first of these, entitled "Democracy," was an attempt to answer Carlyle's attack on democracy in *Shooting Niagara*. But the more Whitman studied the problem, the more he came to agree with Carlyle's charges, though not with his whole condemnation. The second forerunner of *Democratic Vistas* was an essay on "Personalism," the central doctrine in the book, and a philosophical term which the American poet seems to have introduced into America. In writing these papers Whitman's thinking for the past fifteen or twenty years apparently came to a head and he felt the necessity of publishing a more complete treatment. It is interesting also that in doing so he was returning to a purpose which he had once dreamed of achieving through oratory, *i.e.*, leading his country through the eloquence of words.

This purpose is partly indicated by the word *Vistas*: "Far, far, indeed, stretch, in distance, our Vistas!"[124] He is writing more of the future of democracy than of its achievements to date, and makes a powerful homiletic appeal to his countrymen to turn their professed democratic ideals into reality.

Sole among nationalities, these States have assumed the task to put in forms of lasting power and practicality, on areas of amplitude rivaling the operations of the physical kosmos, the moral political speculations of ages, long, long deferr'd, the democratic republican principle, and the theory of development and perfection by voluntary standards, and self-reliance. [362]

But no one is more aware than Walt Whitman that these "moral [and] political speculations of ages" have not yet been honestly tried in America:

... society, in these States, is canker'd, crude, superstitious, and rotten ... Never was there, perhaps, more hollowness at heart than at present ... here in the United States ... The depravity of the business classes of our country is not less than has been supposed,

but infinitely greater . . . Our New World democracy . . . [despite] —
materialistic development . . . is, so far, an almost complete failure in
its social aspects . . . [369]

What kind of people make up the American nation? Looking
around him, Whitman observes almost everywhere low morals, poor
health, and bad manners. Here his dilemma is most acute, but he
attempts to solve it by an analysis of the mass *vs.* the individual. He
agrees that "man, viewed in the lump, displeases, and is a constant
puzzle and affront" to what he calls "the merely educated
classes."[376] Despite the fact, however, that the masses lack taste,
intelligence, and culture, the "cosmical, artist-mind" sees their
"measureless wealth of latent power." The war justified Whitman's
faith in the common man, for the "unnamed, unknown rank and
file" were responsible for the heroic courage, sacrifice, and "labor of
death," and these were "to all essential purposes, volunteer'd," even
in the face of "hopelessness, mismanagement, [and] defeat."[377]
Whitman thinks that the function of government in a democracy
is often misunderstood. It is not merely "to repress disorder, &c. but
to develop, to open up to cultivation."[379] Democracy is not so
much a political system as a "grand experiment"[380] in the development of individuals. He is not concerned either with the romantic
theory of the innate goodness of the masses or with the political
theory of the sovereignty of the people, but with Democracy as a
moral and ethical ideal—in fact, a religion: "For I say at the core of
democracy, finally, is the religious element. All the religions, old and
new, are there."[381] He admits that he has had his doubts, especially "before the war" (around 1860?), and that "I have everywhere found, primarily thieves and scallawags arranging the
nominations to offices, and sometimes filling the offices themselves";
yet he still believes that, "Political democracy, as it exists and practically works in America, with all its threatening evils, supplies a
training-school for making first-class men."
At this point Whitman reiterates, in a more specific context and
as the cornerstone of his democratic idealism, the literary theory
which he had advanced in the 1855 Preface, and continued to reword
in the versions of "By Blue Ontario's Shore." Although the American
people have, he still believes, a great potential capacity for democracy, their genius (or potentiality) is still unexpressed. There is as yet
no Democratic Literature to guide them; hence America's greatest

need is a new school of artists and writers. This call for native authors is subject to misunderstanding, and at times Whitman's own enthusiasm misleads him into an excessive patriotism; but in the larger implications, it is clear that his nationalism is a consequence and not the original motive of his plea for indigenous art. The function of literature is to unite the people with common social and ethical ideals and to establish a moral pattern for its citizens. Thus Whitman's nationalistic poets would combat the greatest enemy of These States, their own moral and, therefore, political corruption. Current literature and "culture" are rejected because they do not provide sufficient moral guidance for a democratic people.

Personalism[125] is the term which Whitman uses to cover his whole program, an all-round development of the self and the individual, including health, eugenics, education, cultivation of moral and social conscience, etc. He rejects institutionalized religion, but a genuine, personal religious life is of paramount importance. Personalism fuses all these developments, including participation in politics and removing the inequality of women. Since the future American democracy depends upon the development of great persons (or personalities) such as the world has never known before, literature and art must not be imitative or derivative of other times or nations, for none of them possessed or attempted to achieve the great American dream of a transcendent democracy.

Here Whitman's Calamus sentiments become completely socialized and emotionally reinforce his democratic idealism:

Many will say it is a dream, and will not follow my inferences: but I confidently expect a time when there will be seen, running like a half-hid warp through all the myriad audible and visible worldly interests of America, threads of manly friendship, fond and loving, pure and sweet, strong and life-long, carried to degrees hitherto unknown—not only giving tone to individual character, and making it unprecedentedly emotional, muscular, heroic, and refined, but having the deepest relations to general politics.[414]

This new democratic literature needs also the help of empiricism and modern science, even necessitating a "New World metaphysics."[417] True, science and materialism have further endangered American democracy by intensifying the greed for things and by "turning out ... generations of humanity like uniform iron castings."[424] But by believing, like all romanticists, in the goodness and friendliness of Nature to man, Whitman thinks that further knowledge of the processes of cosmic melioration will aid mankind in conceiving and establishing a society of perfect equality and human development. Thus Whitman's democracy is finally idealistic and cosmic, and he believes that his social and literary ideals are predestined by the laws of the universe to triumph eventually.

FIFTH EDITION, 1871-72

As with the fourth edition of *Leaves of Grass*, the fifth is difficult to define satisfactorily. The first issue appeared in 1871, and contained 384 pages, but a second issue included "Passage to India" and 74 other poems, 24 of them new, adding 120 extra pages, numbered separately. In 1872 this edition was reissued, from Washington, D.C., dated 1872 on the title page but copyrighted 1870. All the latter copies contain "Passage to India," still with separate pagination, and a later issue includes as supplement "After All Not to Create Only," with 24 extra pages. One of the '72 issues may have been an English pirated edition.[126]

In the following discussion the fifth edition will be regarded as the 1871-72 *Leaves of Grass* (practically identical in all issues), plus the annex, *Passage to India*.[127]

At first glance this does not appear to be an especially important edition, for aside from the annexes it contains only thirteen new poems, all fairly short and individually of no great distinction. But this hasty impression is entirely misleading, for in the revisions and the new poems (including the *Passage to India* supplement) *Leaves of Grass* comes to a great climax, and probably what Walt Whitman intended to be the end of this book and the beginning of a new one, as the prefaces of 1872 and 1876 plainly indicate.

To begin at the first poem of the fifth edition, we notice that the "Inscription" of the fourth edition has now been increased to a whole section containing nine poems, though only two of them are new. Whitman is still trying to clarify the purposes and themes of the book by these prologue poems. "One's-Self I Sing" has become the permanent summary of the themes of *Leaves of Grass*, but the other inscriptions also indicate the nature of the 1871 version.

In 1867 the themes were the great national tragic conflict and the ensuing reconciliation. The war scenes and experiences were naturally still the poet's most vivid memories, though he had come through the tragedy spiritually purged and ennobled. Now the war years have retreated into the background, and both the poet and the nation are busy with reconstruction. In "As I Ponder'd in Silence" a phantom arises and tells the poet that all bards who have achieved a lasting reputation have sung of war. He replies that he too sings of war, the greatest of all, the eternal struggle of life and death. And as we shall see, in his new poems Whitman channels his war emotions and energies into new outlets.

The third "Inscription" (second new poem), "In Cabin'd Ships at Sea," is prophetic not only of the thought of the fifth edition but is also a radical departure from Whitman's former sea imagery. Heretofore, and especially in the great emotional poems of 1860, his imagination always returned to the seashore, where the fierce old mother incessantly moaned, whenever he was deeply moved by an experience or a memory. "Sea-Shore Memories" is an accurate title for the group of poems in the *Passage to India* supplement, which contains "Out of the Cradle" and "Elemental Drifts" ("As I Ebb'd, &c."). In 1871, however, we find the poet venturing beyond the shore, even embarking on ships and vicariously sailing the oceans. Why Walt Whitman was no longer shore-bound we can best decide after further examination of this edition.

But first let us complete the tour of the 1871 *Leaves*. The order of the main part of the book has now become settled, almost as in the final arrangement. After "Inscriptions" come the unclassified "Starting from Paumanok" and "Walt Whitman" (soon to become "Song of Myself"). These are followed by "Children of Adam" and "Calamus." The addition to the latter group of "The Base of All Metaphysics" makes further progress toward the sublimation and reinterpretation of the original personal confessions.

Yet underneath Socrates clearly see—and underneath Christ the
    divine I see,
The dear love of man for his comrade—the attraction of friend to
    friend, . . .

The "Calamus" sentiment is now so generalized that it is to be the foundation, as in *Democratic Vistas*, of a New World "metaphysics."

Drum-Taps, now in *Leaves of Grass* for the first time, has been considerably revised and many of the poems redistributed in sections called "Marches Now the War is Over" and "Bathed in War's Perfume." The title of "Songs of Insurrection" may possibly have been suggested by the war, but the contents are such early poems as "To a Foil'd European Revolutionaire" and "France, the 18th Year of

These States." The new grouping is merely an attempt to give these poems a context in the aftermath of the national struggle.[128]

The fact that in this edition Whitman feels the necessity of giving his poems a topical connotation is of considerable importance, for it offers further testimony that the war enabled him to enter more fully into the life of the nation and think less about himself than he did while writing and editing the 1860 edition. In fact, he is even becoming an "occasional" poet. For example, "Brother of All with Generous Hand" is a memorial to George Peabody, the philanthropist. "The Singer in Prison" records the concert of Parepa Rosa in Sing Sing Prison. Most of the remaining war poems are occasional in a general sense, like "A Carol of Harvest, for 1876" ("Return of the Heroes"), which is a memorial to the Civil War dead on the occasion of a harvest of peace and returning prosperity. (The most *occasional* of all, "Songs of the Exposition" and "Passage to India," will be considered later.)

The 1871 *Leaves of Grass*, exclusive of annexes, ends with the cluster called "Songs of Parting." On the surface there is nothing remarkable in this fact, for the poems are not new, and since 1860 Whitman has been ending his book with "So Long!" However, it rounds out *Leaves of Grass* in such a manner that we wonder if the poet is not planning to make this the last of all the editions. That this is his intention becomes clear during the next six years.

The best of all indications that Whitman was planning a major change in strategy is that nearly a third of his collected poems, including much of his best work, has been removed from *Leaves of Grass* proper and rearranged in *Passage to India*. It is significant that in planning a new collection Whitman did not start out with writing a new book, but began by writing an introductory poem and pulling out of his completed and published work enough pieces to fill out a 120-page pamphlet, which he would presently tack onto the *Leaves* as a supplement. This would be characteristic of his method through the remainder of his life.

The title poem in the supplement, "Passage to India," was occasioned by three events of the greatest international importance: the completion of the Suez Canal, connecting Europe and Asia by water; the finishing of the Union Pacific Railroad, spanning the North American continent; and the laying of the cable across the Atlantic Ocean, thus joining by canal, rail, and cable Europe, North America, and Asia. In celebrating these great scientific and material achievements, Whitman was at last fulfilling one of the announced intentions of his 1855 program: he was now giving expression to the times in which he lived. Thus "Passage to India" is the most important occasional poem in the 1871 edition.

But "Passage to India" is a great deal more than a poetic celebration of nineteenth-century engineering feats, though no other poet of the age seems to have so fully appreciated these materialistic achievements. Having always been fascinated by the history of the human race and its long upward journey through the cycles of evolution, Whitman now sees these events as symbols and spiritual prophecies.

> Lo, soul! seest thou not God's purpose from the first?
> The earth to be spann'd, connected by net-work,
> The people to become brothers and sisters,
> The races, neighbors, to marry and be given in marriage,
> The oceans to be cross'd, the distant brought near,
> The lands to be welded together. [sec. 3]

Once more, as in *Salut au Monde!*, the poet's cosmic vision returns to him:

> O, vast Rondure, swimming in space!
> Cover'd all over with visible power and beauty!

And with the lyric inspiration of his pre-war poems he sketches the history of the race, [sec. 6] saluting the restless soul of man, which has explored the continents and founded the civilizations. Returning to his old poetic conviction, Whitman announces once more that after the engineers, inventors, and scientists

> Finally shall come the Poet, worthy that name;
> The true Son of God shall come, singing his songs. [sec. 6]

All this is repetition in a new context of the poet's great dream of 1855–56, but here both the expression and the application of the theory take on the imagery and meaning of the fifth edition.

> We too take ship, O soul!
> Joyous, we too launch out on trackless seas! [sec. 11; 8 in 1881]

No longer does the poet search for the meaning of life and death in the sibilant waves that wash the shore of Paumanok. Fearlessly he and his soul set out on a voyage, singing their songs of God. Both the theme and mood have changed, for instead of questioning, now the poet affirms. And instead of addressing himself vaguely to "whoever you are up there," he now prays,

Bathe me, O God, in thee—mounting to thee,
I and my soul to range in range of thee.

O Thou transcendant!
Nameless—the fibre and the breath!
Light of the light—shedding forth universes—thou centre of them!
     [sec. 8]

Then comes the final development and culmination of the "Cala-mus" motif: "Waitest not haply for us, somewhere there, Comrade perfect?" First the love poems of 1860 developed into a search for lovers among the readers, then came the creation of an ideal "city of friends," which gradually became a social and patriotic program. Now the poet in his old age looks to God for perfect comradeship.

This is not to say, however, that in "Passage to India" Whitman's religion has become orthodox. Though his language and imagery have profoundly altered, his conception of death and immortality is as pantheistic as in 1855.

> Swiftly I shrivel at the thought of God,
> At Nature and its wonders, Time and Space and Death,
> But that I, turning, call to thee O soul, thou actual Me,
> And lo! thou gently masterest the orbs,
> Thou matest Time, smilest content at Death,
> And fillest, swellest full, the vastness of Space.[sec. 8]

His "soul" is "greater than stars or suns." He and his soul take "passage to more than India"; sounding "below the Sanscrit and the Vedas," they voyage to the shores of the "aged fierce enigmas," plunge to the "secret of the earth and sky," through "seas of God." In 1855-56 Death was a philosophical problem, in 1860 it was chaos and frustration, but now the concept and expectation have become joyous, personal liberation—though still pantheistic in intellectual context.

"Whispers of Heavenly Death," the title poem of a new cluster by this name, comes nearest to returning to the older imagery,

Labial gossip of night—sibilant chorals, . . .
Ripples of unseen rivers—tides of a current, flowing, forever flowing; . . .

But even this poem ends with calling death a "parturition" and an "immortal birth,"

Some Soul is passing over.

"Some Soul is passing over"—soaring, sailing, bidding the shore good-bye (cf. "Now Finale to the Shore"), such are the emotions of the *Passage to India* collection, which ends with "Joy, Shipmate, Joy!" The old poems here grouped as "Sea-Shore Memories" merely emphasize the contrast.

In the other great poem in this collection, "Proud Music of the Storm," we also find the same spiritual exaltation and emotional catharsis. It is not one of Whitman's most famous works, but no-where else did he use his characteristic symphonic structure with greater unity of effect or with richer symbolism. It is his only poem which is literally a symphony of sound, like Lanier's deliberate musical experiments.

The orchestration of the storm ranges through the elemental sounds of all creation and the music of humanity,

Blending, with Nature's rhythmus, all the tongues of nations, . . .

raising allegories with every blast, which it would be tedious to analyze here. It is a private performance, anyway, for the poet's own "Soul":

Come forward, O my Soul, and let the rest retire;
Listen—lose not—it is toward thee they tend;
Parting the midnight, entering my slumber-chamber,
For thee they sing and dance, O Soul. [sec. 2]

First comes a "festival song" of marriage, followed by the beating of war drums and the "shouts of a conquering army," but this gives way to "airs antique and medieval," and then by contrast "the great organ sounds,"

Bathing, supporting, merging all the rest—maternity of all the rest;
And with it every instrument in multitudes,
The players playing—all the world's musicians, . . .[sec. 5]

It is a symphony in which man, who has strayed from Nature like Adam from Paradise, returns,

The journey done, the Journeyman come home,
And Man and Art with Nature fused again.

Section 7 revives the theme of the 1855 "There was a Child Went Forth":

Ah, from a little child,
Thou knowest, Soul, how to me all sounds became music; . . .

But equally sweet to the poet are "All songs of current lands," and the vocalists whom he heard as a young man, best of all the "lustrous orb—Venus contralto," Alboni herself. In section 9 he lists his favorite operas, then passes on (10) to "the dance-music of all nations," Egypt, China, Hindu (11), and (12) Europe.

Finally the poet wakes from his trance, and tells his Soul that he has found the clue he sought so long. What the Soul has heard was not the music of nature or of other lands and times, but

. . . a new rhythmus fitted for thee,
Poems, bridging the way from Life to Death, vaguely wafted in night
    air, uncaught, unwritten,
Which, let us go forth in the bold day, and write.[sec. 15]

Here we have the significance of the supplement to the 1871 *Leaves of Grass*. At this time Walt Whitman plans to close his first life-book, his poems of "physiology from top to toe" and his songs of "Modern Man," described in the first "Inscription," and begin a new collection of "Poems bridging the way from Life to Death." "Proud Music of the Storm" announces the new intention and "Passage to India" was evidently planned to launch this new poetic voyage.

THE 1872 PREFACE

The poems in Whitman's two pamphlet publications of 1871 and '72, "After All, Not to Create Only" ("Song of the Exposition") and "As a Strong Bird on Pinions Free" ("Thou Mother with Thy Equal Brood"), are of distinctly minor importance. The fact that they were both written by invitation, the one for the 40th Annual Exhibition in New York City and the other to be read at the Dartmouth College commencement in 1872—and may therefore have been composed under forced inspiration—might explain their perfunctory tone. Both are poetic restatement of the nationalistic ideas in *Democratic Vistas*.

However, the Preface[129] which Whitman wrote for the latter pamphlet, *As a Strong Bird on Pinions Free*, is highly important in the history and growth of *Leaves of Grass* because in it the poet states unequivocally that he has brought the *Leaves* to an end and is starting a new book. He says, in words that need to be italicized, that his *"New World songs, and an epic of Democracy, having already had their published expression, as well as I can expect to give it, in LEAVES OF GRASS, the present and any future pieces from me are really but the surplusage forming after that Volume, or the wake eddying behind it."* The suspicion that the *Passage to India* supplement was intended to start a new book is here confirmed. In the same paragraph Whitman makes a further confession, no less revealing. He is not sure of his new literary intentions, and he is at least vaguely aware (perhaps subconsciously) that he has written himself out. Now in retrospect he feels sure that in *Leaves of Grass* he "fulfilled ... an imperious conviction, and the commands of my nature as total and irresistible as those which make the sea flow, or the globe revolve." To what extent the "organic" metaphor may have influenced the exaggerated finality of this pronouncement, we cannot say; but never before had Whitman spoken with such finality of *Leaves of Grass*. As for the new project:

But of this Supplementary Volume, I confess I am not so certain. Having from early manhood abandoned the business pursuits and applications usual in my time and country, and obediently yielded

my self up ever since to the impetus mentioned, and to the work of
expressing those ideas, it may be that mere habit has got dominion of
me, when there is no real need of saying anything further . . .

No doubt Whitman intended this comment to apply to the supposedly finished book, but the seven poems of this pamphlet, like
the 1871 "Song of the Exposition," lack the fervor and conviction of
the 1860's. They are the work of a poet who is tired, written out,
and on the brink of physical collapse, for it was only a few months
before he would be stricken down by paralysis, never entirely to
recover.

Even the remainder of this Preface is simply a repetition of the
nationalistic ideal which he had already expressed in *Democratic
Vistas*:

Our America to-day I consider in many respects as but indeed a vast
seething mass of *materials*, ampler, better, (worse also,) than previously known—eligible to be used to carry toward its crowning
stage, and build for good the great Ideal Nationality of the future,
the Nation of the Body and the Soul . . .

The finished book and the projected book are to be differ-
entiated in this way:

LEAVES OF GRASS, already published, [*note!*] is, in its intentions,
the song of a great composite *Democratic Individual*, male or female.
And following on and amplifying the same purpose, I suppose I have
in my mind to run through the chants of this Volume, (if ever
completed,) the thread-voice, more or less audible, of an aggregated,
inseparable, unprecedented, vast, composite, electric *Democratic
Nationality*.

Notice the uncertainty: "I *suppose* I have in my mind"—and "if ever
completed."

Only two of the seven new poems in the 1872 pamphlet are of
sufficient importance to be mentioned, and of these two, "As a
Strong Bird on Pinions Free" ("Thou Mother with Thy Equal
Brood") merely repeats earlier ideas and moods. Once again the poet
declares his function to be the initiator of democratic nationalism,
making "paths to the house."

The motif of the "strong bird on pinions free" is also reminiscent of Shelley's "Skylark," even though Whitman asserts that "The conceits of the poets of other lands I'd bring thee not." But more important: the poem is merely a restatement of the nationalistic literary program of the '55 Preface, "By Blue Ontario's Shore," and other early works.

More significant is "The Mystic Trumpeter," but it is also a summing up rather than a new achievement in thought or lyric expression. Professor Werner has advanced the interesting theory that the poem is an autobiographical record of moods parallel to Whitman's own life: his early fondness for Scott's feudalism; his celebration of love in the early *Leaves*; the Civil War; his post-war despair at the evils of humanity; and his final optimism and ecstasy. Thus interpreted, the poem seems no longer utterly formless, nor an assembly of the chief poetic themes, but a chronological summary of Whitman's poetic life.[130]

"AUTHOR'S EDITION," 1876

Near the end of his first year in Washington, D.C., during the Civil War Whitman hoped to publish a book to be called *Memoranda of a Year (1863)*, and on October 21, 1863, he proposed this title to James Redpath, a Boston publisher who had befriended him during the printing of the 1860 *Leaves of Grass*. The book would contain extracts from Whitman's war diaries and hospital notebooks. Redpath was interested and sympathetic, but found that it would be more expensive to publish than he could afford.[131]

At the end of the war this book was still unpublished, but in 1875, while recuperating in Camden, N. J., from his paralytic stroke in 1873, Whitman employed the print shop of the *New Republic*, a Camden newspaper, to set up and print a small book of 68 pages (ten consisting of notes) entitled *Memoranda During the War*, labeled "Author's Publication." It is estimated that not over a hundred copies were printed.[132] It was indeed a private edition, and Whitman tried in various ways to personalize it, such as printing a page headed "Remembrance Copy," with space for the name of the recipient and giver, and a "Personal Note" (brief autobiography). He also inserted two photographs of himself—though some copies had only one. The main value of this book is bibliographical (and it is a rare collector's item), for the notebooks and diaries were absorbed into *Specimen Days* seven years later.

At this period Whitman's creative energy was at low ebb, but he was restless and frustrated and greatly desired to commemorate the Centennial of the nation (nearby Philadelphia was having an Exhibition) with a new edition of his works. Without any prospects of a publisher, he again employed the *New Republic* printing office. For *Leaves of Grass* he simply reprinted the 1871 edition from the uncorrected electrotyped plates—this making a *new issue* and not a new edition. But on a new title-page he printed a poem from the Christmas 1874 number of the New York *Graphic*:

Come, said my Soul,
Such verses for my Body let us write, (for we are one,)
That should I after death invisibly return,
Or, long, long hence, in other spheres,
There to some group of mates the chants resuming,
(Tallying Earth's soil, trees, winds, tumultuous waves,)
Ever with pleased smile I may keep on,
Ever and ever yet the verses owning—as, first, I here and now,
Signing for Soul and Body, set to them my name,
[signature]

After the signature: "AUTHOR'S EDITION/ *with portraits from life*./ CAMDEN, NEW JERSEY./ 1876." The copyright date was also 1876. Another issue was labeled "Centennial Edition."

The companion volume, *Two Rivulets*, was a hodgepodge of poetry and prose—and of printing methods also. The *New Republic* shop set up a new Preface and fourteen poems collected for the first time—three for the last time.[133] To carry out the motif of the title poem, "Two rivulets side by side," Whitman printed poems on the top half of the page and prose "Thoughts for the Centennial" on the second half: observations on Democracy, nationalism, Darwinism, manners, and other pertinent topics.

About mid-way in the volume Whitman printed a second group of four poems called "Centennial Songs—1876." The first, "Song of the Exposition," was the 1871 American Institute poem, "After All, Not to Create Only," simply retitled. The other three poems were: "Song of the Redwood-Tree," "Song of the Universal," and "Song for All Seas," the first reprinted from *Harper's Magazine* (1874) and the other two from the New York *Daily Graphic*. A new typesetting was required for this group.

For the remainder of the book, Whitman simply used the original plates, without change in pagination, for the pamphlets *Democratic Vistas, As a Strong Bird on Pinions Free, Memoranda During the War*, and *Passage to India*. Thus the 1876 *Leaves of Grass* was entirely a reprint, and *Two Rivulets* mostly reprints in a contrived assemblage.

However, the Preface to *Two Rivulets* has interesting information about Whitman's future plans for editions of his poems. In a footnote Whitman says the Preface "is not only for the present collection, but, in a sort, for all my writings, both Volumes [*Leaves of Grass* and *Two Rivulets*]."[134] He also states that *Passage to India*, which he refers to as "chants of Death and Immortality," was intended "to stamp the coloring-finish of all, present and past. For terminus and temperer to all, they were originally written; and that shall be their office to the last." Having had to give up the plan of making *Passage to India* the nucleus of a new collection of songs, he now plans to regard it as a sort of epilogue of all his poems, but by reprinting it in *Two Rivulets* he postponed the time when it would become a part of *Leaves of Grass*. It is thus still unassimilated, though regarded as an epitome of the *Leaves*. In a long footnote Whitman also says that "*Passage to India*, and its cluster, are but freer vent and fuller expression to what, from the first, and so on throughout, more or less lurks in my writings, underneath every page, every line, everywhere." This is a good example of the way the poet would continue to improvise and compromise in his plans during the remaining editions of *Leaves of Grass*.

In this same footnote he confesses that he has had to relinquish his plan to write a second collection of poems:

It was originally my intention, after chanting in LEAVES OF GRASS the songs of the Body and Existence, to then compose a further, equally needed Volume, based on those convictions of perpetuity and conservation which, enveloping all precedents, make the unseen Soul govern absolutely at last. . . . But the full construction of such a work (even if I lay the foundation, or give impetus to it) is beyond my powers, and must remain for some bard in the future.[135]

Characteristically, however, he does not entirely give up his earlier scheme: "Meanwhile, not entirely to give the go-by to my original plan, and far more to avoid a mark'd hiatus in it, than to entirely fulfill it, I end my books with thoughts, or radiations from thoughts, on Death, Immortality, and a free entrance into the Spiritual world." This intention can be plainly seen in the constant resorting and rearranging of the poems up until the year of Whitman's death.

A note in this Preface, dated May 31, 1875, reveals the second spiritual crisis in Whitman's life (the first being visible in the third edition): "O how different the moral atmosphere amid which I now revise this Volume, from the jocund influences surrounding the growth and advent of LEAVES OF GRASS."[136] As he indicates presently, the "moral atmosphere" to which he refers is his extreme mental depression following his mother's death, a shock from which he seems never to have recovered, and his "tedious attack of paralysis." This depression is also partly responsible for Whitman's interpretation of the first volume (i.e., *Leaves of Grass*) as radiating "Physiology alone," whereas "the present One, though of the like origin in the main, more palpably doubtless shows the Pathology which was pretty sure to come in time from the others." Although the later poems do lack the "vehemence of pride and audacity" to be found in the earlier editions—"composed in the flush of my health and strength—,"[137] it is not strictly true that the first six editions of *Leaves of Grass* dealt exclusively with "Birth and Life."[138] For Death and Immortality are prominent themes in every edition, including the first, though the treatment does vary somewhat from period to period. But in his sickness and old age Whitman was inclined to idealize the physiological vigor and joy of his healthier and happier days.

In another reminiscence, however, he makes one of his most revealing confessions about the psychological origins of much of the earlier *Leaves*:

Something more may be added—for, while I am about it, I would make a full confession. I also sent out LEAVES OF GRASS to arouse and set flowing in men's and women's hearts, young and old, (my present and future readers,) endless streams of living, pulsating love and friendship, directly from them to myself, now and ever. To this terrible, irrepressible yearning, (surely more or less down underneath in most human souls,)—this never-satisfied appetite for sympathy, and this boundless offering of sympathy—this universal democratic comradeship—this old, eternal, yet ever-new interchange of adhesiveness, so fitly emblematic of America—I have given in that book, undisguisedly, declaredly, the openest expression.[139]

Aside from the phrenological term "adhesiveness," which Whitman uses to indicate the "Calamus" emotion, no clearer statement can be found of the fact that the impulse of Whitman's songs came not from the desire to express love experiences but to compensate for the absence of experience. In 1876 Whitman still needs sympathy, but the "terrible, irrepressible yearning" came to a climax in the third edition, was appeased through the activities of the "wound-dresser," and is now almost entirely sublimated in the democratic idealism of such poetry and prose as *Democratic Vistas*, "Thoughts for the Centennial," the centennial songs, and other pieces in *Two Rivulets*, including the Preface, which summarizes Whitman's social and literary theory.

The dominant mood of Whitman during the first years of his invalidism is poignantly mirrored in the chief poems of *Two Rivulets*, the "Prayer of Columbus" and the "Song of the Redwood-Tree." The poet was obviously thinking of himself when he described Columbus in his late years as, "A batter'd, wreck'd old man." Almost with the grief of Job, Columbus reminds God that not once has he "lost nor faith nor ecstasy in Thee." He is resigned to "The end I know not, it is all in Thee." In a climax of pathos he feels mocked and perplexed, but then

> As if some miracle, some hand divine unseal'd my eyes,
> Shadowy, vast shapes, smile through the air and sky,
> And on the distant waves sail countless ships,
> And anthems in new tongues I hear saluting me.

No doubt a similar dream of future reward and recognition in "new tongues" sustained Walt Whitman in the hour of his deepest suffering and discouragement.

We might say that in "Prayer of Columbus" the poet's solution is some variety of religious faith, whereas in "Song of the Redwood-Tree" it is a philosophical consolation, perhaps derived indirectly from Hegel. The subject of this poem is the death-chant of a "mighty dying tree." It too has "consciousness, identity," as "all the rocks and mountains have, and all the earth." In typical Whitmanesque fashion the spirit of the tree is projected into the future—the poet's

"Vistas"—, "Then to a loftier strain" the chant turns to the "occult deep volitions" which are shaping the "hidden national will,"

Clearing the ground for broad Humanity, the true America, heir of
    the past so grand,
To build a grander future.[sec. 6]

The philosophical thought and the imagery of this poem are perhaps more clearly explained in "Eidólons," which in 1881 was shifted to the "Inscriptions" group, thus indicating that Whitman regarded it as one of the keys to *Leaves of Grass*. It is an abstract treatment of Whitman's subjective and idealistic philosophy. Each object, as well as rivers, worlds, and universes, has a spirit, soul, or "eidólon," and the seer tells the poet to celebrate these instead of physical things. This "eidólon" is the poet's "real I myself," and his soul is a part of the great Nature-soul of all creations, so that the only genuine and ultimate reality is eidólons.

The "Song of the Universal" is another Hegelian expression of the *Democratic Vistas* faith in the ultimate triumph of the poet's ideals:

> In this broad Earth of ours,
> Amid the measureless grossness and the slag,
> Enclosed and safe within its central heart,
> Nestles the seed Perfection.

"Nature's amelioration" is constantly evolving the universal "good" out of the "bad majority."

In "Song of Myself" this doctrine was a belief in cosmic evolution, and was then expressed with a plenitude in harmony with the poet's exuberant vigor and audacious ambitions. It is still essentially the same doctrine, but it has now been modified by Whitman's discovery of Hegel and by the calming influence of sickness and old age. In 1855 Whitman gave lyric utterance to philosophical ideas; in 1876 the lyric power has largely evaporated and even the language has become abstract. This is the great change that had taken place over the years. In the 1876 issue of *Leaves of Grass* and *Two Rivulets*, Walt Whitman's poetic fire has notably cooled; but as his inspiration slackens and his vigor ebbs away, he turns more resolutely than ever to critical commentary and editorial revision of his life's work.

SIXTH EDITION, 1881-82

Whitman's bad luck with Boston publishers held until the end, for soon after James R. Osgood and Company brought out the 1881-82 edition of *Leaves of Grass* the District Attorney of Boston threatened prosecution if the book were not withdrawn from the mails or expurgated. When Whitman refused permission to delete any lines whatever, Osgood abandoned publication and turned the plates over to the author, who soon secured a new publisher in Rees Welsh and Company, Philadelphia, and the book was reissued in 1882. Later the same year David McKay took over this edition and remained Whitman's loyal friend and publisher for the rest of his life. McKay imprints of the sixth edition are also dated 1883, 1884, and 1888, but they are from the same plates—though some copies are on larger paper, and in 1888 a small batch was printed with "Sands at Seventy" as an annex.[140]

Whether in 1881-82 Whitman intended this to be the last version of *Leaves of Grass*, we do not know; nevertheless, in this edition the poems received their final revisions of text, their last titles, and their permanent positions. Whitman continued to write poems almost up to his death in 1892, but two installments of these he attached in 1888-89 and 1892 as annexes and he left instructions that his posthumous verse be placed in a third annex, thus leaving the 1881 *Leaves* intact and unaltered. The 1881 edition, therefore, is essentially the final, definitive *Leaves of Grass*, though all modern "inclusive" editions contain also the three annexes, and Blodgett's and Bradley's Comprehensive Reader's Edition includes, besides all the annexes, the poems Whitman dropped from *Leaves of Grass* and his uncollected and unpublished poems.[141]

The sixth edition contains twenty new poems, placed in various groups. All of these new compositions, however, are comparatively short and none is of major importance. Several reflect the old-age activities of the poet, such as his reading Hegel ("Roaming in Thought"), his trip to the West ("The Prairie States," "From Far Dakota's Cañons," "Spirit that Form'd this Scene"), and his anticipations of the end of his life ("As at Thy Portals also Death"). A short poem called "My Picture Gallery" is highly indicative of Whitman's old-age editorial methods. It is actually, as Professor Holloway discovered,[142] a fragment of a very early poem, one of the ur-*Leaves*, parts of the original manuscript having been used in various places. The printing of this unused fragment in 1881 as a new poem indicates that Whitman was salvaging, re-sorting, and editing his old manuscripts—perhaps scraping the bottom of the barrel. The two new bird poems in this edition are also significant. "To the Man-of-War-Bird" is actually a translation from Michelet,[143] and John Burroughs has testified that "The Dalliance of the Eagles" was written from an account which he gave Whitman.[144] As he grew older, Whitman made greater use of borrowed observations, journalistic articles, and events in the day's news.

In 1860 Whitman began groping toward the organization of *Leaves of Grass* which he finally adopted and made permanent in 1881. The nine "Inscriptions" of 1871 have now been increased to 24, though only one, a final two-line dedication to "Thou Reader," is new. Half of these, however, were first published in 1860, before Whitman had started this group, and the final section is thus an improvised prologue rather than a carefully planned unit. At first glance it seems to be a poetic index, or "program," for the contents of *Leaves of Grass*, but on close examination the program-symbolism is vague, unsystematic, incomplete, though some of the intentions and motifs are suggested. The first "Inscription" announces the theme of "One's Self," the third the ship motif (like Shelley's West Wind, the ship carries Whitman's poems to all lands). In "Poets to Come" the "main things" are expected from future bards, and the group ends with a solicitation of friendship and personal intimacy from the reader. Considering the fact that nearly all these poems were first published in other clusters, such as "Chants Democratic," "Drum-Taps," "Calamus," "Two Rivulets," etc., and were transferred to this cluster over a period of ten years, it is surprising that they serve as well as they do to introduce *Leaves of Grass*. And it is characteristic of Whitman that instead of deliberately planning and writing an introductory poem, or series, he selected, like an anthologist, poems already completed under various circumstances and impulses.

The "Inscriptions" also characterize the arrangement of the whole book in a manner that is not obvious to the reader who has not studied the poems chronologically. Since Whitman's avowed purpose was to put on record his own life, which he regarded as typical and representative, we would expect the poems of his life-record to be arranged either in chronology of their composition (which is to say, the chronology of his poetic and emotional development) or classified so that their subject-matter at least suggests a natural bio-graphical sequence. Although the prologue poems are followed by the most ostensibly autobiographical works in the book, "Starting from Paumanok" and "Song of Myself" (new title in 1881), and the collection ends with groups symbolizing old age and approaching death, the life-allegory arrangement is still quite general and unsystematic, and there is little visible attempt at chronology inside the groups.

This observation will become clarified and illustrated as we survey the remaining groups in this final arrangement. The two especially autobiographical and doctrinaire poems are followed by "Children of Adam" and "Calamus," groups which do, of course, typify Whitman's psychology and sentiments from about 1855 to '60, but both groups have since then been considerably revised and edited—and "Calamus," as we have seen, has even been remotivated.

Then come the great songs in an unnamed group. The earliest of these are "Song of the Answerer" and "A Song for Occupations" (1855) and the latest is "Song of the Redwood-Tree" (1874). The group begins with "Salut au Monde!" and contains "A Song of the Rolling Earth," both cosmic in theme and imagery, and they help give unity to these poems in which the poet's universal sympathy and his cosmic lyric inspiration were at white-heat intensity (about 1856, the date of five of these poems). Thus chronologically these poems should precede "Children of Adam" and "Calamus," but they were probably placed after these groups in order that the physiological and sex motifs might precede the cosmic ones—a logical arrangement in terms of Whitman's general philosophy.

The first of the new groups is "Birds of Passage," a title which seems to compare life to the migrations of the bird kingdom. The poems come from various periods, but the general theme of the collection is the evolution and migration of the human race through Time and Space, as in "Song of the Universal," "Pioneers! O Pioneers!," and "With Antecedents." The group has very little personal significance or relation to the life-allegory motif of the whole book. There is, however, a certain appropriateness in placing the "pioneer" motif after the great cosmic songs.

The next group has been renamed "Sea-Drift" (called "Sea-Shore Memories" in 1871). It contains the two major sea poems, "Out of the Cradle Endlessly Rocking" (1859) and "As I Ebb'd with the Ocean of Life" (1860), but also represents different moods from various periods, as in "Tears" (1867), "On the Beach at Night Alone" (1856) and "On the Beach at Night" (1871). In chronological sequence Whitman's seashore poems reveal the major crises of his poetic career and form a psychological drama, but this grouping suggests only that the sea provided much of the poet's inspiration. The group is unified by a common subject and locale, and is not without its own logic, but the student must search through other groups to complete the experiences vaguely hinted here.

Another new group is "By the Roadside," in miscellaneous collection of short poems on many topics and extending from "Europe" (1850) and "Boston Ballad" (1854) to "Roaming in Thought" (1881). They are merely samples of experiences and poetic inspirations along Whitman's highway of life.

Drum-Taps has been considerably revised and enlarged since 1865, and the introductory poem of 1871–76 has been discarded. "Virginia—The West" is a good example of the way Whitman shifted poems around. It first appeared in *As a Strong Bird on Pinions Free* (1872), then in *Two Rivulets* ('76), and now comes to rest in *Drum-Taps*. Also the poem which introduced this group in '71 and '76 is now a part of section 1 of "The Wound-Dresser"—"Arous'd and angry, I'd thought to beat the alarum," etc. Several poems first published in *Sequel to Drum-Taps* have finally been placed in this group, thus making it a record not only of the war but of the aftermath too, except for the memorial poems for President Lincoln, which are now called "Memories of President Lincoln."

The latter group is followed by perhaps the most revised composition in *Leaves of Grass*, now called for the first time, after the sixth change in title, "By Blue Ontario's Shore." In 1856 Whitman incorporated parts of his "55 Preface in this poem, and with each succeeding edition until 1881 made extensive revisions. Perhaps his difficulty in making up his mind what to do with the composition was due in part to his having meanwhile expressed and exemplified his poetic theory in many ways. At any rate, in subject-matter this poem is akin to "Starting from Paumanok" and "Song of Myself," but it now appears after the war and Lincoln poems because in 1867 Whitman had remotivated it as a "Chant . . . from the soul of America," singing the "throes of Democracy" and victory (a transition from *Drum-Taps* to *Democratic Vistas*).

"Autumn Rivulets," another new cluster title, does not signify poems associated with the autumn of the poet's life, although in the introductory "As Consequent, etc." he compares these songs to "wayward rivulets" flowing after the "store of summer rains." He also thinks of his life and the experiences which he has recorded in his poems as "waifs from the deep, cast high and dry" onto the shore. Instead of Emerson's Over-Soul metaphor, Whitman uses "the sea of Time," from whence his own identity has come and toward which it is ever flowing, there to blend finally with "the old streams of death." Thus in the imagery of his group-title Whitman re-expresses his philosophy of life and death through this new poem.

But this symbolism is found only in the lead poem. In the other poems of the group, from the 1855 "There was a Child Went Forth" to the 1881 "Italian Music in Dakota" neither these images nor "Autumn Rivulets" motifs reappear. Furthermore, the majority of the poems date back to 1856 and 1860 and reflect the moods and sentiments of those periods: "This Compost" ('56), "To a Common Prostitute" ('60), "O Star of France" ('71), etc. "My Picture-Gallery" was evidently rescued from the barrel of old manuscripts.

Throughout the remainder of *Leaves of Grass* the poems are in general arranged to emphasize the "spiritual" purposes which Whitman professedly began with "Passage to India." Even here, however, he often places an earlier poem, like "The Sleepers" ('55) or "To Think of Time" ('55), both of which come between "Passage to India" and the 1871 cluster—still retained—, "Whispers of Heavenly Death." Then, after a brief interval, comes the new section called "From Noon to Starry Night," a title which happily permits the poet to follow his usual procedure of selecting typical poems from various periods of his career. The group is introduced by a new poem, "Thou Orb Aloft Full-Dazzling," a prayer to the sun, with which the poet feels a special affinity and a reminder of his own prime:

As for thy throes, thy perturbations, sudden breaks and shafts of
    flame gigantic,
I understand them, I know those flames, those perturbations well.

He adores the sun also because it "impartially infoldest all" and liberally gives of itself. He invokes the sun to prepare his "starry nights." The section ends patly with a short epilogue-poem, "A Clear Midnight," on the images of "Night, sleep, death and the stars."

The final cluster, also with a new title, is the inevitable "Songs of Parting," which of course ends with the 1860 "So Long!" The theme is death in its many connotations: personal anticipation, memory of the poet's mother, the death of soldiers in the war, the assassination of President Garfield, and the triumphant journey of the soul into the realms of eternity. But the anticipated end of the poet's life did not come for eleven years and he was spared to write many more postscripts and epitaphs.

As editor of his own work, Whitman is ingenious. His final group titles are appropriate for this anthology of his life-work, and there is a certain kind of poetic logic in his arrangement of the poems inside the various groups. But the student who has closely examined the growth of the editions will also find serious objections to Whitman's belief that the 1881 *Leaves of Grass* is as unified as a cathedral or as inevitable in structure as an organism in nature. In chronological order his poems do tell the inner story of the poet's long struggle to put on record his own life and the literary ambitions which he was trying to achieve, but in this final arrangement the story is inconsecutive and often obscured by the deletions and emendations which Whitman had made throughout the years as his concept of his own poetic rôle fluctuated. Perhaps he had deliberately obscured it. His arrangement of the poems by subject-matter seems to indicate that this is true. An inconsistency, however, remains. Such cluster titles as "Autumn Rivulets," "From Noon to Starry Night," and "Songs of Parting" suggest a chronology of life-experiences, but the contents of these groups reveal ideational rather than biological sequences. Furthermore, often the symbolism of these titles scarcely carries beyond the introductory poem and possibly an epilogue.

Perhaps critics will never agree upon the poet's success in this final arrangement, for everything depends upon what one wants in an edition of *Leaves of Grass*. The very fact that this was so indisputably Walt Whitman's final choice, and that he was still satisfied with it a decade later, leaves no doubt that this edition does show his intentions—especially his intention to suggest (*indirectly*, as he might have said) that this "is no book" but a man's life, though he reserved the right to erase and emend any parts of the record that violated his later ideals, and to arrange the parts so that they would not suggest the realism of biography. After all, this is a *poetic record*, not objective history or prosaic autobiography. Thus the reader of Whitman will no doubt always cherish the poet's own final edition. But for the student who is interested in the growth of Whitman's thought or the development of his prosodic techniques and artistry, or the solution of psychological mysteries, a chronological text is well-nigh indispensable.

SPECIMEN DAYS, 1882

About one-third of the material in *Specimen Days* had been published in 1875 in *War Memoranda*, but in 1882 Whitman collected this and other prose pieces, including *Democratic Vistas*, into what was historically the second edition of the *Complete Works* in two volumes (volume one being a reprint of the 1881 *Leaves*) but what was now essentially the *Complete Prose*.

Whitman himself called *Specimen Days* a "way-ward book," and it is certainly improvised, much of it having been copied from note-books, diaries, and scraps of manuscript, evidently with little revision—though these notes are perhaps more authentic "specimens" for not having been rewritten. The book covers three main subjects, the first being a brief autobiography which Whitman says he wrote for a friend in 1882; the second being war memoranda, taken from "verbatim copies of those lurid and blood-smutch'd little note-books" written in Washington and Virginia from the end of 1862 through 1865; and the third being diary and nature-notes for 1876–81 and miscellaneous short essays and articles.

The autobiography throws some light on the growth of Whitman as a poet because we can see in the glorification of his ancestry and the importance he attaches to his environment some of the processes by which he transmuted the commonplace into the idealism of his verse. In the war memoranda, however, we get a side of Whitman which is almost entirely lacking in his poems and which therefore supplements the poetry. In his graphic descriptions of the camp of the wounded, with the amputated arms and legs lying under the trees, he anticipates later American realism. And the exact account of many individual cases of the wounded documents the record. Atrocities are told with great anguish of spirit but without partisanship. Without preaching Whitman reveals the bestiality of war. He concludes that, "the real war will never get in the books," and adds that it was so horrible that perhaps it should not. But he comes nearer telling it than anyone else in America was to do for half a century to come, and he tells it all without sentimentality or propaganda for pacifism which followed World War I.

The third part of *Specimen Days* reveals still another side of Whitman's life. Before the war he had been a great nature lover, and nature plays a prominent part in all his poems, but the record of his Timber Creek experiences reads almost like a summer idyl. More amateurish than Thoreau in his botanical and ornithological observations, even priding himself on deficiency in exact information, Whitman's enjoyment of nature is as intimate and personal as one can find in romantic prose. But it is probably not accidental that he now expresses himself in loose, informal language, for he seems to have been living in the most satisfying repose of his life. The great seashore poems were not written in such a mood of quiet resignation. Even in the accounts of his travels of 1889, which he seems to have enjoyed as thoroughly as his youthful trip across the Alleghanies on his way to St. Louis, we find this same repose, this Indian summer atmosphere, which *Specimen Days* more clearly reflects than the old-age poems.

NOVEMBER BOUGHS, 1888

Specimen Days marks the transition to Whitman's final attitude toward life and his art as expressed in *November Boughs*, a large 8 vo book, bound in maroon or green cloth, published in Philadelphia by David McKay. Its 140 pages contain a long Preface, "A Backward Glance O'er Travel'd Roads," twenty essays on literary subjects and personal experiences, and sixty-four new poems grouped in two clusters, "Sands at Seventy" and "Fancies at Navesink." In 1892 these two clusters will become the "First Annex" to *Leaves of Grass* (i.e., annexed to the 1881 text), but the essays will remain outside Whitman's *Prose Works* because he will not live long enough to edit an expanded edition. However, he did append the contents of *November Boughs* to his 900-page quarto, *Complete Poems and Prose of Walt Whitman, 1855-1888*.

The poems in *November Boughs* are mainly the product of old-age reflection, November reminiscences. After completing his poems he is "curious to review them in the light of their own (at the time unconscious, or mostly unconscious) intentions, with certain unfoldings of the thirty years they seek to embody."[145] Gone are the ambitious boastings, the grandiose claims to fame. With tranquil confidence and utmost frankness Whitman now admits in his Preface, "I have not gain'd the acceptance of my own time, but have fallen back on fond dreams of the future." Yet despite the fact that *Leaves of Grass* has always been a financial failure, "I have had my say entirely in my own way, and put it unerringly on record—the value thereof to be decided by time."[146] The work was always an experiment, "as, in the deepest sense, I consider our American Republic itself to be, with its theory." He is content that he has "positively gain'd a hearing."

Once more Whitman reiterates his original purpose: "to exploit [his own] Personality, identified with place and date, in a far more candid and comprehensive sense than any hitherto poem or book." With this part of his original program he is still satisfied, but he is not so sure about another intention:

Modern science and democracy seem'd to be throwing out their challenge to poetry to put them in its statements in contra-distinction to the songs and myths of the past. As I see it now (perhaps too late,) I have unwittingly taken up that challenge and made an attempt at such statements—which I certainly would not assume to do now, knowing more clearly what it means.[147]

It is interesting and a little pathetic that Whitman's failure to gain wide acceptance in his own time and country have convinced him that "in verbal melody and all the conventional technique of poetry, not only the divine works that to-day stand ahead in the world's reading, but dozens more, transcend (some of them immeasurably transcend) all I have done, or could do," though he still believes that "there must imperatively come a readjustment of the whole theory and nature of Poetry. . . ."[148] Today, after such a readjustment has taken place, it is difficult for us to understand the nineteenth-century intolerance in poetic technique.

For the most part, the remainder of this Preface merely reaffirms Whitman's familiar doctrines: that the function of a poem is to fill a person "with vigorous and clean manliness,"[149] that American democratic individuality is yet unformed, and that the great poet will express the goodness of all creation.

The poems in this book scarcely need discussion. They seem to be mainly fragments from unpublished manuscripts (i.e., uncollected in *Leaves of Grass*; some were published in newspapers to earn a few dollars), or stray thoughts and echoes from earlier compositions. Some are ruminations long after the passing of the emotions and

experiences which first gave rise to lyric utterance. Whitman himself
is fully conscious of his true condition. In "Memories" he refers to
the "sweet . . . silent backward tracings," and in "As I Sit Writing
Here" he fears that the old-age vexations of the flesh "May filter in
my daily songs." With conscious effort he tries to make his last days
happiest of all, "The brooding and blissful halcyon days" ("Halcyon
Days").

In his last years the poet also feels close to the sea once more,
and at times both the sight of the ocean and his reflections almost
fan to life the old lyric sparks, as in the group "Fancies at Navesink,"
or "A sudden memory-flash comes back" in "The Pilot in the
Midst." The ocean revives the emotional symbolism of his greatest
poems in "With Husky-Haughty Lips, O Sea":

> The tale of cosmic elemental passion,
> Thou tellest to a kindred soul.

But these are merely echoes too, like "Old Salt Kossabone," based
on the family tradition about the sailor on his mother's side which he
had already used in section 35 of "Song of Myself," and "Going
Somewhere" revives the theme of two 1867 poems, "Small the
Theme of My Chant" and the first "Inscription." As in "After
Supper and Talk" the old poet is "loth to depart" and "garrulous to
the very last."

GOOD-BYE MY FANCY, 1891

In 1891 David McKay published *Good-Bye My Fancy*, a slender
volume of sixty-six pages, uniform in size and style with *November
Boughs*. It was subtitled "2d Annex to Leaves of Grass," but the
book contained both prose and poems, and of course only the thirty-
two poems of the new cluster "Good-Bye My Fancy" constituted the
annex. Gravely ill, Whitman knew that his career as a poet was unmistakably drawing near, and he opened with "Sail Out for Good,
Eidólon Yacht!" In a footnote to the first of his two poems with the
title "God-Bye My Fancy" he asked:

Why do folks dwell so fondly on the last words, advice, appearance, of the departing? Those last words are not samples of the best,
which involve vitality at its full, and balance, and perfect control and

scope. But they are valuable beyond measure to confirm and endorse the varied train, facts, theories and faith of the whole preceding life.

These new poems are permeated with old-age apparitions, twilight, departing ships, funeral wreaths, sunset, the chill of winter, but also "unseen buds" waiting "under the snow and ice" to burst into new life. In the final "Good-Bye" the poet has a kind of agnostic optimism:

Good-bye my Fancy!
Farewell dear mate, dear love!
I'm going away, I know not where,
Or to what fortune, or whether I may ever see you again,
So Good-bye my Fancy.
    .   .   .   .   .

Long indeed have we lived, slept, filter'd, become really blended into
    one;
Then if we die we die together, (yes, we'll remain one,)
If we go anywhere we'll go together to meet what happens,
    .   .   .   .   .

Good-bye—and hail! my Fancy.

In his "Preface Note to 2d Annex,/ concluding L. of G.—1891," Whitman himself wonders, "Had I not better withhold (in this old age and paralysis of me) such little tags and fringe-dots (maybe specks, stains,) as follow a long dusty journey, and witness it afterward?" He is "not at all clear" himself that this new batch of verse and prose "is worth printing," but he begs indulgence because doing so enables him to "while away the hours of my 72d year." Besides, he hopes these "last droplets of and after spontaneous rain" will "filter" to the heart and brain of America. Furthermore, his prose reminiscences of the war years may help "this vast rich Union" to realize and appreciate the cost of its preservation. About half of these prose pieces are autobiographical sketches similar to passages in *Specimen Days*, being, admittedly, items saved from "a vast batch left to oblivion." Yet his final thought is not that he has written himself out, "But how much—how many topics, of the greatest point and cogency, I am leaving untouch'd!"

AUTHORIZED *LEAVES OF GRASS*, 1891-92

The 1891-92 issue of *Leaves of Grass* is widely known as the "death-bed edition" but it is not, as defined at the beginning of this chapter (see note 1), a new *edition*, and the book which his intimate friends called the "death-bed edition" was a book hastily assembled in December, 1891, from unbound sheets of the 1889 reprint so that Whitman might hold the promised "new edition" in his hands before he died. A few copies were bound for the poet's friends, but it was, in a sense, a fake, and certainly not the projected final and definitive 1892 *Leaves of Grass*.

Several months later David McKay did publish the promised volume, dated on the title-page 1891-92, and a uniform volume of the *Complete Prose Works* (reprinted from the 1882 plates of *Specimen Days and Collect*, which in turn had been reprinted with wide margins and bound quarto size as *Complete Poems and Prose of Walt Whitman, 1855-1888*).

The 1891-1892 issue was actually, through page 382, a reprint of the 1881 edition from the James R. Osgood plates, which the Boston publisher had turned over to Whitman after a district attorney threatened prosecution for publishing an obscene book. To the 1881 text Whitman annexed, first, the cluster "Sands at Seventy" from *November Boughs* (using the *November Boughs* plates), and then a second cluster, "Good-Bye My Fancy" from *Good-Bye My Fancy* (using the *Good-Bye ...* plates), designated as the "2d Annex." In 1889 McKay had printed an issue containing the first Annex, but not the second. The 1891-1892 issue also published for the first time the injunction Whitman placed on all future editors and publishers of *Leaves of Grass* (using the untechnical term "editions"):

As there are now several editions of L. of G., different texts and dates, I wish to say that I prefer and recommend this present one, complete, for future printing, if there should be any; a copy and fac-simile, indeed, of the text of these 438 pages. The subsequent adjusting interval which is so important to form'd and launch'd work, books especially, has pass'd; and waiting till fully after that, I have given (pages 423-438) my concluding words.

                                                                    W. W.

The "concluding words" were those of the *November Boughs* (1888)

Preface, "A Backward Glance O'er Travel'd Roads." This "author-ized" text (except for the 1888 Preface) has been honored by nearly all editors of Whitman's poems down to the present time, including Harold W. Blodgett and Sculley Bradley in their "Comprehensive Reader's Edition" (1965).

In 1897 Small, Maynard and Co., in Boston, published an issue with "posthumous additions" called "Old Age Echoes," a title chosen by Whitman himself—held "in reserve," he told Horace Traubel, one of his three literary executors. This cluster of thirteen short poems included some uncollected fragments from 1873–4, and later frag-ments—a regular grab-bag of oddments. On March 16, 1892, ten days before his death, he handed Traubel some slips of paper on which he had written "A Thought of Columbus."[150] It was appropriate that his very last poem should have been a combined salutation and prayer to the martyred explorer with whom he had felt a kindred identity since writing his "Prayer of Columbus" during one of the darkest years of his life (1874).[151]

With the 1897 issue, the official canon of *Leaves of Grass* was now complete: consisting of the 1881 text (sixth edition), plus the cluster "Sands at Seventy" from *November Boughs*, the cluster "Good-Bye My Fancy," from the book of the same title, and the gleanings called "Old Age Echoes," which do not belong in the Whit-man canon.

Chapter III

The Realm of Whitman's Ideas

All these separations and gaps shall be taken up and hook'd
and link'd together,
The whole earth, this cold impassive, voiceless earth, shall
be completely justified.—
"Passage to India"

SOCIETY

Just as the whaling ship was Herman Melville's "Yale and Harvard," so was the newspaper office Walt Whitman's university. In fact, the printing office might also be called his elementary school, for there he learned to spell, punctuate, and compose sentences, rather than in the mediocre public school which he attended until his twelfth year. Later as a reporter and editor of several newspapers he received a practical education in sociology and politics. His moral and intellectual development in printing shop and newspaper office has been traced by several scholars,[1] but fullest and most authoritatively by Joseph Jay Rubin in *The Historic Whitman* (1973). Rubin calls this period of Whitman's life "his Antaen earth,"[2] and certainly it was then that he learned the realities of life in Brooklyn and New York City, and became acutely aware of the larger issues which were already dividing the nation.

Before the Civil War nearly all American newspapers were supported and controlled by political parties. Whitman learned typesetting from Samuel E. Clements, editor of the Long Island *Patriot*, which was Democratic and loyal to the "bosses" of New York City's Tammany Hall. The "Pat" solicited the support of the mechanics and artisans in Brooklyn, who included Walt Whitman's father, a carpenter, and ardent follower of working-men's causes.

Walter Whitman, Sr., was a personal friend of Tom Paine, and a

161

great admirer of the notorious socialist and reformer, Frances Wright, whose lectures Walt attended with his father.[3] At home the boy read Paine's *Age of Reason*, Count Volney's Ruins (a treatise on the ideas which brought about the French Revolution), and Frances Wright's *A Few Days in Athens* (imaginary conversations on the philosophy of Epicurus).[4] At this stage young Whitman's political orientation was passionately proletarian and egalitarian, and in religion Deistic. His political heroes were General Lafayette, whose visit to Brooklyn he witnessed at the age of six,[5] and Andrew Jackson, who made a triumphant tour of the city eight years later.[6] He would always remain a Jacksonian Democrat.

Whitman's Deism, however, was considerably modified by the influence of the radical Long Island Quaker, Elias Hicks, another personal friend of the Whitman family. What might seem like anti-clericalism derived from Paine and Volney was more likely a sympathetic sharing of Hicks's attitude toward all religious institutions as the source of moral authority. As Whitman later recalled, Hicks "believ'd little in a church as organiz'd—even his own—with houses, ministers, or with salaries, creeds, Sundays, saints, Bibles, holy festivals, &c. But he believ'd always in the universal church, in the soul of man, invisibly rapt, ever-waiting, ever-responding to universal truth."[7]

In his childhood Walt Whitman accompanied his parents to hear Hicks preach, and his interest in this unusual Quaker continued into his old age, when he published a long essay on him in *November Boughs* (1888). There he says, "Elias taught throughout [his life], as George Fox began it, or rather reiterated and verified it, the Platonic doctrine that the ideals of character, of justice, of religious action, whenever the highest is at stake, are to be conform'd to no outside doctrine of creeds, Bibles, legislative enactments, conventionalities, or even decorums, but are to follow the inward Deity-planted law of the emotional soul."[8]

All Quakers believed in the moral guidance of the "inner light," but Hicks went further than most of them in sweeping away everything else as nonessential. He had been suspected of holding heretical views on the Divinity of Christ and the Atonement, but he finally created an outright schism in the Society of Friends when he declared at a meeting in Philadelphia in 1829: "The blood of Christ—the blood of Christ—why, my friends, the actual blood of Christ in itself was no more effectual than the blood of bulls and goats...."[9]

Though Walt Whitman never joined a Quaker sect of any kind, and always regarded "churches, sects, pulpits" as lacking "any solid convictions," existing "by a sort of tacit, supercilious, scornful sufferance,"[10] no one believed more devoutly than he in the "inward Deity-planted law of the emotional soul." (By "emotional" he meant *feeling*; one knew what was right by inward, emotional conviction.)

When Whitman first became a political journalist, he supported the candidates and doctrines of the Democratic party in New York State, but he never sold his Quaker conscience to any party or faction, and eventually this brought him into conflict with the party bosses. For a history of Whitman's journalistic career, the reader should consult Rubin's *Historic Whitman*. For the present purpose we need to notice only the major social and political ideas expressed in his editorials in the Brooklyn *Eagle*, which he edited in 1846 and 1847, and later in the *Brooklyn Times* in 1857–59.[11]

Whitman assumed the editorship of the Brooklyn *Eagle* in March 1846 during one of the most momentous periods in American history. Since 1844 the United States had been in a heated dispute with Great Britain over the Northwest boundary line. That year the Democrats had won the Presidential election on the slogan "Fifty-four forty or fight," and fighting was still a real possibility until Britain agreed in June 1846 on what is still the boundary line between the United States and Canada. The line was far short of 54°40′, which would have included British Columbia, but it did extend the territory of the United States clear to the Pacific Ocean, opening up vast possibilities for future economic and demographic growth.

In the spring of 1846 President Polk also ordered the American army to invade Mexico, which had refused to cede California and other Southwest territory (including present New Mexico, Utah, Arizona, Nevada, and parts of Wyoming and Colorado) to the United States. Annexation of Texas the previous December by American citizens living there illegally had precipitated the war with Mexico, but United States imperialists were only too glad of the opportunity to increase the territory of the nation, some calling it the country's "manifest destiny," a phrase coined by the editor of *The United States Magazine and Democratic Review*, John L. O'Sullivan.

Walt Whitman, editor of a prominent Democratic newspaper, might have been expected to support the war with Mexico—which the Whigs called "Jimmy Polk's war"—and to exult over the favorable settlement of the Oregon question. Uncritically, and almost mindlessly, he accepted the "manifest destiny" doctrine with naive idealism. On June 23, 1846, he declared in an editorial that expansion of the United States was natural and inevitable, "and for our part, we look on that increase of territory and power . . . with the faith which the Christian has in God's mystery.—Over the rest of the world, the swelling impulse of freedom struggles, too; though *we* are ages ahead of them."[12] Whitman's imperialist euphoria continued into 1847. On February 8 he shouted that the United States "may one day put the Canadas and Russian America [Alaska] in its fob pocket!" He maintained, however, that his nation "will tenderly regard human life, property and rights" and "*never* be guilty of furnishing duplicates to the Chinese war, the 'operations of the British in India,' or the 'extinguishment of Poland.' "[13]

Partisanship had temporarily blinded Whitman to the fact that Southern slave owners wanted Texas in order to extend slavery, and would strive with all their might to carry slaves into the other territories acquired in the Oregon settlement. He was opposed to slavery as an institution and had published editorials denouncing the slave trade in words that must have pleased the Abolitionists, but he was slow to realize that the war with Mexico strengthened the slave-owner's interests. This was partly because he still believed that slavery could be abolished by peaceful means and he disliked the violent language of the Abolitionists, the chief critics of the Mexican War.

Above all else, Whitman feared that confrontations over abolition might break up the Union, which he regarded as the greatest "political blessing on earth"[14]—exactly the stand Abraham Lincoln would take a decade later. However, Senator Calhoun opened his eyes to the intentions of the Southern Democrats when he proclaimed in the spring of 1847 that "a large majority of both parties in the non-slave-holding States, have come to a fixed determination to appropriate all the territories of the United States now possessed, or hereafter acquired, to themselves, *to the entire exclusion of the slaveholding States.*"[15] Whitman pounced on these italicized phrases, pointing out that with the possible exception of South Carolina, the majority of freemen in the South did not own slaves. "The only persons who will be excluded will be the *aristocracy* of the South— the men who work only with other men's hands."

Whitman, son of a carpenter and friend of the working men, saw the extension of slavery into the new territories as an ominous threat to free labor, especially in the industrial North. "The voice of the North proclaims that *labor must not be degraded*. The young men of the free States must not be shut out from the new domain (where slavery does not now exist) by the *introduction* of an institution which will render their honorable industry no longer respectable."[16]

However, Whitman did not see in the immigration of the poor of Europe a threat to American labor, as the Whig "Nativists" or "Know-Nothing" party did. In actual fact most of the immigrants were ignorant and unskilled and they did flood the labor market with cheap manpower. But here Whitman took an idealistic stand. After describing their wretchedness in the Old World, he asked: "How, then, can any man with a heart in his breast, begrudge the coming of Europe's needy ones, to the plentiful storehouse of the New World?"[17] He advocated raising funds to speed these destitute people to the unsettled West, predicting that the time would come when they would be able to achieve in this country "something of that destiny which we may suppose God intends eligible for mankind. And this problem is to be worked out through the people, territory, and government of the United States."[18] This, of course, was true prophecy, but Whitman did not forsee the Armageddon which would precede the fulfillment.

In advocating "free trade" Whitman was also opposing Whig "protectionism," but again he looked upon this issue from the point of view of the working man. High tariff, he said, would raise prices and restrict trade, thereby depressing wages, contrary to Whig arguments. In one editorial he declared:

When we hear of the immense purchases [bribes], donations, or "movements" of our manufacturing capitalists of the North, we bethink ourselves how reasonable it is that they should want "protection"—and how nice a game they play in asking a high tariff "for the benefits of the working men." What lots of cents have gone out of poor folks' pockets, to swell the dollars in the possession of owners of great steam mills! Molière, speaking of a wealthy physician, says: "He must have killed a great many people to be so rich!" Our American capitalists of the manufacturing order, would *poor* a great many people to be rich![19]

Whitman never wavered on these issues in which his opinions coincided with the liberal principles of the Democratic Party, but on the issue of "free soil" the Democrats of New York State split, and Whitman found himself in the minority faction. This came about as a result of the Wilmot Proviso, a bill introduced by Congressman David Wilmot to prohibit slavery in the new territories. Of course the Southern Democrats were solidly opposed to the Proviso, and in the attempt to preserve Party unity both in the New York Legislature and the Democratic convention at Syracuse in 1847 the New York Democrats refused to take a definite stand on the question. In the November election the Democrats were solidly defeated in New York, and Whitman thought it was because the Party had not been "sufficiently bold, open and radical [liberal], in its avowals of sentiment."[20] Specifically, he blamed it for not having taken a firm and honest stand on the Wilmot Proviso, and he editorialized this warning:

We must plant ourselves firmly on the side of freedom and openly espouse it. The late election is a terrific warning of the folly of all half-way policy in such matters—of all compromises that neither receive or reject a great idea to which the people are once fully awakened.[21]

The owner of the Brooklyn *Eagle* was Isaac Van Anden, one of the conservative leaders of the New York Democrats. When his editor continued to support the "radicals," now called in derision the "Barn-burners" (they would burn the barn to destroy the rats), a rupture was inevitable, though it did not actually take place until about January 4, 1848. General Lewis Cass had written an open letter opposing the Wilmot Proviso. Whitman refused to print it, though he attacked Cass's arguments on January 3. On January 5 the letter was published in full and the *Eagle* was under new editorial management.

A few days after leaving the Brooklyn *Eagle* Whitman was offered an editorial position on a fledgling newspaper in New Orleans, where he spent the spring of 1848. But in the summer he returned to Brooklyn and the free soil Democrats encouraged him to start a weekly newspaper to support their cause. He called his paper the *Freeman* and published the first issue on September 9. That night a fire destroyed the building in which the *Freeman* was edited and printed—arson was strongly suspected. Undaunted, Whitman recouped his resources, bought new type, and continued to publish his paper after a short delay, and was even able to make it a daily in the spring. But by September the New York free soil Democratic politicians had made peace with the conservative faction and Whitman lost his financial support for the *Freeman*. On September 11 he gave up the attempt to keep it going. Had he been willing to compromise his honest conviction, he could no doubt have found another editorial position, but he was a man of principle.

The Whigs, of course, had no use for Walt Whitman either. As a Jeffersonian-Jacksonian Democrat by conviction, he opposed their whole political philosophy. He thought they exaggerated the intricacy of government:

The error lies in the desire after *management*, the great curse of our Legislation: every thing is to be regulated and made straight by force of statute. And all this while, evils are accumulating, in very consequence of excessive management. The true office of government is simply to preserve the rights of each citizen from spoliation: when it attempts to go beyond this, it is intrusive and does more harm than good.[22]

With nowhere to go in journalism, Walt Whitman turned to building houses (mainly as a contractor) in Brooklyn. He felt not only that the politicians in his Party had betrayed him but also the great cause of freedom itself in surrendering to the slave-owning Democrats of the South. In June he published a satirical poem on the Biblical text "I was wounded in the house of my friends" (Zechariah xiii. 6): "If thou art balked, O Freedom,/ The Victory is not to thy manlier foes;/ From the house of friends comes the death stab." He exhorted the "young North" to "arise," because "Our elder blood flows in the veins of cowards."[23]

In Europe, too, reactionaries were again in control after the abortive revolutions of 1848. In the summer of 1850 Whitman expressed his disappointment—and hope—in a poem called "Resurgemus"[24] (resurgence):

Suddenly, out of its state and drowsy air, the air of slaves,
[1855 corrected to read: stale . . . lair . . . lair]

God, 'twas delicious!
That brief, tight, glorious grip
Upon the throats of kings.

But the sweetness of mercy brewed bitter destruction,
And frightened rulers come back:

[Yet] Those corpses of young men,

.　　　.　　　.　　　.　　　.

Cold and motionless as they seem,
Live elsewhere with undying vitality;
They live in other young men, O, kings,

.　　　.　　　.　　　.　　　.

Not a grave of those slaughtered ones,
But is growing its seed of freedom,
In its turn to bear seed,
Which the winds shall carry afar and resow,
And the rains nourish.

Whitman's bitterness of 1848 had now been softened by faith in the ultimate workings of Providence.

Building houses, operating a small printing shop part-time, occasionally contributing verse and articles to New York and Brooklyn newspapers, had enabled him to rise above the political strife and think of ultimate outcomes. He found time to read, attend the opera, visit the studios of Brooklyn artists, and, above all, to think. As a consequence this became the most creative period of his life, during which he conceived and wrote the poems and preface for his remarkable first edition of *Leaves of Grass*, so far superior to anything he had published before that it seemed like the work of a different person—as, psychologically, it was. However, in his passion for political and social equality and justice, the development of character without institutional restraints, and the use of natural resources for the good of every citizen of the nation, Whitman was the same man who wrote editorials welcoming territorial expansion, defended the Wilmot Proviso, and denounced economic exploitation of working men.

Whitman's 1855 Preface inaugurates his revolutionary esthetic program, but it is also social and political, aiming, above all else, to cultivate in every citizen a magnanimity and generosity of spirit to match the territorial expanse and abundance of natural resources of the nation. His ideal "greatest poet" hardly knows pettiness or triviality. "If he breathes into any thing that was before thought small it dilates with the grandeur and life of the universe."[25] This is his impossible goal—no less. He calls the United States themselves a great poem, and he wants every person to make his own life a "poem," that is, a thing of beauty and perfection. He even suggests what might be called a "creed" to attain this self-perfection:

Love the earth and sun and the animals, despise riches, give alms to every one that asks, stand up for the stupid and crazy, devote your income and labor to others, hate tyrants, argue not concerning God, have patience and indulgence toward the people, take off your hat to nothing known or unknown or to any man or number of men, go freely with powerful uneducated persons and with the young and with the mothers of families, read these leaves [Leaves of Grass] in the open air every season of every year of your life, re-examine all you have been told at school or church or in any book, dismiss whatever insults your own soul, and your very flesh shall be a great poem and have the richest fluency not only in its words but in the silent lines of its lips and face and between the lashes of your eyes and in every motion and joint of your body.[26]

Here the "beatitudes" of Christ, Quaker customs and the radical teachings of Elias Hicks, American patriotic arrogance and humility, and the romantic pieties of Walt Whitman mingle in an eclectic creed Whitman intended for his "New Religion." He predicts that "There will soon be no more priests," at least in the church sense:

A new order shall arise and they shall be the priests of man, and every man shall be his own priest. The churches built under their umbrage shall be the churches of men and women. Through the divinity of themselves shall the kosmos[27] and the new breed of poets be interpreters of men and women and of all events and things. They shall find their inspiration in real objects today, symptoms of the past and future.[28]

Whitman's final and ultimate ideal is that "An individual is as superb as a nation when he has the qualities which make a great nation." His own ambition was to achieve this in his own life, or at least in his poetry as a literary archetype, and he ended his Preface with the declaration that, "The proof of a poet is that his country absorbs him as affectionately as he has absorbed it."[29] By this test he would fail during his lifetime, and especially with his 1855 edition,

Ralph Waldo Emerson being one of the few readers to see merit in it.[30] Emerson's praise, however, encouraged him to put out a second edition the following year, which was an even greater failure than the first.

By this time Whitman had also become active in journalism again, but as a free-lance writing special articles for a magazine called *Life Illustrated*. One of his most important contributions, entitled simply "The Slave Trade," was an exposé of the fitting out of ships in the New York harbor to engage secretly in transporting slaves from Africa. He gave explicit details of exactly how the operations were carried out, how much they cost, what the profits were (about 900%), and how the Federal Court in New York permitted the culprits to escape with very light penalties or none at all. Two slavers had left New York for Africa in the past few days (late July, 1856), "and all along they have been slipping off at the rate of a dozen or twenty for every one caught."[31]

Though not a declared Abolitionist, Whitman was nevertheless deeply concerned in the summer of 1856 with events growing out of slavery. His indignation with the political parties became almost frenetic when the Democrats nominated James Buchanan and the Native Americans (Know-Nothing—and late Whigs) Millard Fillmore for the Presidency. Buchanan represented the faction which had betrayed Whitman and the free soil Democrats in 1847–48; and Fillmore, an unsuccessful Whig candidate in 1852, who had succeeded to the Presidency after the death of Zachary Taylor, had signed the Fugitive Slave Law. Whitman knew that neither man would be able to stop the guerilla warfare in Kansas between the free soil settlers and the invading slave owners. The new Republican Party nominated John Charles Frémont, western explorer, adventurer, maverick politician, and no friend of the slave interests. It is possible that Whitman had some hopes for him, though he never gave an open endorsement, and he may have feared that Frémont's election would split the Union, as the election of Republican Abraham Lincoln four years later actually did.

Feeling that someone should speak for the six million "mechanics, farmers, sailors, &c.," Whitman wrote a political tract called "The Eighteenth Presidency!,"[32] which he set up in type and apparently distributed in proof to some "editors of the independent press," hoping that they or "any rich person, anywhere" might "circulate and reprint this Voice of mine for the workingmen's sake."[33] There is no evidence whatever that Whitman was trying to start a new party to represent labor, and if he hoped to aid any of the candidates for President, it would have had to be Frémont, but this was a very ambiguous way to accomplish that. Not surprisingly, his call for reform was ignored; no editor printed his tract, so far as is known, and it was not published until long after Whitman's death. Yet despite his abortive effort, the tract is invaluable as evidence of Whitman's understanding of the political situation in the years immediately preceding the Civil War, and history has corroborated many of his insights.

The main thesis of "The Eighteenth Presidency!" is that under the corrupt party system in the United States of that time government has ceased to be representative, and the ideals of the founding fathers have been betrayed:

At present, the personnel of the government of these thirty millions, in executives and elsewhere, is drawn from limber-tongued lawyers, very fluent but empty, feeble old men, professional politicians . . . rarely drawn from the solid body of the people . . .

I expect to see the day when the like of the present personnel of the governments, federal, state, municipal, military and naval, will be looked upon with derision, and when qualified mechanics and young men will reach Congress and other official stations, sent in their working costumes, fresh from their benches and tools, and returning to them again with dignity.[34]

Whitman, of course, over-simplified the education and skill needed for public office, though four years hence Abraham Lincoln, the "Rail-Splitter," did fulfill part of this expectation—however, he had studied and practiced law. Yet conditions during the campaign for the "eighteenth-Presidency" were not far different from Whitman's description:

To-day, of all the persons in public office in These States, not one in a thousand has been chosen by any spontaneous movement of the people, nor is attending to the interests of the people; all have been nominated and put through by great or small caucuses of the politicians [state primary elections were not general until about 1917], or appointed as rewards for electioneering; and all consign themselves to personal and party interests . . . The berths, the Presidency included, are bought, sold, electioneered for, prostituted, and filled with prostitutes.[35]

One part of the country was no better than the other. In the North were "office-vermin" and "kept-editors"; in the South braggarts who would dissolve the Union. "Are lawyers, dough-faces, and the three hundred and fifty thousand owners of slaves, to sponge the mastership of thirty millions?"[36] This, of course, was the real crux. Even today the democratic majority may be fooled and misled by political trickery, but the immediate cause of the conditions Whitman condemned was that a small band of Southern slave-owning Democrats managed to control the national Party for their own interests. In fact, to preserve party and national unity both the Whigs and the Democrats had yielded to chicanery, subterfuge, expediency, and cowardly compromise on the extension of slavery into the territories throughout the sixteenth and seventeenth Presidencies. And now once more the politicians had nominated "men both patterned to follow and match the seventeenth term," men sworn to "the theories that balk and reverse the main purposes of the founders of These States." One party flaunted "Americanism," using the "great word ... without yet feeling the first aspiration of it"; while the other [he seemed to ignore the Republican] distorted the meaning of "democracy," whereas "What the so-called democracy are now sworn to perform would eat the faces off the succeeding generations of common people worse than the most horrible disease."[37]

Whitman had lost confidence in any party, and thought America had "outgrown parties; hence forth it is too large, and they too small":

I place no reliance upon any old party, nor upon any new party. Suppose one to be formed under the noblest auspices, and getting into power with the noblest intentions, how long would it remain so? ... As soon as it becomes successful, and there are offices to be bestowed, the politicians leave the unsuccessful parties and rush toward it, and it ripens and rots with the rest.[38]

This cynicism explains, perhaps, why Whitman had no enthusiasm for the Republican candidate. And, "Platforms are of no account" either. "The right man is everything." He had not lost faith in all men, or in the "organic compact of These States," which was sufficient platform for any party. He even regarded the Constitution as a sacred and prophetic document, but it could be misused, as it had been in enforcing the Fugitive Slave Act. What was most needed was a great leader with integrity and courage. "Whenever the day comes for him to appear, the man who shall be the Redeemer President of The States, is to be the one that fullest realizes the rights of individuals signified by the impregnable rights of The States, the substratum of this Union."[39] It was not until after Lincoln's election in 1860 that Whitman recognized in him the "Redeemer President," but he did come to that realization and almost worshipped him thereafter.

In spite of Whitman's bitter disappointment with party politics during the Fillmore-Buchanan campaign, he still had faith in the future of democracy because he believed the whole course of world history was against the anti-democratic conduct of the American politicians. "Freedom against slavery is not issuing here alone," he declared, "but is issuing everywhere." He saw in modern inventions and engineering such as the steamship, locomotive, telegraph, mass production of books and newspapers, the means of "interlinking the inhabitants of the earth . . . as groups of one family." All signs pointed to "unparalleled reforms" in society:

On all sides tyrants tremble, crowns are unsteady, the human race restive, on the watch for some better era, some divine war. No man knows what will happen next, but all know that some such things are to happen as mark the greatest moral convulsions of the earth. Who shall play the hand for America in these tremendous games?[40]

When the war came, Whitman soon discovered that it was not "divine," but it was certainly a great moral convulsion which changed the course of American history. During the political and economic corruption following the war, he would find that "democracy" was still more an ideal than a reality in the United States; so he had to make another attempt to analyze the problem and find grounds for continued hope. That he would attempt in *Democratic Vistas*.

NATURE

One can only speak of Walt Whitman's "philosophy" in a loose and colloquial sense, for, like Emerson, he was not a systematic thinker, and his conceptions of the world he lived in and man's place in it came from various sources, some of them contradictory. But by the time he had written what was to be the first edition of *Leaves of Grass* he had found a blend of concepts and abstractions which satisfied his own needs both as a person and a poet. Since they were eclectic, they carried over some connotations from their sources, with consequent ambiguity. Moreover, Whitman used these concepts and terms both as expressions of faith in the things he held sacred and as metaphors for his cosmic visions, but they meshed sufficiently to form the semblance of an intelligible *Weltanschauung*. If he was not a philosopher, he was at least concerned with answers to the most profound questions regarding the destiny of man:

> To be in any form, what is that?
>
> .   .   .   .   .   .
>
> What is a man anyhow? what am I? what are you?[41]

And in his 1855 Preface he declared: "The poets of the kosmos [he may have meant cosmic poets] advance through all interpositions and coverings and turmoils and stratagems to first principles."[42] What these "first principles" were the poet revealed not in a single preface, an ontological poem like Lucretius's *De rerum natura*, or a prose treatise, but piecemeal through the progressive versions of *Leaves of Grass*.

First of all, Whitman was heir to the Cartesian dualism which separated *mind* and *body*, a dualism which no theory has ever satisfactorily explained. Whitman himself often used the word *soul*, in a variety of contexts (some of which will be examined later), always with the conviction that it was "immortal." But exactly what Whitman meant by immortality of the soul is not easy to determine—possibly not survival of personal identity as most Christians believed. When he used the word *heaven* (usually plural) he almost invariably designated the region of the stars and planets. He never referred to a Day of Judgment, or to the Christian *Atonement*, for he did not believe in "original sin," or that men needed to atone for anything except acts of greed and selfishness. We have seen above in his personal social creed striking resemblances to the "Beatitudes" of Jesus. Yet he did not look to a future life for rewards or punishments in any orthodox Christian sense—though in an evolutionary sense he did, as we shall see below. The idea of *resurrection* also occurs frequently in Whitman's poems, but on the analogy of the life cycles of plants and animals: that is, the sequence of seed, germination, growth, organic death, and rebirth from another seed. This favorite theme is prominent in all Whitman's writings and is one of the best clues to his philosophy of man and nature.

What most shocked Whitman's contemporaries was his emphasis on the physicality of life, in which sex was as prominent and necessary as birth and death. Throughout most of its history the Christian Church had tolerated sexual intercourse as a necessity for procreation, but regarded it as shameful, degrading, and sinful if indulged in for pleasure. The Catholic Church had always held chastity to be one of the highest virtues, and in nineteenth-century America several Protestant sects, most conspicuously the Shakers, had founded celibate communities. In practically all Christian denomintions sex was associated with the forbidden fruit in the Garden of Eden.

When Christianity assimilated Neo-Platonism, it exalted mind over body, and gave Nature an inferior position. According to the Platonic myth the soul domiciled in a human body is a homesick exile, longing always to return to its spiritual home, which it might be able to do if not too much defiled by its association with the body and the world of material things. To return, of course, the body must die, but some Neo-Platonists such as Plotinus believed that in a state of mystical ecstasy the soul could catch glimpses of the world of pure spirit. These fleeting experiences were the highest and most desirable possible for the human mind.

Doctrines of the supremacy of the soul over the body had come down to Whitman by too many channels of religious instruction and literary tradition not to have strong impacts on his thinking, but they were rivaled by other, more materialistic, concepts. The most influential of these was eighteenth-century rationalism and early nineteenth-century science. In Tom Paine's *Age of Reason*, which Whitman read in his youth,[43] he was taught that God's true revelation was in Nature, not in the Bible or other religious documents. From science he learned that the world was not six thousand years old, as both the Jewish and Christian churches had taught for centuries, but millions of years old, as the geologists had proven from the strata of rocks and paleontologists from fossils of plants and animals embedded in the ancient rocks. Moreover, the fossils seemed to reveal strong resemblances and gradations of form and structure between the widely distributed specimens of plants and animals of the different geological ages. These resemblances and gradations suggested kinships and systematic variations which led to the idea of "evolution" long before Darwin published his *Origin of Species* in 1859.

In addition to the *Age of Reason*, the discoveries of geologists about the age of the earth, and of prehistoric life by paleontologists, Whitman found in Count Volney's *Ruins* (one of the books he said he had been "raised" on[44]) a complete philosophy of "Natural Religion" and a rationalistic account of the various religions of the world. The title of this book means the "ruins" of great nations,[45] which had fallen because of the greed of their rulers and the ignorance of their peoples. Volney was not a disciple of Rousseau, who believed in the innate goodness of human nature and blamed man's corrupt condition on society. Like Thomas Hobbes, Volney thought that man in a "savage state" was "A brutal, ignorant animal, a wicked and ferocious beast, like bears and Ourang-outangs.[sic] "[46] The strong ruled the weak, and the weak were too ignorant to find means of protecting themselves. Even after the beginning of an organized society, the strong deified themselves and demanded worship and obedience from the ignorant masses. Religion began with men's worship of the stars, and especially of the sun, whose life-giving effects they could see and feel, but tyrannical rulers exploited the natural religious sentiment as a means of gaining power over their subjects.

Aside from the perverse history of religions, Volney pointed out that they all claimed divine origin and presented their doctrines as the only truth. Obviously, with their different gods and theologies, they could not all be right; how then could an honest man choose the *true* religion? Volney said this was easy, that the God who created the universe had revealed his divine truths through his creation. Therefore, to understand God's plan for man, study Nature. The laws of nature were discernible to man's senses, and did not depend upon hearsay traditions or texts which had several times been translated and probably garbled. The laws of nature could be observed and tested. The only authority a man needed was the evidence of his own senses and experiences:

To establish therefore an uniformity of opinion, it is necessary first to establish the certainty, completely verified, that the portraits which the mind forms are perfectly like the originals: that it reflects the objects correctly as they exist. . . . we must trace a line of distinction between those that are capable of verification, and those that are not, and separate by an inviolable barrier, the world of fantastical beings, from the world of realities . . .[47]

Of course Volney's sensational epistemology had its own naive assumptions, as John Locke's critics of his similar theory of knowledge pointed out, but it appealed to men's "common sense." Volney granted that men could be deceived by their senses, but only when they were swayed by ignorance (superstitition) or passion, both of which could be avoided by rational study of the physical world.[48] By "law of nature" Volney meant:

. . . the constant and regular order of facts, by which God governs the universe; an order which his wisdom presents to the senses and to the reason of men, as an equal and common rule for their actions, to guide them, without distinction of country or of sect, towards perfection and happiness.[49]

Like Bishop Paley and the other "Natural Religion" theologians, Volney argued that no intelligent person could examine "the astonishing spectacle of the universe" without believing in "a supreme agent, an universal and identic mover, designated by the appellation of God. . . ." Men whose ideas of God were formed on the "law of nature" would entertain "stronger and nobler ideas of the Divinity than most other men," for they would "not sully him with the foul ingredients of all the weaknesses and passion entailed on humanity."[50] (One example Volney probably had in mind was the jealous and vindictive God of Calvinism.) In deriving a whole code of ethics and morality from the impartial, undeviating, and inexorable "Law of Nature," as Volney did in twelve chapters under this heading, he had to make more assumptions than he realized; and the virtues derived from them resembled those of the Judeo-Christian religion—except for holding pleasure, self-love, and egotism to be positively good so long as they did no harm to anyone.

It was not from Volney, however, that Whitman got his idea of "evolution." Volney believed that societies, or nations, had progressed from barbarism to civilization in various places at various times, but they had also just as frequently regressed. A decadent nation became the easy prey of a stronger nation or of revolt by its oppressed masses, resulting either in social chaos or rejuvenation. Although these cycles could be said to resemble the growth and decay of plants and animals, and thus to obey some law of nature, Volney did not make this connection, perhaps because he regarded the death of a nation as unnatural, man-made, and thus avoidable.

Walt Whitman actually got his ideas of evolution not directly from biologists, but indirectly from lectures and books on geology and astronomy—discussed below. To judge from the nature of his ideas on this subject, they came indirectly from Jean Baptiste Lamarck (1744-1829), who was the most influential evolutionist during the half-century preceding Darwin. Lamarck believed that all plants and animals had continuously evolved throughout the periods of geological time, each species making gradual alterations in structure and form to adapt to its environment.

The most controversial part of Lamarck's theory was that acquired characteristics could be transmitted to the offspring. Moreover, the hypothesis implied purpose, that somewhere in the process of change intelligence was at work making choices. Of course this confirmation of cosmic teleology appealed to religious leaders, who saw in it a means of preserving faith in a benevolent Creator. But before the end of the century most scientists had accepted Darwin's theory of fortuitous mutations, accidental changes in structure which happened to give an individual plant or animal an advantage in the struggle for survival, thereby enabling it to live long enough to produce offspring. This was the Darwinian "law" of "natural selection." Meanwhile Gregory Mendel was discovering the mathematical laws of hybridization, but his work did not become generally known until about 1900.

Although we know today that Darwin never ceased wondering whether some intelligent direction of energy might be aiding the mutations—what came to be called "Vitalism"—he never found any proof that this was actually true, though his *Movement and Habits of Climbing Plants* (1876) has been thought to leave room for the operation of psychic energy.[51] At any rate, by the end of the century the vitalists had lost credibility and Darwinian mechanical chance had won the field. However, in recent years something like Vitalism has been creeping back into speculations on the origin and development of living organisms.[52] A few scientists now suspect that even plants have some sort of mind or psychic energy, and that they, as well as animals, may have survived not because they were lucky but clever. Or as Emerson says, "Nature's dice are always loaded."[53]

Walt Whitman himself would have doubtless approved this speculation on the minds of plants, or Pierre Teilhard de Chardin's theory that every cell and molecule has some kind of innate intelligence, which multiplies and gains in strength with each increase in the combining of cells into more complex organisms, and the process is always toward greater complexity—the true evolutionary trend of the cosmos.[54] The great mystery is how the life of each cell in an organized complex obeys the command of some mysterious center of control. Teilhard speculated that mind is that controlling force, and that cosmic evolution is the order of the universe. Eventually the whole "biosphere" will become a "Noosphere" (realm of mind).[55]

Walt Whitman actually seems to have anticipated Teilhard in some ways—and here no specific source for Whitman is known. In his preparatory notes written between 1847 and the printing of his first edition of *Leaves of Grass* he declared:

The soul or spirit transmits itself into all matter—into rocks, and can live the life of a rock—into the sea, and can feel itself the sea—into the oak, or other tree—into an animal, and feel itself a horse, a fish, or bird—into the earth—into the motions of the suns and stars—[56]

Whitman cautions himself: "Never speak of the soul as any thing but intrinsically great.—The adjective affixed to it must always testify greatness and immortality and purity.—" What he means by "intrinsic" greatness is elaborated in a theory strongly tinged with Neo-Platonism:

The effusion or corporation of the soul is always under the beautiful laws of physiology—I guess the soul itself can never be anything but great and pure and immortal; but it makes itself visible only through matter—a perfect head, and bowels and bones to match is the easy gate through which it comes from its embowered garden, and pleasantly appears to the sight of the world.—[57]

This is a plain statement of the Platonic idea of the "pre-existence of the soul" (expressed by Wordsworth in his "Ode: Intimations of Immortality"), but Whitman's physiological application has the stamp of his own mind and character: "A twisted skull, and blood watery or rotten by ancestry or gluttony, or rum or bad disorders [in Whitman's editorials bad disorders meant venereal disease],—they are the darkness toward which the plant will not grow, although its seed lie waiting for ages.—"[58] Similar to this thought, he says, "Wickedness is most likely the absence of freedom and health in the soul." But if the soul is "pure" (inviolable?) and "immortal," how can matter have any influence on it? We might conclude that a degraded human body has no soul—or at least is not able to expand in it: "the darkness toward which the plant will not grow. . . ." But then in another note Whitman adds: "The universal and fluid soul impounds within itself not only all good characters, and hero[e]s, but the distorted characters, murderers, thieves[.]"[59]

Perhaps these contradictory statements cannot be logically reconciled, and maybe they were only *trial thoughts* anyway. But they reveal attitudes toward mind and matter, and the miraculous nature of both, which carried over into Whitman's poetry and sustained his childlike wonder at existence, "being in any form . . .":

My life is a miracle and my body which lives is a miracle; but of what I can nibble at the edges of the limitless and delicious wonder I know that I cannot separate them, and call one superior and the other inferior, any more than I can say my sight is greater than my eyes.—[60]

In short, these are mysteries which the poet himself does not understand, but he *feels* their existence, and simply accepts them as facts in his experience—an attitude resembling the Buddhist's non-intellectual acceptance of the existence of the unseen God. This faith was also accompanied by an over-belief in what Whitman called "dilation," which he conceived to be a cosmic evolutionary process:

I think the soul will never stop, or attain to any growth beyond which it shall not go.—When I walked at night by the sea shore and looked up at the countless stars, I asked of my soul whether it would be filled and satisfied when it should become god enfolding all these, and open to the life and delight and knowledge of everything in them or of them; and the answer was plain to me at the breaking water on the sands at my feet; and the answer was, No, when I reach there, I shall want to go further still.—[61]

Here are more enormous ambiguities. How will the "soul . . . become god enfolding" the innumerable stars of stellar space? Certainly this is no vision of a Christian heaven or of eternal happiness, for it is the nature of Whitman's "soul" never to be satisfied, or to cease growing. This concept has led many critics and scholars to find parallels to Vedanta and other religious-philosophical concepts of India. While still others are content simply to label Whitman a "mystic." Certainly the far-traveling soul is *migrating* if not transmigrating. But some definite clues both to the source of these huge soul-concepts and to Whitman's future literary use of them are given in some of the poet's trial lines for "Song of Myself":

I am the poet of reality
I say the earth is not an echo
Nor man an apparition;
But that all things seen are real,

The witness and albic dawn of things equally real.

I have split the earth and the hard coal and rocks and the solid bed of
    the sea
And went down to reconnoitre there a long time,
And bring back a report,
And I understand that those are positive and dense every one
And that what they seem to the child they are.

    .   .   .   .   .   .

Afar in the sky was a nest,
And my soul flew thither and squat, and looked out
And saw the journeywork of suns and systems of suns,
And that a leaf of grass is not less than they
And that the pismire is equally perfect, and all grains of sand, and
    every egg of the wren,
And the tree-toad is a chef d'oeuvre for the highest,
And the running blackberry would adorn the parlors of Heaven
And the cow crunching with depressed neck surpasses every
    statue, . . .[62]

SCIENCE

In writing his experimental lines for his 1855 poems Whitman's creative imagination was drawing upon two paradoxical concepts, one animistic in the most primitive sense (everything has a soul), and the other materialistic and naively "common sense": "all things seen are real . . . what they seem to the child they are."[63] And yet they are more than any child could understand, for things are not only "equal," "perfect," and "beautiful," but the whole universe is constructed of the same stuff, which is both material and immaterial—mind and matter—joined in a timeless journey, or as Whitman expressed the thought (or faith) in an old-age poem: "The world, the race, the soul—in space and time the universes,/ . . . all surely going somewhere."[64]

Some light may be thrown on the nature of this journey and its destination by examining how Whitman got his interstellar observations of "the journeywork of suns and systems of suns. . . ." Until Joseph Beaver published his *Walt Whitman—Poet of Science* (1951) most biographers and critics of Whitman had taken too seriously his occasional impatience with the minutiae of exact science and his demanding a "free margin" for his imagination. Most misleading of all was his poem "When I Heard the Learned Astronomer," which describes how the "charts and diagrams" and mathematical demonstrations wearied and sickened him until he left the lecture room and found relief in simply looking up "in perfect silence at the stars." More often, however, he was not bored by the "learned astronomer," who, in fact, as Beaver has shown, gave him a general education in the nineteenth-century scientific view of the universe.

Several astronomers lectured in New York in the 1840s, but the one who particularly attracted Whitman's attention was Ormsby MacKnight Mitchell,[65] who lectured in the Broadway Tabernacle in December, 1848, and published *A Course of Six Lectures on Astronomy* the following year. Whether Whitman attended all six lectures or not, he certainly read the book, drawing upon it many times for imagery and allusions in his poems. He also got his idea of a "nest" in the sky as an observation post from Mitchell's lectures, for the astronomer liked to invite his audience to take imaginary trips with him through interstellar space. In numerous poems Whitman looks down upon the "rolling," "bowling," or "sidelong" revolving earth ("sidelong" referring to the inclined axis). For example, in "Salut au Monde!" he sees "a great round wonder rolling through space," and in "Pioneers! O Pioneers!":

> Lo, the darting bowling orb!
> Lo, the brother orbs around, all the clustering suns and plants, . . .

Beaver found a more specific test of Mitchell's influence in a passage from "On the Beach at Night":

On the beach at night,
Stands a child with her father,
Watching the east, the autumn sky.

Up through the darkness,
While ravening clouds, the burial clouds, in black masses spreading,
Lower sullen and fast athwart and down the sky,
Amid a transparent clear belt of ether yet left in the east,
Ascends large and calm the lord-star Jupiter,
And nigh at hand, only a very little above,
Swim the delicate sisters the Pleiades.

Beaver comments:

Jupiter, in the course of its apparent movement around the zodiac, passes the Pleiades only once every twelve years. This happened in late April and early May, 1870, but Jupiter's slowly changing position made it [the Pleiades] still "only a little above" Jupiter in the early autumn months of the same year. Actually, in September and October, 1870, Jupiter was about 30° from the Pleiades, a fairly large angle. But in 1867, 1868, and 1869, Jupiter would have been *above* the Pleiades, not below them, as that cluster rose in the eastern sky. . . . Whitman, then, first wrote "On the Beach at Night" in the fall of 1870 . . . [Whitman's editors and biographers agree on this date.] Whitman's "only a very little above" seems, in view of the 30° arc which actually separated Jupiter and the Pleiades, to place the bodies closer together than they really were, but it must be remembered that a slight shift in the direction of his vision would have comprehended both. Jupiter was very close to the Pleiades in April and May, 1870, but the Pleiades (and, consequently, Jupiter—in that year) are not visible in the late spring and summer months.[66]

In dozens of passages in his poetry and prose Whitman referred to the position of a planet or constellation. Beaver verified these references with the aid of the *Nautical Almanack* without finding a single error, and he concluded that "Whitman's knowledge of astronomy, though perhaps not technical, was more detailed than has been suspected, and his observations far more accurate than has been admitted or known," and that even his "apparently lush descriptions of celestial objects—of planets in particular—frequently have a basis in natural fact. . . ."[67]

Another example of Whitman's drawing upon Mitchell's lectures is his reference to Saturn in "Song of Myself," sec. 33:

Speeding through space, speeding through heaven and the stars,
Speeding amid the seven satellites and the broad ring, and the
    diameter of eighty thousand miles, . . .

Though Whitman might have learned of the seven satellites from
other books on astronomy, Mitchell's 79,000 miles diameter was
closest to the poet's round 80,000.[68] (Today the diameter of Saturn
is estimated at 75,100 miles, and the number of satellites at twelve
or, possibly, thirteen.)

Whitman also shared Mitchell's enthusiasm for comets. In one
lecture Mitchell said:

There are other mysterious bodies, which seem not to obey the laws
that govern these movements. While the planets are circular in their
orbits and the satellites nearly the same, we find dim, mysterious
bodies, wandering through the uttermost regions of Space,—we see
them coming closer and closer, and as they approach our system,
they fling out their mighty banners, wing their lightning flight
around the Sun and speed away to the remotest limits of vacuity.[69]

The passage from "Song of Myself" quoted above continues:

Speeding with tail'd meteors, throwing fire-balls like the rest,
Carrying the crescent child that carries its own full mother in its
    belly, [answer to the riddle: moon in first quarter]
Storming, enjoying, planning, loving, cautioning,
Backing and filling, appearing and disappearing,
I tread day and night such roads.

Still exploiting the comet metaphor, Whitman continues:

I visit the orchards of spheres and look at the product,
And look at quintillions ripen'd and look at quintillions green.

As interesting as the comet metaphor-vehicle is the "orchard"
metaphor, which in the 1855 version was "orchards of God," thus
anthropomorphizing the astronomical theory of planetary evolution:
some spheres are still in a "green" or early gaseous state of development, while others are more condensed or "ripened." In sec. 44 of
"Song of Myself" Whitman says "the nebula cohered to [i.e., into, or

became] an orb." He was evidently familiar with the "nebular hypothesis."

But it was the comet that most fascinated Whitman, for it seemed to defy all the laws of astronomy, with an orbit of its own so vast that it periodically disappeared into outer space and then returned to swing around our sun and disappear again. The poet liked to think of himself as a comet:

I but advance a moment only to wheel and hurry back in the
    darkness. ("Poets to Come")

Mitchell said that as comets "approach our system, they fling out their mighty banners,"[70] meaning of course the streamers of gases which expand in the heat of the sun. It was also believed that in this process the comet partly consumed itself, an idea which Whitman incorporated in his comet-departure near the end of "Song of Myself":

I depart as air, I shake my white locks at the runaway sun,
I effuse my flesh in eddies, and drift it in lacy jags.

The moon also appealed to Whitman's imagination, but in a less exciting manner. He accepted the astronomer's opinion that it was a dead body, without atmosphere, whose "shine" was only light reflected from the sun. Unlike the romantic poets, he did not usually call the moonlight "yellow," or use it to symbolize beauty and love. In "Song of Myself" (sec. 21) he refers to "the vitreous pour [strained through glass] of the full moon just tinged with blue!," which is an accurate description. In sec. 49 "the ghastly glimmer is noonday sunbeams reflected." The dead satellite is a fit symbol for death and decay, and that is the way Whitman used it in sec. 49, and in "Out of the Cradle. . . " where the light is "brown yellow." In the *Drum-Taps* poem "Look Down Fair Moon" he does call the moon "fair" and "sacred," but he implores it to pour down softly on the purple faces of the soldiers' corpses. Thus his connotations are consistently tinged with factual reality.

For all his celebration of the eternal precision and perfect balance of the stars and planets circling in the fields of gravitation, "wheels within wheels," he knows that "the immortal stars" are

immortal only as his body is, and that they too obey nature's laws of
birth and decay:

(The stars, the terrible perturbations of the suns,
Swelling, collapsing, ending, serving their longer, shorter use, . . .)
    —"Eidólons"

It is surprising to find Whitman aware of a *Nova*, or exploding
star, but still more curious that he should write in "Song of Myself"
(sec. 16):

The bright suns I see and the dark suns I cannot see, are in their
    place,
The palpable is in its place and the impalpable is in its place.

Possibly he meant suns too far away to be seen even with the tele-
scope, but astronomers today believe there are collapsed stars so
dense that they cannot reflect light and are therefore "black holes"
in space. Perhaps here by accident Whitman was prophetic, but at
least the concept shows how attentive he had been to the lectures
(and books) on astronomy, and the awe with which he vicariously
took his position in the observatory in "Song of Myself," sec. 45:

I open my scuttle at night and see the far-sprinkled systems,
And all I see multiplied as high as I can cipher edge but the rim of
    the farther systems.

To summarize the influence of astronomy on Whitman's thinking, he learned, above all else, that physical laws are the basis of all
meaningful theories of man's place and function in nature. In
Whitman's own words in "Song of the Rolling Earth":

There can be no theory of any account unless it corroborate the
    theory of the earth. (sec. 3)

In these laws he saw "the ensemble of the world, and the compact
truth of the world"—"Laws for Creation." In "Solid, Ironical,
Rolling, Orb" he called these *compact truths* the test of his "ideal
dreams."

In specific laws Whitman found also analogies for his subjective life. Thus gravitation in the *Children of Adam* poem "I Am He That Aches with Love": "Does the earth gravitate? does not all matter, aching, attract all matter?/ So the body of me to all I meet or know." Gravitation and magnetism, which seemed somehow akin to gravitation (the relation is still not entirely known to science) always fascinated Whitman, and he saw in both some Divine energy operating "Through Space and Time . . . and the flowing eternal identity" ("As They Draw to a Close").

Of course contemporary pseudo-scientific theories on "animal magnetism" (mesmerism, hypnotism, etc.) mingled in Whitman's mind with the solider aspects of physics, but he was not the only intelligent person of the time to be confused. The confusion was no more serious than his finding analogies between his amorous urges and the attraction of matter for other matter. Thus in "Song of Myself" (sec. 27) the electric "charge" and "conductors":

Mine is no callous shell,
I have instant conductors all over me whether I pass or stop,
They seize every object and lead it harmlessly through me.
I merely stir, press, feel with my fingers, and am happy,
To touch my person to some one else's is about as much as I can stand.

Whitman took pride in his own strong "animal magnetism,"[71] as he did also for a few years in his phrenological chart,[72] but often natural phenomena merely provided him with metaphors for poetizing human experiences, such as the inseminating "touch" in sexual intercourse in "Song of Myself" (sec. 29):

Blind loving wrestling touch . . .
Parting track'd by arriving, perpetual payment of perpetual loan,
Rich showering rain, and recompense richer afterward.

Sprouts take and accumulate, stand by the curb prolific and vital,
Landscapes projected masculine, full-sized and golden.

But it was not entirely from astronomy and physics (then called "natural philosophy") that Whitman derived his deepest insights into the mysteries of nature. In fact, his main concept of evolution came from earth science, as presented by Samuel G. Goodrich in *A Glance at the Physical Sciences* (1844), and a few years later (after the first edition of *Leaves of Grass*) by Richard Owen in *Key to the Geology of the Globe* (1857). From such books as these he learned about "vestiges of creation" (the phrase was popularized by Robert Chambers[73] in *The Vestiges of the Natural History of Creation*, 1844), which had "stucco'd [him] with quadrupeds and birds all over" ("Song of Myself," sec. 31), and made him wonder of the animals "where they got those tokens,/ Did I pass that way huge times ago and negligently drop them?" Though this may seem like evolution in reverse, the poet leaves no doubt in sec. 44 that he is aware of the ages of preparation nature has made for his arrival (or of any human being) on earth:

Immense have been the preparations for me,
Faithful and friendly the arms that have help'd me.

Cycles ferried my cradle, rowing and rowing like cheerful boatmen,
For room to me stars kept aside in their own rings,
They sent influences to look after what was to hold me.

Before I was born out of my mother generations guided me,
My embryo has never been torpid, nothing could overlay it.

For it the nebula cohered to an orb,
The long slow strata piled to rest it on,
Vast vegetables gave it sustenance,
Monstrous sauroids transported it in their mouths and deposited it
    with care.

All forces have been steadily employ'd to complete and delight me,
Now on this spot I stand with my robust soul.

SOUL

At all times Walt Whitman was as much concerned with the health of his soul as the health of his body, and the latter was almost an obsession with him. But what did he mean by "soul" (capitalized or lower case)? In the English language the word has many meanings, and it is not surprising that Whitman used it in various senses and connotations: as a synonym of mind, consciousness, imagination, psychic energy, the self, *élan vital* or "spark of life," or even *God*. Sometimes in "Song of Myself" the "I" is any of these synonyms for *soul*, and the lyrical pronoun might be said (often if not always) to be the poet's faculty of articulation. But these considerations do not help the reader in defining the term. Perhaps the best method by which to do that is to approach the problem inductively.

Unlike Emerson and most poets of the nineteenth century, Whitman always insisted on the equality of the body and soul. In "Starting from Paumanok" (sec. 13) he asks and replies:

Was somebody asking to see the soul?
See, your own shape and countenance, persons, substances, beasts,
    the trees, the running rivers, the rocks and sands.

All hold spiritual joys and afterwards loosen them;
How can the real body ever die and be buried?

Of your real body and any man's or woman's real body,
Item for item it will elude the hands of the corpse-cleaners and pass
    to fitting spheres,
Carrying what has accrued to it from the moment of birth to the
    moment of death.

.   .   .   .   .

Behold, the body includes and is the meaning, the main concern, and
    includes and is the soul;
Whoever you are, how superb and how divine is your body, or any
    part of it!

Though the poet does say in one verse that "the body . . . is the soul," he has previously qualified this statement by "real body." What survives, then, is something less—or more—than the physiological body, which could "elude . . . the corpse-cleaners" only in a conservation-of-energy sense, its chemicals passing into other living organisms. At the end of "Song of Myself" the "I" does say "look for me under your boot-soles," but the "I . . . somewhere waiting for you" is a *self*, or *soul*, or spiritual-identity of some sort.

Emerson has often been thought to have been the main source of Whitman's "transcendental" ideas, but there are marked differences between his doctrines of matter and spirit (or soul) and Whitman's. The "certain poet" in *Nature* (1836) who speaks Emersonian ideas says: "The foundations of man are not in matter, but in spirit. But the element of spirit is eternity [in Plato's sense]. . . . In the cycle of the universal man [Platonic archetype], from whom the known individuals proceed, centuries are points, and all history is but the epoch of one degradation." Thus, "A man is a god in ruins." And "Man is a dwarf of himself."[74]

In "The Poet" Emerson says, "The soul makes the body," and "The universe is the externisation of the soul." Possibly this doctrine could be dialectically reconciled with Whitman's concept of the immortality of the "real body," but the emphasis of the two poets is totally different. Emerson continues: "Our science is sensual and therefore superficial. The earth, and the heavenly bodies, physics, and chemistry, we sensually treat, as if they were self-existent; but these are the retinue of that Being we have."[75]

In "Song of Myself" (sec. 3) Whitman chants:

Clear and sweet is my soul, and clear and sweet is all that is not my
    soul.

Lacks one lacks both, and the unseen is proved by the seen,
Till that becomes unseen and receives proof in its turn.

This statement may be taken as a clue to the relationship of the body and soul, the "seen" and the "unseen." In the lines quoted above from "Starting from Paumanok" Whitman said if you would see the soul, look at the body, and he frequently asserts (as in sec. 48 of "Song of Myself") that "the soul is not more than the body" and "the body is not more than the soul." But he usually mentions them as if they were two, somehow joined in one transitory identity. In fact, "identity" of the self is apparently made possible by this union. That the "soul" is immortal is a belief found in most religions, but few, if any, believe with Whitman "in the flesh and the appetites"—at least not to the extent of declaring ("Song of Myself," sec. 24):

Divine am I inside and out, and I make holy whatever I touch or am
    touch'd from;
The scent of these arm-pits is aroma finer than prayer,
This head is more than churches or bibles or creeds.

Yet he admits (sec. 49) that the body becomes "good manure," though this does not offend his nostrils because this is only a necessary process in the "perpetual transfers and promotions" of the undying self, the "I" of "Song of Myself." This *self* corresponds to the more conventional concepts of the *soul*.

But there is another Neo-Platonic aspect of Whitman's soul-doctrine. In the 1855 poem "To Think of Time" Whitman says (sec. 7):

It is not to diffuse you that you were born of your mother and
     father—it is to identify you,
It is not that you should be undecided, but that you should be
     decided;
Something long preparing and formless is arrived and formed in you,
You are thenceforth secure, whatever comes or goes.

Here identity seems to be more than simply knowing who or what one is—one's place in society and (possibly) history. Several lines later:

The guest that was coming. . . . he waited long for reasons. . . . he is
     now housed,
He is one of those who are beautiful and happy. . . . he is one of
     those that to look upon and be with is enough.

In this context "guest" seems to be the "soul," and *house* the body. But the antecedent of the first "he" is "guest," while the "he" of the second verse seems to be a person: a person who is a proper house for the long-arriving soul. This interpretation is strengthened by the poet's further insistence that "The law of promotion and transformation cannot be eluded. . . ."

Further light is thrown on this Neo-Platonic doctrine in other poems. In "The Sleepers" (sec. 7) the "myth of heaven" indicates the rôle of the soul:

The soul is always beautiful. . . . it appears more or it appears less. . . .
     it comes or lags behind,
It comes from its embowered garden and looks pleasantly on itself
     and encloses the world;

     .   .   .   .   .

The soul is always beautiful,
The universe is duly in order. . . . every thing is in its place,
What is arrived is in its place, and what waits is in its place; . . .

This does not mean that some bodies do not have a soul—that the soul skips around and chooses its abode. It "advances" regardless of the circumstances of the body it is to inhabit. In another 1855 poem, "Faces" (sec. 4):

The Lord advances and yet advances:
Always the shadow in front. . . . always the reached hand bringing up
    the laggards.

"Faces" dramatizes the poet's doctrine of souls. Some faces are hideous from disease, congenital deformities, or self-abuse, but the beauty of the enclosed soul is only temporarily clouded:

In each house is the ovum. . . . it comes forth after a thousand years.

Spots or cracks at the windows do not disturb me,
Tall and sufficient stand behind and make signs to me;
I read the promise and patiently wait.

All persons, "red white or black . . . are deific," but they may not attain the full potentiality of their divine heritage. This is Whitman's message: lct (or aid) your soul attain its "promise." In fact, whether one regards this teaching as trite or profound, it is Whitman's spiritual teaching in *Leaves of G..ass*, which he always maintained was a religious book, a "New Theology" (1872 Preface), a "more splendid Theology" of the "Real . . . behind the Real" (1876 Preface), "poetry suitable to the human soul" (1888 Preface to *November B.·ghs*). He had announced this purpose in his 1855 Preface when he said of his ideal poet that readers had a right to expect him "to indicate more than the beauty and dignity which always attach to dumb real objects . . . they expect him to indicate the path between reality and their souls."[76] Whatever the soul was, Whitman's most serious ambition was to show the "path" to it.

MYSTICISM

Many critics have called Whitman a mystic,[77] and extensive comparisons have been made between his utterances and those of the most renowned mystics. Some have seen in the mating of the poet's body and soul in section 5 of "Song of Myself" the origin of his poetic genius, his visionary power:

I mind how we lay in June, such a transparent summer morning;
You settled your head athwart my hips and gently turned over upon
    me,
And parted the shirt from my bosom-bone, and plunged your tongue
    to my barestript heart,
And reached till you felt my beard, and reached till you held my
    feet.

Swiftly arose and spread around me the peace and joy and knowl-
    edge that pass all the art and argument of the earth;
And I know that the hand of God is the elderhand of my own,
And I know that the spirit of God is the eldest brother of my own,
And that all the men ever born are also my brothers. . . . and the
    women my sisters and lovers,
And that a kelson of the creation is love;
And limitless are leaves stiff or drooping in the fields,
And brown ants in the little wells beneath them,
And mossy scabs of the wormfence, and heaped stones, and elder
    and mullen and pokeweed. [1855 text]

It was this experience, some maintain, which transformed Walt
Whitman from a mediocre literary hack into the most original poet
of his generation. The passage does, indeed, vividly describe the kind
of psychological experience which William James has labeled "mystical states of consciousness,"[78] during which the subject believes himself to be in direct communication with the supernatural, or the
recipient of some miraculous energy from a nonmaterial source.
James calls this kind of mysticism "sporadic,"[79] and, indeed, Whitman's writings contain only this one example. It fits James's definition almost perfectly: it takes place while the poet's will (or the "I"
of the poem) is passive (loafing, lying on the June grass); it is tran-
sient ("Mystical states cannot be sustained for long"[80]); it can be
described only in symbolical language (James's "ineffability"); and it
has "noetic quality" ("states of insight into depths of truth un-
plumbed by the discursive intellect"). Such states of consciousness
are also called "illuminations" and "epiphanies."

Because the epiphany described in "Song of Myself" was so
rare—or even unique—with Whitman, James assumed that he was not
a sporadic mystic: "Whitman in another place expresses in a quieter
way what was probably with him a chronic mystical perception"[81]:

There is, apart from mere intellect, in the make-up of every superior human identity, (in its moral completeness, considered as *ensemble*, not for that moral alone, but for the whole being, including physique,) a wondrous something that realizes without argument, frequently without what is called education, (though I think it the goal and apex of all education deserving the name)—an intuition of the absolute balance, in time and space, of the whole of this multifarious, mad chaos of fraud, frivolity, hoggishness—this revel of fools, and incredible make-believe and general unsettledness, we call *the world*; a soul-sight of that divine clue and unseen thread which holds the whole congeries of things, all history and time, and all events, however trivial, however momentous, like a leash'd dog in the hand of the hunter. Such soul-sight and root-centre for the mind—mere optimism explains only the surface or fringe of it. . . .[82]

Whitman's friend, Dr. R. M. Bucke, called this "soul-sight" by another name, "cosmic consciousness": "The prime characteristic of cosmic consciousness is as its name implies a consciousness of the cosmos, that is, of the life and order of the universe."[83] Dr. Bucke himself had experienced such an "intellectual enlightenment," and he thought that Walt Whitman lived in an almost constant state of this kind of consciousness. Bucke described his own experience as a "sense of exultation, of immense joyousness accompanied or immediately followed by an intellectual illumination, impossible to describe." This sounds more like James's "sporadic" mysticism than Whitman's more "chronic" type.

But whether Whitman experienced "cosmic consciousness," either sporadically or chronically, it was mainly before the Civil War that strong feelings of "elevation, elation, and joyousness" influenced his poetry. Later in old age he fondly recalled those precious times:

In that condition of health, (old style) the whole body is elevated to a state by others unknown—inwardly and outwardly illuminated, purified, made solid, strong, yet buoyant. A singualr charm, more than beauty, flickers out of, and over, the face—a curious transparency beams in the eyes, both in the iris and the white—the temper partakes also. Nothing that happens—no event, recontre, weather, etc.—but it is confronted—nothing but is subdued into sustenance—such is the marvelous transformation from the old timorousness and the old process of causes and effects. Sorrows and disappointments cease—there is no more borrowing trouble in advance. A man realizes the venerable myth—he is a god walking the earth, he sees new eligibilities, powers and beauties everywhere; he himself has a new eyesight and hearing. The play of the body in motion takes a previously unknown grace. Merely *to move* is then a happiness, a pleasure—to breathe, to see, i̇ also. All the beforehand gratifications, drink, spirits, coffee, grease, stimulants, mixtures, late hours, luxuries, deeds of the night, seem as vexatious dreams, and now the awakening;—many fall into their natural places, wholesome, conveying diviner joys.[84]

Roger Asslineau calls Whitman's mysticism of this period his "poetry of the body," and makes a point of the greatest significance in understanding his ecstatic poetry, that though it begins in sensual delight, it leads to spiritual insight:

[Whitman's] sensuality, instead of remaining exclusively carnal, opens out and is sublimated. The spirit, in order to be manifest, cannot do without matter and, of course, all mysticism depends on and is accompanied by emotions of the flesh. But what is original with Whitman, at least in 1855–56, is that, contrary to Wordsworth, Shelley, or Emerson, for instance, he always has the sharp consciousness of the purely sensual source of his mystical intuitions. Instead of proceeding at once to a spiritualization, like the English romantics or the American transcendentalists, he never forgets that his body is the theatre and the point of origin for his mystical states. . . .[85]

Another characteristic of Whitman's mysticism is that he (or the *persona* of his poems) never loses his consciousness of his own unique individuality in contemplation of the Godhead or the realm of spirit. In fact, he is not curious about God, and understands Him "not in the least," yet he hears and beholds God "in every object." In "Song of Myself" (sec. 48) he asks:

Why should I wish to see God better than this day?
I see something of God each hour of the twenty-four, and each
     moment then,
In the faces of men and women I see God, and in my own face in the
     glass?
I find letters from God dropped in the street, and every one is signed
     by God's name,
And I leave them where they are, for I know that others will
     punctually come forever and ever.

In the 1946 edition of this *Walt Whitman Handbook* Whitman's
finding God in His creation was called *pantheism*, and to a certain
extent the term seems to apply (and had frequently been applied by
earlier Whitman scholars), but there is a subtle distinction between
God *in* nature, and God's revealing His power and Beauty *through*
matter. As Sister Flavia Maria has observed in comparing Whitman's
ideas with those of Pierre Teilhard de Chardin, "Song of Myself"
seems almost to presage Teilhard's cosmic theology.[86] She quotes
this significant passage from *The Divine Milieu*:

God penetrates the world as a ray of light does a crystal; and,
with the help of the great layers of creation, he is universally per-
ceptible and active—very near and very distant at one and the same
time.

God truly waits for us in things, unless indeed he advances to
meet us. The manifestation of his sublime presence in no way dis-
turbs the harmony of our human attitude, but, on the contrary, brings
it its true form and perfection. Our lives . . . and the whole of our
world are full of God.[87]

Like Whitman, Teilhard refuses to separate God from the material universe. We have seen above in the discussion of science and
Whitman how strongly contemporary astronomy, geology, and paleontology stirred the poet's imagination and gave him notions of
man's place in cosmic evolution. Teilhard, a reputable geologist and
anthropologist, with considerable knowledge of the other physical
and biological sciences, articulated the "New Theology" which Whitman called for, and in some ways vividly anticipated. Compare, for
example, his vision of the "apices of the stairs" up which the human
soul and body have traveled ("Song of Myself," sec. 44) with
Teilhard's prophecy of the "New Earth":

We live at the centre of the network of . smic influences as we
live at the heart of the human crowd or among the myriads of stars,
without, alas, being aware of their immensity. We should be aston-
ished at the extent and the intimacy of our relationship with the
universe.

The roots of our being plunge back and down into the un-
fathomable past. However autonomous our soul, it is indebted to an
inheritance worked upon from all sides—before ever it came into
being—by the totality of the energies of the earth.

The human soul is inseparable, in its birth and in its growth,
from the universe into which it is born. In each soul, God loves and

partly saves the whole world which that soul sums up in an incommunicable and particular way.

Beneath our efforts to put spiritual form into our own lives, the world slowly accumulates, starting with the whole of matter, that which will make of it the . . . New Earth.[88]

Whitman seems to have anticipated Teilhard's theory of "cosmic influence" in two ways. In the 1860 poem, "With Antecedents," he says, "We touch all laws and tally all antecedents,/. . . We stand amid time beginningless and endless . . ."

All swings around us—there is as much darkness as light,
The very sun swings itself and its system of planets around us,
Its sun, and its again, all swing around us.

Later (1874) in "Song of the Universal," Whitman says that for the soul "the entire star-myriads roll through the sky, /In Spiral routes by long detours. . . ," but always "the real to the ideal tends." Although Whitman would still not dally "with the mystery," his soul in "Passage to India" acknowledges God as the "pulse" and "motive of the stars, suns, systems," the "fibre and breath" creating and animating the universes. Finally in "A Thought of Columbus" (1891) a "breath of Deity" unfolds "the bulging universe" and the "farthest evolutions of the world and man."

The other way in which Whitman anticipated Teilhard—an extension of his "breath of Deity" doctrine—was that the soul itself grows or "dilates" with insatiable ambition (more resembling Milton's Satan or Goethe's Faust than a Christian "soul"). In 1855 "Song of Myself" (sec. 45) all creation is on an evolutionary journey:

There is no stoppage, and never can be stoppage;
If I and you and the worlds and all beneath or upon their surfaces,
    and all the palpable life, were this moment reduced back to a
    pallid float, it would not avail in the long run,
We should surely bring up again where we now stand,
And as surely go as much farther, and then farther and farther.

And again in sec. 46:

This day before dawn I ascended a hill and looked at the crowded
    heaven,

And I said to my spirit, When we become the enfolders of those orbs
    and the pleasure and knowledge of every thing in them, shall we
    be filled and satisfied then?
And my spirit said No, we level that lift to pass and continue
    beyond.

Does this mean that the poet expected after the death of his
body that his soul would pass to other planets? This would be a
fairly literal and simple interpretation of his words, and Kant's
theory of eternal cycles of cosmic evolution and devolution (universes endlessly winding and unwinding themselves, mentioned in
some of the astronomy lectures Whitman had heard) encouraged the
idea that souls might migrate from one cosmic system to another to
continue their evolutionary growth in the "orchards of God." Of
course by mating with Time and smiling at death Whitman could
have meant only to convey the idea of the immortality of the soul.
But the other verse—"fillest, swellest full the vastness of space"—does
seem to mean something more than merely immortality, or a soul
free of time and space.

However, before attempting further to determine the kind of
"immortality" Whitman attributed to the soul, we should notice that
he often used the idea to symbolize his literary "life" after his death.
In such passages he might use "I," "Me," or "Myself" instead of his
"soul," but all of these words were but synonyms for his deeper self,
the "real Me," or as in "So Long!" (1860) the "best of me." Here he
invisions his poems dropping "seed ethereal" into the ground of
posterity, to spread when he is "no longer visible":

I feel like one who has done work for the day to retire awhile,
I receive now again of my many translations, from my avataras as-
    cending, while others doubtless await me,
An unknown sphere more real than I dream'd, more direct, darts
    awakening rays about me, *So long!*
Remember my words, I may again return,
I love you, I depart from materials,
I am as one disembodied, triumphant, dead. [1881 version]

Phrases like "return awhile," "my many translations," "avataras
ascending" (or *descending*?), and "I may return again" carry connotations of Hindu "incarnation." But all the time the poet is thinking of the perennial life of his book, and enjoying vicariously his

expected perpetuity in the minds of his readers.

The second caution is that some of Whitman's boldest assertions of the soul's immortality are incantations resembling "sympathetic magic"—like praying for faith in times of doubt. In "Darest Thou Now O Soul" (1868), for example, the poet (or "I") asks his soul if it is ready to venture into "the unknown region," without "map" or "guide":

> I know it not O soul,
> Nor dost thou, all is a blank before us,
> All waits undream'd of in that region, that inaccessible land.

Yet without further assurances even of the existence of "that inaccessible land," the poet says that when his ties to the earth loosen,

> Then we burst forth, we float,
> In Time and Space O soul, prepared for them,
> Equipt, equipt at last . . .

The real intent of the cluster of poems called "Whispers of Heavenly Death" is perhaps most clearly indicated in "A Noiseless Patient Spider," in which the poet, with a tone of deep pathos and almost desperation, implores his soul to continue throwing out lifelines, like the spider in vacant space,

> . . . throwing, seeking the spheres to connect them,
> Till the bridge you will need be form'd, till the ductile anchor hold,
> Till the gossamer thread you fling catch somewhere, O my soul.

Thus it was not out of confidence in the immortality of his soul (in the sense of a personal identity) that Walt Whitman wrote his invocations to liberating death, but in a desperate attempt to build a "bridge" to belief in the life of the soul in other "spheres" (and note the ambiguity of spheres, ranging from planets to immaterial realms of spiritual existence). In a poem called "The Last Invocation" he begs his soul "to ope the doors" softly:

> Tenderly—be not impatient,
> (Strong is your hold O mortal flesh,
> Strong is your hold O Love.)

To construct a mythology of the "spheres" to which Whitman expects his soul to migrate is to interpret his metaphors too literally and simple-mindedly. He had *hope* of some kind of spiritual life after his mortal end, but his imagination was unequal to visualize it with the vitality of a Blake or a Swedenborg. However, in a less personal, more universal sense, he did have a prophetic vision of the cosmic destiny of the "soul" of the human race, a destiny in which the generic soul of the poet (meaning all true poets) had a special rôle to perform.

In "Passage to India" Whitman calls the poet "the true son of God," by which he means that the poet he himself has tried so hard to be will be the interpreter of the purpose of cosmic creation, as Christ was the intermediary between God and his children. (That Whitman was aware of competing with Milton's Christian epic is also indicated by his repeating *justify*: Milton's "justify the ways of God to men.")

O vast Rondure, swimming in space,
Cover'd all over with visible power and beauty,
Alternate light and day and the teeming spiritual darkness,
Unspeakable high processions of sun and moon and countless
    stars above,
Below, the manifold grass and waters, animals, mountains, trees,
With inscrutable purpose, some hidden prophetic intention,
Now first it seems my thought begins to span thee.

The thought which *spans* cosmology and life on the earth is that the "unsatisfied soul" of God's "feverish children" was responding all along to a divine compulsion. The explorers, scientists, and engineers were predestined to develop the resources of the earth to their utmost possibility, but God's cosmic plan also calls for a humanizing and spiritualizing of these achievements. After the seas are all crossed, the poet's soul (representative, as in "Song of Myself" of all human souls) will "front" God. Then "fill'd with friendship, love complete, the Elder Brother found,/The Younger melts in fondness in his arms." This prophetic wish doubtless does apply to Walt Whitman's own personal hope for his own soul, but the whole context of the poem implies a universal extension. And here again Teilhard seems the best commentator on Whitman's idea. The "religion" defined by Teilhard in *Building the Earth* is strikingly parallel to

Whitman's cosmic theology (the "new religion"[89] he mentions many times in his notes and prefaces):

Religion is not an option or a strictly individual intuition, but represents the long unfolding, the collective experience of all mankind, of the existence of God—God reflecting himself personally on the organized sum of thinking beings, to guarantee a sure result of creation, and to lay down exact laws for man's hesitant activities.[90]

.   .   .   .   .

A substantial part of this tide of available energy will immediately be absorbed in the expansion of man in matter. But another part, and that the most precious, will inevitably flow back to the levels of spiritualized energy.
Spiritualized Energy is the flower of Cosmic Energy.[91]

.   .   .   .   .

To be super spiritualized in God, must not mankind first be born and grow in conformity with the whole system of what we call evolution?
The sense of earth opening and flowering upwards in the sense of God, and the sense of God rooted and nourished from below in the sense of earth. The transcendent personal God and the universe in evolution, no longer forming two antagonistic poles of attraction, but entering into a hierarchic conjunction to uplift the human mass in a single tide.[92]

VISTAS

Whitman predicted as early as his 1855 Preface, as we have seen, that the poet would take the place of the priest and that literature must supply a "new religion" more capable than the old of ministering to the social and moral needs of mankind in a scientific age, and in each succeeding preface he repeated this opinion and stated his own program to meet the need. Although he had no specific social or political program, his literary program was in the broadest and deepest sense both social and political. Finally in *Democratic Vistas* he attempted an extended treatise on his idea of democracy and the means of converting the ideal into reality.

Democratic Vistas is wordy, turgid, and syntactically distracting (partly the result, perhaps, of combining three essays—or condensing three into two),[93] but some distinguished critics have found in it an important contribution to the theory of political democracy. Admitting that "our New World democracy . . . is, so far, an almost complete failure in its social aspects, and in really grand religious, moral, literary, and aesthetic results," Whitman nevertheless points out:

Sole among nationalities, these States have assumed the task to put in forms of lasting power and practicality, on areas of amplitude rivaling the operations of the physical kosmos, the moral political speculations of ages, long, long deferr'd, the democratic republican principle, and the theory of development and perfection by voluntary standards, and self-reliance.[94]

Whitman began *Democratic Vistas* as a reply to Carlyle's attack in *Shooting Niagara* on American democracy,[95] which the Scotchman saw as a degradation of society and an infectious threat to other nations. But as Whitman worked on his reply he became almost as severe as Carlyle on the present reality, with its political hypocrisy, "depravity of the business classes," corruption in government, and general cynicism of "respectable" citizens.[96] Yet it was not, Whitman believed, that democracy had failed; it had, like Christianity, not been tried. That was the problem. How, then, could it be solved?

First of all, Whitman argued, democracy must be understood for what it was: not so much a form of government as a method for men to live together in equality and mutual respect—which must rest on respect for themselves:

Political democracy, as it exists and practically works in America, with all its threatening evils, supplies a training-school for making first-class men. It is life's gymnasium, not of good only, but of all. We try often, though we fall back often. A brave delight, fit for freedom's athletes, fills these arenas, and fully satisfies, out of the action in them, irrespective of success. Whatever we do not attain, we at any rate attain the experiences of the fight, the hardening of the strong campaign, and throb with currents of attempt at least. . . .[97]

Whitman's experiences in the Civil War had convinced him that ordinary people were capable of governing themselves democratically. The trouble was the corruption at the top. The average soldier, from the "unknown rank and file," had shown courage, loyalty, and incredible patience and endurance in spite of the hopeless mismanagement of their officers, and often in the face of defeat and imminent death. In the same way, it was not the average citizen but the professional politician who thwarted political democracy. For this reason Whitman distrusted all parties (as he had in "The Eighteenth Presidency!"). Everyone should enter politics and vote, he advised, but "Disengage yourself from parties."[98] By remaining independent the voter could elect the best man to office. He hoped also that in the future women could participate, for "The day is coming when the deep questions of woman's entrance amid the arenas of practical life, politics, the suffrage, etc., will not only be argued all around us, but may be put to decision, and real experiment." Whitman had always stood for equal rights for women, and he thought their entrance into politics might help the American "experiment" in self-government to work better.

Above all else, however, Whitman looked to literature to aid the production of men and women with sufficient character (sure of their "identity" and with well-developed individualism) to create a viable democratic society. It must be a new literature because that of the past had been tainted by feudalism, caste, and privilege: "Literature, strictly considered [i.e., as literature], has never recognized the People, and, whatever may be said, does not today." Democracy has "a fit scientific estimate and reverent appreciation of the People—of their measureless wealth of latent power and capacity. . . ."[99]

The new literature will be religious in the sense of religion in "Passage to India," which recognizes the importance of both matter and spirit in the development of each individual soul on its cosmic journey. And here again Teilhard's evolutionary process of the "earth opening and flowering upward" (quoted above) both parallels and illustrates Whitman's theory of the future development of democracy—its *vistas*. In *The Future of Man* Teilhard says there are three stages:

The first phase was the formation of proteins up to the stage of the cell. In the second phase individual cellular complexes were formed, up to and including Man. We are now at the beginning of a third phase, the formation of an organico-social super-complex, which, as may easily be demonstrated, can only occur in the case of reflective, personalized elements. First the vitalization of matter, associated with the grouping of molecules; then the hominisation of Life, associated with a super-grouping of cells; and finally the planetisation of

Mankind, associated with a closed grouping of people: Mankind, born on this planet and spread over its entire surface, coming gradually to form around its earthly matrix a single, hyper-complex, hyper-centrated, hyper-conscious arch-molecule, coexistensive with the heavenly body on which it was born. Is not this what is happening at the present time—the closing of this spherical, thinking circuit?[100]

In "Passage to India" Whitman says that after the earth is spanned by man's science and engineering, his thought will return to its spiritual origins, symbolized by India; then he will take passage to "more than India," or "the seas of God." In *Democratic Vistas* (written about the same time) he also has three stages, or subdivisions of Teilhard's "planetisation of Mankind." But Whitman gives more attention than Teilhard to the political process:

For the New World, indeed, after two grand stages of preparation-strata, I perceive that now a third stage, being ready for, (and without which the other two were useless,) with unmistakable signs appears. The First stage was the planning and putting on record the political foundation rights of immense masses of people—indeed all people—in the organization of republican National, State, and municipal governments, all constructd with reference to each, and each to all. This is the American programme, not for classes, but for universal man, and is embodied in the compacts of the Declaration of Independence ... the Federal Constitution—and in the State governments.... The Second stage relates to material prosperity.... The Third stage, rising out of the previous ones, to make them and all illustrious, I, now, for one, promulge, announcing a native expression-spirit, getting into form, adult, and through mentality, for these States ... and by a sublime and serious Religious Democracy sternly taking command, dissolving the old, sloughing off surfaces, and from its own interior and vital principles, reconstructing, democratizing society.[101]

Ray Benoit thinks that Teilhard's stages of evolution point "to just that third stage Whitman envisioned in *Democratic Vistas*"[102] and which he had poetized in "Passage to India":

The linkage "Tying the Eastern to the Western Sea,/ The road between Europe and Asia" heralds the first glimmer of what Teilhard termed the Noosphcre, a layer of mind as the zenith of evolution when physical complexity and sheer plurality are such that psychic unity will be complete and earth will arrive at its Omega Point—"the gradual incorporation of the World in the Word Incarnate." So, in the poem, "The true son of God shall come singing his songs" and

All these separations and gaps shall be taken up and hook'd and
    link'd together,
The whole earth, this cold, impassive, voiceless earth, shall be
    completely justified.

Once again that Miltonic word *justified*, meaning basically that the physical world has fulfilled its divinely-intended purpose. Not believing in man's sinful nature, Whitman could hardly mean justify in the Puritan theological sense of forgiveness and purification of man's soul, though it does have its Whitmanian sublime connotation. In "Song of Myself" he had declared (sec. 24):

Through me many long dumb voices,

.   .   .   .   .

Voices of cycles of preparation and accretion,
And of the threads that connect the stars—and of wombs, and the
    fatherstuff, . . .

For nearly two decades Whitman had been articulating these "dumb voices," attempting both in the imagery of his poems and the theory of a spiritual democracy in *Democratic Vistas* to weave the "threads" connecting the co-equal and co-related worlds of matter and spirit.

[handwritten annotations across top: "? Apostroph Democratic", "take this piece out altogether", "tr to grim tufs", "tr to Drum Taps"]

~~CHANTS~~

~~DEMOCRATIC~~

[handwritten: to Drum taps]

~~AND~~

~~NATIVE AMERICAN.~~

[handwritten: O brood Continental (apostroph.)]

~~Apostroph.~~

~~O mater! O fils!~~

O brood continental! *[handwritten]* !

~~O flowers of the prairies!~~

~~O space boundless! O hum of mighty products!~~

O you teeming cities! ~~O so~~ invincible, turbulent,
 proud!

~~O race of the future! O women!~~

~~O fathers! O you~~ men of passion and the storm!

~~O native power only! O beauty!~~

~~O yourself! O God! O divine average!~~

~~O you bearded roughs! O bards!~~ O all those slum-
 berers!

~~O~~ arouse! the dawn-bird's throat sounds shrill! ~~Do~~
 ~~you not hear the cock crowing?~~ *[handwritten: exultant]*

~~O~~ as I walk'd the beach, I heard the mournful notes
 foreboding a tempest—the low, oft-repeated
 shriek of the diver, the long-lived loon *[handwritten: I heard]*

Chapter IV

Literary Technique in Leaves of Grass

> *The words of my book nothing, the drift of it everything,*
> *A book separate, not link'd with the rest nor felt by the intellect,*
> *But you ye untold latencies will thrill to every page.*
> —"Shut Not Your Doors, Proud Libraries."

THE ANALOGOUS FORM

If it were possible to separate thought from form, we might say that the style of *Leaves of Grass* has puzzled the critics, from 1855 until recent times, even more than the ideas.[1] Certainly many of the most serious efforts of the Whitman scholars and critics have been directed toward the interpretation and rationalization of this poet's art. They have often failed, however, because they did not understand Whitman's ideas and his intentions (though it is by no means certain that he always understood them himself). But some of the ambiguity of both thought and form was implicit in his intentions—either intended or unavoidable. He was right when he claimed in 1876: "My form has strictly grown from my purports and facts, and is the analogy of them."[2] Both his successes and failures as a poet were closely analogous to his theories and literary ambitions.

When Whitman chose to mention style, or someone nudged him into committing himself, he was likely to be disingenuous. To Traubel's questions he replied:

I have never given any study merely to expression: it has never appealed to me as a thing valuable or significant in itself: I have been deliberate, careful, even laborious: but I have never looked for finish—never fooled with technique more than enough to provide for simply getting through: after that I would not give a twist of my chair for all the rest.[3]

On another occasion he claimed that "What I am after is the content not the music of words. Perhaps the music happens—it does no harm."[4]

It is possible that Whitman's form was intuitive. De Selincourt may have been right when he declared romantically that, "His own wild music, ravishing, unseizable, like the song of a bird, came to him, as by his own principles it should have come, when he was not searching for it"[5]—though anyone who has studied Whitman's tortured manuscripts must doubt that this miracle ever happened when the poet "was not searching for it"; he chose the path even if he did not always know the way.

We can never know exactly what went on in Whitman's head either while he composed or while he indefatigably revised and re-edited his manuscripts year after year. As Furness says, "He was imbued more thoroughly perhaps with the 'daemonic' theory of inspiration and execution than any other poet of the nineteenth century."[6] But however unconscious he may have been of technique, he was so concerned with his theory of expression that it became his favorite theme in his various prefaces. The theory has been misunderstood because it was Whitman's avowed purpose in 1855 to achieve a style which would be not only "transcendent and new" but also "indirect and not direct or descriptive or epic,"[7] and "the medium that shall well nigh express the inexpressible."[728] Certainly this is no ordinary demand to make of literary technique. Whitman had no stories to tell, no descriptions of humble life, no melody to sing like Longfellow, Whittier, or Poe. *Poetry* to him was neither words nor beautiful sounds but something within, intangible—"poetic quality ... is in the soul,"[714] and he called "The United States themselves ... essentially the greatest poem."[709]

Whitman's inability or unwillingness to discuss his technique in terms of craftsmanship was imbedded in his fundamental assumptions about his literary intentions. Not only must his form be capable of expressing his mystical ideas, but to admit conscious planning and molding of the expression would have meant casting doubt on its authenticity and his own sincerity. To what extent his literary strategy was conscious, it is difficult to say: nevertheless, his very ambiguity was, for his purposes, clever strategy, as he was not entirely unaware himself:

Without effort and without exposing in the least how it is done the greatest poet brings the spirit of any or all events and passions and scenes and persons some more and some less to bear on your individual character as you hear or read.[716]

What he is attempting, therefore, is not so much the complete "expression" or communication of a thought or an experience as exerting an influence on the reader so that he himself, by willing cooperation with the poet, may have an esthetic-religious experience of his own. It is literally true that Whitman attempts less to create a "poem," as the term is usually understood, than to present the materials of a poem for the reader to use in creating his own work of art. No doubt in a sense, as Croce has argued, this is the manner in which all esthetic experience takes place; but Whitman aims to do nothing more than "indicate," though this is on a grand, mystical scale:

The land and sea, the animals fishes and birds, the sky of heaven and the orbs, the forests mountains and rivers, are not small themes . . .[8] but folks expect of the poet to indicate more than the beauty and dignity which always attach to dumb real objects . . . they expect him to indicate the path between reality and their souls.[714]

There we have the poet's most fundamental literary intention: *to indicate the path between reality and the soul.* And this is why both the theory and the expression must always remain vague and ambiguous. It is also why Whitman attaches so much importance to gestures and "indirections." His ideal poet "is most wonderful in his last half-hidden smile or frown . . . by that flash of the moment of parting the one that sees it shall be encouraged or terrified afterwards for many years."[716] Or again in 1888, after *Leaves of Grass* had been virtually completed:

I round and finish little, if anything; and could not, consistently with my scheme. The reader will always have his or her part to do, just as much as I have had mine. I seek less to state or display any theme or thought, and more to bring you, reader, into the atmosphere of the theme or thought—there to pursue your own flight.[9]

Believing that his function was to hint rather than state, to initiate rather than complete, Whitman adopted and developed for his own purposes the "organic" theory of poetic expression. Poetry should imitate not things but the spirit of things, not God or creation but His creativity. Hence fluency, logical structure, finish, were looked upon as artificial and useless ornamentation: "Who troubles himself about his ornaments or fluency is lost."

The poetic quality is not marshalled in rhyme or uniformity or abstract addresses to things nor in melancholy complaints or good precepts, but is the life of these and much else and is in the soul. The profit of rhyme is that it drops seeds of a sweeter and more luxuriant rhyme, and of uniformity that it conveys itself into its own roots in the ground out of sight. The rhyme and uniformity of perfect poems show the free growth of metrical laws and bud from them as unerringly and loosely as lilacs or roses on a bush, and take shapes as compact as the shapes of chestnuts and oranges and melons and pears, and shed the perfume impalpable to form. The fluency and ornaments of the finest poems or music or orations or recitations are not independent but dependent.[10]

Kennedy was echoing Whitman when in defending the style of *Leaves of Grass* he declared: "it is a truism that Nature, in all her forms, avoids base mechanical regularity."[11] Perhaps Whitman began his prosody with this negative principle: to represent Nature, or the order of creation, he must avoid conventional regularity—which meant of course rime and meter as they were known in the 1850s.

One of the most curious paradoxes in Whitman's literary doctrine is his insistence upon the "simplicity" of this "organic" theory or analogy: "The art of art, the glory of expression and the sunshine of the light of letters is simplicity. Nothing is better than simplicity." This, however, is his idea of stylistic simplicity: "But to speak in literature with the perfect rectitude and insousiance [sic] of the movements of animals and the unimpeachableness of the sentiment of trees in the woods and grass by the roadside is the flawless triumph of art."[12] Equally paradoxical is the added statement that, "The greatest poet has less a marked style and is more the channel of thoughts and things without increase or diminution, and is the free channel of himself."

This conception of the poet as a passive agent, through whom the currents of the universe flow without hindrance or his conscious direction, did not of course, in practical terms, result in a literary form either simple or unmannered. But the theory did determine what the form was not—and perhaps eventually what it was. In the first place, it was not to be restrained, disciplined.

> . . . . I permit to speak at every hazard,
> Nature without check with original energy.[13]

From this doctrine and the resulting uninhibited flow of confessions bubbling up from the poet's inner life came his own apparent belief that he could solve the problem of form by rejecting all conventional techniques. But if he actually did believe this, it was the greatest of all his illusions, for without conventions of some sort there can be no communication whatever. Understanding depends upon the ability of the hearer or reader to recognize some form of order in the linguistic symbols of the speaker or writer.

Of course Whitman did not evolve brand-new techniques. But he did reject and modify or readapt enough conventions to short-circuit communication for many readers for many years, and is not always intelligible even today. He is, however, more easily understood in our day than in his own because critical interpreters have sufficiently clarified his intentions for the reasonably literate reader to know at least what the poet was attempting. For no other American poet has criticism rendered so great a service, or been so necessary.

Before attempting to discover in detail what kind of form and technique Whitman created and adapted for his purposes, we might ask ourselves, by way of summary, what he wanted the "new" style to do. It must, as we have seen, express an inner rather than an outer harmony. He is not so much concerned with things and appearances as with the "spirit" of their relationships. And these are to be suggested or implied rather than explicitly stated. The form must be "organic," though he aims not at describing or imitating external nature but at conveying the creativity of Nature, with her fecundity and variety. It must, therefore, be a democratic-animistic style. Never before, he thought, had "poetry with cosmic and dynamic features of magnitude and limitlessness suitable to the human soul"[14] been possible.

THE EXPANDING EGO

All critics who have seriously tried to understand Whitman have observed that the "I" of his poems is generic: he celebrates himself as a representative man. His "soul" is but a fragment of the World-Soul, and is mystically and animistically related to all the souls of the universe. In asserting his own uniqueness he merely gives expression—at least philosophically and intentionally—to the creative power of the innate soul "identified" through his own personality.

This much is obvious to anyone who is familiar with Whitman's ideas and avowed poetic purposes. The almost inevitable result on his literary technique is that his poetic form is analogous to his "purports and facts." His point of view (except in a few of the shorter and more truly personal lyrics) will not be finite and stationary but ubiquitous and soaring—a migrating soul transcending time and space. It is not in the least unusual for a lyric poet to identify himself with some one object or place, like Shelley in "The Cloud" or "Ode to the West Wind," but Whitman's ego is in constant motion, flitting like a humming bird from object to object and place to place with miraculous speed.

> My ties and ballasts leave me, my elbows rest in sea-gaps,
> I skirt sierras, my palms cover continents,
> I am afoot with my vision.[15]

This is his point of view not only in his spectacular cosmic visions but in nearly all his poems. Even when he is less mystical, not obviously trying to hover over the earth watching the "great round wonder rolling through space,"[16] the imagery is panoramic, unending, flowing, expanding. Whitman's description of the manner in which he "abstracts" himself from the book and stretches his mind (or poetic imagination) in all directions probably gives the best clue to the method by which he developed his style and technique. In the 1855 Preface the "bard" is not only "commensurate with a people" and attempts to "incarnate" flora, fauna, and topography, but he also "spans ... from east to west and reflects what is between them."[17] The point of view of the first section of "Salut au Monde!" is therefore typical of Whitman's art in general:

> O take my hand Walt Whitman!
> Such gliding wonders! such sights and sounds!
> Such join'd unended links, each hook'd to the next,
> Each answering all, each sharing the earth with all.

Although this method results in the long catalogs, in the piling up of image on top of image with meager enumeration of attributes, the poet is not content with merely photographing from an airplane. However unselected the mass of images may seem to some readers, he intended them to symbolize a spiritual unity in himself and all creation.

> What widens within you Walt Whitman?
>
> .   .   .   .   .
>
> Within me latitude widens, longitude lengthens, . . .

The externals, the catalog of concrete details, are transcendental symbols of what he might call "spiritual truths." Thus we have the curious paradox in Whitman's style of snapshot imagery joined to ambiguity. Even in his most vivid realism he is still allegorical and subjective.

The effect of this style has not been unobserved by critics. Paul Elmer More, the late "New Humanist," wrote:

This sense of indiscriminate motion is . . . the impression left finally by Whitman's work as a whole . . . Now the observer seems to be moving through clustered objects beheld vividly for a second of time and then lost in the mass, and, again, the observer himself is stationary while the visions throng past him in almost dizzy rapidity; but in either case we come away with the feeling of having been merged in unbroken processions, whose beginning and end are below the distant horizon, and whose meaning we but faintly surmise.[18]

Reed has called this attempt to present cosmic unity in flux "The Heraclitan Obsession of Walt Whitman."[19] He finds it logically contradictory, however, because the "progressive integration" of form is not "opposed by a contrary disunity of some sort." How can he blend body and soul without a dualism?

But this logical impasse does not appear to have bothered Whitman, and criticism of his thinking need not detain us here. What is of interest . . . is the psychological effect as it is imprinted on the poems. With unification as an ideal, Whitman, one would expect, would show a fine sure insight into the oneness of the phenomenal world. Yet the reader of his poems gains no awareness of such unity. The feeling is rather of disintegration and extreme multiplicity.

This criticism calls attention to the fundamental problem in Whitman's use of the expanding ego. Perhaps the effect depends largely upon the reader's own philosophy. To the Absolutist the effect is no doubt confusion, to the Relativist probably not. Perhaps this is saying that the unity is not in the poem but in the mind of the reader, as it was no doubt in the mind (or intention) of the poet—to whom these "gliding wonders" were "join'd unended links, each hook'd to the next."

This interpretation suggests Whitman's anticipation of both the modern "stream of consciousness" literary technique and the movement known in the 1920s as "Expressionism."[20] Dahlström's characterization of this doctrine in Germany might almost be a summary of Whitman's theory and practice and indicates the need for a study of the American poet's possible influence on the movement:

> Foremost among the elements [of Expressionism] is the concept of the *Ausstrahlungen des Ichs*—the radiation, expansion, and unfolding of the ego. This is partly explained by the phrase 'stream of consciousness' which is current in our English terminology. Yet 'stream of consciousness' offers too frequently the possibility of itemization of the elements of consciousness, lingers too close to the realm of psychology. For the expressionist, consciousness is no manifoldly died punch press turning out countless items of similar or dissimilar pattern. It is rather a unifying instrument that moulds oneness of the countless items poured into it. The ego is the predominant element in our universe; it is, indeed, the very heart of the world's reality. For the artist, the ego is a magic crystal in which the absolute is in constant play. It is the subject that registers the everlasting *state of becoming* that qualifies our world; and this subject has an anti-pole *object* which is functional only in giving meaning to the subject. Conversely, the subject must give meaning to the object. It is this ego, this subject, this magic crystal that actually gathers reality in its ultimate character. [49-50]

The "magic crystal" accurately characterizes Whitman's technique of dynamic, creative, enumeration of the kind of spiritual reality in which he believed, and it was his fundamental purpose to register through the eyes of his expanding ego "the everlasting state of becoming that qualifies our world." For the expression of such basic ideas as his cosmic evolution, his animism, and his adaptation of the "temporalized Chain of Being" concept this technique was astonishingly appropriate.

THE SEARCH FOR A "DEMOCRATIC" STRUCTURE

In so far as the expanding ego psychology results in an enumerative style, the cataloging of a representative and symbolical succession of images, conveying the sensation of subjective unity and endless becoming, it is itself a literary technique. But though this psychology may be called the background or basic method of Whitman's poetic technique, the catalog itself was not chronologically the first stylistic device which he adopted. It emerged only after he had found a verse structure appropriate for expressing his cosmic inspiration and democratic sentiment. Nowhere in the universe does he recognize caste or subordination. Everything is equally perfect and equally divine. He admits no supremes, or rather insists that "There can be any number of supremes."[21]

The expression of such doctrines demands a form in which units are co-ordinate, distinctions eliminated, all flowing together in a synonymous or "democratic" structure. He needed a grammatical and rhetorical structure which would be cumulative in effect rather than logical or progressive.

Possibly, as many critics have believed, he found such a structure in the primitive rhythms of the King James Bible, though some of the resemblances may be accidental. The structure of Hebraic poetry, even in English translation, is almost lacking in subordination. The original language of the Old Testament was extremely deficient in connectives, as the numerous "ands" of the King James translation bear witness.[22] It was a language for direct assertion and the expression of emotion rather than abstract thought or intellectual subtleties. Tied to such a language, the Hebraic poet developed a rhythm of thought, repeating and balancing ideas and sentences (or independent clauses) instead of syllables or accents. He may have had other prosodic conventions also, no longer understood or easily discernible; but at least in the English translation this rhythm of thought or parallelism characterizes Biblical versification.[23]

That Walt Whitman fully understood the nature of these Biblical rhythms is doubtful, and certainly his own language did not tie him down to such a verse system. Despite the fact that he was thoroughly familiar with the Bible and was undoubtedly influenced by the scriptures in many ways, it may, therefore, have been a coincidence that in searching for a medium to express his animism he naturally (we might almost say atavistically) stumbled upon parallelism as his basic structure. Furthermore, parallelism is found in primitive poetry other than the Biblical; in fact, it seems to be typically primitive,[24] and it is perhaps not surprising that in the attempt to get rid of conventional techniques Whitman should have rediscovered a primitive one.

But whatever the sources of Whitman's verse techniques, the style of the King James Version is generally agreed to provide convenient analogies for the prosodic analysis of *Leaves of Grass*.[25]

"The principles which governed Hebrew verse," says Gardiner, "can be recovered only in part, but fortunately the one principle which really affects the form of the English has been clearly made out, the principle of parallel structure: in the Hebrew poetry the line was the unit, and the second line balanced the first, completing or supplementing its meaning."[26]

Even the scholars of the Middle ages were aware of the parallelism of Biblical verse (*Verdoppelten Ausdruck* or "double expression,"[27] they called it) but it was first fully explained by Bishop Lowth in a Latin speech given at Oxford in 1753. Since his scheme demonstrates the single line as the unit, let us examine it.

1. *Synonymous* parallelism: This is the most frequent kind of thought rhythm in Biblical poetry. "The second line enforces the thought of the first by repeating, and, as it were, *echoing* it in a varied form, producing an effect at once grateful to the ear and satisfying to the mind."[28]

> How shall I curse, whom God hath not cursed?
> Or how shall I defy, whom the Lord hath not defied?
> —*Nu.* 23:8.

The second line, however, does not have to be identical in thought with the first. It may be merely similar or parallel to it.

> Sun, stand thou still upon Gibeon;
> And thou, Moon, in the valley of Ajalon.
> —*Josh.* 10:12.

2. *Antithetic* parallelism: The second line denies or contrasts the first:

> A wise son maketh a glad father,
> But a foolish son is the heaviness of his mother.
> —*Prov.* 10:1.

> For the Lord knoweth the way of the righteous;
> But the way of the ungodly shall perish.
>
> *—Ps.* 1:6.

3. *Synthetic* or *constructive* parallelism: Here the second line (sometimes several consecutive lines) supplements or completes the first. (Although all Biblical poetry tends more toward the "end-stopped" than the "run-on" line, it will be noticed that synthetic parallelism does often have a certain degree of *enjambement*.)

> Better is a dinner of herbs where love is,
> Than a stalled ox and hatred therewith.
>
> *—Pr.* 15:17.
>
> Answer not a fool according to his folly,
> Lest thou also be like unto him.
>
> *—Pr.* 26:4.
>
> As a bird that wandereth from her nest,
> So is a man that wandereth from his place.
>
> *—Pr.* 27:8.

"A comparison, a reason, a consequence, a motive, often constitutes one of the lines in a synthetic parallelism."

4. To Lowth's three kinds of parallelism Driver adds a fourth, which for convenience we may include here. It is called *climactic* parallelism—or sometimes "ascending rhythm." "Here the first line is itself incomplete, and the second line takes up words from it and completes them."

> Give unto the Lord, O ye sons of the mighty,
> Give unto the Lord *glory and strength*.
>
> *—Ps.* 29:1.
>
> The voice of the Lord shaketh the wilderness;
> The Lord shaketh the wilderness *of Kadesh*.
>
> *—Ps.* 29:8.
>
> Till thy people pass over, O Lord,
> Till the people pass over *which thou hast purchased*.
>
> *—Ex.* 15:16.

It will be noticed in these examples that parallelism is sometimes a repetition of grammatical constructions and often of words, but the main principle is the balancing of thoughts alongside or against each other. And this produces not only a rhythmical thought-pattern, but also, and consequently, a speech rhythm which we will consider later. This brief summary presents only the most elementary aspects of Biblical rhythm, but it is sufficient to establish the fact that in parallelism, or in the "rhythm of thought," *the single line must by necessity be the stylistic unit.* Before taking up other aspects of parallelism let us see if this fundamental principle is found in Whitman's poetry.

Many critics have recognized parallelism as a rhythmical principle in *Leaves of Grass.* Perry even suggested that *The Lily and the Bee*, by Samuel Warren, published in England in 1851 and promptly reprinted in America by Harpers, may have given Whitman the model for his versification;[29] though Carpenter has pointed out that Whitman's new style had already been formed by 1851.[30] Perry's conjecture is important, however, because parallelism is unquestionably the stylistic principle of *The Lily and the Bee*, and in making the conjecture he is rightly calling attention to this principle of Whitman's style.

But if parallelism is the foundation of the rhythmical style of *Leaves of Grass*, then, as we have already seen in the summary of the Lowth system, the verse must be the unit. Any reader can observe that this is true in *Leaves of Grass*, and many critics have pointed it out. De Selincourt says:

The constitution of a line in *Leaves of Grass* is such that, taken in its context, the poetic idea to be conveyed by the words is only perfectly derivable from them when they are related to the line as a unit; and the equivalence of the lines is their equivalent appeal to our attention as contributors to the developing expression of the poetic idea of the whole.[31]

And Ross adds, more concretely:

Whitman's verse—with the exception that it is not metered—is farther removed from prose than is traditional verse itself, for the reason that the traditional verse is, like prose, composed in sentences, whereas Whitman's verse is composed in lines ... A run-on line is rare in Whitman—so rare that it may be considered a "slip." The law of his structure is that *the unit of sense is the measure of the line.* The lines, in sense, are end-stopped. Whitman employed everywhere a system of punctuation to indicate his structure. Look down any page of *Leaves of Grass*, and you will find almost every line ending in a comma; you will find a period at the end of a group of lines or a whole poem. Syntactically, there may be many sentences in the groups of the whole poem, there may be two or three sentences in one line. But Whitman was composing by lines, not by sentences, and he punctuated accordingly.[32]

WHITMAN'S PARALLELISM

It was only after several years of experimentation that Whitman definitely adopted parallelism as his basic verse structure. In a poem of 1850, "Blood-Money,"[33] he was already fumbling for this technique, but here he was paraphrasing both the thought and the prose rhythm of the New Testament (*Matthew* 26-27):

> Of olden time, when it came to pass
> That the beautiful god, Jesus, should finish his work
>   on earth,
> Then went Judas, and sold the divine youth,
> And took pay for his body.

The run-on lines show how far the poet still is from the characteristic style of *Leaves of Grass*. He is experimenting with phrasal or clausal units; not yet "thought rhythm." But his arrangement of the verse is a step in that direction.

In "Europe," another poem of 1850, we also see the new form slowly evolving. It begins with long lines that at first glance look like the typical verse of the later poems, but on closer observation we see that they are not.

Suddenly, out of its stale and drowsy lair, the lair of slaves,
Like lightning Europe le'pt forth . . . . half startled at itself,
Its feet upon the ashes and the rags . . . . Its hands tight to the throat
    of kings.[1855 Ed.]

The disregard for grammatical structure suggests the poet's mature style—the antecedent of *it* is merely implied and the predicate is entirely lacking—, but the lines are only vaguely synonymous.

We see the next stage of this evolving style in the 1855 Preface, which, significantly, is arranged as prose, but the thought-units are often separated by periods, indicating that the author is striving for a rhythmical effect which conventional prose punctuation can not achieve.

He sees eternity less like a play with a prologue and a denouement . . . he sees eternity in men and women . . . he does not see men and women as dreams or dots. Faith is the antiseptic of the soul . . . it pervades the common people and preserves them . . . they never give up believing and expecting and trusting. [713]

The greatest poet forms the consistence of what is to be from what has been and is. He drags the dead out of their coffins and stands them again on their feet . . . he says to the past, Rise and walk before me that I may realize you. He learns the lesson . . . he places himself where the future becomes present. The greatest poet does not only dazzle his rays over character and scenes and passions . . . he finally ascends and finishes all . . . he exhibits the pinnacles that no man can tell what they are for or what is beyond . . . He glows a moment on the extremest verge. He is most wonderful in his last half-hidden smile or frown. . . .[34]

Notice that the parallelism asserts without qualifications. The poet is chanting convictions about which there is to be no argument, no discussion. He develops or elaborates the theme by enumeration, eliminating so far as possible transitional and connective words. The form is rhapsodic, the tone that of inspired utterance.

In this Preface the third person is used, but the rhetorical form is that of the expanding ego, as clearly revealed in this catalog:

On him rise solid growths that offset the growths of pine and cedar and hemlock and liveoak and locust and chestnut and cypress and hickory and limetree and cottonwood and tuliptree and cactus and wildvine and tamarind and persimmon . . . and tangles as tangled as any canebreak or swamp . . . and forests coated with transparent ice and icicles hanging from the boughs and crackling in the wind . . . and sides and peaks of mountains. . . .[35]

The "ands" are evidently an attempt to convey the effect of endless continuity in an eternal present—the cosmic unity which the poet incarnates as he sweeps over the continent. Here in this rhapsodic Preface, both in the ideas and the manner in which they are expressed, we see the kind of literary form and style which Whitman has adopted as analogous to his "purports and facts."

And in ten of the twelve poems of the 1855 edition of *Leaves of Grass* parallelism is the structural device, chiefly the *synonymous* variety, though the others are found also, especially the *cumulative* and *climactic*. As a matter of fact, it is often difficult to separate these three, for as Whitman asserts or repeats the same idea in different ways—like a musician playing variations on a theme—he tends to build up to an emotional, if not logical, climax. The opening lines of "Song of Myself" are obviously cumulative in effect:

> I celebrate myself, [and sing myself],
> And what I assume you shall assume,
> For every atom belonging to me as good belongs to you.

The following lines are synonymous in thought, though there is a cumulation and building up of the emotion:

> I loafe and invite my soul,
> I lean and loafe at my ease . . . . observing a spear of
> summer grass.

(No doubt much of this effect is due to the pronounced caesura—which we will consider later.)

[In this poem, as in the following ones, the parallelism has three functions. First of all it provides the basic structure for the lines. Each line makes an independent statement, either a complete or an elliptical sentence. In the second place, this repetition of thought (with variations) produces a loose rhythmical chanting or rhapsodic style. And, finally, the parallelism binds the lines together, forming a unit something like a stanza in conventional versification.

This grass is very dark to be from the white heads of old mothers,
Darker than the colorless beards of old men,
Dark to come from under the faint red roofs of mouths.

O I perceive after all so many uttering tongues!
And I perceive they do not come from the roofs of mouths for
nothing.

I wish I could translate the hints about the dead young men and
women,
And the hints about old men and mothers, and the offspring taken
soon out of their laps.

What do you think has become of the young and old men?

And what do you think has become of the women and children?

They are alive and well somewhere;
The smallest sprout shows there is really no death,
And if ever there was it led forward life, and does not wait at the end
     ˙to arrest it,
And ceased the moment life appeared.

All goes onward and outward . . . . and nothing collapses,
And to die is different from what any one supposed, and luckier.[36]

Here Whitman's characteristic structure and rhythm is completely developed and he handles it with ease and assurance. But that he does not yet completely trust it is perhaps indicated by the occasional use of a semicolon (as in next to the last stanza or strophe above) and four periods to emphasize a caesura. In his later verse (including revisions of this poem) he depended upon commas in both places.

In the above extract from "Song of Myself" the similarity of the parallelism to that of Biblical poetry is probably closer than in more typical passages of Whitman's longer poems, for the couplet, triplet, and quatrain are found more often in the Bible than in *Leaves of Grass*; and the Bible does not have either long passages of synonymous parallelism or extended catalogs. The Biblical poets were not, like Whitman, attempting to inventory the universe in order to symbolize its fluxional unity. They found unity in their monotheism, not (or seldom) in a pantheism. But when Whitman's poetic vision sweeps over the occupations of the land, as in section 15 of "Song of Myself," he enumerates dozens of examples in more or less synonymous parallelistic form. And he repeats the performance in section 33 in a kind of omnipresent world-panorama of scenes, activities, and pictures of life, in a strophe (or sentence) of 82 lines.

Another poem in the first edition, later known as "There Was a Child Went Forth," further amplifies both the psychology of the poet's identification of his consciousness with all forms of being and his expression of it through enumeration and parallelism:

There was a child went forth every day,
And the first object he looked upon and received with wonder or
     pity or love or dread, that object he became,

And that object became part of him for the day or a certain part of
the day . . . . or for many years of stretching cycles of years.

Then comes the list—early lilacs, grass, morning glories, March-born
lambs, persons, streets, oceans, etc.—a veritable photomontage. The
catalog and parallelism techniques arise from the same psychological
impulse and achieve the same general effects of poetic identification.
The catalog, however, is most typical of the 1855-56 poems,
when Whitman's cosmic inspiration found its most spontaneous and
unrestrained expression. But even here we find a number of strophes
arranged or organized as "envelopes" of parallelism, a device which
the poet found especially useful in the shorter and more orderly
poems of "Calamus," *Drum-Taps*, and the old-age lyrics. It is essentially a stanzaic form, something like the quatrain of the Italian
sonnet. The first line advances a thought or image, succeeding lines
amplify or illustrate it by synonymous parallelism, and the final line
completes the whole by reiterating the original line or concluding the
thought. For example, in section 21 of "Song of Myself":

Smile O voluptuous coolbreathed earth!
Earth of the slumbering and liquid trees!
Earth of departed sunset! Earth of the mountains misty-topt!
Earth of the vitreous pour of the full moon just tinged with blue!
Earth of shine and dark mottling the tide of the river!
Earth of the limpid gray of clouds brighter and clearer for my sake!
Far-swooping elbowed earth! Rich apple-blossomed earth!
Smile, for your lover comes!

Far more common, however, is the incomplete envelope, the
conclusion being omitted, as in the 1860 "Song at Sunset":

Good in all,
In the satisfaction and aplomb of animals,
In the annual return of the seasons,
In the hilarity of youth,
In the strength and flush of manhood,
In the grandeur and exquisiteness of old age,
In the superb vistas of death.

But of course an "incomplete envelope" is not an envelope at all.
Without a conclusion it is not a container. And it is characteristic of

Whitman, especially in 1855-56, that he more often preferred not to finish his comparisons, analogies, representative examples of reality, but let them trail off into infinity. In his later poems, however, the envelope often provides a structure and unity for the whole composition, as in "Joy, Shipmate, Joy!":

> Joy, shipmate, joy!
> (Pleas'd to my soul at death I cry,)
> Our life is closed, our life begins,
> The long, long anchorage we leave,
> The ship is clear at last, she leaps!
> She swiftly courses from the shore,
> Joy, shipmate, joy!

OTHER REITERATIVE DEVICES

In the above discussion parallelism was referred to as both a *structure* and a *rhythm* in Whitman's verse technique. Since rhythm means orderly or schematic repetition, a poem can have several kinds of rhythms, sometimes so coördinated in the total effect that it is difficult to isolate and evaluate the separate function of each. Thus Whitman's parallelism can give esthetic pleasure as a recognizable pattern of thought, which is to say that it is the basis of the structure of the composition. This does not necessarily result in a repetition or rhythm of sounds, cadences, music, etc. But since thoughts are expressed by means of spoken sounds (or symbols that represent spoken sounds), it is possible for the *thought rhythm* to produce, or to be accompanied by, *phonic rhythm*. The latter need not be a rhythm of accents or stressed syllables (though it often is in *Leaves of Grass* as will be demonstrated later). Rime, or repetition of similar sounds according to a definite pattern, is another kind of phonic rhythm, and may serve several purposes, such as pleasing the ear (which has been conditioned to anticipate certain sounds at regular intervals) or grouping the lines and thereby (in many subtle ways) emphasizing the thought.

Whitman's parallelism, or thought rhythm, is so often accompanied and reinforced by parallel wording and sounds that the two techniques are often almost identical. An easy way to collect examples of his "thought rhythm" is to glance down the left-hand margin and notice the lines beginning with the same word, and usually the same grammatical construction: "I will ... I will ... I will . . ." or "Where . . . Where . . . Where . . ." or "When . . . When . . . When," etc.[37]

These repetitions of words or phrases are often found in modern conventional meters. Tennyson, for example,[38] repeats consecutively the same word or phrase throughout many passages; and the refrain and repetend in Poe's versification is the same device in a somewhat different manner. In conventional meters these reiterations may even set up a rhythm of their own, either syncopating or completely distorting the regular metrical pattern. But there is this very important difference between reiteration in rime and meter and reiteration in *Leaves of Grass*: in the former the poem has a set pattern of accents (iambic, trochaic, anapestic, etc.), whereas in Whitman's verse the pattern of sounds and musical effects is entirely dependent upon the thought and structure of the separate lines.

In every emotionally and intellectually pleasing poem in *Leaves of Grass* these reiterations do set up a recognizable pattern of sounds.[39] Since the line is not bound by a specific number of syllables, or terminated by conventional rime, the sound patterns may seem to the untrained reader entirely free and lawless. It was part of Whitman's "organic" style to make his rhythms freer than those of classical and conventional versification, but they are no freer than those of the best musical compositions of opera and symphony. They can, of course, be too free to recognize, in which case Whitman failed as a poet—and like almost all major poets, he has many failures to his name. But in the best poems of *Leaves of Grass*—such as "Out of the Cradle Endlessly Rocking," "When Lilacs Last in the Dooryard Bloom'd," or "Passage to India,"—the combined thought and sound patterns are as definite and organized as in "Lycidas" or "Samson Agonistes."

Several names have been given Whitman's reiterative devices in addition to the ones used here (phonic reiteration, etc.). Miss Autrey Nell Wiley, who has made the most thorough study of this subject, uses the rhetorical terms *epanaphora* and *epanalepsis*.[40] The nineteenth-century Italian scholar, Jannaccone,[41] calls these reiterations *rima psichica iniziale e terminale* (initial and terminal psychic rime) and *rima psichica media e terminale*. "Psychic rime" is a suggestive term, but it probably overemphasizes the analogy with conventional rime—though it is important to notice the initial, medial, and terminal positions of Whitman's reiterations. The initial is most common, as in the "Cradle" poem:

Out of the cradle endlessly rocking,
Out of the mocking-bird's throat, the musical shuttle,
Out of the Ninth-month midnight.

Although this reiteration might be regarded as "psychic rime," its most significant function is the setting up of a cadence to dominate the whole line, as the "Give me" reiteration does in "Give Me the Splendid Silent Sun," or the "What," "I hear," "I see," etc. in "Salut au Monde!," though scarcely any poem in *Leaves of Grass* is without the combined use of parallelism and reiteration. Often a short poem is a single "envelope" of parallelism with initial reiteration, as in "I Sit and Look Out":

I sit and look out upon all the sorrows of the world, and upon all
    oppression and shame,
I hear secret convulsive sobs from young men at anguish with
    themselves, remorseful after deeds done,
I see in low life the mother misused by her children, dying,
    neglected, gaunt, desperate,
I see the wife misused by her husband, I see the treacherous seducer
    of young women,
I mark the ranklings of jealousy and unrequited love attempted to be
    hid, I see these sights on the earth,
I see the workings of battle, pestilence, tyranny, I see martyrs and
    prisoners,
I observe a famine at sea, I observe the sailors casting lots who shall
    be kill'd to preserve the lives of the rest,
I observe the slights and degradations cast by arrogant persons upon
    laborers, the poor, and upon negroes, and the like;
All these—all the meanness and agony without end I sitting look out
    upon,
See, hear, and am silent.

Initial reiteration, as in the above passage, occurs oftener in *Leaves of Grass* than either medial or final. Miss Wiley has estimated that 41 percent of the more than 10,500 lines in the *Leaves* contains epanaphora, or initial reiteration.[42] But words and phrases are frequently repeated in other positions. "When Lilacs Last in the Dooryard Bloom'd" contains an effective example of a word from the first line repeated and interwoven throughout succeeding lines:

Over the breast of the spring, the land, *amid* cities,
Amid lanes and through old woods, where lately the violets peep'd
    from the ground, spotting the gray debris,
Amid the grass in the fields each side of the lanes, *passing* the endless
    grass,
Passing the yellow-spear'd wheat, every grain from its shroud in the
    dark-brown fields uprisen,
Passing the apple-tree blows of white and pink in the orchards,
Carrying a corpse to where it shall rest in the grave,
Night and day journeys a coffin.

Here the reiterations have little to do with cadences but aid greatly in
the effect of ceaseless motion—and even of *enjambement*, so rare in
Leaves of Grass—as the body of the assassinated president is carried
"night and day" from Washington to the plains of Illinois.

Final reiteration is found, though Whitman used it sparingly,
perhaps because it too closely resembles refrains and repetends in
conventional versification, and also because he had little use for the
kind of melody and singing lyricism which these devices produce.
When he does use final reiteration, it is more for rhetorical emphasis
than music, as in sec. 24 of "Song of Myself":

Root of wash'd sweet-flag! timorous pond-snipe! nest of guarded
    duplicate eggs! *it shall be you*!
Mix'd tussled hay of head, beard, brawn, *it shall be you*!
Trickling sap of maple, fibre of manly wheat, *it shall be you*!
Sun so generous *it shall be you*!

and so on throughout sixteen lines.

Sometimes Whitman uses reiteration through the entire line, as
in "By Blue Ontario's Shore":

I will know if I am to be less than they,
I will see if I am not as majestic as they,
I will see if I am not as subtle and real as they,
I will see if I am to be less generous than they, . . .[Sec. 18]

C. Alphonso Smith in his study of repetitions in English and
American poetry (he does not mention Whitman, however) has
defined the difference between reiterations in prose and poetry:

In prose, a word or group of words is repeated for emphasis; whereas in verse, repetition is chiefly employed not for emphasis (compare the use of the refrain), but for melody of rhythm, for continuousness or sonorousness of effect, for unity of impression, for banding lines or stanzas, and for the more indefinable though not less important purposes of suggestiveness.[43]

Of course, Smith is thinking of conventional versification, but continuousness of effect, unity of impression, joining of lines and stanzas, and suggestiveness all apply to Whitman's use of reiteration.

Although Whitman's reiteration is not musical in the sense that Poe's is (*i.e.*, for melody and harmony), it is musical in a larger sense. Many critics have developed the analogy of music in Whitman's technique, but De Selincourt's comments are especially pertinent here. "The progress of Whitman's verse," he says, "has much in common with that of a musical composition. For we are carrying the sense of past effects along with us more closely and depending more intimately upon them than is possible in normal verse." And he observes that:

repetition, which the artist in language scrupulously avoids, is the foundation and substance of musical expression. Now Whitman . . . uses words and phrases more as if they were notes of music than any other writer . . . it was to him part of the virtue and essence of life that its forms and processes were endlessly reduplicated; and poetry, which was delight in life, must somehow, he thought, mirror this elemental abundance.[44]

Of course Whitman's repetition concerns not only words and phrases (Jannaccone's "psychic rime") but thought patterns as well. In fact, his favorite method of organizing a long poem like "The Sleepers," "Proud Music of the Storm," "Mystic Trumpeter," or even "Song of the Redwood-Tree" is, as remarked elsewhere, symphonic. He likes to advance a theme, develop it by enumeration and representative symbols, advance other themes and develop them in similar manners, then repeat, summarize, and emphasize. Thus Whitman's repetition of thought, of words, of cadences,—playing variations on each out of exuberance and unrestrained joy both in the thought and form—, all combine to give him the satisfaction and conviction that he has "expressed" himself, not logically or even coherently, but by suggestion and by sharing his own emotions with the reader.

Another kind of reiteration which Whitman uses both for the thought and the musical effect is what Jannaccone calls "grammatical" and "logical rime"[45] —though *grammatical rhythm* might be a more convenient and appropriate term. Instead of repeating the same identical word or phrase, he repeats a part of speech or grammatical construction at certain places in the line. This has nearly the same effect on the rhythm and cadence as the reiteration of the same word or phrase, especially when "grammatical rime" is initial. For example, parallel verbs:

Flow on, river! *flow* with the flood-tide, and *ebb* with the ebb-tide!
Frolic on, crested and scallop-edg'd waves!
Gorgeous clouds of the sunset! *drench* with your splendor me or the
        men and women generations after me!
Cross from shore to shore, countless crowds of passengers!
Stand up, tall masts of Mannahatta! . . .
        —"Crossing Brooklyn Ferry," sec. 9.

The following Jannaccone calls "logical rime":[46]

Long and long has the *grass* been *growing*,
Long and long has the *rain* been *falling*,
Long has the *globe* been rolling *round*.
        —"Song of the Exposition," sec. 1.

Not only are *growing, falling,* and *rolling* grammatically parallel, but they are also the natural (and logical) things for the *grass,* the *rain,* and the *globe* to be doing.

Sometimes Whitman reiterates cognates:

The *song* is to the *singer,* and comes back most to him,
The *teaching* is to the *teacher,* and comes back most to him,
The *murder* is to the *murderer,* and comes back most to him, . . .
        —"Song of the Rolling Earth," sec. 2.

In all these examples the various kinds of reiterations produce also a pattern of accents which can be scanned like conventional verse.

Long and long has the grass been growing, . . .

Parallelism gives these lines a *thought* rhythm, but this is reinforced by the phonic recurrences, giving additional rhythm which depends upon *sounds* for its effect. Of course these examples are unusually regular (or simple), whereas the same principles in other passages give a much greater variety and complexity of phonic stress. But the combined reiterations always (at least when successful) produce a composite musical pattern—a pattern more plastic than any to be found in conventional versification, but one which the ear can be trained to appreciate no less than patterns of rime and meter.

"ORGANIC" RHYTHM

As we have repeatedly emphasized, Whitman's parallelism and his phonic reiterations do not exclude accentual patterns. Anyone who examines with care the versification of *Leaves of Grass* will discover many lines that can be scanned with ease, but most critics have regarded such passages as sporadic and uncharacteristic. Several, in fact, have thought the style of *Drum-Taps* inferior to other periods of Whitman's poetry, and a contradiction of his professed theory, because they are much nearer to conventional patterns of verse than his earlier poems.

Sculley Bradley, however, claims accentual patterns as the "Fundamental Metric Principle" of *Leaves of Grass*.[47] He does not challenge the widely accepted interpretations of Whitman's basic parallelism and reiteration, but regards these as obvious—though somewhat incidental. He thinks that many lines in which these devices are not used are also rhythmical and esthetically pleasing. In other words, there must be some other—still more *fundamental*—principle in Whitman's prosody.

Such a principle would have to be an exemplification of the poet's "organic" theory, his belief that form must spring from within, that a poetic experience will find its own natural rhythm in the act of expression. Certainly this was Whitman's most fundamental literary theory, as his various analogies—and those of numerous critics—indicate. Thus he compares his rhythms to the "recurrence of lesser and larger waves on the seashore, rolling in without intermission, and fitfully rising and falling."[48]

Bradley points out the similarity of Whitman's "organic" theory to Coleridge's distinction between "mechanic" and "organic" form, as expressed in his lecture on "Shakespeare, a Poet Generally":

The form is mechanic, when on any given material we impress a pre-determined form, not necessarily arising out of the properties of the material;—as when to a mass of wet clay we give whatever shape we wish it to retain when hardened. The organic form, on the other hand, is innate; it shapes, as it develops, itself from within, and the fullness of its development is one and the same with the perfection of its outward form. Such as the life is, such is the form. Nature, the prime genial artist, inexhaustible in diverse powers, is equally inexhaustible in forms;—each exterior is the physiognomy of the being within,—its true image reflected and thrown out from the concave mirror;—and even such is the appropriate excellence of her chosen poet. . . .[49]

It was on such a theory as this that Whitman's friend, Kennedy, defended the art of *Leaves of Grass* as conforming to the variety and multiplicity of Nature instead of the "base mechanical regularity" of conventional poetry. De Selincourt would agree with this general interpretation, but he also insists that: "The identity of the lines in metrical poetry is an identity of pattern. The identity of the lines in *Leaves of Grass* is an identity of substance."[50] To this statement Bradley objects:

For in the majority of the lines of Whitman, which are not brought into equivalence by repetition of substance and phrases, there is still the equivalence of a rhythm regulated by a periodicity of stress so uniformly measured as to constitute a true "meter." It is a device capable of infinite subtlety, and we must understand it fully in order to appreciate the extent of the poet's craftsmanship.[51]

One of the principal means by which Bradley establishes his "periodicity of stress" is in the use of "hovering accent" in his scansion: "It becomes apparent to the attentive reader of Whitman, especially when reading aloud, that in a great many cases the stress does not fall sharply on a single vowel, but is distributed along the word, or a pair of words, or even a short phrase."[444] As an example:

Which of the young men does she like the best?
Ah the homeliest of them is beautiful to her.

This is, of course, as Bradley himself would agree, a subjective interpretation, but it is undoubtedly a dramatic and effective reading of
the lines. As he himself says, without the glide or hovering accent,
the second line "becomes jocose instead of pathetic."[445]

As an extended example of both organic rhythm and a "unified
organic whole," Bradley scans the poem "Tears" in this manner:[449]

3   Tears! tears! tears!

3   In the night, in solitude, tears,

5   On the white shore dripping, dripping, suck'd in by the sand,

5   Tears, not a star shining, all dark and desolate,[52]

3   Moist tears from the eyes of a muffled head;

5   O who is that ghost? that form in the dark, with tears?

6   What shapeless lump is that, bent, crouch'd there on the sand?

5   Streaming tears, sobbing tears, throes, choked with wild cries;

6   O storm, embodied, rising, careering with swift steps and along
        the beach!

6   O wild and dismal night storm, with wind—O belching and
        desperate!

8   O shade so sedate and decorous by day, with calm countenance
        and regulated pace,

7   But away at night as you fly, none looking—O then the
        unloosen'd ocean,

3   Of tears! tears! tears!

Here Bradley makes a valuable contribution to the understanding and appreciation of Whitman's art by calling attention to the
symmetry of the form. His scansion divides the poem into three
free-verse stanzas, each with its own definite accentual pattern, and
the whole with a pyramidal structure which suggests "a large wave or
breaker with three crests."[449] And he cites several interesting
examples to demonstrate that such structure, especially the pyramidal form, is characteristic of Whitman's more successful versification.

Without in the least denying or detracting from the value of this interpretation, we should also observe, however, that even here Whitman uses repetitions as an integral part of his organic structure. The parallelism and phonic reiteration are less obvious than in "Song of Myself" and the earlier and longer poems, but they are present in this characteristic composition of the 1860s. The word *tears* is "psychic rime" and a kind of refrain, weaving in and out and influencing both the pathos and cadences. There is also a subtle repetition of thought throughout, with the epithets for tears, the references to the "ghost" and the "storm." Furthermore, the parallelism does not entirely divide according to Bradley's stanzaic scheme, but laps over from the second to the third divisions:

(a) O storm, embodied, rising, careering with swift steps along the beach!

(a) O wild and dismal night storm, with wind—O belching and desperate!

The thought structure of the whole is, of course, the envelope, which was mentioned in the section on "Parallelism."

But the fact that Whitman so successfully combines thought, rhetoric, syllabic accent, and stanzaic form in an "organic" whole is sufficient evidence of expert craftsmanship and his ability to adapt technique to his literary purposes. Bradley's reading of the lines with hovering stresses also indicates that Whitman had a keener ear for sound and cadence than has been commonly supposed. Sometimes, indeed, the "subtle patterns are embroidered upon each other in a manner comparable to that of great symphonic music. . . ."[455]

A careful study of Whitman's punctuation will also reveal that it was not erratic or eccentric, as many readers have thought, but that it was an accurate index to the organic rhythm, the musical effects which the poet hoped to have brought out in the reading. We have already noticed that the comma at the end of nearly every line except the last is an indication not of the usual sense-pause but of the end of a prosodic unit—usually ending in a *cadence* or falling of the voice. Perhaps it might be called a final caesura—a slight pause before the voice continues with the recitative. In the first edition Whitman frequently used semicolons at the end of lines which were grammatically complete (either complete predications or elliptical sentences), but later he adopted commas. Inside the line he was still forced to punctuate somewhat according to thought, but his internal commas and dashes are also often caesural pauses.

Whitman has a great variety of caesuras, and an exhaustive study of them would reveal much about his word-music that is still little known. Only a few examples can be given here. We might begin with one of the most rudimentary effects, which may be called a catalog-caesura:

The blab of the pave,/ tires of carts,/ sluff of boot-soles,/ talk of the
    promenaders,/
The heavy omnibus,/ the driver with his interrogating thumb,/ the
    clank of the shod horses on the granite floor,/ . . .[53]

Notice the cumulative effect of the cadences, aided by the slight caesural pauses:

The blab of the pave, tires of carts, sluff of boot-soles,

the omitted unaccented syllable before "tires" and "sluff" breaking the monotony of the pattern and emphasizing the beat, presently giving way to longer sweeps in the following line,

    . . . the driver with his interrogating thumb,
the clank of the shod horses on the granite floor . . . .

A similar caesura, but with many subtle variations:

I hear bravuras of birds,/ bustle of growing wheat,/ gossip of flames,/
    clack of sticks cooking my meals,//
I hear the sound I love,/ the sound of the human voice,//
I hear all sounds running together,/ combined, fused or following,/
Sounds of the city and sounds out of the city,/ sounds of the day
    and night, . . .[54]

Notice how much the shortening or lengthening of the pause can contribute to both the rhythm and the thought. The first line is cumulative in effect, the second balanced, the third suggestive or illustrative, the fourth is emphatic.

Sometimes the caesura divides the parallelism and is equivalent to the line-end pause:

There is that in me—/ /I do not know what it is—but I know it is in
    me.

Wrench'd and sweaty—/ calm and cool/ then my body becomes,/
I sleep—// I sleep long.//

I do not know it—// it is without name—// it is a word unsaid,//
It is not in any dictionary,/ utterance,/ symbol.[55]

Another caesural effect Jannaccone calls "thesis" and "arsis"[56]
because the second half line echoes the thought of the first and
receives a weaker stress and perhaps a lower pitch:

Great are the myths—// I too delight in them,
Great are Adam and Eve—// I too look back and accept them. . .   [57]

This is of course also another example of Whitman's parallelism, and
another indication of why he used parallelism so extensively. The
employment of connectives or subordination would destroy the ring
of inspired authority which he wished to give to his prophetic
utterances.

Whitman's use of the parenthesis in this verse structure throws
further light on his organic rhythms. Although the parenthesis in
Leaves of Grass has been frequently regarded as merely a manerism
without special significance so far as the versification is concerned,
two critics have advanced interesting explanations. De Selincourt
says:

The use of parenthesis is a recurring feature of Whitman's technique,
and no explanation of his form can be adequate which does not
relate this peculiarity to the constructive principles of the whole. He
frequently begins a paragraph or ends one with a bracketed sentence
. . . sometimes even begins or ends a poem parenthetically . . . This
persistent bracketing falls well into the scheme we have laid down of
independent units that serve an accumulating effect. The bracket,
one need not remark, secures a peculiar detachment for its contents;
it also, by placing them outside the current and main flow of the
sense, relates them to it in a peculiar way. And although for the time
being the flow is broken, it by no means follows . . . that our sense of
the flow is broken; on the contrary, it is probably enhanced. We look
down upon the stream from a point of vantage and gauge its speed
and direction. More precisely, the bracket opening a poem or paragraph gives us, of course, the idea which that whole poem or paragraph presupposes, while the closing bracket gives the idea by which

what precedes is to be qualified and tempered. We have thus as it
were a poem within a poem; or sometimes, when a series of brackets
is used, we have a double stream of poetry, as in "By Blue Ontario's
Shore"....[58]

Catel argues, as one proof of his thesis that Whitman's art is that
of the orator, that the parentheses indicate a change of voice or
gesture. Sometimes, he points out, the parenthetical matter is "un
aveu murmuré, comme un aparté, un à-côté personnel,"[59] as in:

The young fellow drives the express-wagon, (I love him, though I do
　　not know him;) . . . .
The canal boy trots . . . .
The conductor beats time . . . .
The child is baptized . . . .
The regatta is spread . . . . (how the white sails sparkle!)[60]

Often, as Catel says, the parenthesis is not necessary for the
thought, and unless it indicates a change in tone, pitch, or emphasis
there is no explanation for its use.

I do not trouble my spirit to vindicate itself or be understood,
I see that the elementary laws never apologize,
(I reckon I behave no prouder than the level I plant my house by,
　　after all.)[61]

Or in the following:

All truths wait in all things,
They neither hasten their own delivery nor resist it, ...
The insignificant is as big to me as any,
(What is less or more than a touch?)[62]
I hear all sounds running together . . . .
The steam-whistle . . . .
The slow march play'd at the head of the association marching two
　　and two,
(They go to guard some corpse, the flag-tops are draped with black
　　muslin.)[63]

As both a summary and supplement to these interpretations, we
can say that almost invariably Whitman's parentheses indicate a
break or change in the organic rhythm. Often, as in the first example

above, the general rhythmical pattern for the passage seems to be suspended momentarily by the bracketed comment: "The young fellow drives .... (I love him though I do not know him) .... The canal boy trots .... The conductor beats time .... The child is baptized .... The regatta is spread .... (how the white sails sparkle!)," etc.

But in some passages Catel's theory of a change of voice or gesture applies only as a thin analogy. In the following example the bracketed passage seems fully as emphatic as the preceding and succeeding lines, although it does not have quite the same cadence as the "to the" reiterations and also presents a specific image in a passage of panoramic and symbolical details:

To the leaven'd soil they trod calling I sing for the last,
(Forth from my tent emerging for good, loosing, untying the tent-
     ropes,)
In the freshness the forenoon air, in the far-stretching circuits and
     vistas again to peace restored,
In the fiery fields emanative and the endless vistas beyond, to the
     South and the North,
To the leaven'd soil of the general Western world to attest my songs,
To the Alleghanian hills and the tireless Mississippi, . . .
To the plains . . .

Such uses of the parenthesis add further proof that Whitman's rhythm is in actuality as well as in theory formed from within, and also controlled and shaped to harmonize with both his thought and emotion. The very fact that so many analogies occur to the critics is evidence both of an "organic form" and at the same time of Whitman's success in subordinating his technique to his "purports and facts." Thus De Selincourt thinks of the punctuation as indicating the ebb and flow of musical composition and Catel as stage directions for an orator. In attempting to explain Whitman's form, Matthiessen uses three analogies—oratory, opera, and the ocean.[65] No poet ever tried more conscientiously to wed sound and sense. As Matthiessen says:

When he spoke of his "liquid-flowing syllables," he was hoping for the same effect in his work as when he jotted down as the possible genesis for a poem: "Sound of walking barefoot ankle deep in the edge of the water by the sea." He tried again and again to describe what he wanted from this primal force, and put it most briefly when he said that if he had the choice of equalling the greatest poets in theme or in metre or in perfect rhyme,

> These, these, O sea, all these I'd gladly barter,
> Would you the undulation of one wave, its trick to me
>   transfer,
> Or breathe one breath of yours upon my verse,
> And leave its odor there.[66]

This ambition, however, should not lead the reader to expect pronounced onomatopoeia in Whitman's verse. Not even in "When Lilacs Last in the Dooryard Bloom'd" does the vicarious bird-singing sound convincingly like the notes of the "gray-brown bird." What the poet does is to convey the spirit, the lyric feeling, of the time and place of his allegory. What he makes is music of the soul, not a literal mimicry of lapping waves or bird-chirping.

> The song, the wondrous chant of the gray-brown bird,
> And the tallying chant, the echo arous'd in my soul,
>
>   .   .   .   .   .
>
> For the sweetest, wisest soul of all my days and lands—and this for
>   his dear sake,
> Lilac and star and bird twined with the chant of my soul,
> There in the fragrant pines and the cedars dusk and dim.

Here the esthetic problem is quite similar to that of "program" vs. abstract music—except for the fact that music depends entirely upon sound, whereas in poetry the words convey ideas and images in addition to rhythms and tones. Many imaginative listeners think they hear in the marvelous symphonies of Sibelius the pine-tree whisperings of Finlandia, but it is doubtful that Sibelius has attempted any literal imitation of these sounds. And seldom is there any indication that Whitman's object is the phonographic reproduction of rustling or splashing water. What he wants in his verse is the "breath" and the "odor" of the sea (abstractions), and "the echo arous'd in my soul." Freneau might capture the rhythms of the "katy-did" or Emerson of the "humble-bee," but Walt Whitman's "organic" rhythms are those of the spirit of Nature "twined with the chant of my soul." This is why he anticipated Expressionism in modern art and was adopted by the French Symbolists as one of their own, though he was neither Expressionist nor Symbolist, but Walt Whitman, poet of a "spiritual democracy."

CONVENTIONAL TECHNIQUES IN *LEAVES OF GRASS*

Although Whitman's "organic" theory of poetic style is commonly assumed to be completely antithetical to conventional techniques, there is no logical reason why the poet might not occasionally have an experience or an emotion which would find natural expression in rime and meter. According to the organic principle, the form must be shaped from within, not from external conventions. But who can say that the inner experience can never find a conventional outlet? At any rate, it is true, as Miss Ware has said, that Whitman "exemplified at some point or other virtually all of the conventions that he professed to eschew, and that he employed some of these conventions on a large scale."[67]

The most obvious conventions against which Whitman was supposedly revolting were rime and meter. Yet we find him using rime in several of his mature poems, all written after the adoption of his "organic" style. The earliest of these is in the first section (or strophe) of "Song of the Broad Axe," which was apparently written in 1856. The rhythm is "organic" in the sense that it varies from line to line, and the lines themselves are often of different lengths, but the accents are surprisingly metrical and the final syllables are so nearly rimed that the pattern is trochaic tetrameter couplets:[68]

Weapon shapely, naked, wan,
Head from the mother's bowels drawn,
Wooded flesh and metal bone, limb only one and lip only one,
Gray-blue leaf by red-heat grown, helve produced from a little seed
    sown,
Resting the grass amid and upon,
To be lean'd and to lean on.

Curiously enough, this effective trochaic movement survives from an early manuscript, in which the poet was apparently trying to imitate the sound of rain drops:

The irregular tapping of rain off my house-eaves at night after the
    storm has lulled, [probably the subject, not a line for a poem],

> Gray-blue sprout so hardened grown
> Head from the mother's bowels drawn
> Body shapely naked and wan
> Fibre produced from a little seed sown.[69]

In this case it would seem, then, that the rhythm was salvaged from a manuscript poem having nothing to do with the subject-matter of the "Broad-Axe"; it did not grow from within but was adapted—not however, inappropriately.

The first section of "By Blue Ontario's Shore" also rimes in almost the same manner, being *aabbcb*. The main part of this poem was also published in 1856, but the version including these rimes was not added until 1867. The conventionality of "O Captain! My Captain!," 1865, has probably been observed by all students of Whitman. The stanza is composed of four long lines and four short ones, the latter being used as a refrain. The meter is iambic and the stanzaic pattern is approximately as follows: $a_5 a_7 b_7 b_7 c_3 d_8 e_4 d_3$. But one of the most conventional of all poems in *Leaves of Grass* is the prisoner's song in "The Singer in Prison," 1869. The first stanza is almost completely regular:

> A soul confined by bars and bands,
> Cries, help! O help! and wrings her hands,
> Blinded her eyes, bleeding her breast,
> Nor pardon finds, nor balm of rest, . . .

Still another poem with a definite rime-scheme is "Ethiopia Saluting the Colors," 1871. The scheme is approximately $(a)a_6 bb_7$ (the first being an internal rime).

In addition to the above poems in more or less conventional stanzas, Whitman also used stanza forms in the following poems: "A Noiseless Patient Spider," 1862–63, a five-line stanza in irregular meter but recognizably metrical; "For You O Democracy," 1860, in a five-line and four-line stanza with a refrain, ending with a free-verse couplet (of parallelism); "Pioneers! O Pioneers!," 1865, in four-line trochaic stanzas, the first line being mainly three-stress and the fourth line being the refrain of the title; "Dirge for Two Veterans," 1865–66, in four-line stanzas, the scheme being mainly *3-4-3-6*; "Old War Dreams," 1865–56, in a four-line stanza, the fourth being a refrain; "Gods," 1870, in short unrimed strophes (mainly triplets) with refrain; "In Cabin'd Ships at Sea," 1871, in iambic eight-line stanzas, each first and last line being shorter than the others; and "Eidólons," 1876, in four-line stanzas, the first and fourth lines being dimeters and trimeters and the second and third being longer, of indefinite length.

Nearly half of these poems are, as indicated, in conventional meters. Especially interesting is the anapestic-iambic "Beat! Beat! Drums!"

Beat! beat! drums—blow! bugles! blow!

Over the traffic of cities—over the rumble of wheels in the streets;

Are beds prepared for sleepers at night in the houses? no sleepers

    must sleep in those beds,

No bargainers' bargains by day—no brokers or speculators—would

    they continue?

One of the most metrical poems in *Leaves of Grass* is the trochaic "Pioneers! O Pioneers!," 1865. The number of stresses in the second and third lines varies from seven to ten, and occasionally an iamb is substituted for a trochee, but the pattern is almost as regular as in conventional verse.

    For we cannot tarry here,

We must march my darlings, we must bear the brunt of danger,

We the youthful sinewy races, all the rest on us depend,

    Pioneers! O Pioneers!

Most of Whitman's poems contain occasional lines that scan easily as iamblic, trochaic, anapestic, or—very rarely—dactyllic. The poems mentioned above are nearly all that adhere closely to a definite conventional metrical pattern—though most of the *Leaves* can be scanned by Bradley's method.

But it will be observed that most of these examples were first published in the 1860s. Both *Drum-Taps* and *Sequel to Drum-Taps* are a great deal more conventional in form and style than earlier poems in the *Leaves*. Apparently the poet found more conventional metrics either convenient or necessary for the expression of his experiences and emotions connected with the war. Even "Pioneers! O

Pioneers!" is a marching poem. But what is more natural than that the poet's heartbeat would throb to the rhythms of marching feet—especially a poet who aspired to give organic expression to his own age and country?

Throughout most of his poems, of all periods, Whitman made extensive use of other conventional devices, such as alliteration, both vowel and consonantal, and assonance, but these are rather embellishments (perhaps often unconscious) than fundamental techniques. They are interesting in view of Whitman's determination in the 1855 Preface not to use any ornamentation in his verse, but they have so long been taken for granted in English poetry that they can hardly be called a contradiction of the poet's doctrines. In a poem like "Tears" they are almost inevitable, and it is not surprising to find them in the more onomatopoetic description of seashore experiences and memories. Although Miss Ware probably attaches too much importance to these particular conventions, her conclusion is no doubt sound:

A comparison of the results found by a study of *Leaves of Grass* and the *Uncollected Poetry and Prose of Walt Whitman* would seem to indicate that when Whitman discarded the more obvious poetic devices—like regular stanza forms, meter, and rhyme,—he unconsciously adopted the less obvious conventions, such as alliteration, assonance, repetition, refrain, parallelism, and end-stopped lines.[70]

Whether these survive in Whitman's versification unconsciously or not, it is difficult to say, but it is quite certain that he could not very well write intelligible poetry without retaining some conventions—and adapting or creating some basic prosodic techniques not altogether "transcendent and new." But they were sufficiently new to puzzle his own generation, and as the many critics have demonstrated, need to be explained and interpreted even today.

THE ORGANIC THEORY OF WORDS

Since the publication of the first edition of *Leaves of Grass*, critics have been interested in Whitman's bold use of words and have tried to discover the secret of his large but indiscriminate vocabulary. Wordsworth's poetic reform, as set forth in the Preface to *Lyrical Ballads*, was mainly concerned with diction, with the rejection of artificial "poetic diction" of neo-classicism and the adoption of living speech of ordinary people (though pruned of the grossest crudities).

Many critics have assumed that Whitman was completing the reform begun by Wordsworth. Catel says, "Whitman a retrouvé, par un instinct très sûr de poète, la source vive du langage qui est le style oral, ce qu'il a appelé lui-même 'a vocal style.' "[71]

Whitman himself anticipated modern linguistic theory by declaring in his *American Primer* that "Pronunciation is the stamina of language,—it is language,"[72] and there is no doubt that he tried to make extensive use of the vernacular in his poems. Perhaps it would not have been inconsistent with his other literary theories for him to have cultivated almost exclusively a vernacular vocabulary. But it is a notorious fact that he did not do so. True, he greets the earth as "top-knot"[73] and he likes to close his poems with a "so long"[74] to the reader, but he practically ransacks the dictionaries for literary words like "chyle," "recusant," and "circumambient."[75] And he is almost childishly fond of foreign words, especially French[76] and Spanish ones, which he sometimes uses with a reckless disregard for correct spelling or meaning.[77] English biographers and critics, especially,[78] still cringe at the democratic "mélange" which often resulted from Whitman's indiscriminate mixture of all levels of linguistic usage. No one with literary taste can deny that this self-styled poet of democracy often brewed a linguistic concoction as strange as the barbaric rituals of Melville's Quequeg. Possibly, too, many of his philological indiscretions were due to ignorance or primitive delight in verbal displays; but his theory of language was more fully developed than some critics have realized, and it harmonizes surprisingly well with his "organic" conception of poetic form.

And nowhere do we find evidence of Whitman's indebtedness to Emerson and Transcendentalism more than in his theory of words. In "The Poet" Emerson says that,

Things admit of being used as symbols, because nature is a symbol, in the whole, and in every part. Every line we can draw in the sand, has expression; and there is no body without its spirit or genius. All form is an effect of character; all condition, of the quality of the life; all harmony, of health; (and, for this reason, a perception of beauty should be sympathetic, or proper only to the good).

From this Swedenborgian point of view, "the world is a temple, whose walls are covered with emblems, pictures and commandments of the Deity," and it is also interesting to see that here, as in Whitman's cosmic equalitarianism, "the distinctions which we make in events, and in affairs, of low and high, honest and base, disappear when nature is used as a symbol."

The poet is the man, above all others, who has the power to use symbols, and thus to indicate men's relationships to nature, God, and the universe they inhabit. "We are symbols and inhabit symbols; workmen, work, and tools, words and things, birth and death, all are emblems. . . ." But the poet gives to words and things "a power which makes their old use forgotten, and put eyes, and a tongue, into every dumb and inanimate object." Thus to Emerson, words are symbols of symbols. Above all they are images with spiritual significance. Even more to him than to the philologist, "Every word was once a poem," and language itself "is fossil poetry."

On the basis of this theory Emerson declares that:

The vocabulary of an omniscient man would embrace words and images excluded from polite conversation. What would be base, or even obscene, to the obscene, becomes illustrious, spoken in a new connection of thought. The piety of the Hebrew prophets purges their grossness. The circumcision is an example of the power of poetry to raise the low and offensive. Small and mean things serve as well as great symbols. The meaner the type by which a law is expressed, the more pungent it is, and the more lasting in the memories of men . . . Bare lists of words are found suggestive to an imaginative and excited mind . . .

There we have Whitman's complete theory and attitude toward words. He added little if anything to it, but it was he, not Emerson, who made the broadest application of the theory. Here we find the foundation of Whitman's doctrine in the 1855 Preface that words reveal the character and the inner harmony of the speaker, and that "All beauty comes from beautiful blood and a beautiful brain. If the greatnesses are in conjunction in a man or woman it is enough."[79] Or as he later expressed it in *An American Primer*, "Words follow character."[80] And thus in his great faith in the future of the Democratic Republic he envisions a nation of people who will be "the most fluent and melodious voiced people in the world . . . the most perfect users of words." Some critics have thought Whitman an atavistic savage who believed in the magic of words. Actually, however, he worships neither words nor images, but the mystic powers and relationships which they feebly signify. If the meaning is not in the user of words, it cannot be in the verbal symbols which he employs. As Matthiessen comments, "Whitman's excitement [in naming things] carries weight because he realized that a man cannot use words so [as Whitman did] unless he has experienced the facts that they express, unless he has grasped them with his senses."[81]

Whitman's propensity for inventorying the universe is, therefore, evidence of his desire to know life—*being*—in all its details, the small and the mean as well as the great and the good. Locked in the words is the vicarious experience of the poet, to whom even bare lists are suggestive and exciting.

A perfect writer would make words sing, dance, kiss, do the male and female act, bear children, weep, bleed, rage, stab, steal, fire cannon, steer ships, sack cities, charge with cavalry or infantry, or do anything, that man or woman or the natural powers can do.

Latent, in a great user of words, must actually be all passions, crimes, trades, animals, stars, God, sex, the past, might, space, metals, and the like—because these are the words, and he who is not these, plays with a foreign tongue, turning helplessly to dictionaries and authorities.—How can I tell you?—I put many things on record that you will not understand at first—perhaps not in a year—but they must be (are to be) understood.—The earth, I see, writes with prodigal clear hands all summer, forever, and all winter also, content, and certain to be understood in time—as, doubtless, only the greatest user of words himself fully enjoys and understands himself.[82]

Although Whitman's poetic form and technique throughout *Leaves of Grass* exemplify both his theory and attitude toward words, he treated the problem specifically in the 1856 "Poem of the Sayers of the Words of the Earth."[83]

Earth, round, rolling, compact—suns, moons, animals—all these are words,
Watery, vegetable, sauroid advances—beings, premonitions, lispings of the future, these are vast words.

Were you thinking that those were the words—those upright lines? those curves, angles, dots?
No, those are not the words—the substantial words are in the ground and sea,
They are in the air—they are in you.[84]

Though this doctrine is mystical and transcendental, it is also *semantic*. What Whitman is trying to get at is "meaning," and meaning, he says, is in cosmic processes (evolution: "sauroid advances" and "lispings of the future"), in things, and "in you." Language is conduct and words are merely gestures:

> A healthy presence, a friendly or commanding gesture, are words,
>   sayings, meanings,
> The charms that go with the mere looks of some men and women are
>   sayings and meanings also.[85]

But though the meaning of words is subjective, it must tally with objective fact. Whitman anticipated modern semantic doctrine in his insistence on this harmony between the inner and outer meaning:

> I swear the earth shall surely be complete to him or her who shall be
>   complete!
> I swear the earth remains broken and jagged only to him or her who
>   remains broken and jagged!
>
> I swear there is no greatness or power that does not emulate those of
>   the earth!
> I swear there can be no theory of any account, unless it corroborate
>   the theory of the earth![86]

Far from worshipping words or mistaking them for reality, Whitman sees their inadequacy and searches for the meaning behind words:

> I swear I begin to see little or nothing in audible words!
> I swear I think all merges toward the presentation of the unspoken
>   meanings of the earth!
> Toward him who sings the songs of the body, and of the truths of
>   the earth,
> Toward him who makes the dictionaries of the words that print
>   cannot touch.

As a poet Whitman must make carols of words, but he knows that these are only "hints of meanings" which "echo the tones of Souls, and the phrases of Souls." This attitude toward words and the form of his poems he never renounced, but continued to regard his poems as mere hints and "indirections," and, as Hermann Bahr says, to present and arrange the materials of poems instead of finished products.[87] In 1855 he liked to think of the poet (or himself as a poet) as a "kosmos,"[88] or a kind of microcosm symbolizing the macrocosm. But it is just as accurate to say that he thought of a poem itself as a mirror-like monad (to use Leibniz's term) which reflected in itself the form, structure, and spiritual laws of the universe.

In a manuscript dating from around 1850 Holloway has discovered[89] a great deal about the nature of Whitman's inspiration and the manner in which he composed his poetry. The poem, only a fragment of which was included in *Leaves of Grass*, was called "Pictures." Bucke printed four lines in *Notes and Fragments*:

O Walt Whitman, show us some pictures;
America always Pictorial! And you Walt Whitman to name them
Yes, in a little house I keep suspended many pictures—it is not a
    fixed house.
It is round—Behold! it has room for America, north and south,
    seaboard and inland, persons . . .[90]

This crude picture-gallery allegory was not published as a single poem because the various images and catalogs which it contained were expanded into a number of separate poems—in fact, might be thought of as the genesis of the first editions of *Leaves of Grass*. In an outline for the original "Pictures," we glimpse the poet's method:

Poem of Pictures. Each verse presenting a picture of some characteristic scene, event, group or personage—old or new, other countries or our own country. Picture of one of the Greek games—wrestling, or the chariot race, or running. Spanish bull fight.[91]

Of the finished "Pictures" Holloway says:

Each is a microcosm of the whole "Leaves of Grass," which the author looked upon less as a book than as a picture of himself in all his cosmopolitan diversity. And the more we learn of the facts of Whitman's comprehensive life, whether experience, reading, or meditation, the more we realize that before each thumb-nail picture was set down on paper it had really been hung, as a personal possession, on the walls of his "Picture-Gallery."[92]

Thus in his desire to explore life, personality, and the inner meaning of Being, Whitman turned to Emerson's theory of symbols for guidance in the development of a literary technique. By imaginative identification of his own ego with the creative processes of nature, and by the vicarious exploration of all forms of existence, he evolved the technique of panoramic imagery, "organically" echoing a subjective harmony and rhythm of his own "Soul," and revealing by "hints" and "indirections" the spiritual truths of the universe. Both in form and content *Leaves of Grass* is primarily cosmic, animistic, and democratic, and Walt Whitman's literary technique is admirably adapted for his "purports and facts and is the analogy of them."

Chapter V

Walt Whitman and World Literature

My spirit has pass'd in compassion and determination around the whole earth,
I have look'd for equals and lovers and found them ready for me in all lands . . .
                                                                —"Salut au Monde!"

WORLD POET

Walt Whitman was the first American poet to gain world recognition, and he is still one of the best-known of American authors in nearly every country of the globe, with complete translations of his *Leaves of Grass* in France, Germany, Spain (and Latin America), Italy, Greece, and Japan, and selections of his poems in nearly all other languages, but especially in the Soviet Union, where editions of his writings sell far better than they do in the United States. Professor Harold Blodgett, who has taught in Holland, India, and Iran, says "one cannot travel anywhere in the world without coming upon distinguished and sensitive people to whom Whitman is the greatest American poet."[1]

In the Preface to his first edition of *Leaves of Grass* Whitman declared that the "bard" of the United States should be "commensurate" with his nation, his spirit responding to "his country's spirit," and that he should incarnate "its geography and natural life."[2] Such a poet would be nationalistic in every sense of the term, and Whitman left no doubt that this was his ambition. In fact, he ended his 1855 Preface with the confident assertion that, "The proof of a poet is that his country absorbs him as affectionately as he has absorbed it."[3] But he failed by his own test. His country did not "absorb" him during his lifetime—not to any great extent, in fact, until about 1955,[4] when his country celebrated the first centennial

of the 1855 edition, as did admirers in Moscow, Tokyo, New Delhi, and elsewhere.

In his old-age preface to *November Boughs* ("A Backward Glance O'er Travel'd Roads") Whitman admitted candidly, "I have not gain'd the acceptance of my own time, but have fallen back on fond dreams of the future."[5] Because of this realization the aged poet was pathetically grateful to the British authors, under the leadership of William Rossetti and Mrs. Alexander Gilchrist, who came to his financial rescue in 1876 during a period of illness and extreme discouragement.[6]

Discussions of Whitman in Great Britain actually resulted in his first extensive literary reputation, with helpful "feedback" results in the United States. It was about this time also that he began to receive encouragement from several foreign countries. While in exile in Great Britain, Ferdinand Freiligrath became acquainted with Whitman's poems, and after his return to Germany he published an appreciative newspaper article in 1868.[7] Four years later Rudolf Schmidt in Denmark began writing articles on Whitman, which he mailed to the ailing poet in Camden, N. J. In 1876 he published a Danish translation of *Democratic Vistas*.[8]

This did not mean that Whitman had fulfilled his "Salut au Monde!" prophecy (see epigraph at the head of this chapter), but he began to have hopes, especially in 1881 when an Irishman, Dr. John Fitzgerald Lee, wrote him from Dresden asking for permission to do a translation of *Leaves of Grass* into Russian.[9] What qualification Dr. Lee had for this difficult undertaking is not known, but Whitman assumed that he was Russian (the name should have told him that the man was Irish), and he replied enthusiastically with his blessing and greetings to the Russian people. In this letter Whitman confessed:

As my dearest dream is for an internationality of poems and poets binding the lands of the earth closer than all treaties and diplomacy—as the purpose beneath the rest in my book is such hearty comradeship, for individuals to begin with, and for all the Nations of the earth as a result—how happy I should be to get the hearing and emotional contact of the great Russian peoples.[10]

Dr. Lee had become acquainted with Whitman's poems through his Dublin friend Thomas W. Rolleston, who also wanted to make a translation of selected poems into German. On April 5, 1884, Rolleston wrote Whitman that his translation was nearly finished, and received this reply:

...I had more than my own native land in view when I was composing Leaves of Grass. I wished to take the first step toward calling into existence a cycle of international poems. The chief reason for being of the United States of America is to bring about the common good will of all mankind, the solidarity of the world. What is still lacking in this respect can perhaps be accomplished by the art of poetry, through songs radiating from all the lands of the globe. I had also in mind, as one of my objects, to send a hearty greeting to these lands in America's name. And glad, very glad, should I be to gain entrance and audience among the Germanic people.[11]

Just when in composing Leaves of Grass Whitman began to have more than his own land in view is not easily determined, but by the 1870s the words and acts of friends abroad did make him feel that his 1856 prophecy that he would find "equals and lovers . . . in all lands" was coming true.

Today the abundance of foreign criticism of Whitman, the number of translations of his poetry and prose, and his influence on poets in other lands make his importance in world literature so vast a subject that only the highlights can be presented in a single chapter. It is a field for a richly-detailed book, or several books. The chapter on "Walt Whitman and World Literature" in the 1946 edition of this *Handbook* was the first systematic attempt to cover the subject. W. S. Kennedy's *Fight of a Book for the World* (1926)[12] contained a good deal of scattered information, but it was so poorly organized and amateurishly presented that it did not give a coherent account. Frederik Schyberg's *Walt Whitman* (1933) had a highly valuable chapter on "Whitman in World Literature,"[13] but he was particularly interested in "those he resembled and those who resembled him"—a comparative literature approach. Much valuable information was obtained from Schyberg for the chapter in the *Walt Whitman Handbook*. In fact, it was through Schyberg's influence that the chapter was undertaken at all. Praise of his work led to the translation and publication of his book in this country,[14] where it is still admired and used.

In 1955 *Walt Whitman Abroad*[15] made available in English some of the best critical essays on Whitman in nine languages. This anthology also contained surveys (introductions to the selections) by competent scholars of Whitman's reputation and influence in Germany, France, Denmark, Norway, Sweden, Russia, Italy, Spain and Latin America, Israel, and India, with some inadequate notes on Japan, for Whitman had had a far greater reception in Japan than the editor knew at the time. These introductory essays still remain the fullest survey of Whitman in the countries covered, but they need to be updated, for in every major country there has been great activity during the past twenty years in translating and interpreting Whitman.

In 1954 Fernando Alegría published a model study in his *Walt Whitman en Hispanoamerica*,[16] but this, too, needs updating. Charles Grippi's exhaustive dissertation, *The Literary Reputation of Walt Whitman in Italy* (1971) remains unpublished—though available on microfilm. Obviously much remains to be done, and it is hoped that this revised—but necessarily inadequate—survey of "Walt Whitman and World Literature" will serve as a guide to what has been done and indicate where more scholarly work still needs to be done.

AMERICAN TRANSCENDENTALISM

One reason both for the many striking parallels to Whitman's thought and expression in World Literature and for his dynamic influence on later writers is that his own major literary sources were international in origin. The first and most important of these was ostensibly American, being the "transcendentalism" of Emerson, Thoreau, Alcott, Margaret Fuller, Channing, Hedge, etc., that group of congenial minds which came together informally in the 1830s and 40s and generated not a school but a fermentation of ideas and attitudes which became the major stimulation of literary activity in the United States during the "American Renaissance."[17] This group followed no single master, creed, or even philosophy, but all members were profoundly interested in speculative thinking and in the great minds of the past. Most of them read and translated writings from Plato to Goethe and George Sand. They were especially interested in German Idealism, which came to them directly from the study and discussion of the Kantian school and indirectly through Coleridge and Carlyle, who were also reading and interpreting the poetry and philosophy of the German Romantic School.

To complete the international cycle, the Germans were, in turn, influenced by the mysticism both of Neo-Platonism and of the Orient. In fact, many of the leaders of the Romantic School in

Germany, like the Schlegels, were philologists and Orientalists. The American Transcendentalists, however, became sufficiently interested in the literature and religion of Asia, especially of the Hindus, to make some explorations of their own. Sanskrit was taught at Harvard, and India was frequently discussed in newspapers and popular magazines—to judge by the large number of clippings which Whitman amassed in his own scrapbooks.[18] American Transcendentalism was not a creed, a "school," or a systematic philosophy, but its basic assumptions came simultaneously from East and West, modified, of course, by American experience and Yankee character.[19]

One of the first Transcendentalist assumptions was the Rousseauistic belief in the innate goodness of human nature. The Emersonian absolute moral and intellectual self-reliance might also be regarded as the ultimate in Protestantism, the last phase of the Reformation, and a reaction against Calvinism. The greatest single philosophical influence on this group of American thinkers was probably the "transcendentalism" of Immanuel Kant, or at least the interpretations which they (partly following Coleridge and Carlyle) made of the *Critique of Pure Reason* (1781). In this work Kant, attempting to establish the limits of human reason, concluded that the finite mind could deal reliably only with phenomena. He did not deny the possible reality or existence of *something* behind appearances or phenomena, but insisted that it was unknowable. Kant admitted, however, the human need for belief in such supra-rational ideas as God, Immortality, Freedom, etc., and the result was that, especially in Great Britain and the United States, speculative minds were stimulated to explore the realm of the unknowable, the hypothetical "world-beyond-phenomena." W. F. Taylor has summarized the result in this manner:

The transcendentalists, then, were mystics. They hoped to "transcend" the realm of phenomena, and receive their inspirations toward truth at first hand from the Deity, unsullied by any contact with matter. Spiritual verities alone were of great importance to the transcendentalists; and, like the "divine and supernatural light" of Jonathan Edwards, these were immediately imparted to the soul from God. Yet God, the Over-Soul, was revealed also in nature, which was a beautiful web of appearances veiling the spirituality of the universe, a living garment, half concealing, half revealing, the Deity within.[20]

Some of the close parallels between Whitman's thought and the ideas of the Transcendentalists may be due to the fact that he also wrote as a mystic; but it would have been impossible for him to escape some direct influence from such members of the group as Channing, Hedge, Parker, Margaret Fuller, Thoreau, and Emerson, who wrote for the very magazines and newspapers which Whitman read and to which he also contributed during the 1840s. In fact, nearly all scholars now agree that Emerson himself was the one single greatest influence on Whitman during the years when he was planning and writing the first two or three editions of *Leaves of Grass*. Arvin was probably right when he declared that Emerson was for Whitman what Epicurus was for Lucretius or Spinoza for Goethe.[21] Another critic, who made a special investigation of the relationship, decided that, "Whitman was more indebted to Emerson than to any other for fundamental ideas in even his earliest *Leaves of Grass*."[22] Despite the fact that "on certain occasions [he] endeavored to minimize his debt to Emerson ... Whitman ultimately arrived at an open, almost undeviating, allegiance both to Emerson as a person and to Emersonian ideas in general."[23]

A later critic, however, has pointed out what he regards as a significant difference between the thought of Emerson and Whitman. This difference, as presented by Leon Howard,[24] is parallel to the contrast which we have already mentioned between true Kantian transcendentalism and Coleridge and Carlyle's interpretation of Kant. It is the old question of the *reality* of phenomena, "appearances," matter, etc. Howard regards transcendentalism as monist, the true *reality* being spirit or Soul: "Running through Whitman's poetry is the constantly iterated idea of equalitarianism, one aspect of which is the avowal of equality between body and soul."[25] From this point of view the famous argument which Emerson gave Whitman on the Boston Common against the inclusion of the sex poems in the third edition was a struggle "between militant materialism combined with idealism and idealism in its transcendental purity."[26] However, it is still a moot question whether Emerson was a monist, a pure idealist, or a dualist. The humanistic critics argue that Emerson placed neither mind nor matter over the other. This argument merely indicates the close parallels between Emerson and Whitman's mystical pantheism. As F. I. Carpenter says, Emerson always "expressed his mystical belief in 'the eternal ONE.' By religion, rather than by philosophy, he was a monist, as 'The Over-Soul' and 'Brahma' bear witness."[27]

We see these tendencies further in two more of Emerson's theories which are also parallel to Whitman's ideas. One is the Plotinian theory of *emanation*, and the other is cosmic evolution:

Emanation may be described as an idealistic monism; evolution as a materialistic monism. The first readily adapted itself to the theory (then merely a suggestion, but now well established), of the identity of energy and matter—energy continually "emanating" from God, and condensing itself, as it were, in the forms of the material world. The second, describing the gradual evolution of life from inanimate to animate matter, and from lower to higher forms until it issues at last in the intelligence of man, also seemed to furnish such a satisfactory monistic theory, and recommended itself especially to Emerson as confirming his idea of progress, or melioration.[28]

WHITMAN, CARLYLE, AND GERMAN IDEALISM

In the case of Carlyle, however, it is easier to differentiate. Whitman's interest in Carlyle was perhaps second only to his interest in Emerson, but he usually found himself combatting Carlyle's ideas, though he finally came around to a grudging admiration of the dour Scotsman who was so critical of American democracy. In fact, almost all Whitman knew about German philosophy he got either from American popularizations or from Carlyle. Thus Carlyle was one of Whitman's main sources. But the following differences should be clearly borne in mind: (1) For Whitman *things* are real (even though they may be symbolized by pantheistic metaphors); for Carlyle nature is illusory and dream-like. (2) To Whitman, the poet of democracy, every man is a hero; whereas to Carlyle the average are merely "hodmen," whom the "heroes" have the divine right to rule. (3) Though Whitman believes that all symbols are in a sense religious, he does not, like Carlyle, think that the highest symbol is the Church. (4) There is in Whitman, unlike Carlyle, no renunciation, no hatred of evil, no need for expiation for sins.[29]

Yet despite these contrasts, Whitman undoubtedly owed a great debt to Carlyle—especially, as remarked above, for arousing his curiosity in German philosophy. It is difficult to assess this debt, for Carlyle was only one of Whitman's sources of information about German Idealism, others being Gostwick's popular handbook, *German Literature*, Hedge's *Prose Writers of Germany*, and of course Emerson. But Whitman's manuscript notes on Kant, Fichte, Schlegel,

Hegel, etc., show considerable knowledge of Carlyle's discussion of these men.[30]

John Burroughs declared (undoubtedly with Whitman's approval) that *Leaves of Grass* "tallies ... the development of the Great System of Idealistic Philosophy in Germany,"[31] and in 1884 Whitman called himself "the greatest *poetical* representative of German philosophy."[32] Although these pretentious claims may amuse the scholars, there is no reason to doubt the poet's sincerity, and there is even some truth in the claim. Arvin remarks that,

At some indeterminate period—though the chances are that it was after two editions of *Leaves of Grass* had appeared and perhaps mainly during the sixties—Whitman began looking more closely and more curiously into the significance of certain stupendous names that had recurred invitingly in so much that he had heard and read, in Coleridge, in Carlyle, in Emerson too; and these were the names of the great German metaphysicians of idealism, Leibniz, Kant, Fichte, Schelling, Hegel. . . .[33]

Probably he actually read little of the "Critiques," "Systems," and "Encyclopaedias"; however, though Whitman "was certainly neither a professional nor a formal thinker, [he] was responsive enough to these activities of the ideologues to go into the subject at his own leisure and in his own way."[34]

What the poet got primarily from Leibniz, Kant, and Hegel seems to have been, in his own words, "the religious tone, . . . the recognition of the future, of the unknown, of Diety over and under all, and of the divine purpose, [which] are never absent, but indirectly give tone to all."[35] Though this "tone" may be vague, it is important because it indicates not only Whitman's assumptions and attitudes but also the scope and application of his ideas. However general his borrowings, the German names and theories gave him confidence in the ideas which he had already adapted for his "message." As Riethmuller puts it, "His comprehensive mind affectionately absorbed the great literary ideas of the Germanic countries and rejected or moulded them to fit his compass of a national American literature."[36] The route by which Whitman derived these ideas cannot be clearly traced, and is perhaps best indicated by the figurative language of Woodbridge Riley: "The migrations of the Germanic mysticism form a strange story. It began with what has been called the pantheism of the Rhine region; it ended, if it has ever ended, with the poetic pantheism of Walt Whitman, for in this modern American may be found traces of a remote past, and echoes of a distant land."[37]

As for specific authors, Hegel has often been cited as both source and parallel for Whitman's ideas. Boatright made the first extensive investigation of the subject, and he came to the conclusion that Hegel at least "strengthened Whitman's convictions"[38] — especially in his cosmic evolution, his pantheistic "unity," and his synthesis of Good with which the antithesis, Evil, merges and disappears. But he thought that the poet's knowledge of Hegelianism came more from Gostwick than Hegel's own writings, a deduction which Fulghum has since then amplified and further demonstrated.[39] Falk has also studied the relationship and decided that:

In the case of Hegel, Whitman certainly buttressed, and possibly largely derived, his evolutionary conception of a universe, exhibiting conflict and struggle, yet tending toward a vague divine culmination in the return of the individual souls to the Absolute. But most of all, he saw in the Hegelian metaphysic a logical rationalization of the New World Democracy which he aimed to glorify.[40]

A later investigator of this subject, however, Miss Parsons, believes that "many of the likenesses [between Whitman and Hegel] cited from time to time are misleading, if not fallacious, or are too general to be of significance."[41] Her argument is based mainly on Whitman's failure, or perhaps inability, to understand the Hegelian dialectic. In this contention she is probably quite correct, but this admission does not contradict the popularized Hegelianism which the American poet derived indirectly, through Gostwick and others. At any rate, Whitman's relations to Hegel seem closer than those with other philosophers of the Rhineland. Falk says,

In the case of the other German metaphysicians, we can ascribe no certain influence; yet, it is true that Whitman reveals parallels in thought and even phrase with most of the transcendental philosphers from Kant on down. In all of them Whitman sees lessons for American Democracy.[42]

Alfred H. Marks thinks that the test of Whitman's Hegelianism should be his use of Hegel's Dialectic, indicated by his frequently

. ing terms of "fusing," "blending," "uniting," "joining," suggestive of the "dialectical 'synthesis.' " Whitman frequently "calls up paired contradictories or 'thesis' and 'antithesis' and handles them as if there were no opposition between them."[43] As an example: "Do I contradict myself?/ Very well then I contradict myself,/ (I am large, I contain multitudes.)" If critics would pay attention to Whitman's dialectical "synthesis" they would find fewer contradictions than they imagine. Furthermore, Marks finds this process of two contradictory images (or ideas) resolved in a third employed throughout *Leaves of Grass*. Though one may wonder whether Whitman actually learned this way of thinking from Hegel, Marks does succeed in showing a basic Hegelian "dialectic" in Whitman's poems, giving the poet the right to call Hegel *his philosopher*.

WHITMAN AND INDIA

Whitman's indebtedness to Oriental literature and Hindu mysticism is even more difficult to trace than his relations with German philosophy; and yet almost from the first edition students of Oriental thought have recognized in *Leaves of Grass* such striking parallels to the *Bhagavad Gita* and other Indian poems that they have speculated on Whitman's use of translations as primary sources for his poems. In 1856 Thoreau, an amateur but ardent Orientalist, called *Leaves of Grass* "wonderfully like the Orientals ... considering that when I asked [Whitman] if he had read them, he answered, 'No: Tell me about them.' "[44] Later, on numerous occasions, Whitman evinced some knowledge of Hindu and other Oriental translations. In *A Backward Glance*, for example, he claims to have read "the ancient Hindoo poems"[45] in preparation for *Leaves of Grass*—i.e., apparently before publishing the first edition. Whether in his reply to Thoreau's question he was trying to conceal this source, or whether Thoreau's question directed his attention to this field and stimulated his curiosity to explore it, we can at present only guess. But as with the German influence, this Orientalism was very much in the American intellectual atmosphere of the 1840s and 50s,[46] and it would have been impossible for Whitman to escape at least some indirect influence. Indeed, American Transcendentalism, as we have seen, received it from two directions: German Idealism and Romanticism were strongly indebted to Oriental mysticism,[47] and American Transcendentalism might be called the offspring of a German father and a Hindu mother.

In 1866 Viscount Strangford, an Oriental scholar, observed similarity of Whitman's rhythms to those of Persian poets,[48] and the same year Moncure D. Conway found Asia the key to both Whitman and the Transcendentalists.[49] In 1889 Gabriel Sarrazin declared that "Walt Whitman in his confident and lofty piety, is the direct inheritor of the great Oriental mystics, Brahma, Proclus, Abou Saïd."[50] In 1906 Edward Carpenter cited interesting parallels (which he did not claim as sources) between the Upanishads and *Leaves of Grass*.[51]

The first extensive investigation of the similarities between the *Bhagavad Gita* and *Leaves of Grass* was made by Dorothy Frederica Mercer in a doctoral dissertation at the University of California (Berkeley) in 1933, parts of which she later published in *Vedanta and the West*.[52] Labeled a "Comparative Study," this thesis did not claim the *Bhagavad Gita* as an actual source, though the author quoted an Indian scholar who believed Whitman "must have studied the *Bhagavad Gita*, for in his *Leaves of Grass* one finds the teaching of Vedanta; the Song of Myself is but an echo of the sayings of Krishna."[53]

The first striking parallel between Whitman's ideas and the Vedantic teaching is the doctrine of the *self*. "Whitman's soul, like the self of the *Bhagavad Gita*, is the unifying energy."[54] The self is not material, but spiritual; "it is the passive spectator; it is Brahma incarnate in the body; and it is permanent, indestructible, eternal, all-pervading, unmanifest." In the same way Whitman's "Me, Myself" is immortal, and through his cosmic "I" he merges with all creation, feeling himself to be at one with the spirit of the universe.

Other Vedanta doctrines Dr. Mercer found paralleled in *Leaves of Grass* were reincarnation, intuition in place of learning, and knowledge through love.[55] The most important parallel was on God and the self. It may be objected, however, that all of these terms and ideas are sufficiently ambiguous as to be capable of various interpretations. The importance of Dr. Mercer's study was that she interpreted Whitman as various Indian minds had seen him; there was—and is—something in Whitman's poems to provoke these responses.

In 1959 the major American critic, Malcolm Cowley, decided after reading Heinrich Zimmer's *The Philosophies of India* (1951): "Most of Whitman's doctrines, though by no means all of them, belong to the mainstream of Indian philosophy."[56] Unlike the Indian

ᵢsistent idealist; he did not despise the body,
ᵢion with the Over-Soul by "subjugating the
ᵧogis and Buddhists alike. . . ." Yet at times he
ᵤᵢhayana Buddhist "promising nirvana for all after
ᵢncarnations, and also sharing the belief of some Maha-
ᵢᵢcts that the sexual act can serve as one of the sacraments."[57]
ᵢc other times he proclaims "joyous affirmation" like an apostle of
Tantric Brahmanism. In *The Gospel of Sri Ramakrishna* Cowley
found "this priest of Kali, the Mother Goddess . . . delivering some of
Whitman's messages in—what is more surprising—the same tone of
voice."[58] To Cowley the importance of these resemblances was that
they help the modern reader to understand Whitman. For example,
his idea of God:

In "Song of Myself" as originally written, God is neither a person
nor, in the strict sense, even a being; God is an abstract principle of
energy that is manifested in every living creature, as well as in "the
grass that grows wherever the land is and the water is." In some ways
this God of the first edition resembles Emerson's Over-soul, but he
seems much closer to the Brahman of the *Upanishads*, the absolute,
unchanging, all-enfolding Consciousness, the Divine Ground from
which all things emanate and to which all living things may hope to
return. And this Divine Ground is by no means the only conception
that Whitman shared with Indian philosophers, in the days when he
was writing "Song of Myself."[59]

In 1964 V. K. Chari, a graduate of Benares Hindu University and
a superbly-trained scholar in Vedanta, published a closely and subtly
reasoned study of *Whitman in the Light of Vedantic Mysticism.*[60]
Like Cowley, Chari was less interested in possible sources than in
useful interpretation. "The theme of self, of relating the self to the
world of experience, is central to the comprehensive intent of Whitman's poems. . . ."[61] The subject matter of Whitman's poetry is no
other than the nature of experience itself, . . . the fact of human
consciousness." The way to read "Whitman's poetry is . . . as a direct
dramatization of the act of consciousness." Whitman's "intuitional
sense enables man to realize the oneness of the universe." This sense
is what Dr. Bucke called "cosmic consciousness," which Chari defines as "the consciousness of the self that is the cosmos."[62] This
view places in a new light Whitman's calling himself "kosmos"[63]—
because the self and *Atman* are one—and his statement in the 1855

Preface that, "The poets of the cosmos advance through all inter-positions and coverings and turmoils and strategems to first principles."[64]

In Vedantic mysticism there is no duality of subject and object, and Whitman's imaginative identification with everything and everyone is based on this principle. His conception of the self is not that of the post-Kantian idealists, because "for all these philosophers dialectic is the vehicle of their thought," and for them the self is also dialectical: "The self is a dialectical and antithetical being to which dualism and opposition become a necessary condition of existence."[65] For Hegel, "The self subsists by subduing the opposition of the non-self."

Whitman's essentially mystical thinking would be opposed to any doctrine that accords to the individual but a dependent and inferior status. Whitman asserts, "And nothing, not God, is greater to one than one's self is." A true doctrine of self is that which holds that the individual is coeval and coeternal with the absolute and accords to every particle of the universe the status of the supreme.[66]

Chari opposes all those critics who derive both Emerson's and Whitman's thought from German philosophy. Whether one agrees with him or not, it must be conceded that Chari's interpretation is consistent, penetrating, and more illuminating than the dialectical approaches. He is especially good on Whitman's democratic philosophy:

Whitman's democratic faith is born out of his conception of the mystical self. Since the central problem of democracy is the resolution of the inherent conflict between the individual and the universe, Whitman resolves it at the level of the transpersonal self, where the individual being himself is also the self of all. . . . The faith that there is a central identity of self running through all life is the foundation of democracy and freedom. Each individual is unique, and yet he is identical with the all. It is this conviction of the uniqueness and intrinsic worth of every human being that accounts for Whitman's individualism and his espousal of democracy as the surest guarantee of individual values.[67]

In 1966 another Hindu, Professor O. K. Nambiar, of Mysore University, published a study called *Walt Whitman and Yoga*.[68] Nambiar did not claim that Whitman knew or practiced Yogic discipline.

"Patanjali, the greatest authority on Yoga Sastra mentions . . . those rare geniuses born with the Yogic gift—the natural Yogis—who rise to cosmic consciousness or *Brahma Chit* without religious striving."[69] Whitman did that, Nambiar contends, in section 5 of "Song of Myself."[70] There he describes attaining Kundalini, "a psycho-physical energy present in every individual," but usually attained only by those who employ Yogic techniques of meditation and breath control. One who attains the Kundalini level of consciousness, as described in "Song of Myself," experiences the "unitive life based on Love."[71]

Nambiar says that he does not regard his book as cultist, though he does think that Whitman is a good example of the religious life possible for everyone, and greatly needed by all people. He would use *Leaves of Grass* as a text which the Western world could understand, with such aid as his book provides. In view of Whitman's ambition to write a "New Bible" for Democracy, this view is interesting, and gives Whitman credit for more than most Western critics have seen in his poems—that is, since the "hot little prophets" of the poet's Camden era.[72]

However, another Indian, T. R. Rajasekharaiah, has tried in *The Roots of Whitman's Grass* (1970)[73] to settle the question of Whitman's actual indebtedness to Indian sources—with results quite different from those of Chari and Nambiar. He began by making a list of the books and articles in English on Eastern literature, philosophy, and religion available to Whitman in the years immediately preceding 1855. He found that the Astor Library, which Whitman used, had over 500 items on this subject. Rajasekharaiah then went through each of these looking for parallels to passages in Whitman's poems. He found many, some of which he thought were so close that he decided, like Esther Shepherd,[74] he had discovered Walt Whitman's closely-guarded "secret." Whitman had borrowed his ideas, much of his imagery, and his fake "mysticism" from translations and popularizations of Oriental literature, especially Hindu. Though, again like Shepherd, this author insists that he is not attacking Whitman's position as a great poet, his accusations do question not only the poet's honesty but also his talent, if his power rested on plagiarism.

Some of Rajasekharaiah's examples are striking and may, indeed, indicate the possibility of actual source material, but many of them seem far-fetched and doubtful. Some, too, could be coincidence, such as Whitman's symbolical "leaves" of grass and the sacred Kusa grass of a Hindu sect. As a source study *The Roots of Whitman's Grass* is a failure, yet it still has value because of the parallels cited. It is unfortunate that the author did not use his material for a comparative study—but that did not fit his strong conviction. If read for comparisons, this book does have value and may contribute to further understanding of Whitman in relation to the literature of India.

During the 1950s and 60s there was so much interest in Whitman in India that the Sahitya Akademi (National Academy) began publishing translations of Whitman, with the assistance of UNESCO, into the eighteen languages of the country. So far only two have been published, 101 poems into Kannada by M. Gopalakrishna Adiga in 1966;[75] and 114 poems into Punjabi by Gurbakhsh Singh in 1968[76]—both with an Introduction by Gay Wilson Allen.[77] Since nearly all educated Indians read English, Whitman's reception in that nation is not limited to his availability in the native languages; nevertheless, the translations should create more interest in the American poet.

THE FRENCH BACKGROUND

These American, English, German, and Indian parallels—and possible origins—provide clues and analogues for Whitman's "mysticism" and philosophical idealism. But there was also another side of his thought and expression, which Arvin refers to as "a kind of Transcendental atheism."[78] This is the Whitman of French rationalism, skepticism, and "free thought," who declares in the 1855 Preface that, "There will soon be no more priests. Their work is done.... A new order shall arise and they shall be the priests of man, and every man shall be his own priest."[79] This is partly Emersonian "self-reliance" and the ultimate result of the Reformation, but it is also the offspring of the French Revolution, and of Thomas Jefferson and Tom Paine in America.

As the heir of this tradition Whitman wrote such early poems as "Europe," "Boston Ballad," and "To a Foil'd European Revolutionaire," and felt great sympathy for the defeated revolutionists of France (and other European countries) of 1848. He too shouts "Equality!" and "Liberty!" At this time the "headsman" is a symbol to him of reactionary Europe, where the oppressors of mankind are "hangman, priest, tax-gatherer." Whitman's realization that the ideals

of the American and French Revolutions had been thwarted in
Europe intensified his own nationalism and increased his conviction
that, politically, the United States was the only hope of the world
for freedom and equality.

Even his Christ-rôle, his vicarious sympathy, was to some extent
the product of these times and influences.

> Through me many long dumb voices,
> Voices of the interminable generations of slaves,
> Voices of prostitutes, and of deformed persons . . .[80]

The above interpretation is strengthened by the fact that he was
more exercised over abstract political slavery than the concrete
example of racial slavery in his own nation.

Whitman's interest in comparative religion and his attempt to
construct a theology which would fuse and extract the best of all
religions probably also came to a considerable degree from French
deism and rationalism, both directly and indirectly (see Chap. III,
"Nature").

> Magnifying and applying come I,
> Outbidding at the start the old cautious hucksters,
> [*i.e.*, priests of historical religions].[81]

He will accept only "the rough deific sketches to fill out better in
myself." Bibles and religions "have all grown out of you . . . It is not
they who give the life . . . . it is you who give the life."[82] Institutionalized religion is dead and ought to be buried:

> Allons! From all formulas!
> From your formulas, O bat-eyed and materialistic priests!
> The stale cadaver blocks up the passage—the burial waits no longer.[83]

And the only guide is each person's own conscience:

> I only am he who places over you no master, owner, better, God,
> beyond what waits intrinsically in yourself.[84]

Of course there are many possible sources for Whitman's "free
thought" and "natural religion." In Chapter III the influence of
Thomas Paine's *Age of Reason*, Frances Wright's *A Few Days in*

Athens, and Volney's *Ruins* on Whitman in his youth were pointed out. Certainly these were important in the formative stage of Whitman's mind, though a source for only one aspect of his thought, a distinctly limited aspect which does not entirely harmonize with all his ideas. But when we come to the romantic as distinguished from the rationlistic French authors, it is still more difficult to separate source from parallel. Bliss Perry regarded Whitman as an heir of Rousseau,[85] but what romantic poet in Europe or America was not? No one can deny the influence of the doctrines of innate goodness of human nature and "primitivism" on *Leaves of Grass*. Of course Whitman was well acquainted with Rousseauism, but it is not an influence which can be weighed objectively.

Of the French Romantic School, George Sand has been claimed not only as a major but even as Whitman's main source. Professor Esther Shephard[86] thought that in the wandering carpenter poet of the *Countess of Rudolstadt* Whitman found the literary rôle (she called it a "pose") which he was thereafter to adopt as his own through all the editions of *Leaves of Grass*. That he read and admired this and other novels by George Sand, there can be no doubt. It is even possible that George Sand's carpenter poet aroused in Walt Whitman the literary ambitions which he sought to achieve in *Leaves of Grass*, but Professor Shephard's claims for this source lose much of their strength when we discover equally striking parallels in the works of other French romanticists.

One of these is Victor Hugo—though Whitman seems not to have admired him as much as he admired George Sand.[87] However, they had much in common, as Kennedy has pointed out:

> Walt Whitman continually suggests another great humanitarian poet,—Victor Hugo. That which chiefly affines them is sympathy, compassion. To redeem our erring brothers by love, and not inflexible savage justice, is the message of each. Who is worthy to be placed beside these two as promulgators of the distinctive democratic ideas of these times,—the thirst for individual growth, space for the expansion of one's own soul, and equal rights before the law? . . . They have the same love of the sea and the immensities, and the same ingrained love of freedom.[88]

More specifically, one might compare Hugo's assertion that everything has a soul with Whitman's animism, or his including the ugly as a necessary part of his esthetic[89] with Whitman's complete

equalitarianism, or his belief that the spirit is always advancing toward something better[90] with Whitman's cosmic meliorism. Although these parallels indicate not so much sources or direct
influences as a general literary movement to which both belonged,
the very fact that the American poet shared these fundamental
resemblances with one of the major poets of nineteenth-century
France indicates that the ground was already partly prepared for
Whitman's later reception in France.

Another French writer of the period whose thought and expression parallel Whitman's to an astonishing degree is the historian, Jules
Michelet. In 1847 Whitman reviewed his *History of France*[91] and in
1876 he paraphrased (one might almost say plagiarized) a passage
from Michelet's *The Bird* in his poem, "To the Man-of-War Bird."
Before he published the first edition of *Leaves of Grass* Whitman
probably also read Michelet's *The People*,[92] but there is no conclusive evidence. Nevertheless, the literary theory on which Michelet
wrote this book is completely analogous to Whitman's poetic program. In his preface Michelet says, "This book is more than a book;
it is myself, therefore it belongs to you . . . Receive, then, this book
of *The People*, because it is you, because it is I . . ."[93] Compare:

> Camerado, this is no book,
> Who touches this touches a man, . . .[94]

"Son of the people," says Michelet, "I have lived with them, I know
them, they are myself . . . I unite them all in my own person."[95]
Whitman:

In all people I see myself, none more and not one a barley-corn less,
And the good or bad I say of myself I say of them.[96]

Through Michelet's historian and Whitman's poet "the people"
find their voice:

The people, in the highest sense of the word, is seldom to be
found in the people . . . it exists in its truth, and at its highest power
in the man of genius; in him resides the great soul . . . the whole
world [vibrates] at the least word he utters . . . That voice is the

voice of the people; mute of itself, it speaks in this man, and God in him.[97]

This "genius" is Whitman's ideal poet, who "is to be commensurate with a people . . . He is a seer . . . he is individual . . . he is complete in himself . . . the others are as good as he, only he sees it and they do not."[98] Throughout the 1855 Preface Whitman insists that only the poet, who is the true man of genius, can express the heart of the people; only through the poet can the people become articulate.

Michelet also anticipates Whitman in the cult of the barbarian:

> The rise of the people, the progress, is often nowadays compared to the invasion of the *Barbarians!* yes! that is to say, full of sap, fresh, vigorous, and for ever springing up . . . travellers toward the Rome of the future.[99]

As one of the barbarians, he glories in their crude, untutored, natural strength of expression,

> striving to give everything at once—leaves, fruit, and flowers—till it breaks or distorts the branches. But those who start up thus with the sap of the people in them, do not the less introduce into art a new burst of life and principle of youth; or at least leave on it the impress of a great result.[100]

We could easily imagine that these are Whitman's words, he who sounds his "barbaric yawp over the roofs of the world,"[101] and would have his verse break forth loosely like lilacs on a bush.[102] Even more than Michelet he strives "to give everything at once . . . till it breaks or distorts the branches."

There is another curious parallel between Michelet's sentimental story in *L'Oiseau* of a nightingale during a storm near Nantes and Whitman's mocking-bird on Long Island.[103] If a translation[104] of *L'Oiseau* had been available to Whitman in 1859, this story might be regarded as a possible source for the bird motif in "Out of the Cradle . . ." Nevertheless, the parallels do show that the two authors shared a common intellectual world in which birds and animals could speak the language of "Art and the Infinite,"[105] to use Michelet's term. This is less important, however, than the fact that Whitman attempted in his rôle of poet of Democracy to embody Michelet's ideal of the literary genius of the people who would be the articulate voice of the masses—in which Michelet succeeded better than the American poet.

WHITMAN IN THE BRITISH ISLES
RECEPTION AND INFLUENCE

In beginning a survey of Whitman's reception, reputation, and influence in foreign countries, we inevitably start with the British Isles, where he was first appreciated and first recognized as a major poet.[106] The story need not be told in complete detail, however, for it is familiar to most students of American literature, and much of it has already been covered in this book in the account of the biographies. Furthermore, it is largely the story of Whitman's reputation in Great Britain (and the poet's reflected fame at home), for even to the present time he has had less actual literary influence in England than in France or Germany.

The introduction of *Leaves of Grass* to the British Isles began more or less by accident. Several months after the almost complete failure of the first edition to gain sales or recognition in America, Thomas Dixon, a cork cutter of Sunderland, bought a copy from a peddler, James Grinrod, a veteran of the American Civil War. Dixon sent this copy to his friend William Bell Scott, a minor poet and sculptor. Scott gave a copy to William Rossetti for a Christmas present in 1856, and Rossetti was so pleased with the work that he immediately began telling his friends about it.[107] In the same year Emerson sent a copy, with an apologetic note, to Carlyle, but until his death Carlyle remained either indifferent or merely irritated by Whitman's poems.[108]

English criticism of Whitman did not get under way, however, until about 1866. Lord Strangford published a critical essay in *The Pall Mall Gazette*, February 16, 1866,[109] in which he recognized the American poet's Oriental style without approving his use of it. Whitman, he says, "has managed to acquire or imbue himself with not only the spirit, but with the veriest mannerism, the most absolute trick and accent of Persian poetry."[110] Instead of wasting his gifts on *Leaves of Grass*, he should have translated Rumi. This observation might have started interesting and fruitful discoveries in comparative literature, but no one at the time, not even Lord Strangford, pursued the comparison any further. In October of the same year, Moncure

Conway, who had visited Whitman in America, wrote a personal sketch of the poet for the October *Fortnightly Review*.

Over ten years after his introduction to *Leaves of Grass*, Rossetti published his first article on Whitman in the *Chronicle*, July 6, 1867. He attempted to enlarge the theory of poetry by declaring that, "Only a very restricted and literal use of the word, rhythm, could deny the claim of these writings to being both poetic and rhythmical." He called *Leaves of Grass* "incomparably the largest poetic work of our period."[111] But in the introduction to his edition of *Selections*[112] published the next year, he was cautious and judicious, perhaps the best strategy for increasing Whitman's reputation in England. Also the fact that his poems were edited in England at this time by Rossetti, a man known and respected by the literary profession, who carefully eliminated the most daring sex poems, accounts to a considerable extent for Whitman's greater fame in Britain than at home.

It was this edition of selected poems which Mrs. Anne Gilchrist read in 1869, having borrowed a copy from Madox Brown. She was not satisfied, however, with a censored edition and borrowed the complete *Leaves* from Rossetti himself. So profoundly affected was she that she wrote the famous "An Englishwoman's Estimate of Walt Whitman," published in the *Boston Radical*, May, 1870. To her, *Leaves of Grass* was not only sacred literature but also a personal plea for love. It is doubtful that anywhere else in the whole range of Whitman criticism any other person ever responded to the poet's message with such absolute sympathy and understanding—such sympathy, in fact, that she fell in love with the man through the book, and after this one article the story belongs to biography rather than to criticism.[113]

Ironically, one of Whitman's most ardent and impetuous friends and critics in England at this time was that eccentric enemy of the Rossetti-Swinburne circle, Robert Buchanan. This son of socialist and "infidel" parents was the first in Great Britain to accept Whitman unreservedly as a prophet and a modern Socrates. Blodgett calls his first criticism, published in *The Broadway Magazine* (1868) and reprinted in the same year in the book *David Gray*, "the most exhilarating that had yet appeared on Whitman in England."[114] But Buchanan worked himself into an embarrassing position in 1871 in an attack on the sensuality of Swinburne, Dante Gabriel Rossetti, Baudelaire, and others, which he called "The Fleshly School of

Poetry."[115] When Swinburne inquired why Buchanan "despised so much the Fleshly School of Poetry in England and admired so much the poetry which is widely considered unclean and animal in America,"[116] he was hard pressed for a defense of "Children of Adam," and even admitted that *Leaves of Grass* contained about "fifty lines of a thoroughly indecent kind."[117] But the controversy only intensified his loyalty to Whitman, whose cause he did at least two good services. In the first place, he was one of the earliest foreign critics to recognize the literary quality of Whitman's "wonderful poetic prose, or prose-poetry,"[118] and in the second place, in 1876 he started a storm of controversy over Whitman's neglect which stimulated the sale of his books and raised a substantial sum of money for him. Hearing that the poet, "old, poor, and paralyzed,"[119] was shamefully neglected in America, Buchanan wrote a letter to *The London Daily News* hotly denouncing the poet's unappreciative countrymen. Naturally many Americans resented the charge and Whitman's cause thereby became entangled with Anglo-American antagonisms which lingered on for years. After visiting the United States in 1885, Buchanan poured more oil on the fire with a satirical poem against the Bostonians for their indifference to Whitman, and in 1887 he added that in his native land Whitman was "simply *outlawed*":

In a land of millionaires, in a land of which he will one day be known as the chief literary glory, he is almost utterly neglected. Let there be no question about this; all denial of it is disingenuous and dishonest. The literary class fights shy of him.[120]

Swinburne's criticism of Whitman illustrates anew the fortuitous and erratic reception of *Leaves of Grass* in Great Britain. A copy of the 1855 edition found its way into the hands of George Howard, the ninth Earl of Carlyle, who passed it on to Swinburne.[121] It interested Swinburne so much that he ordered a copy for himself, and then later procured a copy of the 1860 edition. In the latter volume he greatly admired "Out of the Cradle Endlessly Rocking" (then called "A Word Out of the Sea").[122] In his biography of Blake (1868) he compared the Universal Republic and the spiritual democracy of the two poets. Their writings seemed to him like "fragments . . . of the Pantheistic poetry of the East."[123] After *Drum-Taps* was published, Swinburne declared the threnody on Lincoln to be "the most sweet and sonorous nocturne ever chanted in the church of the world." The height of his admiration for Whitman was reached in 1871 when in *Songs Before Sunrise*, dedicated to Mazzini, he addressed a poem "To Walt Whitman in America." Whitman and his friends took the poem as a personal greeting, but as Blodgett points out, Swinburne's "interest in political freedom, never realistic, took the form of a passtionately expressed idealism in which Walt Whitman appeared as the prophet of liberty, the 'strong-winged soul with prophetic lips hot with the blood-beats of song.' " Whitman and his country were "apostrophized as symbols of the freedom which with Swinburne was a seductive abstraction. . . ."[124]

The following year (1872), in *Under the Microscope*, Swinburne's admiration for Whitman's poetry became more restrained and judicious. While still accepting the American poet's democracy, he began to find fault with his style and his lapses from good taste. *Under the Microscope* was directed especially at Buchanan, and it is understandable that Swinburne would begin to have his doubts about the poet so noisily praised by the enemy of Swinburne's circle.

Edmund Gosse thought Watts-Dunton was responsible for the cooling of Swinburne's enthusiasm for the American poet,[125] but later investigators found nothing either remarkable or treacherous in his increasing impatience with Whitman as formalist and thinker, the two special deficiencies mentioned in *Under the Microscope*. Even the notorious "Whitmania," published first in *The Fortnightly Review*, August, 1887, and reprinted in *Studies in Poetry and Prose* (1894), is, as Cairns says, "directed primarily against those enthusiasts who give Whitman a place 'a little beneath Shakespeare, a little above Dante, or cheek by jowl with Homer.' "[126] It was no outright "recantation," for Swinburne still admired Whitman's "genuine passion of patriotic and imaginative sympathy" and his "earnest faith in freedom,"[127] but he objected to the weakness of thought, the unpoetic style, and the manner of treating sex. It is not surprising that a poet of Swinburne's temperament and culture would eventually find the self-appointed poet of American Democracy uncongenial, and his objections are essentially those of the later British biographers, such as John Bailey and Hugh I'Anson Fausset.[128]

The biographical and critical contributions of John Addington Symonds to Whitman literature in England have been treated in a previous chapter,[129] but we may note here that he became acquainted with Whitman's writings in 1865 at Trinity College, Cambridge, through his friend Frederic Myers. Young university men in

Great Britain seem to have been especially attracted by Whitman at this time. Other bookish men drawn to him were Lionel Johnson, Robert Louis Stevenson, and Edward Dowden.

Edward Dowden, Professor of English Literature and Oratory at Trinity College, Dublin, was one of the most gifted and remarkable critic-admirers of Whitman in the British Isles. What especially attracted him to *Leaves of Grass* were the spiritual values. In his first book on Shakespeare (1879) he ranked Whitman with the "spiritual teachers": Wordsworth, Coleridge, Shelley, Carlyle, Browning, and others.[130] Whitman's form, however, was a challenge to his powers of analysis and he attempted to rationalize it.

Dowden's essay, "The Poetry of Democracy: Walt Whitman," was rejected in 1869, as too dangerous to print, by *Macmillan's Magazine* and *The Contemporary Review* but was finally published by *The Westminster Review* in July, 1871 (reprinted in *Studies in Literature*, London, 1878). In this essay Dowden accepted the view that America lacked native literature before Whitman and regarded *Leaves of Grass* as democratic art, which must reject aristocratic form and make its own rules and techniques. However, he valued Whitman as a poet despite his unconventional form, not because of it. Though he admitted guardedly that Whitman might not have been sufficiently reserved in the treatment of sex, he did not think that the poet exalted the body over the soul. On the whole, Dowden accepted Whitman on his own terms, but brought to his interpretations a literary skill and critical background which greatly advanced the American poet's reputation abroad—and even influenced the course of his reception at home. The distinguished Dublin professor found himself embarrassed and repulsed by Whitman's American disciples, but this did not affect his critical opinions or published support. He reviewed *Specimen Days* in *The Academy*, November 18, 1882, and arranged for an English edition of Dr. Bucke's biography, for which he collected and arranged an appendix, "English Critics on Walt Whitman."

Despite Dowden's championship of Whitman, however, *Leaves of Grass* was removed from the Trinity College library after Boston banned the 1881-82 edition. But meanwhile other Irish scholars were also active in spreading Whitman's fame in the British Isles. Standish O'Grady ("Arthur Clive") published "Walt Whitman: the Poet of Joy" in the December, 1875, *Gentleman's Magazine*. With Irish exuberance he elaborated in the vein of O'Connor and

Bucke: "Often we think one of the elements of nature has found a voice, and thunders great syllables in our ears."[131] O'Grady's friend, Thomas W. Rolleston, discovered Whitman in 1877. After four years in Germany, he published at Dresden a study called *Über Wordsworth und Walt Whitman* (1883). Rolleston was one of the first critics to perceive Whitman's connection with German philosophy and to interpret him not as a "primitive" but in terms of comparative literature—an important step toward the recognition of Whitman as a "world poet." However, like the American disciples, he thought that criticizing Whitman was like criticizing Nature. Rolleston also translated a book of "selections" from *Leaves of Grass* into German (1884), but it was not published until Dr. Karl Knortz, a German-American scholar, revised it and finally got J. Schabelitz, of Zürich, to bring it out in Switzerland in 1889.

Scotland was slow in accepting Whitman. John Nichol, Professor of English Literature at the University of Glasgow, discussed him in an article on "American Literature" in the ninth edition of the *Encyclopaedia Britannica* (1875) in the following tone:

... although this author on various occasions displays an uncouth power, his success is in the main owing to the love of novelty, wildness, and even of absurdity, which has infected a considerable class of critics and readers on both sides of the Atlantic. ... he discards not only rhyme, but all ordinary rhythm. ... "The Leaves of Grass" is redeemed by a few grand descriptive passages from absolute barbarism both of manner and matter. It is a glorification of nature in her most unabashed forms, an audacious protest against all that civilization has done to raise men above the savage state.

These views were amplified in Nichol's book, *American Literature* (1882), in which he decided that "If Shakespeare, Keats, and Goethe are poets, Whitman is not."[132] He regretted Swinburne's favorable comparisons of Blake and Whitman. The Earl of Lytton and Sir Leslie Stephen also, as Blodgett says, "felt the need of British austerity toward American literary bumptiousness,"[133] and many Scottishmen seem to have shared their attitudes. One of these was Peter Bayne, a prominent editor of the day, who in the December, 1875, *Contemporary Review* "pounced upon Whitman like a Sunday school superintendent upon a bad boy, and he plainly intimates, in doing so, that he is exposing the hoax that Dowden, Rossetti, and Buchanan had been playing off on the British public." Blodgett also rightly calls this "A very plausible Tory attack," stating "the formid-able case that all respectable persons have against *Leaves of Grass*."[134] But another Scotsman, John Robertson, published a kind and sympathetic though undistinguished pamphlet, *Walt Whitman: Poet and Democrat*, at Edinburgh in 1884.

Despite the Tory opposition, Whitman made steady progress in England, partly, as Blodgett suggests, because, "In the seventies or eighties a young critic or journalist, trying to get a foothold in the London literary world, would be quite likely to seize upon Whitman for 'material.' "[135] Among these young critics were H. Buxton Forman, Ernest Rhys, and Edmund Gosse. Forman observed similarities between Whitman and Shelley and tried, without much success, to interest Whitman in Shelley. At the age of twenty-five Rhys turned from mining engineering to literature in order to advance the cause of labor, and he thought he saw in Whitman the enemy of "the stronghold of caste and aristocracy and all selfishness between rich and poor."[136] Consequently Rhys gave popular lectures on Whitman and edited, with a good critical introduction, a pocket edition of selected poems. It was Rhys's intention to make Whitman known to the common people, the very kind of audience which the poet had originally attempted to address in his own country. Gosse, like Swinburne, passed from ardent admiration to cool objectivity in his criticism of Whitman and was regarded with increasing hostility by the Camden circle. But he was one of the most competent critics that Whitman had in Great Britain.

There were, however, other distinguished critics. One was George Saintsbury, who reviewed *Leaves of Grass* in *The Academy*, October 10, 1874. He admired Whitman as poet and artist, though demurring somewhat at his idealization of the animal. He found Whitman's rhythm "singularly fresh, light, and vigorous," and praised his technique in the great *History of Prosody* (1910). Another critic, George C. Macaulay, gave a more philosophical analysis in *The Nineteenth Century*, December, 1882, describing Whitman's religion as pantheistic, his ethics as Greek, and his sympathy as universal. Still earlier William Kingdon Clifford, Professor of Mathematics at the University College, London, had made one of the first contributions to the understanding of Whitman's mysticism by citing him as an illustration of "Cosmic Emotion" in *The Nineteenth Century*, October, 1877. In 1886 even the staid *Quarterly Review* (in a review of Stedman's *Poets of America*, published in the October number) called Whitman "a lyric genius of the highest order," praising especially his cosmic qualities.

Though Walt Whitman was befriended by such famous men in England as William Rossetti, John Addington Symonds, and Lord Tennyson (who remained a steadfast friend and correspondent though not a public critic), and had what might be called a strong personal following, his actual literary influence in the British Isles was negligible. In fact, it included only one well-known writer and a small group of left-wing socialists and reformers in Lancashire. The one writer was Edward Carpenter, a young poet, socialist, and idealistic reformer who, in Blodgett's words, "felt himself dedicated, heart and soul, to the life work of interpreting and expanding Whitman's dream of democratic brotherhood."[137] *Toward Democracy* is such an expansion, and *My Days and Dreams* outlines in detail a social program inspired by *Leaves of Grass*, though it probably goes far beyond anything Whitman ever dreamed.

The one group of ordinary folk who organized a club to study and apply Whitman's doctrines was known as "Bolton College," a satirical name adopted by the members, middle-class Lancashire business men, professional men, and artisans. Two of the members visited Whitman and wrote books about the meeting.[138] The group had no great influence on the course of Whitman criticism, but, as Blodgett remarks, "it is strangely interesting that the story of Whitman's English following should begin with the effort of Thomas Dixon, cork-cutter, to call attention to him, and end with the homage of a middle-class coterie in the cotton-manufacturing town of Bolton."[139]

What pleased and encouraged Walt Whitman most about his reception in Great Britain was the friendly praise and the personal comradeship of both the professional writers and the disciples. This recognition sustained him during the dark hours of his neglect in America. But it can not be said that many of these critics made permanent contributions to Whitman criticism, except for some psychological interpretations which the poet could never appreciate.

It was the British who first tried to penetrate the mystery of the "Calamus" emotions, first Symonds, then Carpenter, and finally Havelock Ellis. Carpenter, like Symonds, seems to have felt in himself something of the same emotion and he never gave up the attempt to understand both himself and Whitman, and to discover the social value of "manly love." He did not shrink from the analysis of "sexual inversion,"[140] but he also thought that "The Comradeship on which Whitman founds a large portion of his message may in course of time become a general enthusiasm. . . ."[141] It was Ellis, however, who came nearest getting to the bottom of this question and who analyzed Whitman's psychology with the most penetrating insight. But he also warned that:

> It is as [a prophet-poet] that Whitman should be approached, and I would desire to protest against the tendency, now marked in many quarters, to treat him merely as an invert, and to vilify him or glorify him accordingly. However important inversion may be as a psychological key to Whitman's personality, it plays but a small part in Whitman's work, and for many who care for that work a negligible part.[142]

Out of Whitman's emotional sensitivity came a more sane and wholesome attitude toward the physical basis of life: "Whitman represents, for the first time since Christianity swept over the world, the re-integration, in a sane and whole-hearted form, of the instincts of the entire man, and therefore he has a significance which we can scarcely over-estimate."[143] Here we have the foundation for the later growth of reputation and understanding of the message of Walt Whitman in both Europe and America.

The question of "inversion" may also have been involved in the reaction of Gerard Manley Hopkins when his friend Robert Bridges accused him in 1882 of having been influenced by Whitman. Hopkins replied that he knew Whitman only from two or three articles in the *Athenaeum* and *Academy*. One of these was a review by George Saintsbury with short extracts from *Leaves of Grass*. These few lines were hardly enough to influence his style, but he admitted that Whitman attracted him, for:

> . . . I always knew in my heart Walt Whitman's mind to be more like my own than any other man's living. As he is a very great scoundrel this is not a pleasant confession. And this also makes me the more desirous to read him and the more determined that I will not.[144]

In spite of denying that Whitman's savage style had influenced his own "sprung rhythm," Hopkins admitted resemblances, especially in his and Whitman's fondness for the alexandrine. But the important point is that Hopkins respected Whitman as a poet, felt attracted to him personally, and admitted, "His 'savage' style has advantages. . . ."

In 1910, in his monumental *History of English Prosody*, Saints-bury also defended Whitman's right to compose poems in his own original manner. He thought that if Whitman had chosen, "he could have written beautiful verse proper [i.e., according to convention]. Yet it is clear also, that in passages, and many of them, the marriage of matter and form justifies itself as a true marriage."[145]

Edith Sitwell agreed with Saintsbury, and *A Poet's Notebook* (1943) contains a considerable number of quotations from Whit-man's prefaces and notebooks on "The Nature of Poetry," "Techni-cal Matters," "The Natural World and Inspiration," etc. Miss Sitwell includes him with Dunbar and Dryden as one of the "giants of our poetry." In her Preface to the anthology *The American Genius* she calls Blake and Whitman "Pentecostal Poets." Both "were born at the time when their characteristics were most needed"; Blake when eighteenth-century materialism "was freezing poetry," and Whitman "after a time of vague misty abstractions, to lead poetry back to the *'divine, original concrete.'* "[146] But in one respect they were dif-ferent: "Blake could not forgive the Fool, or believe that he could enter Heaven." Whitman tolerated even the fool, "and believed it to be the mission of the great poet to lead men back from the delusion of Hell."

One poet could scarcely admire another to this extent without being influenced, but Whitman's literary influence on Edith Sitwell is not obvious or easily traced. All that can be said truthfully is that this gifted and eccentric member of the Sitwell family aided in sustaining Whitman's reputation in Great Britain during the first half of the twentieth century. William Butler Yeats made a similar contri-bution, and was perhaps influenced even less, but a recent observer quotes from Yeats's letters to prove a "sustained interest" in the American poet during most of Yeats's adult life.[147]

One British writer who was unmistakably influenced by Whit-man was D. H. Lawrence.[148] His satire on Whitman's *merging* was quoted in Chapter I on "Whitman in Biography." But he was also as strongly attracted as repelled. Edwin H. Miller correctly calls Law-rence's interpretation of Whitman in *Studies in Classic American Literature* "brilliantly insightful but also brilliantly wrongheaded," and adds, in Lawrence's criticism "the author of *Leaves of Grass* becomes the author of *Women in Love*, an extraordinary novel which the poet of 'Calamus' could not have written."[149]

James E. Miller, Jr., with his colleagues Karl Shapiro and Bernice Slote, in *Start with the Sun*, see both Lawrence and Whitman as two of the great "Cosmic Poets" of modern literature. By this term they mean poets of "pagan joy and wonder in the natural world, the living cosmos."[150] They are the poets of the carnal self and the unconscious. Lawrence called Whitman "the first heroic seer to seize the soul by the scruff of her neck and plant her down among the potsherds."[151] He agreed with Whitman that the soul and body are one, and that "the root of poetry" is "phallic consciousness," not "cerebral sex-consciousness."[152] Lawrence called the Freudian unconscious "the cellar in which the mind keeps its own bastard spawn."[153] In *Start with the Sun* the "Laurentian unconscious" is described as "the unconscious *pristine*, primitive, elemental, unsullied by mind: this unconscious, asserts Lawrence, *is* the soul."[154] This was Whitman's concept also, though he did not use the term "unconscious" for it. He did, however, in his 1855 Preface seem to anticipate Jung's "collective unconscious" or "racial memory," when, after enumerating the traits of character needed by a great poet, he declared, "these are called up of the float of the brain of the world to be parts of the greatest poet from his birth out of his mother's womb and from her birth out of her mother's."[155]

The authors of *Start with the Sun* also claim Dylan Thomas as not only a "cosmic poet," but also as one strongly, and admittedly, influenced by Whitman. The tradition to which both belong is "affirmative, physical, intuitive, incantatory."[156] As a Welshman Thomas inherited the "bardic" tradition, but it was reinforced by Whitman's "body poetry," emphasizing "birth and procreation." Thus Thomas's metaphors, rhythms, and themes were the offspring of Welsh paganism and the "neo-paganism" of Walt Whitman.

In the opinion of some critics the great literary innovator, James Joyce, also made use of Whitman. About 1926 Sylvia Beach, the American expatriate and first publisher of Joyce's *Ulysses*, staged an exhibition of Whitman in her Paris bookshop. " 'The Crowd' [American writers]," she reports in *Shakespeare and Company*, "couldn't put up with him, especially after T.S. Eliot aired *his* views about Walt. Only Joyce and the French and I were still old-fashioned enough to get along with Whitman. I could see with half an eye Whitman's influence on Joyce's work."[157] Richard Chase found strong evidence of that influence in *Finnegans Wake*. For example, Joyce alludes to "old Whiteman self," and has him say: "I foredreamed for thee and more than full-maked: I prevened for thee in the haunts that joybelled frail light-a-leaves for sturdy traemen.

...."[158] In this passage Joyce parodies Whitman's tolerance for prostitutes, rowdies, "prater brothers," his comradeship with everyone, and his "evangel of good tidings."

This may not sound very friendly to "old Whiteman," but Chase thinks the " 'panromain' which 'Watllwewhistlen sang' may easily have suggested to Joyce how a work of literature might picture 'the soul of everyelsebody rolled into olesoleself.' "[159] Joyce's protagonist Earwicker "has the same capacity as the 'I' of 'Song of Myself' to merge ('at no spatial time') with and become anyone and anything in the universe." The reincarnation motif in "Song of Myself," sec. 27-31, parallels Joyce's revolving cycles. "In a very real sense, then, *Finnegans Wake* is the ultimate development of a literary method 'foredreamed' in 'Song of Myself.' " Moreover, "The references to Whitman in *Finnegans Wake* (brief as they are) are fresher and more moving to the modern reader than are those, for example, in Hart Crane's *The Bridge*, where Whitman is understood only as the aspirational prophet."[160]

At this point it becomes unprofitable to consider Whitman's reputation and influence in England and the United States separately. In Hart Crane the influence of Whitman, Eliot, and the French Symbolists (some of whom were Whitman's greatest admirers in France) mingle inextricably. Allen Tate did not think Whitman's influence on Crane altogether fortunate,[161] and Yvor Winters blamed Whitman for Crane's suicide.[162] Then, to increase the tangle, Eliot, who strongly disliked Whitman's "ideas" but grudgingly admitted some pleasure in his imagery and music,[163] was in turn thought by a New Zealand scholar, S. Musgrove,[164] to have been influenced by Whitman, an opinion in which Pearce concurs.

Then there is Pound, the American poet with the international and tragic career, who found difficulty in acknowledging his debt to his "pig-headed father,"[165] but nevertheless did. As early as 1909 he confessed that, "Mentally I am a Walt Whitman who has learned to wear a collar and a dress shirt. ...."[166] And in his famous "truce" (later changed to "pact") he declared, "We have one sap and one root—/ Let there be commerce between us." In 1934 in his *ABC of Reading* he called Whitman's faults "superficial," and said he had written the *histoire morale* of nineteenth-century America.[167] As for direct influence, Roy Harvey Pearce finds evidence in some of the *Cantos*, especially 82, 85, and 93, and in the "gross structure" of the *Cantos*, as difficult to define as the structure of "Song of Myself," with which they have definite analogues.[168] Thus throughout the English speaking world Walt Whitman's fame and influence continued to grow through the twentieth century—and still continues.

WHITMAN IN FRANCE: RECEPTION AND INFLUENCE

The first critics of Walt Whitman in France used him as a horrible example of the cultural chaos to be expected of rampant "democracy" and "republicanism" in a semi-civilized country like the United States of America. This was the opinion, during the reign of Emperor Napoleon III, of Louis Etienne in his "Walt Whitman, poète, philosophe et 'rowdy,' " *Revue européenne*, November, 1861, adding, however, "mais gardons-nous de confondre la nation de Washington et de Franklin avec les héros de ce nouveau Tyrtée."

In 1872, soon after the founding of the Third Republic, Mme. Blanc (Thérèse Bentzon) still held essentially the same view:

Soi-même et en masse, l'égoïsme et la démocratie, voilà les sujets favoris des chants de Whitman; à ce titre, ils sont essentiellement modernes. Certes aucun écrivain européen, poète ni prosateur, n'est tombé dans les excès d'énergique mauvais goût que voudraient inaugurer sur les ruines de l'idéal Walt Whitman et ses sectaires; mais enfin il existe malheureusement chez nous, depuis quelques années, une tendance marquée vers ce réalisme qui est le contraire du naturel et de la vérité, une disposition à confondre les muscles avec le génie.[169]

But despite the fact that she associated Whitman's "muscle and pluck" with the school of realism, Bentzon was fully aware of Whitman's mystic identification of himself with the universe—though she regarded this as a "pretension":

Une des prétentions de Walt Whitman est non seulement de représenter un citoyen de l'univers, comme il nous le fait entendre en déclarant qu'il est un vrai Parisien, un habitant de Vienne, de Pétersbourg, de Londres (tant de villes sont énumérées dans son hymne *Salut au monde* qu'on croirait lire une leçon de géographie ancienne et moderne), mais encore de contenir en lui-même l'univers tout entier.[170]

In such comments as these Bentzon did not misunderstand or misrepresent Whitman; she was merely unsympathetic and afraid of the "tendencies" which he represented in literature. Immediately Émile Blémont, a Parnassian poet, replied to Bentzon in a series of articles on "La Poésie en Angleterre et aux États-Unis," published in *Renaissance littéraire et artistique*. He understood and approved Whitman's new "ensemble" of body and soul and the significance of his *one's-self* and *en-masse*, accurately summarizing the thought in this concise manner:

Il est biblique, mais comme Hegel, il admet le principe de l'identité dans les contraires. Il est réaliste et optimiste, il est spiritualiste aussi; pour lui le mal n'existe pas, ou s'il existe, il est utile. Il a les vigoureuses conceptions d'une forte santé, chaste et sobre. Il est le champion sans honte de la sainteté de la chair, et des instincts charnels.[171]

Following the poet's own clues, Blémont idealized him as a man of the people, a prophet, and an original genius. This of course prevented the critic from a full comprehension of Whitman's literary antecedents and his relations to other writers. It is significant, though, that Blémont did understand fairly well the "organic style," for it was Whitman's form perhaps more than anything else that for many years prevented most French critics from appreciating *Leaves of Grass*.

Five years later Henri Cochin, in "Un poète américain, Walt Whitman," *Le Correspondant*, November 25, 1877, still thought that Whitman's democracy and friendship degraded society and threatened the safety of all nations. He saw in *Leaves of Grass* "democracy run wild, a form of insanity and megalomania."[172] Whitman, he thought, had no moral code at all, advocating chaos and license; and his form was equally contradictory and incoherent. But even in the attacks of Etienne, Bentzon, and Cochin on Whitman as a materialist, vulgarian, and political menace, "they recognized," as Pucciani says, "his growing stature in world literature, and that he was at all events a figure to be coped with."[173]

By 1884 Whitman was no longer feared in France. The violent opposition had spent itself, but his form was still a major difficulty. Léo Quesnel thought that Whitman fooled himself in believing that poetic sentiments intuitively generated artistic form: "N'est-ce pas une naïveté que de croire que parce qu'un poète aura le coeur plein

de beaux sentiments, l'esprit rempli de hautes pensées, la rime et la
césure viendront d'elle-mêmes se ranger sous sa plume?"[174] Quesnel
predicted that Whitman would be slow in winning the recognition in
France that he had already received in Great Britain. In the first
place, his "langue riche et libre" is difficult to translate; in fact,
"Whitman traduit n'est plus Whitman." And in the second place, the
French are still children of Greece, from whence they have inherited
a sense of delicacy and elegance in language. He regards Whitman as a
great poet for Americans (who are not "children of Greece"!), but
not for Frenchmen.

Still, discussions such as Quesnel's brought Whitman to the attention of French men of letters and prepared the way for appreciation of him. This appreciation came during the period of Symbolism,
during the 80s and 90s. It was the Symbolists "who brought Whitman to France, who espoused him, translated him, and to some
extent recognized in him a literary parent,"[175] and he is still associated with the "decadents," as Rockwell Kent's illustrations bear
witness.[176] Catel thinks Whitman a forerunner of Symbolism, but
Pucciani points out, for example, Whitman's dissimilarities to Mal-
larmé.[177] It seems, in fact, to have been mainly the "decadent"
aspect of Whitman which the Symbolists adopted. In the broader
aspects he and they were quite different, for Whitman's symbols
were universal, theirs specialized and often so subjective that they
had little meaning for anyone except the author.

Although the early critics translated fragments of Leaves of
Grass in their articles, it was the Symbolist poet, Jules Laforgue, who
in 1886 published three numbers of translations in La Vogue and
thus stimulated interest in Whitman among the young poets of
France. The following year the American expatriate, Francis Vielé-
Griffin, translated the entire "Song of the Broad-Axe" for La Revue
indépendante. It was through Laforgue, however, that Whitman most
strongly influenced the vers-libristes.[178]

In 1888 a comprehensive, scholarly critique of Whitman was
published by Gabriel Sarrazin, first in the Nouvelle Revue, May 1,
1888, and a year later in his book, La Renaissance de la poésie
anglaise. Especially valuable for the assimilation of Whitman in
France was Sarrazin's comprehension of the poet's pantheism, which
revealed an inheritance from the mysticism of the East and linked
him in modern times to German Idealism, especially Hegel. Unlike
most of Whitman's contemporary admirers in America, this learned

French critic did not regard him as an untutored "original genius" but as a man who knew his way around Parnassus. "Non seulement il n'était point un illettré, mais il avait lu tout ce que nous avons lu nous-mêmes. Il avait vu aussi beaucoup plus que nous, et bien plus distinctement. . . ."[179] Pucciani thinks Sarrazin's special virtue the fact that he sees Whitman as "an event in world literature that has already been operative for some time."[180]

The Symbolists, themselves influenced by the free verse of the Bible, were the first critics fully to appreciate the Biblical style of *Leaves of Grass*. Rémy de Gourmont mentions it in 1890: "en Whitman, le grand poète américain, se régénère l'esprit ancien de simplicité, l'esprit biblique. . . ."[181] This "Biblical spirit" has a curious international relationship to the Symbolists because they were also influenced, especially through Gustave Kahn, the editor of *La Vogue*, by the style of the German Bible, as Rémy de Gourmont has pointed out in *Le Problème du style* (1902)[182] and *Promenades littéraires* (1904).

Walt Whitman was sufficiently known in France in 1892 for news of his death to arouse a new flurry of critical activity. We are thus enabled to see that Sarrazin's effort had been only partly successful. For example, Paul Desjardins, in "Walt Whitman," *Journal des Débats*, April 4, 1892, still regards the American poet as "a kind of beautiful primitive,"[183] to use Pucciani's phrase, lacking in restraint and self-control—and this amoral interpretation was also repeated by Téodor de Wyzewa[184] and B. H. Gausseron,[185] the latter thinking that Whitman had rejected all laws and all traditions. But Desjardins admires Whitman's patriotism, understands his doctrine of good and evil, and thinks the poet a *précurseur* of future popular literature.

At this time Henri Bérenger, who had quoted Whitman as early as 1873 in his novel *L'Effort*, and had shown an interest in his themes—though not his forms—in *L'Ame moderne* (1890), translated Havelock Ellis's essay on Whitman (*L'Ermitage*, June, 1892). Thus the course of French criticism was influenced by this English sexologist, whose brilliant and sensible interpretation has seldom been equalled in Whitman scholarship. Ellis understood even better than Sarrazin Whitman's mysticism, his cosmic philosophy, his doctrine of the equality of matter and spirit, and the immortality of the Ego. It is safe to say that no previous critic had been so well prepared to appreciate the sanity of the poet's attitude toward sex. He saw also the similarity between Whitman and Millet. On the subject of Whitman's reading he struck a happy medium, somewhere near the real truth. Without being either a blind admirer or a skeptical detractor, Ellis fully appreciated Whitman's personality. This essay did a great deal for the American poet's reputation on the continent.

It was also in *L'Ermitage* (December, 1902) that Henri Davray undertook to present Whitman to French readers through faithful, accurate translations, with little or no interpretation. Before Whitman could be widely known in France, such translations as these were needed, and they prepared the way for others.

During the next two decades Walt Whitman became almost a major force in French literature. But he continued to be identified with special groups and movements, each finding some special doctrines, attitudes, or tricks of style to admire or to confirm its own theories. Whitman's importance in World Literature is in great measure due to his astonishing adaptability. Just as the Symbolists found much in him to support their own program, so also did two of the three movements of reaction against Symbolism: *naturisme* and *unanimisme*. The *romanisme* of Moréas and Maurras, with its attempt to restore classicism, had of course no use for Whitman. But the whole generation of *naturisme* poets and critics adopted the pantheism, the glorification of physical joy and health, and the anti-art-for-art's-sake attitude of the American poet. The Unanimist school, led by Jules Romains, was interested especially in Whitman's mystic and cosmic *ensemble*. The influence is particularly evident in the section of Romains' *La Vie unanime* which he entitled, significantly, "L'Individu."[186] Baldensperger is authority for the statement that, "The movement known as *l'unanimisme*, aiming at a sort of pantheistic and pan-social vision where the poor individual is more or less absorbed, claimed [Whitman] as a master."[187]

The Unanimist who did most for Whitman in France was Léon Bazalgette,[188] whose first biography, *Walt Whitman: l'homme et son oeuvre*, appeared in 1908, followed in 1909 by his complete translation, *Feuilles d'herbe*. Both the biography and the translation highly idealized Whitman and his language, but they influenced a whole generation of young writers, among them the Abbaye group, which included Georges Duhamel, a later Whitmanesque poet. During this period, however, it is difficult to separate influence from parallels, for as Pierre de Lanux has emphasized,[189] Whitman's point of view exactly suited the new twentieth century, especially his mysticism, his humanism, his belief in the present, and his functional style without ornamentation.

On June 1, 1912 a critic in *Nouvelle Revue Française* mentioned *le Whitmanisme* as a real force in French poetry. About the same time Henri Ghéon declared, "Il a nourri notre jeunesse."[190] Jean-Richard Bloch, in *L'Anthologie de l'Effort* (1912) praised Whitman as "the prophet from whom Vildrac and Duhamel, André Spire and Jules Romains, have learned most."[191] Duhamel himself said in *Les Poètes et la poésie* (1914), "J'ai dit que Walt Whitman fut et demeure un grand introducteur à la vie poétique."[192]

In 1914 Valery Larbaud traced the history of Whitman criticism in France, giving a factual and sensible account up to that date. In 1918 this essay was used as the preface to a book of translations called *Walt Whitman: Oeuvres choisies*, composed of poetry and prose rendered into French by Jules Laforgue, Louis Fabulet, André Gide, and Francis Vielé-Griffin. André Gide himself had been highly displeased by Bazalgette's "prettified" version and had spent much time during the first World War on a translation of his own, which finally appeared in 1918 in the "Important World Literature" series of *Nouvelle Revue Française*. In 1918 Eugène Figuière also gave a series of lectures on Whitman, accompanied by recitations by various people, at the Odéon Theatre in Paris; and the following year, June 10, 1919, John Erskine lectured on him at Dijon. There was no longer any doubt in France about Whitman's being a poet. An interesting side-light on his reputation was provided in January, 1919, by Jean Guéhenno in an article in *Revue de Paris* entitled "Whitman, Wilson et l'esprit moderne," in which the author accused President Wilson of having borrowed his "Fourteen Points" from Walt Whitman—a charge repeated in Germany several months later.[193]

The culmination of outright Whitman worship in France was reached in 1921 when Bazalgette published the last of his studies, *Le Poème-Évangile de Walt Whitman*. Although the attitude had been anticipated in Bazalgette's earlier biography, it is difficult to imagine how any one could go further in deifying the poet-prophet and his evangel-poem. As Schyberg remarks, this latest "idealization of the Whitman figure was too much even for the prophets in America."[194] Both this new interpretation and the re-publication of Bazalgette's translation of *Leaves of Grass* in 1922 raised a fresh protest from Gide and his friends.

Throughout these years the name of the American poet was

frequently mentioned in Baldensperger's *Revue de Littérature Comparée*, and in 1929 Baldensperger's former student, Jean Catel, published his great study, *Walt Whitman: La Naissance du poète* (discussed in Chap. I),[195] followed in 1930 by a penetrating analysis of style, *Rythme et langage dans la première édition des* "Leaves of Grass." Both are interesting contributions to Whitman scholarship—and testify anew to the fact that this scholarship has become truly international.

In his critical biography Catel attempted to discover the reality hidden beneath Whitman's imagery, or poetic symbols. His basic theory is that here we have a poet isolated from humanity by his genius. *Leaves of Grass* is a plea for love, an attempt to solve the personal problem. Failing to identify himself with humanity or nature, the poet tried *identité* exclusively (i.e., attempted to pierce to the soul of things, to understand the phenomenon of being). Whether or not later critics would accept this psychological interpretation, they could hardly ignore it. In subtlety and suggestiveness the French criticism of Whitman had thus surpassed the English or American—but after Catel it is uninspired until Asselineau.

In the above rapid survey of Whitman's reception in France several references have been made to his influence on French literature. Some idea of its extent and importance may be gained by a brief discussion of a few key examples.

The Unanimist lyric socialism closely parallels Whitman's "adhesiveness" and "comradeship," and was at least in part inspired by "Calamus." Schyberg refers to Jules Romains' novel of brotherly love, *Les Copains* (1913) as "the half glorification of the 'manly friendship' which is at once Calamus-sentimentality and devil-may-care swaggering"; but Romains' lyric poetry shows a greater Whitman influence, "with its wholly religious worship of life and its entirety and democratic multiplicity."[196] The four prophets and masters of the Unanimists were Hugo, Whitman, Verhaeren, and Claudel, "and usually all the Unanimist lyricism can be traced to the influence of one of these four." Bazalgette was mainly responsible for the group's admiration for Whitman. Other Unanimists who used Whitman themes were Georges Duhamel, Pierre Jean Jouve, and Charles Vildrac. Duhamel's *Vie des martyrs* (1917), written from his experiences as a doctor in the first World War, is reminiscent of Whitman's *Drum-Taps* and Civil War diaries. Both Jouve and Vildrac adopted the loose verse-form of *Leaves of Grass*, as Vildrac plainly indicated in *Verslibrisme* (1902) and *La Technique poétique* (1910).

Closely related to the Unanimists was another group of writers who were united through their internationalist sympathy and Gide's *Nouvelle revue francaise*, the organ of a number of French intellectuals during World War I. Two of these who were especially affected by Whitman's influence were Panaït Istrati and Valéry Larbaud.[197] Istrati, who wrote romances of an Oriental nature—cf. *Dyra Kyralina* and *Mikail*—used the vagabond friendship motifs in the Whitman manner, even to the length of phrase and cadence. Larbaud, whose preface has already been mentioned, was one of the revolutionary leaders of his literary generation, a champion in France of D. H. Lawrence and James Joyce in addition to Walt Whitman.

Most revealingly Whitmanesque is Larbaud's *Les Poésies de A. O. Barnabooth* (definitive edition, 1923). The irony and satire in the character of Barnabooth is un-Whitmanesque—or perhaps rather like a parody of Whitman—but the vicarious desire to cover continents, to share every human experience, to embrace all knowledge, and to live in his verses after his death are extremely close in theme and spirit to many poems in *Leaves of Grass*. Schyberg calls "Europe" a "reworked Whitman poem" in which the poet greets in turn the great cities, the seas, and the rivers of Europe, all of which he wished to embrace simultaneously in one grand panoramic vision. "This is 'Salut au Monde' in a modern French version. A fastidious artist has fallen so deeply in love with Whitman's poetry that he has copied it not only in content but also in form, with catalogues, participles, shouts, hails, parentheses, everything."[198]

For this brief period of post-war internationalism in France, Larbaud's Whitmanism appealed to a small coterie of intellectuals. But for a more deep and sustained influence we turn back to André Gide, who first became interested in the American poet in 1893 through Marcel Schwob, a distinguished Symbolist critic, poet, and romancer, who had discovered consolation in Whitman after deep personal bereavement. Like Symonds in England, these men found *Leaves of Grass* a spiritual tonic. According to Rhodes, who has made a close study of the influence of Whitman on André Gide,[199] in 1893 Gide was struggling to emancipate himself from two great handicaps, puritanism and the sort of physical *anomalie* which Whitman expressed in "Pent-up Aching Rivers" and other poems in "Calamus" and "Children of Adam." These poems "gave Gide the assurance he needed that 'la perversion de [son] instinct était naturelle. . .' Morally as well as spiritually, he felt he had been saved; he felt he was a new man, reborn to life as well as to art."[200]

This experience turned Gide from Symbolism, his nihilistic cynicism, and his earlier "Christian concept of the duality of human passion." In *Les Nourritures terrestres* (1897),

He turned away from reading and dreaming to desiring and living. His emotions blossomed out; he felt every sensation with the fervor of a religious experience. He hungered for a fresh awareness of the world about him to be apprehended not only by his reason but also by his senses. "Il ne me suffit pas de *lire* que les sables des plages sont doux; je veux que mes pieds nus les sentent." To be alive, merely to be, had become a voluptuous and intense satisfaction to him.[201]

In addition to the emancipation of his senses, Gide also found in Whitman "an attachment similar to that he was finding in Dostoievsky 'for the precious image of Christ before us,' who 'worked His first miracle to help men's gladness. . . .' "[202] Thus he could share the religious joy of life and love of all things of Whitman's "Song of Joys" or "Song of the Rolling Earth." "Je n'ai jamais rien vu de doucement beau dans ce monde, sans désirer aussitôt que toute ma tendresse le touche. Amoureuse beauté de la terre, l'effloraison de ta surface est merveilleuse. O paysage où mon désir s'est enfoncé!"[203] Also Whitman's doctrine of the inseparability of good and evil healed Gide's divided spirit and convinced him of the goodness and unity of all creation. Freed from "the metaphysics of symbolist ideologies 'en dehors du temps et des contingences,' uttering the shadows of words instead of their substance," Gide "took up and lived the life of *Les Nourritures terrestres*, and sang it subsequently."[204]

Whitman was of course not solely responsible for Gide's spiritual and literary growth:

He had started moving in the same direction from the beginning. His moral and social preoccupations have become not less but more intense with the passing of time . . . The ideal both he and Whitman have pursued has been the same: the salvation of the individual soul in the modern world. The course Gide has followed describes thus a spiritual curve that runs somewhat parallel to that of Whitman. Having discovered him at the start of his career, and felt his influence, he meets him again at its close.[205]

Here we have not only the clue to the growth of Whitman's reputation in France from Etienne to Gide, but also a clue to his importance in the modern world. The American poet was in the strong currents of a world stream of social and artistic change. Like André Gide, the twentieth century mind and spirit might have arrived at the same conclusions without Whitman, but he quickened the human sympathy and strengthened the social conscience of democratic writers in all countries—and in none more than France.[206]

In the great socialistic Belgian poet, Émile Verhaeren, we find a literary artist so like Whitman in temperament, in lyric inspiration, and in oratorical style (with its catalogues, parallelisms, and reiterations), that it is hard to believe he was not an adoring disciple; yet he apparently had no direct knowledge of the American poet, and in the words of his biographer, "independently and unconsciously arrived at the same goal from the same starting point."[207] But as Schyberg remarks, "the influence of Jules Laforgue on him, as on all 'La Jeune Belgique,' was important in helping him to revolt against all traditional forms, to find his 'free form,' 'this free verse so satisfying to the contemporary soul' . . ."[208]

Verhaeren's first poems, written under the inspiration of Symbolism, were not Whitmanesque, being protests against modern life, against industrialism and the city. But he soon threw off the shackles of Symbolism, or at least its "décadence," and in *Les Visages de la vie* (1899), *Les Forces tumultueuses* (1902), *La Multiple splendeur* (1906), and *Les Poèmes ardents* (1913) he celebrated the joy of existence in the modern world. Schyberg says:

The poet wants to feel the whole rhythm of life in his verse, the wind, the forest, the water, and "the thunder's loud roar," the entire world unfolding from North to South, from East to West, from the cities of India and China to the "gleaming cities" along the shores of America and Africa. He wants to share the life of each individual person, whether priest, scientist, soldier, moneychanger, swindler, or sailor.

Il faut admirer tout pour s'exalter soi-même,[209]

and

Je ne distingue plus le monde de moi-même,

he writes in *La Multiple splendeur*.

In this collection he writes hymns to work and to words, to the

wind, which, full of love, roams over the earth, to the grass, into
which he throws himself in an excess of happiness, to the enthusiasm
which inspires the poets of his day and produces "the new forms for
the new time," to the joy in which he, in Whitmanesque phrases,
celebrates all parts of his body . . .[210]

Professor P. M. Jones summarizes the Belgian poet's major
points of view in three of his most important works:

In *Les Forces tumulteuses* he has sung the mysterious union which
pervades all forms of reality; in *La Multiple splendeur* the ethical role
of admiration; while *Les Rythmes souverains* gives the world its most
august ideal of the struggle of man to reach divinity and free himself
from the sway of chance and the supernatural.[211]

Jones finally decides, however, that Verhaeren went far beyond
Whitman, though in a way that fulfilled and developed Whitman's
program:

Broadly speaking, Whitman theorizes, Verhaeren achieves. In spite of
all the former has said on the subject of science and industry, he has
written no poems like "La Science" or "Les Usines." Many themes
which have received full treatment from Verhaeren exist as hints or
indications in Whitman's works. And although Emile Verhaeren is
considered one of the most original of living [*i.e.*, in 1914] Continental poets, his work so often appears to realize the ideals of the
American prophet-poet that he seems, all unconsciously, to be the
first to have answered Whitman's appeal to the "poets to come."

> *I myself but write one or two indicative words for the
> future*[212]

Another Belgian poet who also reflects the reputation and influence of Whitman is Charles van Lerbherge (1861-1907). His *Chan-
son d'Eve* (1904) has the themes and sentiments of *Children of
Adam* and a verse form that reminds one of *Leaves of Grass*. This is
especially apparent in "Eve's discovery of the beautiful earth, her
pantheistic feeling about God, and her yearning for death as a release, the sound, a note in the whistle and roar of the universe."[213] It
is, however, Whitman's "decadent" aspects which suggest the comparison. As Schyberg says, "There is a consistent parallel between

Whitman and the *fin de siècle* poets that is astonishing."[214] But it is not the whole of Whitman, and to an English reader *Leaves of Grass* is more unlike than like Symbolist and "decadent" poetry. The most remarkable thing about Walt Whitman's influence abroad, however, is his adaptability. He could provide inspiration for Symbolists, *fin de siècle* poets, Unanimists, and democratic humanitarians like Verhaeren and Gide (in their "redeemed" phases). Each group found something to admire or adopt from the American poet, thus testifying to his fertility and his perennially dynamic vision of life and its meaning.

Those French writers still living who admired Whitman so much earlier in this century are still loyal to his memory. In 1972 Roger Asselineau, the present leading French authority on Whitman, invited several to contribute to a symposium, called *Walt Whitman in Europe Today*.[215] Jules Romains, now a member of the *Académie Française*, remembered how he and his friends "discovered" Whitman in Bazalgette's translation. "Our enthusiasm was aroused by the fact that the American poet renewed the relationship between poetry and man. . . ." Jean Guehenno, also a member of the *Académie* and a former co-editor with Bazalgette of *Europe*, "loved" Whitman for the same reason he loved Montaigne, who also wrote one of "the most intimate, the most carnal of books." Furthermore, Whitman "perceived men as more similar than different and all ruled by the same fate." Jean Marie Le Clezio first read *Leaves of Grass* at fifteen, and "it struck me as a miracle. . . . What Whitman has told us we still do not know completely, but he has shown the way, as Rimbaud did with the same words: the straight, unutterable beauty of the modern world. . . ."

If one can judge from these examples, it is Whitman's personality and his serving as a symbol of democracy which remains most alive in France today. In 1948 Paul Jamati[216] in a spirited but inaccurate introduction to a mediocre translation of major selections of *Leaves of Grass* revived Bazalgette's glorified saintly prophet, and condemned all studies of Whitman's psychological aberrations, exclaiming, "*O psychanalyse, que de ravages!*" The "Calamus" poems are simple celebrations of comradeship and brotherly love. All attempts to find pathology in this kind of affection Jamati called a "*contre-légende*" perpetrated by antidemocratic critics to discredit Whitman. This was the conviction—or strategy—of most Communist champions of Whitman in the 1940s and 50s.

However, objective Whitman scholarship continued in France. In 1956 Roger Asselineau followed his excellent biographical-critical study with the best translation France had yet had.[217] Asselineau knew Whitman as well as any contemporary scholar anywhere, and he had also mastered not only the English language but even the American idiom. His *Feuilles d'herbe* does not contain all of *Leaves of Grass*, but all of "Song of Myself" and the major poems, with well-chosen selections from the shorter poems. As he has explained, French is more prolix than English, and Whitman is very difficult to translate into French. In German and other cognate languages of English it is easier to reproduce the sound and rhythm of Whitman's verse. Nevertheless, Asselineau has succeeded in conveying the spirit and core meaning of *Leaves of Grass*. His translation provides a sound foundation for further French criticism and understanding of Whitman. Yet, aside from Asselineau, there are no outstanding critics of Whitman in France today. However, translation continues. In 1959 Alain Bosquet,[218] a poet of considerable distinction, published a volume of selected translations in an excellent literary style, faithful to the tone of Whitman's verse, but not as strictly accurate as Asselineau's. To introduce Whitman to the French-speaking African nations (République du Congo, Guinée, Mali, Maroc, Tunisie) Asselineau made a special selection from his translation in 1966, with the title *Chants de la terre qui tourne*.[219] In his Introduction he stresses the Whitman of "Salut au Monde!":

> *O toi, Africain à l'âme divine, aux origines obscures, grand, noir, à la tête et aux formes nobles, promis à un destin superbe à égalité avec moi!*

Thus, through France, Whitman now moves to Africa, where perhaps a chapter in his reception is beginning. The President of the Republic of Senegal, Léopold Sédar Senghor, known in France for his poetry, says that "with Whitman it is truly primeval man and *natura naturans* which get expressed to the rhythm of days and nights, of ebb and flow, a rhythm which, for all its freedom, is strongly stressed." This, he thinks, is "why Whitman's poetry immediately gripped me."[220]

In French-speaking Canada the well-known Franco-American poet Rosaire Dion-Lévesque (winner of several decorations and prizes from both the French Academy and the Royal Society of Canada) published his first translation, *Walt Whitman: ses meilleures pages*, in 1933 in Montreal, and a revised edition in Quebec in 1965.[221] His translation has been praised in France by Vielé-Griffin, Valéry Larbaud, F. Delattre, and Auguste Viatte.

WHITMAN IN GERMANY: RECEPTION
AND INFLUENCE

In no other country in the world has Walt Whitman been so extravagantly admired and even worshipped as in Germany. But from England came the initial impetus, for while a political exile in Great Britain Ferdinand Freiligrath read the Rossetti edition of Whitman's poems and felt moved, as one critic has expressed it, "to contribute toward the realization of Goethe's ideal of 'Welt-Literatur' "[222] by publishing an appreciative account in a German newspaper, April 24, 1868.[223] This enthusiastic essay aroused little interest, but it is significant that in the "ego" of *Leaves of Grass* Freiligrath found a "part of America, a part of the earth, of humanity, of the universe."[224] The structure of the poems reminded him of the "Northern Magus," of Hamann, of Carlyle, and, above all, of the Bible, and he thought they might, like Wagner's music, shatter "all our canons and theories." It was thus as a world poet that Walt Whitman gained his first, though obscure, recognition in Germany. Freiligrath followed up this article with some undistinguished and inaccurate translations from the Rossetti edition, which seems to have been the only one he knew; and when he returned to Germany in 1869 he encouraged his friend, Adolf Strodtmann, who had also been exiled and had spent 1852–56 in the United States, to undertake other translations from *Leaves of Grass*.[225] These translations, however, attracted almost no attention.

For two decades after this unpromising beginning, Whitman was almost completely ignored in Germany—perhaps not surprising when one considers the period, which was a time of intense nationalism, of scientific interest, and of social agitation. Meanwhile in 1882 a German-American, Karl Knortz, published an essay on the American poet in a German language newspaper in New York, later reprinted as a monograph, *Walt Whitman, der Dichter der Demokratie*.[226] His biographical interpretation was based on Bucke and O'Connor, and he himself wrote like a member of the "inner circle." Thus Knortz helped to lay the foundation for the Whitman cult in Germany. But he, too, did not stop with criticism. After T. W. Rolleston was unable to get his translations of *Leaves of Grass* published in Germany,[227] Knortz revised the manuscript and found a publisher in Switzerland in 1889. Knortz's contribution to this book seems to have been mainly editorial, but he added some translations of his own to a third edition of his *Walt Whitman, der Dichter der Demokratie* (1889). Not only were these versions superior to Freiligrath's, though still literal and crude, but German readers also got for the first time such long, characteristic, poems as "Song of Myself," "Starting from Paumanok," and "Out of the Cradle."

As early as 1883 Rolleston had tried to call attention to Whitman's embodiment of democratic ideals, but the time was not yet ripe for the appreciation in Germany of a "democratic" poet. By the time the Rolleston-Knortz edition appeared, however, the ground had been prepared. Especially among the young socialists and revolutionaries there was a great desire to break with the traditions of the past and to find new forms and expression for art and society. Both the ideas and the style of *Leaves of Grass* quickly became vitalizing symbols for many of the young writers. Eduard Bertz felt that the high point of his visit to the United States was making the acquaintance of Whitman's poetry, which he considered naturally religious, with a gnarled originality and strength. J. V. Widmann[228] declared in the same tone: "Walt Whitman is to be understood as a Jacob Boehme, an Angelus Silesius. In him the basic principle of his ideas and creations is always an overwhelmingly strong feeling of the sacredness and innate nobility of all existence."[229] This complete acceptance of Whitman as a prophet of a new natural religion, or ontological monism, was the central faith of the Whitman cult in Germany—and "cult" is not too strong a term.[230]

The most ardent disciple of this cult was Johannes Schlaf, who, much like Carpenter in England—though more uncritical—was to make the promotion of Whitman the great work of his life. The American poet's doctrine of the unity of all creation, of man and nature, of spirit and matter, strongly influenced Schlaf's volume of poems, *Der Frühling* (1896). Among his many publications on Whitman, the best known are his monograph, *Walt Whitman*, first published in 1896 and reissued in 1904,[231] and his translation, *Grashalme, in Auswahl* [selection], 1907, 1919. He also adapted or improvised upon O'Connor's work in his essay, *Vom Guten Grauen Dichter*, 1904, and made an attempt to translate the English biography of Binns. But unfortunately Schlaf knew English so imperfectly that he botched all his translations, both prose and poetry, and drew down upon his head scathing denunciations, especially from

Eduard Bertz, who attempted to expose Schlaf's ignorance and pretence.[232] But this infatuated disciple was undaunted by such attacks and was still "promoting" Whitman as late as 1933.[233]

There would have been a "Whitman movement" in Germany without Schlaf's efforts, though it might not have been so fanatical. In 1904 Karl Federn published a collection of selected poems in translation,[234] using as Introduction an essay which he had written five years before.[235] He called the poems "simple and crude" like the Psalms or the Eddas. Goethe and Whitman were said to be alike in that "the man and his work are inseparably united." Here we find also an observation which explains not only Whitman's appeal to these German admirers but also his astonishing world-wide reception: he "possessed one secret, which is the profoundest secret of the real poet, namely that of calling forth in the reader his own mood."

Federn's translations are more poetic than those of Knortz and vastly superior to Schlaf's, though Law-Robertson has pointed out serious inaccuracies.[236] Especially noteworthy is the fact that Federn arranges the poems chronologically. His text is based on the 1881 edition. The same year (1904) Wilhelm Schölermann published still another translation, but in his attempt to make his version poetic he resorted to rhyme and omitted some of the repetitions from "Song of Myself." Needless to say, the result was not characteristic of the original. But in his introductory essay Schölermann provided an interesting illustration of the German deification of Whitman during this period:

Whitman belongs to a class of individuals who are more than life size, who spring into existence in a moment of lavish exuberance on the part of procreative nature ... Beethoven and Bismarck are men of similar calibre; Whitman also betrays a number of traits in common with that awe-inspiring man-of-men (*Ganzmenschen*) Jesus of Nazareth, for example, his exalted, tender kindness, his heroic love ... The healing power of this kindness and goodness, that ancient miracle-performing gift which causes the blind to see and the lame to walk, that gift Whitman also possessed.[237]

Less exalted but no less ardent was the declaration in 1905 of O. E. Lessing, who had spent a year on the faculty at the University of Illinois, that Whitman "is the center, summit, and fountain-head of a first great epoch in the intellectual life of the new world."[238] He called Whitman "the greatest poet since Goethe ... He is the embodiment, the representative, and the illuminator of American Literature in the same sense that Dante is of the Italian, Shakespeare of the English, and Goethe of the German." Several years later in his retraction Lessing could truthfully say that he had "made Whitman *only* a superman instead of a God as my predecessors had done."[239] But in 1905 his prose translations, in the main accurate and competent, were a great boon to the Whitman movement in Germany. In his sound introduction he quoted from Whitman's notebooks, especially, as Law-Robertson remarks, "those which show his cosmic world outlook as well as his personal opinions about personal and human relationships."[240]

From about 1895 to 1905 or 1907, Whitman's name was a convenient literary and social symbol for many of the more revolutionary German writers, but aside from Schlaf, his actual influence is difficult to assess. Schlaf eagerly adopted Whitman's religious and cosmic ideas and attempted to re-express them in his own lyrics. *Frühling* was written under the direct inspiration of Schlaf's secondhand knowledge of *Leaves of Grass*. *Sommerlied* (1903), though more conventional in form, showed strong influence of "Children of Adam," while *Das Gottlied* (1922), an attempt to treat the theme of the origin of the world, was consciously Whitmanesque in manner. Like Whitman, Schlaf expected a new poetic language to emerge from the age of science and materialism, a view which he shared with his friend Arno Holz, who deliberately tried to establish a modern theory and technique in his *Revolution der Lyrik* (1899). Because Holz was friendly both to Schlaf and Whitman at the time he was experimenting with free (Whitman's "organic") rhythms, he has often been accused of indebtedness to the American poet. But Holz admired Whitman as a personality and ethical leader, not as a poet. In a letter he explained:

Quite a different man from Goethe or Heine was Whitman. I shall never write the name without taking off my hat to this American. He is one of the names dearest to me in the literature of the world. He wanted the change which has now taken place. But although he broke the old forms, he did not give us new ones.[241]

Amelia von Ende, in the best article on the subject in English, says of Whitman:

His aim was to give us new values of life, not new forms of art. This he has accomplished; he has given us a view of life, which it will take generations to accept, to assimilate and to put into practice. Whitman is a man among men, a poet for mankind. Holz is a poet among poets, a poet for poets.[242]

To the present writer, the chief link between Whitman and Holz seems to be their cosmic mysticism and evolutionary transmigration. Holz projects himself backward and forward in time, identifying himself with various objects in Whitman's manner, but decidedly not in his poetic form.[243]

Law-Robertson thinks that in the impressionistic school, which regarded Schlaf's *Frühling* as something of a "program," Whitman did influence the form of certain German lyricists.[244] He mentions especially Alfons Paquet's *Auf Erden* (1904-05). "Paquet's impressionistic sketches are compressed into compact pictures and therefore lack the strong exuberance of the cosmic breadth of Whitman's verse. Otherwise he uses the same stylistic methods—repetitions, enumerations, participle constructions."[245] In a letter to Law-Robertson, Paquet acknowledged his indebtedness to Whitman, whom he regarded as the "Great American poet, the great prototype ... and as often as I read his poetry, there always streams out something of the infinite space, of the simplicity and brave goodness of humanity, such as I felt in a few unforgettable happy days [in the United States], especially in the wilderness of Colorado."[246] But other impressionists, like Karl Röttger, found the basis for their "free rhythms" in older German literature, and some members of the group broke with conventional rules without knowing Whitman.[247]

The reaction against Whitman began as early as 1900 when Knut Hamsun's savage attack in a Danish paper was translated into German,[248] though the editor felt compelled to insert a footnote saying, "We who love Whitman prefer to learn about him from Johannes Schlaf."[249] Hamsun's argument was simply that of the literary conservatives of all countries, not least of Whitman's own contemporary Americans: he is not a poet, but an uncouth fraud. He is modern only in his brutality. In short, Hamsun attempted with heavy irony to demolish every one of the poet's literary pretentions.

Eduard Bertz was first an admirer but later a disillusioned critic of Whitman. In 1881-83 he lived in Tennessee (in one of the numerous American social experiments similar to Brook Farm) and later settled in London. He was thus better prepared than most of the German critics for genuine understanding of Whitman. In 1889 he wrote: "As the greatest benefit which I derived from my sojourn in America, nay as one of the happiest events of my life, I regard the acquaintance with the writings of the most original and deepest of all American poets."[250] Bertz sent this article to Whitman, who responded so eagerly—bombarding the author with material for future articles—that Bertz was shocked and wrote a reserved account of the poet for Spemann's *Goldenes Buch der Weltliteratur* (1900). Now suspicious, he re-examined Whitman's claims—and the claims made in his name by his over-zealous disciples—to being the founder of a new religion. In 1905 he attempted to reveal what he now regarded as Whitman's sex pathology,[251] agreeing with Edward Carpenter in the verdict. In *Der Yankee-Heiland* Bertz attempted further to destroy the "prophet myth," though he still regarded Whitman as a great lyric poet.[252] Schlaf replied to these attacks upon his "saint," and it was as a result of this quarrel that Bertz so mercilessly exposed Schlaf's pretentions as a translator and scholar.

O. E. Lessing was likewise drawn into the controversy, against Schlaf. In 1910 he confessed "to the guilt of a serious attack of Whitman"—as previously mentioned.[253] Many critics had tried to couple Whitman's name with Nietzsche's, partly, no doubt, because Nietzsche was a great name to conjure with in the late nineteenth and early twentieth century, but also because these Germans could think of no one else who had created a literary form so daring and impressive. Lessing, however, now used this comparison to "debunk" Whitman:

As artists [Nietzsche and Whitman] have fallen below many a less famous poet. Neither *Zarathustra* nor *Leaves of Grass* are, strictly speaking, poetical compositions. They contain a wealth of esthetic material. . . . Accepting Sainte-Beuve's view[254] that a work of art should rather suggest emotions than give definite form to an esthetic experience, Whitman, in true romantic fashion, meets the critic's objection to the hazy vagueness of the majority of his poems.[255]

But Whitman's poetry in "its final effect is enervating rather than invigorating. In this Whitman resembles a vastly superior artist: Richard Wagner, whom Nietzsche justly calls the great sorcerer."[256] Both "possessed . . . an indomitable sensuality, the magnetism of which, vibrating through all their compositions, causes an ecstatic intoxication invariably followed by utter exhaustion."[257]

Although the first great wave of Whitman enthusiasm in Germany had ebbed by 1910, he was not forgotten. In 1906 the Alsatian, Friedrich Lienhardt, considered the American poet the successor of Goethe.[258] A year later the proletarian poet of Austria, M. R. von Stern, hailed him as an Hegelian conditioned by a "strong autochthonic democratic instinct. There is no other poet who is so consistently permeated by democratic ideas."[259] In 1911 Knortz entered the controversy over Whitman's abnormality by publishing *Walt Whitman und seine Nachahmer, Ein Beitrag zur Literatur der Edelurninge*. He agreed in the main with Carpenter and Bertz on the subject, which he said he deliberately ignored in his *Dichter der Demokratie* in order to secure a favorable response to Whitman in Germany. This admission was an indication of the passing of the "cult."

In only a few years, however, the second Whitman movement in Germany began when the labor press discovered him at the beginning of the first World War. He was hailed by the people as he had never been in America. As Jacobson remarks, *Drum-Taps* and "Whispers of Heavenly Death" "struck upon the ear and heart of an era that experienced a similar disaster."[260] These writers were interested not so much in the poet as in the "wound-dresser" and social prophet. He became, in fact, a kind of official spokesman for the Social Democrats. Franz Diedrich thought the poet of *Drum-Taps* could be "consoler, physician, pathfinder" to the enslaved and oppressed,[261] and Max Hayek praised him in the same way in the *Sozialistische Monatsheft*, in which he frequently published translations from *Leaves of Grass* between 1914–1931. In emphasizing this aspect of Whitman, the Social Democrats were also strongly influenced by Schlaf—thus to some extent reviving the "cult."

Of the World War I poets who were influenced by Whitman, one of the most interesting was Gerrit Engelke, a young German poet who read Whitman in the trenches and was killed in battle. His posthumous book, *Rhythmus des neuen Europa* (1923), shows us, as Jacobson remarks, "how Whitman's message became his gospel,"[262] though "his racing through all continents is not a mere imitation of Whitman, but an inevitable outcome of his inner feeling." Karl Otten's song "An die Besiegten" is also reminiscent of *Drum-Taps*. And though the poems of Heinrich Lersch are more conventional in form than Whitman's, we find in them many of the themes and sentiments of *Leaves of Grass*, especially significant being the eternal now, embracing past, present, and future.

When the war ended, Whitman became in Germany the poet of peace, and also more than ever the symbol of Democracy. Hugo Wolf, reviewing Hayek's translation, "Ich Singe das Leben," in *Der Friede*, July, 1919, declared that President Wilson's "fourteen points" had been plagiarized from Whitman.[263] Many celebrations were held in honor of the poet's centenary. Schlaf hailed him again as the perfect social and religious leader.[264] The Socialists of the November Revolution considered him as a comrade, and the Communist poet, Johannes Becher, wrote a poem to "Bruder Whitman." Max Hayek called *Leaves of Grass* "in fact the Bible of Democracy. . . . Walt Whitman's time has only now arrived. He is the poet of the modern day . . . of the year that now unfolds [1919]."[265] Whitman not only wrote of Democracy, but he lived it himself; therefore, he is a perfect example for "Social Democracy" in Germany. The working men were summoned to study Whitman.[266] But in Austria and Hungary, translations of Whitman's works were suppressed[267]—the proletariat had found in him the power of the masses. *Freie Jugend*, a very radical paper, published a translation of Whitman's "To a Foil'd European Revolutionaire." "Here," as Jacobson says, "Whitman is celebrated as the enemy of the state because of his love for order among men, as the enemy of the church because of his religion and conscience."[268]

This new cult led to Whitman evenings, "with slides and recitations, as for instance, in Vienna, where an actor makes out of Whitman's 'Mystic Trumpeter' a symphony of drama and lyricism, or in Munich, in Frankfort, and in Berlin, where Hans Reisiger and a great Reinhardt actress try to introduce Whitman into larger circles, the actress even over the radio."[269] Meanwhile the "expressionists" had also taken up Whitman,[270] and René Schickele included three of his poems (in Landauer's translation)[271] in *Menschliche Gedichte im Kriege* (1918). In fact, during the turbulent years in Germany from about 1918 to 1922 the American poet of Democracy seems to have been all things to all men.

Despite the great critical excitement over Whitman, however, no really good translations of his poems existed in Germany until the gifted Munich poet, Hans Reisiger, undertook the task. His first small volume of selections appeared in 1919, and was followed in 1922 with a greatly expanded translation in two volumes, with an eloquent

Introduction.[272] This work is now regarded as a classic. Herman Stehr declared: "it is as if the great American had written not in English, but in German."[273] And Law-Robertson, who has pointed out serious faults in all previous attempts to turn Whitman's poems into German, is almost lyrical in praise of this one. In his now-famous Introduction Reisiger idealized Whitman almost as much as Schlaf had done, but he wrote from full knowledge of the poet and his work and his eloquence is due not to subjective fictionizing but to his deep, intelligent conviction of Walt Whitman's importance. In his psychological approach he also anticipated Catel, Schyberg, and Canby: "Walt Whitman was one of the fortunate people who, even in ripe old age, remained wrapped in a strong and warm mother-world...."[274] At the heart of Walt Whitman's being was the fact that he had never lost the miraculous twilight gleam of childhood, the gleam of the first delightful surprise in mere existence."[275] Like many of his contemporaries in Germany, Reisiger appreciated more deeply than most Americans what the Civil War had meant to the author of *Leaves of Grass*, and he thought that *Democratic Vistas* had a special meaning for the post-war generation in Germany.

Had political history in this nation followed a different road from the one the people were already unconsciously choosing even in 1922, Reisiger's great work might have been the beginning of a long and fruitful Whitman epoch in Germany rather than the crest of the interest which would soon recede. With unconscious irony Reisiger declared at this time:

The quick success of my first selected translation in 1919 and the fact that I can now bring out this larger work are proofs of the ever-growing interest taken by the German speaking intellectuals of Europe in this man who is being recognized with increasing certainty as the most powerful, purest, and most virile embodiment of a truly cosmo-democrat.

In the developing democracy of Germany—I use the word democracy in its political as well as its social sense—Walt Whitman will be more and more regarded as *the* poet of a new community of mankind, who has, by his truly magnetic personality, succeeded in blending most completely the contrast between individuality and the mass; who, fully conscious of the wonder of his existence in the midst of the universe, the wonder of Now and Here, expresses it with the highest power of love, and, dwelling thus in his Self, embraces All; whose work is nothing less than the natural, wild, and sweet language of an exalted type of future humanity, totally liberated in himself, lovingly housed in the Seen and Unseen; in a word, a Columbus of the Soul, who truly leads on God's seas to a New World.[276]

The irony of these optimistic hopes first appears in the use which the renowned novelist, Thomas Mann, made of the American poet in 1922. Mann seems to have discovered Whitman in the early 1920s at a time when he despaired of his own negative inheritance from Schopenhauer, Nietzsche, and Wagner. In thanking Reisiger for a copy of his two-volume translation Mann called it a "holy gift" and declared it to be of special benefit "to us Germans who are old and unripe at one and the same time, to whom contact with this powerful member of humanity, the humanity of the future, can prove a very blessing if we are able to receive his message."[277] But could Germany receive the message? No one was more fearful than Mann himself, for in the same year he saw the tragic necessity of beginning a personal fight to prolong the life of the young Republic. In his historic speech, *Von Deutscher Republik*,[278] delivered in 1922 to strengthen popular approval of the new democratic experiment in Germany, he hailed the identity of American Democracy with German Humanity, and cited Whitman and Novalis as the archetypes of each, as in his letter to Reisiger he had cited Whitman and Goethe. Mann also tried to contribute to this *rapprochement* by extoling Whitman's "athletic" Democracy, an appeal which even a National Socialist might understand; but from this time on Whitman's influence in Germany rapidly faded. The American poet was still loved by Stefan Sweig,[279] Franz Werfel,[280] and the Mann family[281] —but they were soon writing in exile, like the first German critic and translator three-quarters of a century before, Ferdinand Freiligrath.

World War II was not followed by another surge of interest in Whitman, though *Leaves of Grass* continued to be translated, read, and quietly studied. Of course Whitman was included in the various American Studies programs which have flourished in German universities during the past two decades. Georg Goyert, the famous translator of James Joyce, published a well-received volume of selections of *Grashalme* in 1948,[282] and he also translated Henry Seidel Canby's biography of Whitman the same year.[283] Herbert Pfeiffer in *Der Tages Spiegel* (April 21, 1948) thought Canby's book lacked objectivity, but he envied a country in which an individual could still be a hero in biography. In 1961 Rowohlt published in its Monographien series a translation by Kurt Kusenberg of Gay Wilson Allen's brief biography *Walt Whitman*.[284] But Professor Hans-Joachim Lang, of the University of Erlangen-Nuremberg, in his contribution to *Walt Whitman in Europe Today* (1972) can not point to any important recent publications on Whitman. He ends his essay with this rhetorical question: "Is it an academic illusion to believe that more people in Germany today have a surer grip on the original text of Whitman and a better personal acquaintance with American life ... than 50 years ago?"[285] —when so many German writers were deifying "the Poet of Democracy."

WHITMAN IN SCANDINAVIA

Denmark, as Schyberg has pointed out with some pride,[286] discovered Whitman almost as soon as England and Germany, and contemporaneously with France. In 1872 Rudolf Schmidt began writing articles on him in Copenhagen and two years later he published a translation of *Democratic Vistas*. His "Walt Whitman, the Poet of American Democracy" is a sympathetic but fair summary and analysis of the poet's ideas and art, well worth reading today.[287] In 1888 Niels Møller translated *Autumn Rivulets*, but Schyberg says that because of its "remarkably complicated rhythmic diction," it did not contribute to the future understanding of Whitman's poetic art.[288] However, the fact that Whitman had no influence on Danish writers of the late nineteenth century is probably attributable to the complete indifference to him of Georg Brandes,[289] the critical dictator of the period; and Knut Hamsun, of Norway, was openly hostile.[290] Johannes V. Jensen counteracted this indifference and hostility when he published his novel, *Hjulet (The Wheel)*, in 1905. This is a very unusual contribution to Whitman criticism, for both the hero and the villain represent the American poet's doctrines on two planes, that of a social idealist and of a charlatan "prophet." The book contains long translated passages from *Leaves of Grass*, which Jensen and Otto Gelsted edited in an enlarged edition in 1918, with a critical Introduction by Gelsted. This collection is said to have had considerable influence on the generation of World War I lyricists in Denmark.[291]

In 1929 Børge Houmann translated "Song of Myself" and some other poems, with a highly romantic Introduction. And in 1933 Frederik Schyberg published his biographical and critical study, which has been mentioned so frequently in this *Handbook* that little more need be said about it. In the same year he also published another book of translations.[292] There were at this time, according to this competent witness, several Whitmanesque Danish poets, notably Harald Bergstedt, "a kindred spirit of Whitman's—not only in his great democratic declamations" but also in his lyric style. Bergstedt denies the influence, though he admits that he has known Whitman since he began writing.[293]

Jørgen Erik Nielsen, in the latest summary and evaluation of Whitman in Denmark, reports Torben Brostrøm's assertion in *Dansk Litteraturhistorie* (IV, 1966) that "the 'modernism' in Danish literature in the 1930s was inspired by Whitman rather than Baudelaire."[294] Although there is still no complete translation of *Leaves of Grass* into Danish, translation of his poetry and prose continues: a selection of *Specimen Days* (*Fuldkomme Dage*) by P. E. Seeberg in 1950; in 1965 Poul Sørensen's 64 pages devoted to Whitman translations and critical comment in his *Moderne amerikansk lyrik: Fra Whitman til Sandburg*; and Emma Cortes's volume of selections, *Til Graesset ved Søens Bred Er Jeg Flygtet* ("I Have Fled to the Grass by the Edge of the Water") in 1970. Professor Neilsen's evaluation is that this translation has some merit, but shows insufficient familiarity with the Danish language. As for the other translations, Houmann's is faithful but prosaic; Schyberg's "runs smoothly and pleasantly" but is not always accurate, "and the reader is forced to consult the original." Jensen's and Gelsted's rank somewhere between these two. "Poul Sørensen's translations have a modern ring; they are reliable and contain some extremely beautiful renderings." Since the study of English in Denmark begins in grammar school, the "original" offers most Danes little difficulty, and this may explain the lack of a complete translation of *Leaves of Grass*.

Rudolf Schmidt's Danish translation of *Democratic Vistas* in 1872 was the means of Whitman's first introduction to Norway (the literary languages of the two countries were then essentially the same). Schmidt's *Demokratiske Fremblik* aroused the enthusiasm of Bjørnstjerne Bjørnson,[295] and also influenced Kristofer Janson to visit America.[296] After his return Janson praised the American poet in *Amerikanske Forhold* (American Culture), published in Copenhagen in 1881. However, Knut Hamsun, whose trip to the United States disillusioned him, made a speech in the Copenhagen Student Union in 1889 in which he satirized Whitman's claims to being a poet, calling *Leaves of Grass* "not poetry at all; no more than the multiplication tables are poetry."[297] Hamsun called Whitman "a savage" and "a voice of nature in an uncultivated land." Apparently Hamsun and Georg Brandes stifled any further interest in Norway until he twentieth century.

Schyberg's 1933 translation and his biographical-critical study called Whitman again to the attention of Norway. One result was the translation of the complete "Song of Myself" into Landsmaal (or Nynorsk), the more colloquial of the two official Norwegian languages, by Per Arneberg in 1947.[298] This is still probably the most successful of all Scandinavian versions of Whitman, perhaps partly because of the compatibility of Landsmaal with Whitman's language, but more to the skill of the poet-translator.[299] Kjell Krogvig immediately recognized the similarities between Whitman and Norway's great early nineteenth century poet, Henrik Wergeland (1808–1845), especially in Wergeland's long epic-drama (1830) *Skabelsen, Mennesket og Messias* (*Creation, Mankind, and Messiah*). Krogvig recommended that Norwegians approach Whitman through Wergeland, who offered parallels in ideas, imagery, and even rhythms; and "if one did not know it to be impossible, one might be tempted to speak of direct influences."[300] But how many Norwegian readers followed his advice is not known. Whitman is also, as in Germany, taught in the country's university American Studies programs.

Frederic Fleisher says that probably the first mention of Walt Whitman in Sweden was "in 1895 in a poem by Gustaf Uddgren, a minor author and journalist."[301] Culturally Sweden has long been closer to Finland than to Denmark or Norway, and it was through a group of modern Finnish authors that Whitman began to arouse some interest in Sweden in the twentieth century. "The influence of Whitman on Edith Sölergran, perhaps the outstanding Finnish-Swedish poet of this century, is quite marked." The Swedish author Arthur Lundkvist, novelist, poet, and critic, though not a champion of Whitman, helped to make him known to the literary world. Schyberg's Danish translation stimulated Roland Fridholm to publish an essay in 1934 called "Pindarus från Paumanok" ("Pindar from Paumanok"),[302] and the following year K. A. Svensson published a selected translation, *Strån av gräs*.[303] Fleisher says it was not very good and received little attention. In 1937 Erik Blomberg, poet, art historian, and critic, published a "far superior" translation. He was a well-known socialist, and was interested in Whitman for ideological reasons, as were many other European socialists in the 1930s. The first Finnish translation of selected poems was made by Viljo Laitinen in 1954, but Fleisher does not mention it. "During the past three decades," he says, "Whitman's name has been mentioned on numerous occasions, but he has not gained much attention. He has assumed the role of a classic who is respected but [is] no longer a major source of inspiration."

It is different, however, in Iceland. There, "where grass is prized as the ultimate in vegetation and every third intellectual is a poet," writes Leedice Kissane, a visiting professor in the University of Iceland, writers have "responded understandably to *Leaves of Grass.*"[304] Editions of Whitman's poems in English reached the National Library in the 1880s, and later in complete editions of his works. Many single poems have been translated at various times into Icelandic, and around mid-twentieth century Whitman became a strong influence on several of the *Atomskald* poets, "a name coined by Nobel Prize winner Halldor Laxness to designate their modern obscurity and flouting of poetic conventions." Among these, Einar Bragi Sigurdsson recently translated "What Think You I Take My Pen in Hand," which describes the emotional parting of two men on a pier.

One Icelandic poet who makes no secret of Whitman's influence on him is Matthias Johannessen, who is also editor of Reykjavik's leading newspaper, *Morgunblade.* Kissane writes:

He recalls reading *Leaves of Grass* voraciously in his youth and points to the initial poem in his first book, *Borgin Hlo* (*The City Laughs*), as clearly echoing Whitman's "Song of Myself." This poem begins in the manner of Whitman—"I sing of you, City"—and continues with descriptions of Reykjavik, its harbor, streets, buildings, and sea gulls, thus recalling the American poet's many tributes to his own harbor cities of Brooklyn and Manhattan. . . . Though he attributes to Whitman's influence the freedom won in breaking the strictures of rhyme and alliteration, he respects the spareness and integrity of the Saga tradition, and his later poetry may be said to revert to that tradition in a sort of "revolution within a revolution."[305]

WHITMAN IN RUSSIA

In the summer of 1955 the first centennial of *Leaves of Grass* was celebrated in various parts of the world: in the United States by the publicaton of biographies and interpretations of Whitman by television programs, exhibitions, and lectures; in Russia by a mass meeting in the Academy of the Soviet Union. Before an enlarged fifty-foot portrait of the poet addresses were given by the Secretary of the Union of Soviet Writers and the two leading Russian authorities on Whitman, M. Mendelson and Kornei Chukovsky. The Soviet Embassy in Washington supplied the Library of Congress with published accounts of this meeting, and after studying them Mary McGrory wrote in the Washington *Star*:

> The Russians, one gathers from a study of such papers as *Pravda,* *Izvestia* and the *Literary Gazette* of the Union of Soviet writers, discovered Whitman much earlier than his fellow Americans. Turgenev in the 1870's was translating "this remarkable and striking poet" and Tolstoy, who particularly admired Whitman's "Leaves of Grass" recommended translation of all his works.[306]

The tone of this American report reflected the tension of the "Cold War" years, as perhaps the Russian speeches did also. In fact, the Voice of America radio station in New York countered some of the Russian claims by a broadcast given by the author of this *Handbook* on Whitman's concept of individual freedom, which the Russians had overlooked. Thus Whitman was used for propaganda purposes on both sides of the Iron Curtain. But the Russians had a right to celebrate "their" Whitman, for he did enter Russian literature early and may have been a vital influence in Soviet culture before he was in his own. What Russians value in Whitman is not exactly what Americans find in him, but this has been true of his reception in every country, as we have seen.

Whitman was mentioned in Russian journals as early as 1861,[307] but the first Russian critical notice occurred as a result of a lecture by Whitman's friend John Swinton in 1882, which was translated in *Zagranichnyi Vestnik (Foreign Herald)*.[308] This caused N. Popov to publish an article on "Uolt Guitman" in the *Herald* in March, 1883, in which the critic asked and attempted to answer: "Who is this Walt Whitman? He is the spirit of revolt and pride, Milton's Satan. He is Goethe's Faust, but a happier one. . . . he has solved the riddle of life; he is drunk with life, such as it is; he extols birth equally with death because he sees, knows, senses, immortality."[309] In his first response to the question Popov hit the keynote of Whitman's appeal in pre-revolutionary Russia: "He is the spirit of revolt." In tsarist Russia this statement might have been enough to get the critic into trouble, but he added something else that the censor pounced upon. In "This Compost" Whitman had wondered how the earth can grow "such sweet things out of such corruptions"—diseased corpses and decaying matter. Popov paraphrased: "Every life is composed of thousands of corpses," without indicating the redeeming transformation Whitman found in Nature. Consequently, Popov's essay was classified as "decadent," the author thrown into prison, and the magazine suspended. For many years thereafter it was dangerous to praise or translate Whitman in Russia. Perhaps this hazard made him more tempting to young writers.

Yet for all Whitman's admiration of American men and women in the mass, and his ambition to be a representative common man, the hero of his epic cycle of poems, there were enormous differences between his experiences and those of the Russian revolutionary writers (i.e., both those who preceded the abortive revolt in 1905 and the great revolution of 1917). In the United States Black people were enslaved until Lincoln's Emancipation Proclamation in 1863 (effective date), though it did not bring economic freedom. But slavery was a Southern institution, and Brooklyn-reared Whitman had no firsthand experience with slavery—with the exception of two months observation in New Orleans. As editor of the Brooklyn *Eagle* he did fight to prevent the extension of slavery to the new territories (see Chapter III), thereby causing his journalistic career to come to an end, or very nearly so.

It was during this time that Whitman wrote his impassioned poem "To a Foil'd European Revolutionaire."[310] This poem established his credentials in radical Russian circles in the last quarter of the nineteenth century. But most of his poems were not of this kind. He did not write abolitionist poems like Whittier. His revolution was mainly of the heart and mind; it was religious, philosophical, and esthetic rather than directly political. This the Russians could appreciate also, but they needed a more militant activist—or a poet who could be so used—and they partly recreated Whitman.

Like Nikolai Nekrasov, Whitman was also a poet-democrat and a poet-patriot, but the United States did not have an enslaved peasantry similar to Russia's. Negro slavery was certainly as reprehensible, and Whitman opposed it, at least in principle, but it was not the main substance of his experience or the subject-matter of his poems. As Chukovsky says, the hero of Nekrasov's great poem *Who Lives Happily in Russia?* is "the whole Russian people."[311] Whitman attempted to make his persona the symbolical voice of the American people, but most critics agree that *Leaves of Grass* is personal, lyrical, and for the most part joyous, and only occasionally the anguished voice of protest over unbearable social conditions, as Nekrasov's voice was. In America Whitman was condemned. Once an edition of *Leaves* was suppressed because of his free treatment of sex, but he was never officially persecuted, as Nekrasov was, for his literary attacks on political autocracy. Thus from the very beginning, the Russians selected what they most wanted or needed from Whitman, and magnified his rôle as "poet of the people." As has often been observed, Whitman's fondest wish was to be that kind of poet, but he never succeeded because he was more literary than he knew. Nor could he have reached the Russian people even if Fitzgerald Lee[312] had been able to make his proposed translation. Aside from likely censorship, the Russian masses were illiterate.

But a few of Russia's intellectuals did begin to discover Whitman fairly early. One of these was Turgenev. In 1872, in Paris, where Turgenev was living in exile, Whitman's poems were called to his attention, and he was so deeply moved by them that he offered to make some translations for *Nedeli* (*The Week*), but soon found his linguistic skills unequal to the task. The manuscript of his attempt to translate "Beat! Beat! Drums!" still exists in the National Library in Paris.[313] Turgenev is said to have told Henry James that Whitman's poems contained much chaff but also some sound grain.[314]

Tolstoy's first reaction to Whitman was unfavorable, but later found pleasure in the "Calamus" poems—interpreting them, of course, as all Russians have, as poems of comradeship. However, Tolstoy still thought Whitman lacked a coherent philosophy of life.[315]

The news of Whitman's death in 1892 was widely reported in Russian newspapers, and Russian émigrés in Switzerland learned about the poet in their Russian-language newspaper. The Russian Symbolists, like the French, were attracted by Whitman. Russia had Symbolists too, and in 1905 Konstantin Balmont published the first book of selected Whitman poems in translation.[316] It was immediately denounced by Kornei Chukovsky as weak, inaccurate, and in a style wholly unsuitable. Chukovsky himself then began translating Whitman, and soon established himself as the poet's major Russian translator, publishing edition after edition for the rest of his life, ending with a thoroughly revised posthumous edition in 1970 (he died in 1969). Three years earlier he had published *My Walt Whitman*, containing a personal account of his long experience in reading, translating, and interpreting Whitman, with a selection of his favorite poems, and a critical bibliography of books he had used.

In *My Walt Whitman* Chukovsky says, "Walt Whitman was the idol of my youth."[317] In 1901 he bought a copy of Whitman's poems from a sailor in Odessa for 25 copecks. He was "shaken to the core by the novelty of [Whitman's] perception of life," and responded "fervently to his call for ecstatic friendship, his paeans to equality, labour and democracy, his joyful intoxication with life, and his daring words glorifying the emancipation of the flesh, which had terrified the hypocrites of that time."

Chukovsky's first translation was published in 1907 in a St. Petersburg University student magazine, *Circle of Youth*.[318] Later he realized how poor his versions were, but he continued to learn and improve, until he had published ten editions by 1944, to which he added others in 1953, 1955, and 1970. "I continued to preach the gospel of Whitman everywhere, and there was no publication, it seemed, in which I did not print an article about him or translations of *Leaves of Grass*."[319] Meanwhile, Chukovsky became not only Whitman's leading translator in Russia, but also the leading translator of Shakespeare, Defoe, Mark Twain, Kipling, and other British and American authors. He was also the most popular author of children's books, read in every school and most homes of the land. In 1962 Oxford University awarded him an honorary degree of Doctor of Literature.[320]

In spite of his great admiration for Whitman, Chukovsky strove to present both the man and his work with the greatest fidelity possible. He depended mainly upon the "mythmakers," Bucke, Burroughs, O'Connor, and Horace Traubel, for his facts until he read Asselineau's *L'Evolution de Walt Whitman* and Allen's *The Solitary Singer*. In a letter addressed to *Walt Whitman in Europe Today* he says that with these books "the Whitman chronicle was finally purged of the myths and legends with which it had been cluttered."[321] By this time he had also used the newly edited volumes in the New York University edition of Whitman's *Collected Writings*; and he expressed his gratitude to the editor of the *Correspondence*, Edwin H. Miller, as well as to Floyd Stovall, editor of the

Prose Works 1892. Thus it appears that Russian Whitman scholarship is profiting from the American.

Chukovsky had all along welcomed intelligent criticism of Whitman. In 1935 he printed D. S. Mirsky's essay, "Walt Whitman: Poet of American Democracy," as an Introduction to his current translation. And Mirsky did not see Whitman as the prophet of a new society, but as "the last great poet of the bourgeoise era of humanity, the last in the line that begins with Dante."[322] He "is the poet of American democracy of the Fifties and Sixties, in all its organic strength. . . . He accepted it as something already existent in the nature of the American people and needed only to be brought to light. . . . Later on, in the Seventies, he had to confess that America of the present was yet far from the ideal. . . ,"[323] though he continued to hope for the future.

Whitman, of course, believed that democracy would be saved—or attained—by the character of individual Americans. But the Marxists believed that society must be remade before the individual could improve. This was the great chasm between Whitman and the Marxists. Mirsky found Whitman's importance not in his thought but his artistry: "It is not as to a prophet with a system that we should come to Whitman, but as to an artist. . . . those concrete forms to which he brought all the depth and strength of his emotion, all that he as an artist had learned from the American scene."[324] This Whitman "occupies an honorable place with the great poets of the past, who have afforded us . . . a vision of that full man who in reality is only able to exist as at once the builder and the creator of constructive socialism."[325]

In the same year Leonard Spier, writing in the English-language magazine published in Moscow, *International Literature*, gave a similar interpretation: "Whitman was a great critic of his nation who essayed to probe its future and influence it. His major deficiency, however, lay in his recourse to a false or pseudo dialectic."[326] This condemnation of Whitman's Hegelian mysticism had been voiced earlier in Germany by Bertz, and Arvin repeated it in the United States in 1938. But Spier concluded that "the best in Whitman belongs to the future and 'the future rests in the hands of the radicals' . . . what gold there is in this mountain is ours."

Whitman's greatest influence on Soviet poetry, according to Chukovsky, was in the 1920s and 30s, especially in the work of Mayakovsky and Khlebnikov.[327] He does not mention Yevtushenko and the poets of his generation.

POLAND, HUNGARY, CZECHOSLOVAKIA, YUGOSLAVIA AND RUMANIA

In other Communist countries of Eastern Europe there has been sporadic interest in Whitman, with numerous translations of single short poems or fragments of longer poems. In Poland Whitman was discussed as early as 1887, and after World War I a group of poets called "Skamander" espoused the American poet and experimented with his free rhythms.[328] Stanislaw de Vincenz published *Trzy Poematy* (*Three Poems*) in 1921, and S. Napieralski *75 Poematów* (*75 Poems*) in 1934. Two recent editions have appeared, *Walt Whitman, Poezje Wybrane* (*Selected Poems*) by several hands, edited by Hieronim Michalski, 1973, and *Źdźbla Trawy, Wybrane (Leaves of Grass, Selected Poems)*, edited with Introduction by Juliusz Zuławski, 1965. Zuławski has also published a biographical study, of nearly four hundred pages, *Wielka Podróz Walta Whitmana*, 1971, based on the latest American scholarship. He stresses the contribution of Poles in American history in order to arouse the interest of his fellow countrymen in America's most representative poet.[329]

Of all Eastern European countries Hungary is perhaps best supplied with modern translations. Keszthelyi Zoltán published a small volume in Budapest in 1947.[330] Kardos László and Szenczi Miklós edited a greatly augmented edition, over 400 pages, by various translators, in 1955,[331] and Országh László a still larger edition of nearly 800 pages in 1964.[332]

Czechoslovakia has the problem of two languages. Professor Ján Boor reports that "Czech literature is quite rich indeed in Whitman translations."

The great national poet Jaroslav Vrchlický was the first translator of the great American poet as early as in 1895. Later he made a representative selection of Whitman's poetry, published separately in 1906. Another Czech poet, Emanuel z Leshradu, translated poems of Whitman at the same time as Vrchlicky. Among other translators Arnost Vanecek and Pavel Eisner must be mentioned. Their modern translations—especially that of Pavel Eisner in 1945—made Whitman widely known throughout Czechoslovakia. Finally, the biggest choice of both poetry and prose of Whitman was given by two Czech translators, Jiri Kolár and Zdenek Urbánek, in 1955 and reprinted several times since then.[333]

The Slovak language has only one translation, *Pozdrav svetu*

("Salut au Monde!"), published in 1956; it contains fifty poems and all of *Democratic Vistas*. In 1969 a Whitman jubilee was held in Bratislava, for which the American (now living in Japan) William Moore wrote a drama, produced on Czechoslovakian television. Professor Boor says that a revival of interest in Whitman is taking place among the younger Czechoslovakian poets.

In Yugoslavia the language problem is still more complicated, but there have been translations of selections from Whitman's poems in Croatian (in 1900, 1909, and 1919); a lecture on Whitman in Serbian (1919); and, according to Sonja Bašić, "a series of remarkable translations by the great Croatian Bohemian poet and translator Augustin Ujević," was published in Zagreb in 1951, "retaining the powerful rhetorical flow of Whitman's poetry and his unconventional, rich vocabulary."[334]

Janez Stanonik has been translating and writing about Whitman in Slovenian since the first World War, and his latest translation appeared in 1962. There have also been translations of some poems into Macedonian and Serbian. Several Yugoslav poets are thought to have been influenced by Whitman but the subject has not been closely studied.

The most versatile volume of translations of Whitman in Eastern Europe is Rumania's *Opera Alese* (*Selected Work*) translated and edited by Mihnea Gheorghiu (Bucharest, 1956).[335] It contains a long historical and critical introduction, 234 pages of poems, 224 pages of prose (including early prose, autobiography, prefaces, and literary essays), two critical studies of Whitman (comparing him with Tolstoy and Mayakovsky), some letters, and poems to Whitman by García Lorca, Pablo Neruda, and Geo Bogza of the Rumanian Academy.

WHITMAN IN ITALY

Italy has also been hospitable to Walt Whitman, as Charles S. Grippi shows in his *The Literary Reception of Walt Whitman in Italy*, (1971).[336] Whitman has been translated, subjected to extensive critical analysis, and used as a symbol in the ideological conflicts. The bibliography of Whitman in Italy is so voluminous that a short sketch can do little more than name the major translators and critics.

There are two complete translations of *Leaves of Grass* in Italian, the first by Luigi Gamberale, *Foglie di erba*, in 1907 and 1923 editions;[337] the second by Enzo Giachino, *Foglie d'erba e prose*, 1950.[338] In 1972 Mariolina Meliadò Freeth wrote of the latter: "This beautiful translation, which also had the merit of bringing to the public's notice a selection from the prose, completely superseded Gamberale's old version and did much to stimulate criticism on Whitman."[339] Mrs. Freeth herself has translated the entire *Specimen Days*[340] (the only complete edition of this work in a foreign language), which Professor Roger Asselineau calls "a brilliant translation."[341]

As early as 1872 Enrico Nencioni discovered Whitman by way of French criticism, and interested his friends in the strange new American poet. In 1879 Nencioni published his first article on Whitman, in which he warned his readers that the poet was rude, shocking, and violated good taste, but had primitive strength and magnetism.[342] These traits, of which Whitman boasted himself, were the main attractions for his first Italian readers. Giovanni Papini, the leader of an Italian school of Pragmatism, declared that in discovering Whitman in his youth he had discovered poetry. He thought Italian poetry had become over-refined and effete, and, "If we would find again the poetry we have lost, we must go back a little toward barbarism—even toward savagery."[343]

When Giosuè Carducci read Nencioni's article he also responded with enthusiasm, declaring that "Italy has need to heal itself," and Whitman sounded like good medicine.[344] "The healing reference," says Grippi, "was a reaction to 'consumptive Leopardianism' and 'dropsical Manzonianism' of the ugly aspects of romantic sentimentalism that he saw in contemporary Italian literature."[345] Actually, Whitman seemed to answer several needs: recovery from sickly romanticism, from cultural insecurity, and from moribund literary conventions. It is curious, and doubtless significant, that most of the early Whitman enthusiasts in Italy were classical scholars, several of them teachers, like Carducci, who first thought of trying to translate Whitman's poems into Homeric hexameters.[346] Perhaps the long lines and Whitman's rhythms suggested this form, but the comparison also showed a desire to find Homeric qualities in this New World poet.

Carducci, D'Annunzio, and Giovanni Pascoli, the dominant triad of Italian poetry at the end of the nineteenth century, found Greek characteristics in Whitman to counteract their own exhausted Latinity. This attitude also made them more receptive to Whitman's open-ended prosody and new esthetics. They saw that his art was not lawless, but simply innovative in the use of old forms. Pascoli said the rhythms of *Leaves of Grass* resembled those of the Bible.[347]

But it remained for a young precocious scholar, Pasquale Jannaccone (who later became an economist and a statesman, not a poet) to observe parallels between Whitman's rhythms and those of primitive Greek hymns.[348] He was so taken by this discovery, and resemblances to other primitive poetry, that he proceeded to analyze the principles of Whitman's prosody—at a time when nearly everyone thought he had no prosody, though some of his friends in America had defended his verse-forms as "organic," operating on their own internal laws.[349] Jannaccone's *La Poesia di Walt Whitman e l'Evoluzione delle Forme Ritmiche* has been discussed in Chapter IV. Some of the poets disagreed with Jannaccone's methodical analysis, though they were apparently influenced by the very patterns of sounds and rhythms he dissected. One of these poets was Pascoli, especially in his "Il fanciullim," which Mariolina Meliadò has shown to resemble Whitman's "Out of the Cradle Endlessly Rocking."[350] This critic, in fact, sees in Giovanni Pascoli's poetry the "subterranean influence" of Whitman which provided the transition to modern Italian poetry.

The three major twentieth-century critics of Whitman in Italy have been Cesare Pavese (1908–50), Carlo Bo, and Glauco Cambon. Pavese discovered Whitman in his youth, wrote a university dissertation on him, and continued until his suicide in 1950 to write about Whitman. He challenged the usual sentimental image of Whitman— the old man with a white beard holding a butterfly on his index finger—and anticipated American critics by several decades in his opinion that Whitman's best poetry was in his earliest editions, and that with declining health his poetry degenerated. Pavese also rejected Whitman's claims to having put his own country and the nineteenth century "on record" in his book:

Walt Whitman lived out the idea of this mission so intensely that, though not avoiding the fatal failure of such a design, he yet avoided through it the failure of his work. He did not write the primitive poem of which he dreamed, but the poem of that dream. He did not succeed in his absurd attempt to create a poetry adapted to the democratic and republican world and to the character of the newly discovered land—because poetry is one—but as he spent his life repeating this design in various forms, he made poetry out of this very design, the poetry of the discovery of a world new in history and of the singing of it. To put the apparent paradox in a nutshell, he wrote poetry out of poetry-writing.[351]

This was a very acute observation, but critics of Pavese accused him of being highly subjective and of writing more about himself than Whitman. Carlo Bo, however, went even further in subjectivity by insisting on a "hermetic" or private reading of *Leaves of Grass*, a theory heavily indebted to French Symbolism and Surrealism. He took seriously Whitman's ambition to create poetry which would indicate "the paths between reality and the soul," or as he declared in his 1855 Preface: "The poets of the kosmos advance through all interpositions and coverings and turmoils and stratagems to first principles."[352] Bo's "hermetic" criticism linked Whitman to Symbolism in an entirely new way, one which no American critic attempted until Charles Feidelson wrote his *Symbolism and American Literature* (1953).[353]

In *Walt Whitman Abroad* the present author remarked apropos Giachino's translation that "Evidently Whitman still has a future in Italy."[354] Cambon retorted, "We can agree with Allen that Whitman has an open account with us for the future because he has already had an excellent past, both distant and recent."[355] Cambon himself studied the American idiom and literature in the United States and in a series of articles attempted to interpret Whitman's language and to explicate key poems. He also traced "Whitman's fortune in Italy," as Mrs. Freeth expresses it.[356] She herself praises Cambon for having called attention to the "literary worth" of Whitman's prose in "La parola come emanazione" (1959). Italian critics have been especially interested in Whitman's language. S. Perosa's study, Mrs. Freeth says, "shows Matthiessen's influence in establishing Whitman as a classic in Italy," and it is natural that they would have been affected by Matthiessen's theories about *Leaves of Grass* as "a language experiment."[357]

Not all Italian criticism, however, has been favorable. Mario Praz, of the University of Rome, had little use for Whitman, classifying him with Proust as "men-women, or better, human beings who have remained infantile in an essential part of their psyche."[358] Mario Alicata, like Paul Jamati in France,[359] branded all such interpretations of Whitman as the attempts of political reactionaries to discredit Whitman's "humanism and democracy."[360] Thus in Italy, as in other countries, Whitman criticism has been affected by the conflict of social and political ideologies.

WHITMAN IN SPAIN, PORTUGAL,
LATIN AMERICA AND GREECE

The cultural interchange between Spain and the Spanish-speaking South American countries, as well as Portugal and Brazil, makes the Spanish and Portuguese reception of Whitman the most extensive geographically of any languages. Both Spain and Ecuador have complete translations of *Leaves of Grass*, by Concha Zardoya in Madrid, 1946, and Francisco Alexander, Quito, 1953.[361] There are also numerous selections in Spanish, ranging from the Catalan version of Cebría Montoliu, Barcelona, 1909, reprinted in Buenos Aires in 1943, to Armando Vasseur's in Valencia, 1912, reprinted in Montevideo in 1939, and numerous others.[362] *Democratic Vistas* has been translated in Spain by Concha Zardoya (1946) and in Argentina by Luis Azua (1944).[363]

Both Spain and Latin America first became interested in the mythical Whitman of Bazalgette, and Cameron Rogers's fictionized *The Magnificent Idler*, as the biographical introductions of the various translations reveal. Even the Prologue by John Van Horne in Concha Zardoya's translation—and her own Introduction too—show the glorified Whitman against which Pavese in Italy protested;[364] however, the more realistic biographies of Asselineau and Allen had not yet been published—and there was also the usual cultural lag. Whitman, in fact, as a person was not very real to his Latin hosts. While making his study of Whitman in Latin America, Fernando Alegría wrote:

To study Whitman in Spanish American poetry is to trace the wanderings of a ghost that is felt everywhere and seen in no place. His verses are quoted with doubtful accuracy by all kinds of critics; poets of practically all tendencies have been inspired by his message and have either written sonnets celebrating his genius or repeated his very words with a somewhat candid self-denial.[365]

In Spain, at least, one major poet has been definitely influenced by Whitman. Miguel de Unamuno began translating and writing about him as early as 1906. In his own poems he adopted some of Whitman's mannerisms, echoed him in his "credo poético," and, as Concha Zardoya testifies, "In writing his great poem *El Cristo de*

Velázquez, he had very much in mind—as is known—Whitman's rhythmic liberties."[366] In "El canto adámico" ("Adam's Song") he wrote the most eloquent and imaginative defense of Whitman's "catalogs" ever published.[367]

Usually the Spanish poets most interested in Whitman had visited the United States. While studying at Cornell University, León Felipe Camino was attracted by Whitman. Later he translated, or paraphrased, "Song of Myself" with such freedom that he did not know himself whether his versions of sections 44 and 45 "are from the Bible, from Whitman or are mine."[368] In "Resumen" he declared, "I am Walt Whitman. In my blood there is an American romantic. . . ."[369] His own poems have enumerations, repetitions, epic lyricism, and "prosaism" which Zordoya says came from Whitman.

Federico García Lorca also became acquainted with Whitman's poems in New York, and wrote "Oda a Walt Whitman,"[370] which is generally agreed to be one of the greatest poems ever addressed to this American poet. Yet Lorca's own poems show no influence of Whitman in his themes or style. His ode is merely the heart-felt tribute of one poet to another.

In Jorge Guillén's Castilian *Cántico* (Madrid, 1926, 1928) there are resemblances to Whitman's cosmic pantheistic lyricism, though it is not known whether he was acquainted with Whitman before he wrote this book. Guillén came to the United States in 1940, and may have read Whitman then. His collection of all his poems in one volume, *Aire nuestro* (1968), reminds Concha Zardoya of Whitman's final *Leaves*.[371]

The realism and social consciousness of Rafael Alberti also "recalls Walt Whitman. In 'Siervos,' for example: 'I send you a greeting/ and I call you comrades.' " Since the Spanish Civil War poetry has become more social and humanistic. "Gabriel Celaya is, perhaps, the most representative poet of this tendency, not only for his subject matter but for his use of enumeration (occupations, things, places.")[372]

In Latin America three literary movements of modern times have, according to Alegría, responded in different ways to Whitman.[373] First the Modernista period: in 1887 José Martĭ, the Cuban poet and journalist, wrote an article on Whitman after hearing him read his Lincoln address in New York. The Nicaraguan poet, Rubén Darío addressed a sonnet to Whitman in his book, *Azul* (1888), and

Armando Vasseur translated the bulk of *Leaves of Grass* in 1912. But most of these writers knew Whitman very superficially, even Darío. Alegria says, "Whitman's voice is present throughout the modernist movement, but not his spirit."[374] The Chilean poet, Pablo de Rokha, comes nearest, in Alegría's opinion, of matching the genius and expression of Whitman. Today Alegría would probably agree that another poet of his country, the Nobel Prize winner, Pablo Neruda, has profited even more from Whitman's nourishing influence—though he is no imitator. Neruda himself gladly acknowledges the "internal debt," which began when he was barely fifteen. Whitman not only helped him become a poet, he "has helped me to exist." Then this remarkable tribute from one of the greatest poets of the twentieth century:

> There are many kinds of greatness, but let me say (though I be a poet of the Spanish tongue) that Walt Whitman has taught me more than Spain's Cervantes: in Walt Whitman's work one never finds the ignorant being humbled, nor is the human condition ever found offended.[375]

In these words Neruda pays tribute to Whitman not so much as a poet but as a moral force (which of course Whitman exerted through his poems), and that is the kind of tribute the American poet would have valued. Neruda defined his own poetry as "impure," meaning his esthetics was "confused [with the] impurity of the human condition."[376] Doubtless he hoped his poetry would help to sanitize and humanize that condition, but he pessimistically anticipated the "predators gnawing within"[377] who overthrew the Allende regime a few days before Neruda's own death from natural causes. Allende was his friend, whom he had served as Ambassador to France until illness forced his resignation. In his prophetic poem, "Fin de mundo" ("World's End") he had sorrowfully admitted, "Walt Whitman doesn't belong to us. . . ."[378] The point is that Whitman belongs to a free world—though at times men in bondage have turned to him for help in gaining freedom, as they did in Russia before and after the Revolution, in Italy under Fascism, in Spain during and since the Civil War. It is significant that *Democratic Vistas* is admired both in Spain and Latin America. *O Camarada Whitman*, by the great Brazilian sociologist, Gilberto Freyre, is ostensibly about the "good gray Whitman," but its main subject is his *Democratic Vistas*, in which Freyre finds a faith for both North and South America.[379]

To turn back to Europe briefly for Whitman's reception in another Latin country, an ardent but eccentric admirer of Whitman flourished in Portugal both before and during its political dictatorships. He was Fernando Pessoa (1888–1935), born in South Africa of Portuguese parents, but returned to Portugal for his career. Some of his poetry expresses social protest, and possibly all of it in subtle ways, but Pessoa was not an "activist." Whitman influenced him only in finding his own poetic form and idiom. Pessoa created several heteronyms under which he could express his private emotions without inhibitions, for which he was perhaps more indebted to Valéry Larbaud's A. O. Barnabooth than to Walt Whitman, but Whitman meant a great deal to him.

Pessoa's "Salutation to Walt Whitman"[380] is a clever parody, but without rancor, and can easily be taken for homage. From Portugal, with "all the ages" in his brain, Pessoa salutes his "brother in the universe," who, he is sure, knows him, "clasping hands, with the universe doing a dance in our soul." (Not two souls joined, but the one soul they share in common.) The following stanza is a fair sample of the poem:

O singer of concrete absolutes, always modern and eternal,
Fiery concubine of the scattered world,
Great pederast brushing up against the diversity of things,
Sexualized by rocks, by trees, by people, by their trades,
Rutting on the move, with casual encounters, with mere observations,
My enthusiast for the contents of everything,
My great hero going to meet death by leaps and bounds,
Roaring, screaming, bellowing greetings to God.[381]

The poet tells Walt he is not his disciple, not his friend, or his singer:

You know that I am You, and you are happy about it!

[Reprinted from *Selected Poems by Fernando Pessoa*, trans. Edwin Honig, with permission of The Swallow Press. © 1971 by Edwin Honig.]

He regrets not having Whitman's "self-transcending calm," and that is why he is crying out—saluting the "Great Liberator." The poem ends:

Goodbye, bless you, live forever, O Great Bastard of Apollo,
Impotent and ardent lover of the nine muses and the graces,
Cable-car from Olympus to us and from us to Olympus.[382]

[Reprinted from *Selected Poems by Fernando Pessoa*, trans. Edwin
Honig, with permission of The Swallow Press. © 1971 by Edwin
Honig.]

No one who could write like this could be called a disciple of
Whitman, and though Pessoa was liberated by him from certain literary conventions, and echoed him in some poems, such as "Triumphal
Ode," he hated the machine age which Whitman innocently welcomed. As Octavio Paz says in a Preface to Pessoa's poems, "*Triumphal Ode* is neither romantic nor Epicurean [like the poems of
Larbaud and Whitman] nor triumphant; it is a song of hate and
defeat. And this is the basis of its originality."[383] Here also we have
the vast distance between Whitman and Pessoa, in spite of the
American poet's influence.

In another southern European country, Greece (not Latin but
the mother of Latin tongues), *Leaves of Grass* has been admired sufficiently to be translated by the poet Nick Proestopoulos and published in an edition of selections and in a complete version.[384] The
language used is demotic Greek, perhaps because the translator
thought it to be equivalent to Whitman's language. But whether
appropriate or not, the two volumes show that Whitman has aroused
some interest in Greece, even during the great turmoils since World
War II.

WHITMAN IN OTHER COUNTRIES:
JAPAN, ISRAEL, CHINA

Several Japanese scholars have written articles on the reception
and influence of Walt Whitman in Japan.[385] They give abundant
titles, dates, and names of translators—a surprising number—and
critics. Evidently Whitman has attracted wide attention in Japan, at
least in academic circles. But beneath the smoke, how brightly does
the fire burn? For one who does not read Japanese, it is a guessing
game. Translating poetry into any language is, as Roger Asselineau
says, "an impossible task."[386] If that is true of translating Whitman
into French, how much more difficult it must be in a language using
idiographs instead of an alphabet.

In Japan, however, most of the scholars interested in American literature—and there have been many since World War II—can read English, so that they are not entirely dependent upon Whitman in Japanese. Perhaps it is for this reason that interest in Whitman seems to be largely, though not entirely, in the academic world. In Professor Shigenobu Sadoya's bibliography[387] the first article on Whitman appeared in 1892 in the University of Tokyo *Journal of Philosophy*.[388] By 1914 ten more articles had been published in magazines of limited circulation. After World War I the pace increased, and then rapidly multiplied after World War II, explained in part by the introduction of American literature in university studies during the years of reconstruction.

The major translator of *Leaves of Grass* has been Shigetaka Naganuma, though he was not the first. He became interested in Horace Traubel's work in 1917, and visited him in 1919 to secure his blessing for a translation of his poems, but Traubel persuaded him to translate Whitman instead.[389] After several editions of selections, Naganuma was able to publish a complete *Leaves of Grass* in Japanese in 1950, and a revised edition in 1954.[390] In 1958 he finished a translation of Walt Whitman's letters to his mother during the Civil War.[391]

As early as 1898 a literary critic, Rinjiro Takayama, at Waseda University, "passionately admired Whitman," especially his doctrine that "there is no soul apart from the body."[392] A Christian professor in Tokyo, Kanzo Uchimura, thought Whitman "must be a true Christian or prophet, not a poet." He concluded that "no racial discrimination nor expansion of armaments will be raised in America when Americans have attained to the height of Whitman's ideal."[393] Takeo Arishima, who became a novelist of note before his early suicide, published literary interpretations of Whitman and some translations. Arishima belonged to the Shirakaba (White Birch) literary circle, which opposed the dominant Naturalism of the early twentieth century (influenced by Flaubert, Dostoevsky, and Zola).[394] This group also associated Whitman with Blake and briefly published a magazine devoted to the two poets.

Since World War II Whitman has, of course, been treated in the various Japanese surveys of American Literature and included in anthologies of English and American poetry. In 1953 Masaru Shiga's translation of *Democratic Vistas* was published, and the following year Kinichi Ishikawa's translation of Van Wyck Brooks's *The Times of Melville and Whitman.*[395] During the 1950s visiting American scholars lectured on Whitman in universities and American Cultural Centers.[396]

Also since World War II a very enthusiastic American Whitmanian, Professor William Moore, has given many lectures on his favorite poet at the International Christian University in Tokyo and elsewhere. In 1967 Professor Moore made what will probably be a lasting contribution to the study of Whitman in Japan by publishing (in English) Whitman's complete *Leaves of Grass*, with "Prose Essences and Annotations."[397] The subject-matter of Whitman's poems is often so alien to a Japanese student that he has difficulty in understanding "what the poem says." Here, out of his long experience both in studying and in teaching Whitman to youthful readers in Japan, Professor Moore is uniquely qualified to aid, encourage, and stimulate. He deserves a special note in the history of Walt Whitman in Japan.

In Israel, too, university professors have made the most significant contributions to the reception of Whitman. One is Professor Simon Halkin, well-known poet, novelist, critic, and teacher in the Hebrew University of Jerusalem, who published a translation of *Leaves of Grass* (not complete but full) in 1952.[398] There have been numerous other translations of single poems or brief selections, but Halkin's version remains the fullest and most respected. Then in critical interpretation there are the studies of Professor Sholom Kahn, also of the Hebrew University, who studied at Columbia University under Mark Van Doren before becoming an Israeli citizen.[399]

Among the other poets who have been translating Whitman is S. Sholom. In 1950 he explained his fondness for Whitman in an interview for the New York *Herald Book Review*: "Whitman's pioneering is very close to us, and so are his Biblical rhythms. To translate him into Hebrew is like translating a writer back into his own language."[400]

Some of Israel's leading poets, such as Uri Zvi Grinberg, were writing about Whitman before Israel became a nation. In 1964 Benjamin Krushovski, author of an authoritative study of free verse in modern poetry, published a long essay called "Theory and Practice in U. Z. Grinberg's Expressionist Poetry." A summary in English states:

Grinberg's two-level rhythm is compared to the rhythm of Maya-kovsky and Whitman. In Mayakovsky's poetry there is uniformity on the upper level and freedom on the lower one, while in Grinberg's Expressionist poetry it is vice versa. Whitman's long lines are free to an extent on both levels, but this freedom is limited.[401]

Several years ago Professor Kahn wrote that he had been finding reminders of Whitman in the collected poems of Moshe Bassok (1907–66), a Lithuanian with Hassidic ancestry who joined a col-lective farm in Israel in 1936.[402] Kahn is not sure that Bassok had read Whitman, but the Hassidic background reminds one that Fred-erik Schyberg in 1933 compared Whitman to the Hassidic poets.[403] And recently E. Fred Carlisle has based a book-length study on similarities between Whitman's "drama of the soul" and Martin Buber's Hassidic philosophy, in *The Uncertain Self: Whitman's Drama of Identity* (1973).

In a survey of Whitman in Israel in 1961 Kahn found his shadow in many places, but he wondered about the presence of the real man. Eight years later he wrote: "I find much more to report: presence, spirit, scholarship—on all levels, Whitman seems very much alive in Israel today."[404] This is an opinion which he still holds in 1974.[405]

It is perhaps appropriate to end this chapter on Whitman and World Literature with a note on the People's Republic of China. Little is known about Chinese interest in Whitman, but a translation of selections from Whitman's *Leaves of Grass* (324 pages) published in 1955 lifts the bamboo curtain slightly.[406] In his preface the trans-lator, T'u-nan Ch'u, says he began translating Whitman's poems thirty years ago (1925), sending out "the rendered pieces, a few at a time, to the periodicals that would accept them. Later they were collected and published in book form." (Does this mean before 1955?) The bibliographical details are missing. But the earlier trans-lations have obviously been revised, for the reviewer of this inter-esting volume, Angela Chih-Ying Jung Palandri, says that the simplified written characters have been used, which of course were introduced by Mao Tse-tung. Also in a few places Whitman's words have been slightly slanted to favor Chinese Communist politics—or what was the country's politics in 1955—though on the whole the reviewer finds the translation accurate. Furthermore, the preface ends with these sentences:

Whitman is indeed the most distinguished poet of realism and democracy. His poetry serves not only as a warning flare to ward off the American ruling reactionary groups in their military expansion, racial prejudice, and abuse of human rights, but it also serves as a shining banner guiding all the peoples, including the American people, who strive for real democracy that leads to world peace and progress.[407]

In view of the thaw in Chinese-American relations, it will be interesting to see what Walt Whitman's future will be in the People's Republic of China.*

*Note: See Introduction, p. xiv.

NOTES

NOTES FOR CHAPTER I

1. *The Good Gray Poet: A Vindication* was first published for O'Connor in pamphlet form by Bunce and Huntington, New York, 1866, but was reprinted in Richard Maurice Bucke's *Walt Whitman* (Philadelphia: David McKay, 1883), pp. 99-130. References in this chapter are made to the original pamphlet.

2. John Burroughs, *Notes on Walt Whitman as Poet and Person* (New York: American News Co., 1867). A second revised and enlarged edition was published in New York by J. S. Redfield, 1871, but references in this chapter are given to the 1867 edition. For argument that Whitman wrote earlier chapters of this book see F. P. Hier, Jr., "End of a Literary Mystery," *American Mercury*, I, 471-78 (April, 1924).

3. Edward Carpenter, *Days with Walt Whitman* (London: George Allen, 1906), 37.

4. Horace Traubel, *In Re Walt Whitman* (Philadelphia: David McKay, 1893), v.

5. See *Specimen Days*, in *Prose Works 1892*, ed. Floyd Stovall (New York University Press, 1963), I, 5. Dr. Bucke says 1635 [p. 13], but there is no evidence for this date. Bliss Perry discovered that the Rev. Zechariah Whitman had no children, *Walt Whitman: His Life and Works* (Boston: Houghton Mifflin, 1906), p. 2, note 2.

6. *Prose Works 1892* (ed. Stovall), I, 288.

7. Hippolyte Adolphe Taine expressed this doctrine in his famous introduction to his *L'Histoire de la littérature anglaise* (1864), translated into English by H. Van Laun in 1873.

8. Richard Maurice Bucke, *Cosmic Consciousness: A Study in the Evolu-*

tion of the Human Mind (Philadelphia: Innes and Sons, 1901). Fourth ed., New York: E. P. Dutton, 1923.

9. Charles N. Elliot, *Walt Whitman as Man, Poet and Friend* (Boston: Richard G. Badger, 1915), 50.

10. Harold Blodgett, *Walt Whitman in England* (Ithaca: Cornell University Press, 1934).

11. Moncure D. Conway, "Walt Whitman," *The Fortnightly Review*, VI, 538-48 (Oct. 15, 1866).

12. See William Sloane Kennedy, *Reminiscences of Walt Whitman* (London: Alexander Gardner, 1896), 51-74.

13. Conway (see note 11 above) omitted this implausible statement in his *Autobiography* (Boston: Houghton, Mifflin and Co., 1905), I, 218.

14. "Walt Whitman's Poems," *The London Chronicle*, July 6, 1867.

15. *Poems by Walt Whitman* (London: John Camden Hotten, 1868).

16. See Blodgett, 25-30.

17. *Poems* (ed. Rossetti), 3-4.

18. Emory Holloway, *Walt Whitman* (New York: Alfred A. Knopf, 1926), 257-64.

19. *In Re Walt Whitman*, 41-55.

20. *The Westminster Review*, XCVI, 33-68 (July, 1871); reprinted in *Studies in Literature* (London, 1878).

21. Published in the Canterbury Poets Series (London: Walter Scott, 1886).

22. William Gay, *Walt Whitman: His Relation to Science and Philosophy* (Melbourne: Firth and M'Cutcheon, 1895).

23. John Addington Symonds, *Walt Whitman: A Study* (London: George Routledge, New York: E. P. Dutton, 1893), 41.

24. Quoted by Edward Carpenter, 142-43.

25. J. A. Symonds, 92-93.

26. See note 19 above.

27. Chap. V.

28. Thomas Donaldson, *Walt Whitman, the Man* (New York: Harper, 1896).

29. John Burroughs, *Walt Whitman, A Study* [not to be confused with *Notes*, see note 2 above] (Boston: Houghton Mifflin, 1896), 4.

30. *Birds and Poets* (Boston: Houghton Mifflin, 1877, 1895), 188.

31. *The Complete Writings of Walt Whitman*, issued under the editorial supervision of his literary executors, Richard Maurice Bucke, Thomas B. Harned, and Horace L. Traubel; with additional bibliographical and critical material by Oscar Lovell Triggs (New York and London: G. P. Putnam's Sons, 1902).

32. Kennedy, 76.

33. John Townsend Trowbridge, *My Own Story: With Recollections of Noted Persons* (Boston: Houghton Mifflin, 1903), 366-67.

34. Cf. testimony of Whitman's friends on his "unconscious fabrications" regarding the mysterious "children"—Clara Barrus, *Whitman and Burroughs: Comrades* (Boston: Houghton Mifflin, 1931), 336-38.

35. See Introduction to *Calamus* [Whitman's letters to Peter Doyle], ed. R. M. Bucke (Boston: Laurens Maynard, 1897), 25. Also *Complete Writings*, VIII, 7.

36. *In Re Walt Whitman*, 34.

37. Quoted by Edward Carpenter, 150.

38. Şculley Bradley, "Walt Whitman on Timber Creek," *American Literature*, V, 235-46 (Nov., 1933).

39. Henry Bryan Binns, *A Life of Walt Whitman* (London: Methuen, 1905), 51.

40. Oscar L. Triggs, *Browning and Whitman: A Study in Democracy* (Chicago: University of Chicago, 1893).

41. Cf. Chap. V, 295.

42. Schlaf's best known work is his monograph *Walt Whitman*, 1904, published as Vol. XVIII of *Die Dichtung*.

43. Eduard Bertz, *Der Yankee-Heiland: Ein Beitrag zur Modernen Religionsgeschichte* (Dresden: Verlag von Carl Reissner, 1906), 100.

44. W. C. Rivers in *Walt Whitman's Anomaly* (London, 1913) makes a similar classification: "If Walt Whitman was homosexual, then, to what variety of male inversion did he belong? Essentially the *passive* kind, as one might expect from his pronounced feminine nature," p. 64. Edward Carpenter in *Some Friends of Walt Whitman: A Study in Sex-psychology* (London, 1924), accuses Rivers of having accentuated "the petty or pathological marks," p. 14. Carpenter thinks that Nature may be evolving a new form of humanity, "inclusive of male and female."

45. Bertz finds striking parallels between Novalis and Whitman's doctrine that "there is really no evil in the world," 146-47.

46. William Sloane Kennedy, *The Fight of A Book for the World* (West Yarmouth, Mass.: Stonecroft Press, 1926), 93.

47. *With Walt Whitman in Camden: January 21—April 7, 1889* (Carbondale: Southern Illinois University Press, 1959). (Counted as Vol. IV in ser.)

48. See note 34 above.

49. George Rice Carpenter, *Walt Whitman* (New York: Macmillan, 1909), 64 (note).

50. *Walt Whitman: the Man and His Work*, translated from the French by Ellen FitzGerald (Garden City: Doubleday, Page and Co., 1920). The translator states: ". . . I have felt justified in abridging M. Balzagette's treatment of the New Orleans episode, not that it may not be true but that it is a mystery which neither H. B. Binns nor he can clear by elaborate guess work; I have also as much as is consistent with the unity of the book lightened his emphasis on the *Leaves of Grass* conflict," viii. The warm description of Whitman's supposed first sexual ecstasies are freely deleted.

51. Léon Bazalgette, *Walt Whitman: L'Homme et son oeuvre* (Paris: Mercure de France, 1908), 92. Quotations from these passages which Miss Fitzgerald so discreetly omitted are kept in the original in order to avoid any confusion between the French and American versions of Bazalgette's biography.

52. Cf. note 42 above. Johannes Schlaf also wrote *Walt Whitman Homosexueller*, Kritische Revision einer Whitman-Abhandlung von Dr. Eduard Bertz (Minden: Bruns' Verlag, 1906).

53. FitzGerald trans. of Bazalgette, 220-21.

54. Basil De Selincourt, *Walt Whitman: A Critical Study* (London: Martin Secker, 1914), 18.

55. *Walt Whitman: Oeuvres choisies, poémes et proses*, traduits par Jules Laforgue [et autres], précédes d'une étude par Valéry Larbaud (Paris: Gallimard, 1930—6 éd.), 43.

56. D. H. Lawrence, "Whitman," *Studies in Classic American Literature* (New York: Albert Boni, 1923), 260; Doubleday Anchor Book, 188. The earlier, "Uncollected Versions," of this book has been edited by Armin Arnold, with a Preface by Harry T. Moore, *The Symbolic Meaning* (London: Centaur Press, 1962); Whitman, 253-64.

57. Gerald Bullett, *Walt Whitman: A Study and a Selection* (London: Grant Richards, 1924), 27. Bullett has in mind Cleveland Rodgers and John Black's *The Gathering of the Forces* [editorials from Brooklyn *Eagle*] (New York: G. P. Putnam's Sons, 1920), 2 vols.; and Emory Holloway's *Uncollected Poetry and Prose of Walt Whitman* (New York: Doubleday, 1921), 2 vols.

58. John Bailey, *Walt Whitman* (New York: Macmillan, 1926), 197.

59. See note 57 above.

60. Emory Holloway, "Walt Whitman's Love Affairs," *The Dial*, LXIX, 473-83 (Nov., 1920). In this article Holloway also discusses the evidence for an affair with a married woman in Washington.

61. Emory Holloway, *Whitman* (Biog.), 66.

62. Jean Catel, *Walt Whitman: La Naissance du Poète* (Paris: Les Éditions Rieder, 1929), 41. (Trans. by G. W. A.)

63. "Il est certain, d'un côté, que Walt n'entretenait pas avec les jeunes filles de ces relations sentimentales (à la Byron) dont il s'est moqué et que, d'un autre côté, Walt Whitman fréquentant les lieux de plaisir, il ne pouvait rester étranger aux joies sexuelles ... Il est probable que le jeune Walt connut la plaisir des sens et que, sans doute, New-York lui offrit les facilités de l'amour professionel ...", 254.

64. Frederik Schyberg, *Walt Whitman* (København: Gyldendalske Boghandel, 1933). Translated by Evie Allison Allen, with Introduction by Gay Wilson Allen (New York: Columbia University Press, 1951). All references are to the translation.

65. See Schyberg, 53 and 75; Clara Barrus, 339.

66. Notebook entry for April 16, 1861, first quoted by Binns, 181.

67. Schyberg, 342, note 77.

68. Edgar Lee Masters, *Whitman* (New York: Charles Scribner's Sons, 1937), 142. The authorities used by Masters are: Edward Carpenter, *The Intermediate Sex*; De Joux, *Die Enterbten des Liebes-glückes*; and Havelock Ellis, *Psychology of Sex*.

69. Esther Shephard, *Walt Whitman's Pose* (New York: Harcourt, Brace, 1938), 141. Mrs. Shephard was not the first, however, to exploit the "pose" theory. That doubtful honor goes to Harvey O'Higgins for his attack on the poet in "Alias Walt Whitman," *Harper's Magazine*, CLVIII, 698-707 (May, 1929), later published (same title) in New York: W. W. Stone, 1929, 49 pp.; limited edition, 1930. For a good critique of both Shephard and O'Higgins see F. I. Carpenter, "Walt Whitman's 'Eidólon'," *College English*, III, 534-45 (March, 1942).

70. Whitman "never possessed a great poet's imagination" nor "mastery over his materials," and "he revised and rejected not as an artist but rather as the poseur that he was, fame-greedy and fearful lest his secret be betrayed," —Shephard, 242.

71. Cf. Gay Wilson Allen, "Walt Whitman and Jules Michelet," *Études anglaises*, I, 230-37 (May, 1937); and "The Foreground" in *A Reader's Guide to Walt Whitman* (New York: Farrar, Straus, and Giroux, Noonday ser., 1970), 17–44.

72. Haniel Long, *Walt Whitman and the Springs of Courage* (Santa Fe: Writers Editions, 1938).

73. Edward Hungerford, "Walt Whitman and His Chart of Bumps," *American Literature*, II, 350-84 (Jan., 1931). See also Arthur Wrobel, "Whitman and the Phrenologists: the Divine Body and the Sensuous Soul," *PMLA*, LXXXIX, 17-23 (Jan., 1974).

74. Newton Arvin, *Whitman* (New York: Macmillan, 1938), 161.

75. *Ibid.*, 33: "We shall find no other dose so acrid or so hard to swallow . . . [as] his rather inglorious record in the days of the Abolitionists."

76. Clifton J. Furness, *Walt Whitman's Workshop: A Collection of Unpublished Manuscripts* (Cambridge: Harvard University Press, 1928).

77. *American Literature*, XIII, 423-32 (January 1942).

78. Privately printed for the author.

79. The description of the "capricious and headstrong—but tender and very affectionate—sister Mary" in Whitman's juvenile story, "The Half Breed," is evidently his own sister. See Molinoff, 4 ff.

80. Published by Macmillan in 1955; reprinted by Grove Press in 1959; revised edition, New York Universtiy Press, 1967, 1972.

81. Furness did indeed complete a manuscript, but over a dozen publishers found it unworthy of publication. After Furness's death I acquired his manuscript and notebooks into which he had transcribed unpublished holographs. These copies were useful in locating manuscript material (and for

some not located), but the biography was useless—a pathetic failure, perhaps partly the result of Furness's rapid decline in health. I have deposited this unpublished biography in the Fales Collection of the Bobst Library, New York University, where anyone who is interested may examine it.—G.W.A.

82. See note 64 above.

83. Constance Rourke, *American Humor: A Study in National Character* (New York: Harcourt, Brace, 1931), esp. Chap. VI, "I Hear America Singing."

84. D. H. Lawrence, Chap. 12. See note 56 above.

85. The "I" in "Song of Myself is "half-heroic, half-ironic," Leslie Fiedler, Introduction to *Whitman*, Laurel Poetry Series (New York: Dell Publishing Co., 1959), 16.

86. Introduction to *Walt Whitman's Leaves of Grass: The First (1855) Edition* (New York: Viking, 1959), esp. x-xiv.

87. Letter dated February 7, 1882, in *The Correspondence of Walt Whitman*, ed. Edwin H. Miller (New York University Press, 1964), III, 266. (Whitman wrote "pourtray.")

88. "Death of Thomas Carlyle," *Prose Works 1892* (ed. Stovall), I, 248-62.

89. Chase quotes only part of the sentence in Whitman's letter to Bucke (see note 87 above); it ends: "...but let that pass—I have left it [the biography] as you wrote it." It is now known, however, that Whitman did write and emend a considerable part of the book—see *Walt Whitman's Autograph Revision of the Analysis of Leaves of Grass* (For Dr. R. M. Bucke's *Walt Whitman*), New York: New York University Press, 1974. This edition reproduces the second part of Bucke's *Walt Whitman*, the analysis of *Leaves of Grass* and the quotations in the Appendix supplied by Whitman. Quentin Anderson has written a long Introduction for this edition, which is based only on the manuscript owned by Daniel Maggin; other manuscript versions are in the Duke University Library and the Charles E. Feinberg Collection in the Library of Congress.

90. Jan Christian Smuts, *Walt Whitman: A Study in the Evolution of Personality*, ed. Alan L. McLeod (Detroit: Wayne State University Press, 1973), 26. In 1895 Smuts submitted the manuscript of this book to two British publishers, both of whom rejected it. The manuscript remained unpublished until this posthumous edition.

91. See above pp. 277-278.

92. Joseph Jay Rubin, *The Historic Whitman* (University Park: The Pennsylvania State University Press, 1973).

NOTES FOR CHAPTER II

1. For many years Whitman scholars have counted *nine* editions of

Leaves of Grass, but William White, who is preparing the definitive bibliography for *The Collected Writings of Walt Whitman* (New York University Press) says only *six* fit the strict definition of bibliographical authorities. See "Editions of *Leaves of Grass*: How Many?", *Walt Whitman Review*, XIX, 111 (September 1973). Ronald B. McKerrow in *Introduction to Bibliography for Literary Students* (Oxford, 1927) defines an edition as "the whole number of copies of a book printed at any time or times from one setting-up of type (including copies printed from the stereotype or electrotype plates made from the setting-up of type)....," 175. By this definition the true editions of *Leaves of Grass* were printed in 1855, 1856, 1860, 1867, 1871, and 1881. All other so-called editions are reprints or "issues," using a former setting of type (or unbound sheets from a former printing) to which some new (or revised) poems were added in a new setting of type. More bibliographical details will be given below in descriptions of the "issues" of 1876, 1892, and 1897. The Comprehensive Reader's Edition of *Leaves of Grass*, edited by Harold W. Blodgett and Sculley Bradley (New York University Press, 1965), contains all the poems ever included in an edition or issue of *Leaves of Grass*, plus the posthumous "Old Age Echoes" and other unpublished or uncollected poems. This is the most complete and scholary of all editions of *Leaves of Grass*.

2. For example: "['Leaves of Grass' must be] considered as a growth and as related to the author's own life process.... Succeeding editions have the character of expansive growths, like the rings of a tree...." Oscar Triggs, "The Growth of 'Leaves of Grass,' " *The Complete Writings of Walt Whitman* (New York and London: G. P. Putnam's Sons, 1902), X, 102. But Frederik Schyberg declares that: "Bogen er nok et levende Hele, men dens Historie fremgaar ikke af Ringene i den som de nu er lagt," 17. (The book is a living unit but in its present state [i.e., final text] its history is *not* shown by annual rings of growth.)

3. Reader's Ed. of *L. G.* (see note 1 above), 713.

4. In "Passage to India" Whitman uses "justify" in the Miltonic sense several times.

5. Reader's Ed. of *L. G.* 713.

6. *Ibid.*, 728.

7. From a manuscript draft of an unpublished preface first dated May 31, 1861, then redated May 31, 1870. Printed in Clifton J. Furness, *Walt Whitman's Workshop* (Harvard University Press, 1928), 135-37.

8. Found in a rejected passage for "A Backward Glance," printed in "Notes and Fragments," ed. Dr. R. M. Bucke, in *Complete Writings* (see note 2 above), IX, 17.

9. Furness, *Workshop*, 9-10.

10. R. M. Bucke, *Walt Whitman* (Philadelphia: David McKay, 1883), 147.

11. Quoted by Clara Barrus, *Whitman and Burroughs, Comrades* (Boston:

Houghton Mifflin, 1931), 318: letter dated Feb. 12, 1896.

12. See note 2 above.

13. See note 8.

14. Reader's Ed. of *L. G.*, 560, note.

15. Stuart P. Sherman's chronological edition of *Leaves of Grass* (New York: Charles Scribner's, 1922), contains none of the poems published after 1881. The revised *Viking Portable Whitman* (New York: Viking Press, 1974) reprints texts of some 1855, 1856, and 1860 poems, but it is a selected anthology. Blodgett and Bradley in their Reader's Ed. include the rejected and unpublished poems, but they base their text on the one "authorized" by the poet in 1892.

16. Basil De Selincourt, *Walt Whitman: A Study* (London: Martin Secker, 1914), 164.

17. Jean Catel, *Walt Whitman: La Naissance du Poète* (Paris: Éditions Rieder, 1929).

18. Floyd Stovall, "Main Drifts in Whitman's Poetry," *American Literature*, IV, 3-21 (March 1932).

19. Killis Campbell, "The Evolution of Whitman as Artist," American Literature, VI, 254-63 (November 1934).

20. See note 1 above.

21. Schyberg (trans.), 12.

22. Irving C. Story, "The Growth of *Leaves of Grass*: A Proposal for a Variorum Edition," *Pacific University Bulletin*, XXXVII, 1-11 (February 1941).

23. *Ibid.*, 4.

24. "The Problem of a Variorum Edition of Whitman's *Leaves of Grass*," *English Institute Annual, 1941* (New York: Columbia University Press, 1942), 128-37.

25. *Pacific University Bulletin*, XXXVIII, No. 3, pp. 1-12 (Jan., 1942).

26. "The Poet," second paragraph.

27. Carl F. Strauch, "The Structure of Walt Whitman's Song of Myself," *English Journal* (College Ed.), XXVII, 597-607 (September 1938).

28. *Leaves of Grass: The First (1855) Edition* (New York: Viking, 1959).

29. James E. Miller, *A Critical Guide to Leaves of Grass* (Chicago: University of Chicago, 1957), 6-35.

30. Evelyn Underhill, *Mysticism: A Study in the Nature and Development of Man's Spiritual Consciousness* (London: Methuen, 11th ed., 1926).

31. V. K. Chari, *Walt Whitman in the Light of Vedantic Mysticism* (Lincoln: University of Nebraska Press, 1965).

32. *Walt Whitman's Poems*, eds. Gay Wilson Allen and Charles T. Davis (New York University Press, 1955), 9.

33. Chari, 124.

34. Roy Harvey Pearce, *The Continuity of American Poetry* (Princeton: Princeton University Press, 1961), 73.

35. Schyberg (trans.), 124.

36. Edwin H. Miller, *Walt Whitman's Poetry* (New York University Press, 1968), 72.

37. Schyberg (trans.), 59.

38. Cowley, x.

39. See letter to Mrs. Sarah Tyndale quoted by G. W. Allen in *The Solitary Singer* (New York: Macmillan, 1955), 217. *Correspondence*, I, 42.

40. This version is printed from the holograph letter now in the Charles E. Feinberg Collection at the Library of Congress. Whitman printed it in his 1856 *Leaves of Grass* (345-46) with slight alterations in punctuation.

41. See "Mutations in Whitman's Art," *Walt Whitman as Man, Poet, and Legend* (Carbondale: Southern Illinois University Press, 1961), 46-62; reprinted in *Walt Whitman: A Collection of Criticism*, ed. Arthur Golden (New York: McGraw-Hill, 1974).

42. Chari, 41.

43. Edwin H. Miller, 200.

44. Richard Chase, *Walt Whitman Reconsidered* (New York: William Sloane, 1955), 107.

45. For interpretation of Whitman's phrenological vocabulary, see Edward Hungerford, "Walt Whitman and His Chart of Bumps," *American Literature*, II, 350-84 (January 1931).

46. See Willie T. Weathers, "Whitman's Poetic Translations of His 1855 Preface," *American Literature*, XIX, 21-40 (March 1947).

47. *Nature* (1836), "Language."

48. See Fredson Bowers, *Whitman's Manuscripts: Leaves of Grass (1860): A Parallel Test* (Chicago: University of Chicago Press, 1955), xxxv.

49. *Complete Writings*, IX, 6.

50. Sarah Tyndale letter, *Correspondence*, I, 42 (Miller points out that Whitman's date of "July 20" was a mistake for June 20.

51. See note 48 above.

52. Bowers, 3.

53. *Ibid.*, xxxvi, 100. Whitman numbered these twelve poems with Roman numbers, but Bowers found them scattered throughout the "Calamus" MSS.

54. No. VIII, Bowers, 82.

55. *Ibid.*, 88-89; quoted in *Solitary Singer*, 223.

56. Nos. IV and VIII; *Solitary Singer*, 223-24.

57. Bowers, 69.

58. *Ibid.*, 115.

59. *Ibid.*, 122.

60. Reader's Ed. *L. G.*, 751, 160n.

61. *Complete Writings*, X, 18.

62. *Ibid.*,IX, 150.

63. *Ibid.*, 125.

64. *Ibid.*, 134.

65. *Ibid.*, 145; in "Chants Democratic," No. 8, changed to "Song at Sunset" in 1867, and thereafter, 1. 39.

66. Bowers, 161.

67. *Ibid.*, 173.

68. *Ibid.*, 85-86.

69. *Ibid.*, 192.

70. *Ibid.*, 211.

71. "Bardic Symbols" was not in the manuscripts Bowers edited, an indication that it was written after Whitman had the Rome Brothers set up poems he hoped to use in a third edition, and he did not revise the *Atlantic Monthly* text before printing it in his third edition about the same time it appeared in the magazine.

72. Schyberg (Allen translation) comments on the significance of this passage, 147-48; also on the conclusion, which read in 1859 and '60: "Which I do not forget,/ But fuse the song of two together," changed later to "song of my dusky demon and brother, . . ."

73. Quoted by Bowers, xxxii; G. W. Allen, *The Solitary Singer*, 236-37.

74. See *The Solitary Singer*, 237; *Correspondence*, I, 49.

75. *Correspondence*, I, 48, n. 7: Thayer and Eldridge to W. W., June 14: "The first edition is nearly all gone, and the second is all printed and ready for binding. . . ."

76. The first binding was probably yellow; a later, green; and another, plum-colored. As many as twelve different bindings have survived, according to Carolyn Wells and Alfred F. Goldsmith in *A Concise Bibliography* (Boston: Houghton Mifflin Co., 1922), 8. After the bankruptcy of Thayer & Eldridge the plates came into the possession of a piratical printer in New York, Richard Worthington, who printed many copies without the poet's permission. On the verso of the title-page the Thayer & Eldridge edition bears these words: "Electrotyped at the Boston Stereotype Foundry. Printed by George C. Rand and Avery." Spurious copies lack these words.

77. Esther Shephard, *Walt Whitman's Pose* (New York: Harcourt, Brace & Co., 1938), discovered that the butterfly was a photographer's prop, p. 250-52.

78. The drawing could be of either a sunrise or sunset, but the latter was probably intended because of the sunset in "Crossing Brooklyn Ferry."

79. Whitman also used a butterfly on the backstrip of his 1881 edition of *Leaves of Grass*, and a famous photograph taken of him in 1883 shows him posing with the same cardboard butterfly on his forefinger: See *The Artistic Legacy of Walt Whitman*, edited by Edwin H. Miller (New York University Press, 1970), figure 18 and p. 134.

80. The old poems are: No. 1, adaptations from 1855 preface; "Poem of Many in One," 1856; "As I Sat Alone by Blue Ontario's Shore," 1867; "By Blue Ontario's Shore," 1881. No. 2, "Broad-Axe Poem," 1856; "Song of the Broad-Axe," 1867. No. 3, second poem in 1855; "Poem of The Daily Work of The Workmen and Workwomen of These States," 1856; finally "A Song for Occupations," 1881. No. 5, "Poem of the Proposition of Nakedness," 1856; "Respondez," 1867; dropped 1881—parts transferred. No. 6, "Poem of Remembrance for a Girl or Boy of These States," 1856. No. 15, "Poem of The Heart of The Son of Manhattan," 1856; "Excelsior," 1867.

81. New poems, to use later titles, were: "Apostroph" (never reprinted); "Our Old Feuillage"; "With Antecedents"; "Song at Sunset"; "Thoughts," sec. 1; "To a Historian"; "Thoughts," sec. 2; "Vocalism," sec. 1; "Laws for Creation"; "Poets to Come"; "Mediums"; "On Journeys through the States"; "Me Imperturbe"; "I Was Looking a Long While"; "I Hear America Singing"; "As I Walk these Broad Majestic Days."

82. Schyberg (translation), 171.

83. In a letter to Harrison Blake, Dec. 7, [1856], *The Correspondence of Henry David Thoreau*, eds. Walter Harding and Carl Bode (New York University Press, 1958), 444.

84. "Appreciation of Walt Whitman," *The Nation* (London), XXIX, 617 (July 23, 1921).

85. Emory Holloway, "Walt Whitman's Love Affairs," *The Dial*, LXIX, 473-83 (Nov., 1920). Holloway discusses, among other hypotheses, a love affair with a married woman in Washington, D. C.

86. Schyberg (trans.), 158.

87. The great Brazilian sociologist Gilberto Freyre says Whitman's "fraternalistic sense of life" was "so vibrant as to seem at times homosexualism gone mad whereas it was probably only bisexualism sublimated into fraternalism," in *O Camarada Whitman*, translated in *Walt Whitman Abroad*, ed. Gay Wilson Allen (Syracuse University Press, 1955), 229.

88. John Addington Symonds, *Walt Whitman: A Study* (London: George Routledge & Sons, 1893), 158.

89. Emory Holloway, *Whitman: An Interpretation in Narrative* (New York: Knopf, 1926), 81.

90. *Leaves of Grass By Walt Whitman: Facsimile Edition of the 1860 Text*, ed. with Introduction by Roy Harvey Pearce (Ithaca: Cornell University Press, 1961).

91. Quentin Anderson in his Introduction to *Walt Whitman's Revision of the Analysis of Leaves of Grass (For Dr. R. M. Bucke's Walt Whitman)*, (New York University Press, 1974), says "this sentimental poem . . . has proved a trap for critics," 35.

92. "Whitman's Awakening to Death," in *The Presence of Walt Whitman: Selected Papers from the English Institute*, ed. with a Foreword by R. W. B. Lewis (New York: Columbia University Press, 1962), 22.

93. Facsimile 1860 Ed., xxxiii.

94. *Presence of Walt Whitman*, 80.

95. *Correspondence*, I, 48, note 7.

96. Arthur Golden, editor, *Walt Whitman's Blue Book: the 1860-61 Leaves of Grass Containing His Manuscript Additions and Revisions* (New York Public Library, 1968), xxxiv.

97. "Banner at Day-Break," retitled "Song of the Banner at Day-Break"; "Washington's First Battle" became "The Centenarian's Story, Volunteer of 1861 (At Washington Park, Brooklyn, assisting the Centenarian)"; "Pictures," not published by Whitman but edited by Emory Holloway (New York, 1927); "Quadrel," probably "Chanting the Square Deific"—also "Quadriune" or "Deus Quadriune," written over CONTENTS (p. iii) in Blue Book; "Sonnets," probably some of the "Calamus" poems. See note 53 above.

98. These manuscripts, now in the Oscar Lion Collection of the New York Public Library, have been edited by Furness (see note 7 above), 117-37; 167-74—"paths to the house," 135.

99. See Gay Wilson Allen and Charles T. Davis, eds., *Walt Whitman's Poems* (New York University Press, 1955), 16-21.

100. Furness, *Workshop*, 137.

101. *Workshop*, 127.

102. *Workshop*, 130.

103. *Workshop*, 131.

104. *Workshop*, 136.

105. Pearce, *Facsimile Edition of the 1860 Text*, xlvii.

106. The copy is now in the Lion Collection of the NYPL. See note 104 above.

107. Vol. I contains the facsimile; Vol. II, Golden's Introduction and Textual Analysis.

108. Golden, *Blue Book*, II, lvi ff.

109. Golden, *Blue Book*, II, lii.

110. Charles I. Glicksberg, *Walt Whitman and the Civil War* (Philadelphia: University of Pennsylvania Press, 1933), 8.

111. Schyberg (trans.), 181.

112. The "Drum-Taps" of the final edition of *Leaves of Grass* contains only about half of the original collection; thirty-three poems were shifted to other sections and six were added to the group after 1865.

113. Letter dated March 31, 1863, *Correspondence*, I, 85-86.

114. However, Clara Barrus in *Life and Letters of John Burroughs* (Boston: Houghton Mifflin, 1925) says that Miss Juliette H. Beach was "The friend to whom Whitman wrote 'Out of the rolling ocean.' She wrote many beautiful letters to Walt which J. B. tried in vain to get her consent to publish. She died many years ago." I, 120, note.

115. Wells and Goldsmith, 11.

116. G. L. Sixbey, "Chanting the Square Deific—A Study in Whitman's Religion," *American Literature*, IX, 174 (May, 1937).

117. *Ibid.*, 72.

118. They are: "Inscription (One's Self I Sing)," "The Runner," "Tears! Tears! Tears!," "Aboard at a Ship's Helm," "When I Read the Book," "The City Dead-House."

119. With its separate title-page and pagination this annex appears to be an independent publication, though it has no copyright notice.

120. Wells and Goldsmith, 14.

121. In his final revision (1871) of this poem Whitman reversed the order of 1 and 2 as summarized here.

122. The context indicates that "offspring" means national results, not biological—as in the American war in Viet Nam.

123. An 84-page pamphlet, with green cover, printed by J. S. Redfield, New York. Title page: *Democratic/ Vistas./* Washington, D. C./ 1871.

124. Quotations from "Democratic Vistas" in *Prose Works 1892* (Stovall), II, 389. Bracketed numbers in subsequent quotations refer to this edition.

125. Whitman never defined "personalism," but he used it to include his whole program of all-round development of the self and the individual, including health, eugenics, education, moral and social conscience.

126. Pamphlet of 24 pages, published by Roberts Brothers, Boston, 1871. See Wells and Goldsmith, 18.

127. A 120-page pamphlet, with green cover, printed by J. S. Redfield, New York. Title page: *Passage/ to/ India./* Washington, D.C./ 1871.

128. Lines 4, 5, 6 of "The Wound Dresser" (1881) were used in 1871 and 1876 as epigraph for the "Drum-Taps" cluster: "(Arous'd and angry . . . watch the dead;)."

129. *Prose Works 1892* (Stovall), II, 458-64.

130. W. L. Werner, "Whitman's 'The Mystic Trumpeter' as Autobiography," *American Literature*, VII, 455-58 (January 1936).

131. Redpath letter, dated October 28, 1863, quoted by Roy Basler in Introduction to his facsimile edition of *Walt Whitman's Memoranda [&] Death of Abraham Lincoln* (Indiana University Press, 1962), 11-12, *Correspondence*, I, 170n, 171-72.

132. Wells and Goldsmith, 19.

133. The three poems which Whitman did not include in any later collections: "Two Rivulets," "From My Last Years," "In Former Songs." Another poem, "Or from That Sea of Time," was incorporated into "As Consequent, Etc." (1881), with omissions. The other poems in this group of *TR*: "Eidolons," "Spain, 1873-'74," "Prayer of Columbus," "Out from Behind This Mask," "To a Locomotive in Winter," "The Ox-Tamer," "Wandering at Morn," "An Old Man's Thoughts at School," "With All Thy Gifts," "After the Sea-Ships."

134. Reader's Ed. *L. G.*, 744-54.

135. *Ibid.*, 746.

136. *Ibid.*, 747.

137. *Ibid.*

138. "In Former Songs" (1876, *Two Rivulets*, p. 31) stresses this division in Whitman's poems, but it was dropped after 1876, probably because the poet had given up dividing his poems into two books.

139. Reader's Ed. *L. G.*, 751.

140. This issue contains 404 instead of 382 pages. See Wells and Goldsmith, 27.

141. See note 1 above.

142. See Emory Holloway, "Whitman's Embryonic Verse," *Southwest Review*, X, 28-40 (July 1925); also Introduction to *Pictures: An Unpublished Poem by Walt Whitman* (London: Faber and Gwyer, 1928).

143. See Adeline Knapp, "Walt Whitman and Jules Michelet, Identical Passages," *Critic*, XLIV, 467-68 (1907); also Gay W. Allen, "Walt Whitman and Jules Michelet," *Études Anglaises*, I, 230-37 (May 1937).

144. Barrus, xxiv.

145. Reader's Ed. *L. G.*, 712.

146. *Ibid.*, 562.

147. *Ibid.*, 564.

148. *Ibid.*, 566.

149. *Ibid.*, 570.

150. *Ibid.*, 581, note.

151. *Solitary Singer*, 459.

NOTES FOR CHAPTER III

1. By most biographers, but especially by Emory Holloway in Introduction to *The Uncollected Poetry and Prose of Walt Whitman* (New York: Doubleday, Doran, 1921).

2. Joseph Jay Rubin, *The Historic Whitman* (Pennsylvania State University Press, 1973), xii.

3. Horace Traubel, *With Walt Whitman in Camden* (New York: Appleton, 1908), II, 205.

4. For influence, G. W. Allen, *A Reader's Guide to Walt Whitman* (Farrar, Straus & Giroux, 1970), 21-22.

5. *Prose Works 1892* (Stovall, ed.), I, 13.

6. *Ibid.* 17.

7. *Solitary Singer*, 13.

8. *Prose Works 1892*, II, 639.

9. *Ibid.*, 645.

10. *Ibid.*, 647.

11. *Solitary Singer*, 208.

12. *Gathering of the Forces*, edited by Cleveland Rodgers and John Black (New York: G. P. Putnam's Sons, 1920), I, 23.

13. *Ibid.*, I, 33.

14. *Ibid.*, 229; cf. also 234-39.

15. *Ibid.*, 203.

16. *Ibid.*, 205-06.

17. *Ibid.*, 18.

18. *Ibid.*, 28.

19. *Ibid.*, II, 70-71.

20. *Ibid.*, I, 218.

21. *Ibid.*, 222.

22. *Ibid.*, 54.

23. "The House of Friends," New York *Tribune*, June 14, 1850; collected by Thomas L. Brasher in *The Early Poems and the Fiction of Walt Whitman* (New York University Press, 1963), 36-37.

24. *Ibid.*, 38-40.

25. Reader's Edition of *LG*, 713.

26. *Ibid.*, 714-15.

27. In "Song of Myself" Whitman called himself a "kosmos," perhaps meaning that his "greatest poet" in the 1855 Preface is an all-inclusive system, independent of outside forces. His preference for the Greek spelling, Κόδμος, which came from Sanskrit *cad*, "to distinguish one's self," indicates emphasis on independent order and harmony as an attribute of his own "divinity."

28. Reader's Edition of *LG*, 727.

29. *Ibid.*, 729.

30. *Ibid.*, 729-30.

31. Reprinted in *New York Dissected*, edited by Emory Holloway and Ralph Adimari (New York: Rufus Rockwell Wilson, 1936), 108.

32. *The Eighteenth Presidency!* A Critical Text [with an Introduction] edited by Edward F. Grier (University of Kansas Press, 1956).

33. *Ibid.*, 42.

34. *Ibid.*, 19-20.

35. *Ibid.*, 22.

36. *Ibid.*, 23.

37. *Ibid.*, 30.

38. *Ibid.*, 33.

39. *Ibid.*, 39.

40. *Ibid.*, 44.

41. "Song of Myself," sec. 27 and sec. 20.

42. Reader's Edition of *LG*, 721.

43. Traubel, II, 205. See also David Goodale, "Some of Walt Whitman's Borrowings," *American Literature*, X, 202-13 (May 1938).

44. Traubel, II, 445.

45. Full title: *The Ruins; or Meditation on the Revolution of Empires*, by Count C. F. Volney, Count and Peer of France. . . . To Which is Added *The Law of Nature*. . . . (New York: Calvin Blanchard, n.d.) The French edition was published in 1791; the American translation after Volney's visit to Philadelphia in 1797—probably around 1800.

46. *Ruins*, 184.

47. *Ibid.*, 173.

48. *Ibid.*, 182.

49. *Ibid.*, 175.

50. *Ibid.*, 179.

51. See Peter Tompkins and Christopher Bird, *The Secret Life of Plants* (New York: Harper & Row, 1972), 125-26.

52. In addition to Tompkins and Bird (note 51, above), see also Arthur Koestler's discussion of "Evolution" (Chaps. XI and XII) in *The Ghost in the Machine* (New York: Macmillan, 1967), 151-71.

53. *Nature* (1836), part V. In *The Collected Works of Ralph Waldo Emerson*, edited by Robert E. Spiller and Alfred R. Ferguson (Harvard University Press, 1971), I, 25.

54. This is the argument of Pierre Teilhard de Chardin in *Man's Place in Nature: The Human Zoological Group*, translated by René Hague (New York: Harper & Row, 1966); and *The Phenomenon of Man*, translated by Bernard Wall (New York: Harper & Row, 1961).

55. *Man's Place in Nature*, 79-121.

56. *Uncollected Poetry and Prose of Walt Whitman*, II, 64.

57. *Ibid.*, 65.

58. *Ibid.*

59. *Ibid.*, 65-66.

60. *Ibid.*, 66.

61. *Ibid.*

62. *Ibid.*, 69-70.

63. *Ibid.*, 70. Floyd Stovall thinks that these trial lines of verse may have been written as late as 1854: See "Dating Whitman's Early Notebooks," *Studies in Bibliography* (University of Virginia), XXIV, 197-204 (1971).

64. "Going Somewhere" (1887).

65. Joseph Beaver, *Walt Whitman—Poet of Science* (New York: King's Crown Press, 1951; Octagon Press, 1974), 44.

66. *Ibid.*, 37-38.

67. *Ibid.*, 38.

68. *Ibid.*, 58.

69. Quoted by Beaver, 59-60.

70. *Ibid.*, 60.

71. See Edmund Reiss, "Whitman's Debt to Animal Magnetism," *PMLA*, LXXVIII, 80-88 (March 1963).

72. See Edward Hungerford, "Walt Whitman and His Chart of Bumps," (*American Literature*, II, 350-84) and Haniel Long, *Walt Whitman and the Springs of Courage* (Santa Fe, N. M.: Writers Editions, 1938). Also Arthur Wrobel, "Whitman and the Phrenologists: The Divine Body and the Sensuous Soul," *PMLA*, LXXXIX, 17-23 (January 1974).

73. *Vestiges* was published anonymously and Robert Chambers's authorship was not established until 1884. *New Century Cyclopedia of Names* (New York: Appleton-Century-Crofts, 1954). The book was so popular that the idea of "vestiges of creation" was known to many people who had not read the book.

74. *Nature* (1836), part viii; *Collected Works* (1971), I, 42.

75. "The Poet," first essay in second series (1844) of *Essays*, 15.

76. Reader's Edition of *LG*, 714.

77. Two recent examples: James E. Miller, " 'Song of Myself' as Inverted Mystical Experience," *A Critical Guide to* Leaves of Grass (University of Chicago Press, 1957), 6-35; and Malcolm Cowley, Introduction to *Walt Whitman's* Leaves of Grass: *The First (1855) Edition* (New York: Viking Press, 1959), esp. p. xii ff.

78. William James, *The Varieties of Religious Experience* (New York: Longmans, Green, and Co., 1902), 379.

79. *Ibid.*, 395.

80. *Ibid.*, 381.

81. *Ibid.*, 396, n.1.

82. *Prose Works 1892* (Stovall, ed.), I, 257-58.

83. Richard Maurice Bucke, *Cosmic Consciousness: A Study in the Evolution of the Human Mind* (New York: E. P. Dutton, 1901), 3.

84. *Prose Works 1892* (Stovall, ed.), II, 678.

85. Roger Asselineau, *The Evolution of Walt Whitman: The Creation of a Book* (Harvard University Press, 1962), 4.

86. Sister Flavia Maria, C. S. J., " 'Song of Myself': A Presage of Modern Teilhardian Paleontology," *Walt Whitman Review*, XV, 43-49 (March 1969).

87. Pierre Teilhard de Chardin, *The Divine Milieu* (New York: Harper & Row, 1960), 47. (Quoted by Sister Flavia Maria, 44.)

88. See Ray Benoit, "The Mind's Return: Whitman, Teilhard, and Jung," *Walt Whitman Review*, XIII, 21-28 (March 1968). However, Benoit does not mention *Building the Earth*, quoted below, and Benoit's parallels in Jung are omitted here.

89. Cf. Bucke, *Notes and Fragments*, 57; note No. 14.

90. Pierre Teilhard de Chardin, *Building the Earth* (Wilkes-Barre, Pa.: Dimensions Books, 1965), 63. (In this special edition, designed and illustrated by Sister Rose Ellen, Teilhard's sentences are printed as poetry; here they are quoted as prose.)

91. *Ibid.*, 71.

92. *Ibid.*, 117.

93. *The Galaxy* published "Democracy" in December, 1867, and "Personalism" in May 1868. Whitman intended to publish a third essay to be called "Literature," but it was not published, and possibly was not finished, though Whitman added his thoughts on literature to his book, *Democratic Vistas*, privately printed in Washington, D. C., in 1871. It was added to his *Prose Works* in 1882. See bibliographical note by Stovall in *Prose Works*, II, 361-62.

94. *Prose Works 1892* (Stovall, ed.), II, 362.

95. See Whitman's note, *Prose Works*, II, 375.

96. *Prose Works 1892*, II, 386.

97. *Ibid.*, 385.

98. *Ibid.*, 399.

99. *Ibid.*, 376.

100. Pierre Teilhard de Chardin, *The Future of Man* (New York: Harper & Row, 1964), 100.

101. *Prose Works* (Stovall, ed.), II, 409-10.

102. Quoted by Benoit, *WWR* XIII, 22, from *The Future of Man*, 35.

NOTES FOR CHAPTER IV

1. Hermann Bahr, in his Introduction to Max Hayek's translation, *Ich Singe Das Leben* (Leipzig, Wien, Zürich: E. P. Tall & Co., 1921), 7, says: "[*Grashalme*] ist kunstlos, es bringt eigentlich nur das Material für ein Kunstwerk, diesen Eindruck hat man immer wieder."

2. *Prose Works 1892*, ed. Floyd Stovall (New York University Press, 1964), II, 473.

3. Horace Traubel, *With Walt Whitman in Camden* (New York: Mitchell Kennerley, 1914), III, 84.

4. *Ibid.*, I, 163.

5. Basil De Selincourt, *Walt Whitman: A Critical Study* (London: Martin Secker, 1914), 73.

6. Clifton Joseph Furness, *Walt Whitman's Workshop* (Cambridge: Harvard University Press, 1928), 30.

7. Reader's Ed. *L. G.*, 712.

8. The three periods do not indicate editorial omission but Whitman's punctuation to indicate a caesura in the 1855 edition; sometimes four periods—the number was inconsistent.

9. Reader's Ed. *L. G.*, 570.

10. Preface to 1855 edition. Reader's Ed. *L. G.*, 714.

11. W. S. Kennedy, *Reminiscences of Walt Whitman* (London: Alexander Gardner, 1896), 151.

12. Reader's Ed. *L. G.*, 717.

13. "Song of Myself," 1. 13.

14. "A Backward Glance," Reader's Ed. *L. G.*, 566.

15. "Song of Myself," sec. 33.

16. "Salut au Monde!," sec. 4.

17. Reader's Ed. *L. G.*, 711.

18. Paul Elmer More, *Shelburne Essays*, 4th ser. (Boston: Houghton Mifflin, 1922), 203.

19. Harry B. Reed, "The Heraclitan Obsession of Walt Whitman," *The Personalist*, XV, 125-38 (April 1934).

20. For definition and history of the term, see Carl Enoch William Leonard Dahlström's Introduction to *Strindberg's Dramatic Expressionism* (Ann Arbor: University of Michigan, 1930), 3-10; 35-38; 221-26.

21. "By Blue Ontario's Shore," sec. 3.

22. See A. S. Cook, "The 'Authorized Version' and Its Influence," *Cambridge History of English Literature* (New York and London: G. P. Putnam's Sons, 1910), IV, 29-58.

23. See S. R. Driver, *Introduction to the Literature of the Old Testament* (New York: Charles Scribner's Sons, 1910), 361 ff. Also see E. Kautsch, *Die Poesie und die poetischen Bücher des Alten Testaments* (Tübingen und Leipzig, 1902), 2. Bishop Lowth first pointed out the prosodic principles of parallelism in the Bible in *De sacra poesi Hebraeorum praelectiones academiae Oxoni habitae*, 1753. See Driver, 362. In the main the Lowth system is the basis for R. G. Moulton's arrangement of Biblical poetry in his *Modern Reader's Bible* (New York: Macmillan, 1922). See also note 25 below.

24. For example, in American Indian rhythms. Cf. Mary Austin's *The American Rhythm* (New York: Harcourt, Brace, 1913).

25. Observed by many critics, but first elaborated by Gay Wilson Allen, "Biblical Analogies for Walt Whitman's Prosody," *Revue Anglo-Americaine*, X, 490-507 (Aug., 1933). Basis for same author's chapter on Whitman in *American Prosody* (New York: American Book Co., 1935), 217-43.

26. J. H. Gardiner, *The Bible as English Literature* (New York: Charles Scribner's Sons, 1906), 107.

27. Kautsch, 2.

28. Driver, 340.

29. Bliss Perry, *Walt Whitman* (Boston: Houghton Mifflin, 1906), 92.

30. George Rice Carpenter, *Walt Whitman* (New York: Macmillan, 1924), 42.

31. De Selincourt, 103-4.

32. E. C. Ross, "Whitman's Verse," *Modern Language Notes*, XLV, 363-64 (June 1930). Autrey Nell Wiley demonstrates this view in "Reiterative Devices in 'Leaves of Grass,' " *American Literature*, I, 161-70 (May 1929). She says: "In more than 10,500 lines in *Leaves of Grass*, there are, by my count, only twenty run-on lines," 161.

33. Whitman himself misdated this poem 1843. It was published in The New York *Tribune*, Supplement, March 22, 1850, and the occasion of the

satire was Webster's speech on March 7, 1850, regarding the Fugitive Slave Law.

34. Reader's Ed. *L. G.*, 716.

35. Reader's Ed. *L. G.*, 711.

36. "Song of Myself," sec. 6.

37. Cf. "Song of Myself," sec. 33, and "Salut au Monde!"

38. Cf. Emile Lauvriere, *Repetition and Parallelism in Tennyson* (London: Oxford University Press, 1901).

39. Here again Emerson's theory preceded Whitman's practice. In the section on "Melody, Rhyme, and Form," in his essay "Poetry and Imagination" Emerson wrote: "Another form of rhyme is iteration of phrases. . . ."

40. See note 32 above.

41. P. Jannaccone, *La Poesia di Walt Whitman e L'Evoluzione delle Forme Ritmiche* (Torino, 1898), 64 ff. Translated by Peter Mitilineos. *Walt Whitman's Poetry and the Evolution of Rhythmic Forms* (Washington, D. C.: Microcard Editions, 1973).

42. Wiley, 161-62.

43. C. Alphonso Smith, *Repetition and Parallelism in English Verse* (New York, 1894), 9.

44. De Selincourt, 104-9.

45. Jannaccone (trans.), 70.

46. *Ibid.*, 74.

47. Sculley Bradley, "The Fundamental Metrical Principle in Whitman's Poetry," *American Literature*, X, 437-59 (January 1939).

48. Quoted by Perry from unpublished preface, 207; cf. Traubel, I, 414.

49. Samuel Taylor Coleridge, *Essays and Lectures on Shakespeare and Some Other Old Poets and Dramatists* (London: Everyman Library, n.d.), 46-47.

50. De Selincourt, 96-97.

51. Bradley, 447.

52. Would it not increase the pathos to read "all dark" and "desolate" with hovering accent? But this scansion would not affect Bradley's accent count.

53. "Song of Myself," sec. 8.

54. "Song of Myself," sec. 26. Compare the similar idea (and "I hear . . ." reiteration) in "Salut au Monde!," sec. 3, with caesural effect.

55. "Song of Myself," sec. 50.

56. Jannaccone (trans.), 93.

57. "Great are the Myths," sec. 1.

58. De Selincourt, 106-08.

59. Jean Catel, *Rythme et langage dans la 1re édition des "Leaves of Grass," 1855* (Paris: Rieder, 1930), 126.

60. "Song of Myself," sec. 15.

61. *Ibid.*, sec. 20.

62. *Ibid.*, sec. 30.

63. *Ibid.*, sec. 26.

64. "To the Leaven'd Soil They Trod."

65. F. O. Matthiessen, *American Renaissance* (New York: Oxford University Press, 1941), 549-77.

66. *Ibid.*, 565: poem quoted, "Had I the Choice."

67. Ware, 47.

68. Since "bone—one" and "grown—sown" are approximate rimes, the third and fourth lines are also tetrameter couplets.

69. *Complete Writings*, III, 161.

70. Ware, 53.

71. Catel, 84.

72. *An American Primer*, ed. Horace Traubel (Boston: Small, Maynard and Co., 1904), 12. Ed. William White, *Walt Whitman's Day-Books and Notebooks.* (New York University Press, 1975).

73. "Song of Myself," sec. 40 (1. 990).

74. Closing poem in third edition.

75. See Matthiessen, 517-32. In the first edition of *Leaves of Grass* Whitman was especially fond of such rare or obsolete words as *exurge* (p. 60), *caoutchouc* (p. 83), and *albescent* (p. 84).

76. See Louise Pound, "Walt Whitman and the French Language," *American Speech*, I, 421-30 (May 1926). Also Asselineau, II, 225-38.

77. Cf. Louise Pound, "Walt Whitman's Neologisms," *American Mercury*, IV, 199-201 (Feb. 1925). Louis Untermeyer, "Whitman and the American Language," New York *Evening Post*, May 31, 1919, calls Whitman "the father of the American language."

78. Cf. John Bailey, *Walt Whitman* (New York: Macmillan, 1926), 87 ff. Hugh l'Anson Fausset, *Walt Whitman: Poet of Democracy* (New Haven: Yale University Press, 1942) shares Bailey's lack of sympathy and understanding of the principles on which Whitman chose his diction and form. He simply regards the poet as ignorant and careless.

79. Reader's Ed. *L. G.*, 714. Cf. Jean Gorely, "Emerson's Theory of Poetry," *Poetry Review*, XXII, 263-73 (Aug. 1931), and Emerson Grant Sutcliffe, "Emerson's Theory of Literary Expression," *University of Illinois Studies in Language and Literature*, VIII, 9-143 (1923).

80. *American Primer*, 2.

81. Matthiessen, 518.

82. *American Primer*, 16-17.

83. Renamed in 1881 "Song of the Rolling Earth."

84. Version of 1856 edition; first three lines in this passage were dropped in 1881. See also "Song of Myself," sec. 25.

85. "Poem of the Sayers of the Words of the Earth" (1856); "Song of the Rolling Earth," sec. 1.

86. *Ibid.*, sec. 3.

87. See note 1, above.

88. See Reader's Ed. *L. G.*, 718; also "Song of Myself," sec. 12.

89. First published in "Whitman's Embryonic Verse," *Southwest Review*, X, 28-40 (July 1925), later in *Pictures: an Unpublished Poem by Walt Whitman*, Introduction and Notes by Emory Holloway (London: Faber and Gwyer, 1927); reprinted in Reader's Ed. *L. G.*, 642-49.

90. Richard Maurice Bucke, *Notes and Fragments* (London; Ontario, printed for the editor, 1899), 27.

91. *Ibid.*, 179.

92. Holloway, *Pictures*, 10-11. See also Allen and Davis, *Whitman's Poems*, 5-8.

NOTES FOR CHAPTER V

1. Harold W. Blodgett, "Whitman in 1960," *Walt Whitman Review*, VI, 23 (June 1960).

2. Reader's Ed. of *L. G.*, 711.

3. *Ibid.*, 729.

4. As early as 1900 Whitman was accepted as a major poet. See, for example, Barrett Wendell's *A Literary History of the United States* (New York: Charles Scribner's Sons, 1901), 465-79. But Randall Jarrell's defense of Whitman in "Walt Whitman: He Had His Nerve," *Kenyon Review*, XIV (Winter 1952), 63-71, marked a turning point in Whitman's reputation with leading poets and critics.

5. Reader's Ed. of *L. G.*, 562.

6. See *The Solitary Singer*, 472.

7. *Allgemeinen Zeitung*, Augsburg, April 24, 1868; reprinted in *Gesammelte Dichtung* (Stuttgart: Goschen'sche, 1877), IV, 86-87.

8. See Frederik Schyberg, *Walt Whitman*, trans. by Evie Allison Allen (New York: Columbia University Press, 1951), 220-24.

9. *Correspondence*, III, 259.

10. *Ibid.* Quoted by Kornei Chukovsky in "Walt Whitman's Greeting to the Russian People," *Sputnik*, June, 1967, pp. 88-93; reprinted in *Walt Whitman in Europe Today*, edited by Roger Asselineau and William White (Detroit: Wayne State University Press, 1972), 35-40. Whitman's letter, dated "Dec. 20, '81," quoted by Horst Frenz, editor, *Whitman and Rolleston: A Correspondence* (Indiana University Press, 1951), 49.

11. *Ibid.*, 89.

12. William Sloane Kennedy, *The Fight of a Book for the World: A Companion Volume to Leaves of Grass* (New York: privately printed, 1926); Part I, "Story of the Reception of 'Leaves of Grass' by the World."

13. Frederik Schyberg, *Walt Whitman* (Copenhagen: Gyldendalske Boghandel, 1933); "Whitman i Verdenlitteraturen."

14. See note 8, above. Professor Lionel Trilling read the praise of Schy-

berg in the *Walt Whitman Handbook* and recommended that the Columbia University Press publish a translation; Mrs. Allen was invited to do a translation.

15. Gay Wilson Allen, editor, *Walt Whitman Abroad: Critical Essays from Germany, France, Scandinavia, Russia, Italy, Spain and Latin America, Israel, Japan and India* (Syracuse University Press, 1955).

16. Fernando Alegría *Walt Whitman en Hispanoamerica* (Mexico: Ediciones Studium, 1954).

17. The phrase is used by F. O. Matthiessen in one of the best interpretations of the period, *The American Renaissance: Art and Expression in the Age of Emerson and Whitman* (New York: Oxford University Press, 1941).

18. See *Notes and Fragments*, Part V, 193-534—especially items no. 210-36, 332-39, and 395.

19. This is essentially Arthur Christy's attitude toward the Orientalism of Emerson and Thoreau in *The Orient in American Transcendentalism* (New York: Columbia University Press, 1932).

20. Walter F. Taylor, *A History of American Letters* (New York: American Book Co., 1936), 145-46.

21. Newton Arvin, *Whitman* (New York: Macmillan and Co., 1938), 190.

22. John B. Moore, "The Master of Whitman," *Studies in Philology*, XXIII, 77 (January 1926). See also Clarence Gohdes, "Whitman and Emerson," *Sewanee Review*, XXXVII, 79-93 (January 1929).

23. Moore, 77.

24. Leon Howard, "For a Critique of Whitman's Transcendentalism," *Modern Language Notes*, XLVII, 79-85 (February 1952).

25. *Ibid.*, 83.

26. *Ibid.*, 85.

27. F. I. Carpenter, *Emerson: Representative Selections* (New York: American Book Co., 1934), xxxiii.

28. *Ibid.* However, as pointed out in Chap. III (see p. 190), whereas Emerson's evolution starts from spirit or soul, Whitman's starts from matter impregnated by spirit—always co-equal.

29. For a good summary of Carlyle's ideas, see Charles Frederick Harrold, *Carlyle and German Thought* (New Haven: Yale University Press, 1934), esp. Chap. IV, "Carlyle's Universe."

30. See *Notes and Fragments*, 132-41. In his notes on Goethe and Schiller (105-06) Whitman mentions Carlyle several times, as if he were taking notes from Carlyle's books.

31. Richard Maurice Bucke, *Walt Whitman* (Philadelphia: David McKay, 1883), 211. Bucke attributes the quotation to Burroughs.

32. Clifton Joseph Furness, *Walt Whitman's Workshop* (Cambridge: Harvard University Press, 1928), 236, note 138.

33. Arvin, 191.

34. *Ibid.*

35. *Prose Works 1892* (Stovall, ed.), II, 418, note.

36. Richard Riethmuller, "Walt Whitman and the Germans," *German American Annals*, New Ser., IV (1906), 126.

37. Woodbridge Riley, *The Meaning of Mysticism* (New York: Richard R. Smith, 1936), 64.

38. Mody C. Boatright, "Whitman and Hegel," *Studies in English*, No. 9, University of Texas Bulletin, July 8, 1929, p. 150.

39. W. B. Fulghum, Jr., "Whitman's Debt to Joseph Gostwick," *American Literature*, XII, 491-96 (January 1941).

40. Robert P. Falk, "Walt Whitman and German Thought," *Journal of English and Germanic Philology*, XL, 329 (July 1941).

41. Olive W. Parsons, "Whitman the Non-Hegelian,"*PMLA*, LVIII, 1073 (December 1943).

42. Falk, 330.

43. Alfred H. Marks, "Whitman's Triadic Imagery," *American Literature*, XXIII, 99 (March 1951).

44. Henry Thoreau, *Familiar Letters* (Boston: Houghton Mifflin Co., 1894), 347. Quoted by Bliss Perry, *Walt Whitman* (Boston: Houghton Mifflin Co., 1906), 121-22.

45. *Prose Works 1892* (Stovall, ed.), II, 722.

46. See Christy, note 19, above. Also F. I. Carpenter, *Emerson and Asia* (Cambridge: Harvard University Press, 1930); O. B. Frothingham, *Transcendentalism in New England* (New York: Putnam's Sons, 1876), Chaps. I-III; H. C. Goddard, *Studies in New England Transcendentalism* (New York: Columbia University Press, 1908).

47. Cf. Friedrich von Schlegel, "The Indian Language, Literature, and Philosophy," reprinted in *Aesthetic and Miscellaneous Works* (London: George Bell and Sons, 1900), 425-526. Edwyn C. Vaughn says, in *The Romantic Revolt* (New York: Charles Scribner's and Sons, 1907), that this work "forms nothing short of an epoch in the history of European learning, and even of letters and philosophy." See also Arthur F. J. Remy, *The Influence of India and Persia in the Poetry of Germany* (New York: Columbia University Press, 1910).

48. Lord Strangford, "Walt Whitman," *The Pall Mall Gazette*, February 16, 1866; reprinted in *A Selection from the Writings of Viscount Strangford* (London, 1869), II, 297 ff. See Harold Blodgett, *Walt Whitman in England* (Ithaca: Cornell University Press, 1934), 198.

49. Moncure D. Conway, "Walt Whitman," *The Fortnightly Review*, VI, 538-48 (October 15, 1866).

50. Gabriel Sarrazin, translated by Harrison B. Morris from *La Renaissance de la Poésie Anglaise, 1798–1889,* in *In Re Walt Whitman* (Philadelphia: David McKay, 1893), 161 ff. French text reprinted in *The*

Universal Review (London), No. 22, February 15, 1890, pp. 247-69.

51. Edward Carpenter, *Days with Walt Whitman* (London: George Allen, 1906), 94-102.

52. Dorothy Frederica Mercer, "Walt Whitman on Reincarnation," *Vedanta and the West*, IX, 180-85 (November-December 1946); "Walt Whitman on Learning and Wisdom," X, 57-58 (March-April, 1947); "Walt Whitman on God and the Self," X, 80-87 (May-June 1947); "Walt Whitman on Love," X, 107-13 (July-August 1947).

53. Mercer (thesis), 51.

54. *Ibid.*, 110.

55. See note 52, above.

56. Malcolm Cowley (editor), Introduction to *Walt Whitman's* Leaves of Grass: *The First (1855) Edition* (New York: Viking Press, 1959), xxii.

57. *Ibid.*

58. *Ibid.*

59. *Ibid.*, xiv.

60. V. K. Chari, *Whitman in the Light of Vedantic Mysticism: An Interpretation*, With an Introduction by Gay Wilson Allen (Lincoln: University of Nebraska Press, 1964).

61. *Ibid.*, 18.

62. *Ibid.*, 34.

63. *Ibid.* "Walt Whitman, a kosmos," "Song of Myself," sec. 24, 1. 1.

64. Reader's Ed. of *L. G.*, 721.

65. Chari, 54.

66. *Ibid.*

67. *Ibid.*, 127.

68. O. K. Nambiar, *Walt Whitman and Yoga* (Bangalore: Jevan Publications, 1966).

69. *Ibid.*, vii.

70. *Ibid.*, viii.

71. *Ibid.*,

72. See Chap. I of this *Handbook*, p. 27.

73. T. R. Rajasekharaiah, *The Roots of Whitman's Grass* (Madison, N. J.: Fairleigh Dickinson University Press, 1970).

74. See Chap. I of this *Handbook*, p. 45.

75. *Hullina Dalagalu* [101 selected poems from *Leaves of Grass*], translated by M. Gopalakrishna Adiga [New Delhi]: Sahitya Akademi, 1966), 222 pp.

76. *Ghah Diyan Pattiyan*: Punjabi translation by Gurbakhsh Singh; Selected Poems from Whitman's *Leaves of Grass* ([New Delhi]: Sahitya Akademi, 1968), 260 pp.

77. "Walt Whitman: Passage to India," *Indian Literature*, II, 38-44 (April-September 1959). Half-yearly Journal of Sahitya Akademi, New Delhi.

78. Arvin, 201.

79. Reader's Ed. of *L. G.*, 727.

80. "Song of Myself," sec. 24 (1855 edition).

81. *Ibid.*, sec. 41.

82. "Song of Occupations," sec. 3 (1855 edition).

83. "Poem of the Road" (1856 edition); "Song of the Open Road."

84. "Poem of You" (1856); 1881 title, "To You."

85. Perry, 277-80.

86. Esther Shephard, *Walt Whitman's Pose* (New York: Harcourt, Brace and Co., 1936).

87. *Uncollected Poetry and Prose*, II, 53.

88. W. S. Kennedy, *Reminiscences of Walt Whitman* (London: Alexander Gardner, 1896), 106.

89. Cf. Hugo's Preface to *Cromwell.*

90. See Schyberg (trans.), 268-70.

91. See *Uncollected Poetry and Prose*, I, 134.

92. Gay Wilson Allen, "Walt Whitman and Jules Michelet," *Études Anglaises*, I, 230-37 (May 1937). Whitman's paraphrase of Michelet's poem on the Man-of-War bird was first pointed out by Adeline Knapp, "Walt Whitman and Jules Michelet, Identical Passages," *Critic*, XLIV, 467-68 (1907).

93. Jules Michelet's *The People*, translated by G. H. Smith (New York: Appleton, 1846), 6.

94. "So Long!," ll. 53-54.

95. *The People*, 25.

96. "Song of Myself," sec. 20.

97. *The People*, 135.

98. Reader's Ed. of *L. G.*, 713-16.

99. *The People*, 24.

100. *Ibid.*

101. "Song of Myself," sec. 52.

102. Reader's Ed. of *L. G.*, 714.

103. Discussed by Gay Wilson Allen in "Whitman and Michelet—Continued," *American Literature*, XLV, 428-32 (November 1973). The "Continued" refers to an article by Arthur Geffen, "Walt Whitman and Jules Michelet—One More Time," *American Literature*, XLV, 107-13 (March 1973). "One More Time" refers to Allen's article listed in note 92, above.

104. *L'Oiseau* was published in France in 1857, and T. Nelson and Sons published a translation in 1869. Scholars agree that Whitman could not read French. "Out of the Cradle Endlessly Rocking" (final title) was composed and published in 1859.

105. Michelet's two chapters in *The Bird* on the nightingale are entitled "Art and the Infinite."

106. Blodgett. See note 48, above.

107. *Ibid.*, 14 ff.

108. *Ibid.*, 163-66.

109. Reprinted in *A Selection from the Writings of Viscount Strangford* (London, 1869), II, 297 ff. Blodgett, 198.

110. *Ibid.*

111. Quoted from *Chronicle* article by Blodgett, 22.

112. See Chap. I, pp. 10-11.

113. *Ibid.*, p. 48.

114. Blodgett, 78.

115. Published in *The Contemporary Review*, October 1871, and reissued in an expanded pamphlet, London, 1872.

116. Quoted by Blodgett, 79.

117. *Ibid.*

118. *The Fleshly School of Poetry* (London: Strahan, 1872), 97.

119. Article in *The Athenaeum*, March 11, 1876, partly reprinted from *The West Jersey Press* (Camden), January 26, 1876. The original article on the American neglect of Whitman may have been written by the poet himself. See Furness, *Workshop*, 245.

120. Robert Buchanan, "The American Socrates," *A Look Round Literature* (London: Ward and Downey, 1887), 344.

121. Blodgett, 105.

122. Swinburne used the 1867 title.

123. Algernon Charles Swinburne, *William Blake* (London: Hotten, 1868), 335.

124. Blodgett, 108.

125. See especially W. B. Cairns, "Swinburne's Opinion of Whitman," *American Literature*, III, 125-35 (May 1931). Also W. S. Monroe, "Swinburne's Recantation of Walt Whitman," *Revue Anglo-Américaine*, IX, 347-51 (March 1931).

126. Cairns, 131.

127. Quoted by Cairns, 131-32, from *Fortnightly Review*.

128. See Chap. I, p. 51.

129. See pp. 33 and 51.

130. Edward Dowden, *Shakespeare: A Critical Study of His Mind and Art* (London: C. Kegan Paul and Co., 1879), 40. Mentioned by Blodgett, 43.

131. Reprinted in part by Traubel *et al, In Re*, 284.

132. Quoted by Blodgett, 185.

133. *Ibid.*, 186.

134. *Ibid.*, 199.

135. *Ibid.*, 190.

136. *Ibid.*, 193.

137. *Ibid.*, 201.

138. John Johnston and J. W. Wallace, *Visits to Walt Whitman in 1890-1891 by Two Lancashire Friends* (London: Allen & Unwin, 1917).

139. Blodgett, 215.

140. Cf. *Homogenic Love* (1894), *Love's Coming of Age* (1896), *An Unknown People* (1897), *Some Friends of Walt Whitman* (1904), *The Intermediate Sex* (1912).

141. *The Intermediate Sex* (New York: Mitchell Kennerley, 1912), 117.

142. Havelock Ellis, *Sexual Inversion* (Philadelphia: David McKay, 1915, 3rd ed.), 51.

143. Havelock Ellis, *The New Spirit* (New York: Modern Library, 1921), 31.

144. *The Letters of Gerard Manley Hopkins to Robert Bridges*, ed. Claude C. Abbott (London: Oxford University Press, 1935), 155. Reprinted by Edwin H. Miller (ed.), *A Century of Whitman Criticism* (Bloomington: Indiana University Press, 1969), 77-80.

145. George Saintsbury, *A History of English Prosody* (London: Macmillan, 1910), III, 492. Reprinted by Edwin H. Miller, 56 f.

146. *The American Genius: An Anthology of Poetry and Some Prose.* Selected with a Preface by Edith Sitwell (London: John Lehmann, 1952), x-xi.

147. James E. Quinn, "Yeats and Whitman: 1887-1925," *Walt Whitman Review*, XV, 106-08 (September 1974).

148. See Schyberg (Allen translation), 321-26; D. H. Lawrence, *Studies in Classic American Literature* (New York: Doubleday—Anchor Books, 1953), Chap. 12.

149. Edwin H. Miller (see note 144, above), xxxiv.

150. James E. Miller, Jr., Karl Shapiro, and Bernice Slote, *Start with the Sun* (Lincoln: University of Nebraska Press, 1960), 4.

151. *Studies in Classic American Literature*, 184.

152. Quoted by Miller, Shapiro, Slote, 80, from letter to Harriet Monroe, March 15, 1928.

153. Miller, Shapiro, Slote, 106.

154. *Ibid.*, 47.

155. Reader's Ed. *L. G.*, 723.

156. Miller, Shapiro, Slote, 170.

157. Sylvia Beach, *Shakespeare and Company* (New York: Harcourt, Brace, 1959), 128.

158. *Finnegans Wake* (New York: Viking Press, 1959), 263. Reprinted by Edwin H. Miller, *A Century &c*, 171.

159. *Finnegans Wake*, 551. Reprinted, *Ibid.*

160. Richard Chase, *Whitman* (New York: Sloane Associates, 1955). In a note on p. 89 Chase explains Joyce's *panromain*: "Presumably—pan-Roman (i.e., "universal") and pan-romaine (i.e., a vegetable: 'Leaves of Grass') and pan-*roman* (the universal novel).

161. Cf. Brom Weber, *Hart Crane* (New York: Bodley Press, 1948), 303.

162. Yvor Winters, *In Defense of Reason* (New York: Swallow Press & William Morrow, 1947), 590.

163. T. S. Eliot, "Whitman and Tennyson," *The Nation and Athenaeum*, XL, 426 (Dec. 18, 1926). Reprinted Edwin H. Miller, 162-63.

164. S. Musgrove, *T. S. Eliot and Walt Whitman* (Wellington: University of New Zealand Press, 1952).

165. "A Pact," poem written in 1913.

166. Herbert Bergman, "Ezra Pound and Walt Whitman," *American Literature*, XXVII, 56-61 (March, 1955). An unpublished 1909 essay.

167. Quoted by Roy Harvey Pearce, *The Continuity of American Poetry* (Princeton: Princeton University Press, 1961), 84.

168. *Ibid.*

169. "Un poète américain, Walt Whitman: 'Muscle and Pluck Forever,' " *Revue Deux Mondes*, XLII, 566-67 (June 1, 1872).

170. *Ibid.*

171. Quoted by O. F. Pucciani, "French Criticism of Walt Whitman" (Harvard University doctoral dissertation, 1943—unpublished), 70-71, from Émile Blémont, "La Poésie en Angleterre et aux États-Unis," III: "Walt Whitman," *Renaissance littéraire et artistique*, 1872. The article ran in three numbers: June 8, July 6, July 13, 1872.

172. Quoted by F. Baldensperger, "Walt Whitman and France," *Columbia University Quarterly*, Oct., 1919, p. 302.

173. Pucciani, 58.

174. Léo Quesnel, "Poètes américains: Walt Whitman," *Revue politique et littéraire*, Feb. 16, 1884, p. 215.

175. Pucciani, 94.

176. *Leaves of Grass*, with one hundred drawings by Rockwell Kent (New York: Heritage Press, 1936).

177. Pucciani, 141.

178. Édouard Dujardin, in "Les premiers poètes du vers libre," *Mercure de France*, March 15, 1921 (vol. 146, pp. 577-621), denies that Whitman had any influence on "free verse" in France, pointing out: "Exactement parlant, le vers de Walt Whitman, du moins celui des *Brins d'Herbe*, n'est pas le vers libre, mais le verset ... Nous avons vu que le vers libre et le verset sont de la même famille, et qu'on pouvait considérer le verset comme un vers libre élargi, le plus-souvent composé lui-même de plusieurs vers libres étroitement associés," 606. It would seem significant, however, that Laforgue was experimenting with the new form at the same time that he was translating Whitman (see *La Vogue*, II, No. 7; III, Nos. 1, 3, 8, 1886); and the following year Gustave Kahn, editor of *La Vogue*, published "La Belle au château revenant" in *Revue indépendante*, Sept., 1887. And even Dujardin admits that "le vers libre et le verset sont de la même famille." It seems likely, therefore, that Whitman's form had some effect on the French experiments. See also P. M. Jones, "Influence of Walt Whitman on the 'Vers Libre,' " *Modern Language Review*, XI, 186-194 (April, 1916). "Perhaps it would be safest to say that in the days when the first *vers libres* were being written, the poets who knew Whitman—and they were few, though important—were attracted mainly

through the appeal made by his brusque originality to their pronounced taste for literary novelties."194.

179. Gabriel Sarrazin, *La Renaissance de la poésie anglaise, 1778-1889*, (Paris: Perrin, 1889), 236-37. Translation in *In Re Walt Whitman*, 160.

180. Pucciani, 103.

181. In a review of Havelock Ellis's *New Spirit* in *Mercure de France*, June 1890, tome 1, p. 220.

182. "Le vers libre, tel que le comprend ce dernier poète [Francis Vielé-Griffin], vient en partie de Whitman; mais Whitman était lui-même un fils de la Bible et ainsi le vers libre, ce n'est peut-être, au fond, que le verset hébraïque des prophètes; c'est bien également de la Bible, mais de la Bible allemande, cette fois, que semble nous venir une autre nuance du vers libre, celle qui a valu sa réputation à M. Gustave Kahn," *Le Problème du style* (Paris: Mercure de France, 1924 [first ed. 1902], p. 159.

183. Pucciani, 118.

184. Téodor de Wyzewa, "Walt Whitman," *Revue politique et littéraire*, XLIX, 513-19 (April 1892).

185. B. H. Gausseron, "Walt Whitman," *Revue encyclopédique*, May 15, 1892, pp. 721-26.

186. Jules Romains, *La Vie unanime* (Paris: "L'Abbaye," 1908), 121-236.

187. Baldensperger, 307.

188. See Dominique Braga, "Walt Whitman," *Europe nouvelle*, anné 5, N. 35 (August 19, 1922), 1042.

189. Pierre de Lanux, *Young France and New America* (New York: Macmillan, 1917).

190. Baldensperger, 307.

191. *Ibid.*

192. Georges Duhamel, *Les Poètes et la poésie, 1912-1914* (Paris: Mercure de France, 1914), 141.

193. See p. 287.

194. Schyberg (trans.), 355, note 70.

195. See Chap. I, p. 36.

196. Schyberg (trans.), 300-1.

197. *Ibid.*, 302.

198. *Ibid.*, 304.

199. S. A. Rhodes, "The Influence of Walt Whitman on André Gide," *Romanic Review*, XXXI, 156-71 (April 1940). See also Huberta F. Randall, "Whitman and Verhaeren—Priests of Human Brotherhood," *French Review*, XVI, 36-43 (1942).

200. Rhodes, 159.

201. *Ibid.*, 161.

202. *Ibid.*, 162.

203. *Ibid.*, 163.

204. *Ibid.*, 170.

205. *Ibid.*, 170-71.

206. This conclusion is supported by Klaus Mann, *André Gide and the Modern Spirit* (New York: Creative Age Press, 1944).

207. Stefan Zweig, *Emile Verhaeren* (Boston: Houghton Mifflin Co., 1914), 108.

208. Schyberg (trans.), 297.

209. *La Multiple Splendeur.*

210. Schyberg (trans.), 298.

211. P. M. Jones, "Whitman and Verhaeren," *Aberystwyth Studies* (University College of Wales), II, 82-83 (1914).

212. *Ibid.*, 106.

213. Schyberg (trans.), 297.

214. *Ibid.*, 300.

215. *Walt Whitman in Europe Today*, eds. Roger Asselineau and William White (Detroit: Wayne State University Press, 1972).

216. *Walt Whitman, Une étude, un choix de poèmes* par Paul Jamati (Paris: Pierre Seghers, 1948). 229 pp.

217. *Walt Whitman: Feuilles d'herbe* (Choix), Introduction et traduction de Roger Asselineau (Paris: Societé d'Édition "Les Belles Lettres," 1956). 358 pp. A bilingual edition with introduction by Roger Asselineau, Paris: Aubier-Flammarion, 1972. 511 pp.

218. *Whitman*, by Alain Bosquet [long introduction on the man and his work, with translation of selected poems and prose] (Paris: Gallimard, 1959). 270 pp.

219. Walt Whitman: *Chants de la terre qui tourne*, Préface et Traduction de Roger Asselineau (Paris: Nouveaux Horizons, 1966). 303 pp.

220. *Walt Whitman in Europe Today*, 33.

221. *Walt Whitman, ses meilleures pages traduites de l'anglais par* Rosaire Dion-Lévesque (Montreal: Les Elzévirs, 1933). 240 pp. Same title (Québec: Les Presses de l'Université Laval, 1965). 240 pp.

222. O. E. Lessing, "Walt Whitman and His German Critics prior to 1910," *American Collector*, III, 7 (October 1926).

223. First published in *Allgemeinen Zeitung*, Augsburg, April 24, 1868; reprinted in *Gesammelte Dichtung*, Stuttgart, 1877.

224. Lessing, 7.

225. These were published in 1870 in *Amerikanische Anthologie*; see Harry Law-Robertson, *Walt Whitman in Deutschland* (Giessen, 1935), 13-14.

226. The paper was *New Yorker Staatszeitung*. The essay was translated for *In Re Walt Whitman* (Philadelphia: David McKay, 1893), 215-30. *Walt Whitman, der Dichter der Demokratie* appeared in several German editions, 1882, 1886, 1889, and 1899.

227. On September 9, 1884, Rolleston wrote Whitman that he had not been able to find a German publisher for his translation and had been told

"there would probably be difficulties with the police, who in Germany exercise a most despotic power."—*Whitman and Rolleston: A Correspondence*, ed. Horst Frenz (Bloomington: Indiana University Press, 1951), 94. See also Horace Traubel, *With Walt Whitman in Camden* (Boston: Small, Maynard, 1906), I, 18. Earlier, Rolleston had discussed Whitman's democratic ideas in *Über Wordsworth und Walt Whitman* (Dresden, 1883), written in collaboration with C. W. Cotterill.

228. Quoted by Law-Robertson, 39, from *Deutsche Presse*, Jg. II, No. 23, 1889.

229. Quoted by Law-Robertson, 39, from *Magazin für Literatur des In- und Auslandes*, No. 37, p. 584 (1889).

230. "Most of the references to Whitman [1889–1909] are characterized by a supreme admiration which, in some instances, rises in intensity even to the point of fanaticism or deification. It is this extravagant admiration for the poet which justifies the term cult as a name for the agitation as a whole." Edward Thorstenberg, "The Walt Whitman Cult in Germany," *Sewanee Review*, XIX, 77 (January 1911).

231. Lessing, 10, says, "This little book is an unparalleled example of high-handed arrogance, cowardly imposition, and utter ignorance." Lessing claims (following Bertz, see note 232 below) that Schlaf had read no more than 15 percent of Whitman's writings, and those in German translations.

232. In *Jahrbuch für sexuelle Zwischenstufen*, IX, 551-64 (Jg. 1908). Law-Robertson, 51, discusses the controversy.

233. See Law-Robertson, 85.

234. *Grashalme, Eine Auswahl*, Leipzig, 1904.

235. Written for *Aus Amerikanischen Kriegszeiten*. See Lessing, 10.

236. Law-Robertson, 20.

237. Translated by Thorstenberg, 79, from Schölermann's *Grashalme*, xiv.

238. *Walt Whitman: Prosaschriften*, Auswahl übersetz (Munich and Leipzig: R. Piper & Co., 1905), xxvi.

239. Lessing, 11.

240. Law-Robertson, 21.

241. Quoted by Amelia von Ende, "Walt Whitman and Arno Holz," *Poet Lore*, XVI, 63 (Summer 1905).

242. *Ibid.*

243. For example, one of the poems quoted by Amelia von Ende (from *Phantasus*), 65:

> Seven billions of years before my birth
> I was an iris.
> My roots
> Were imbedded
> In a star.
> Upon its dark waters floated
> My large blue blossom.

244. Law-Robertson, 65-66.

245. *Ibid.*, 65.

246. *Ibid.*, 66-67.

247. Cf. *Ibid.*, 68.

248. "Walt Whitman," translated by Rudolf Komadina, for *Die Gesellschaft Halbmonatschrift für Litteratur, Kunst, und Sozialpolitik*, XVI, Bd. I, pp. 24-35 (Jg. 1900).

249. *Ibid.*, 24.

250. "Walt Whitman zu seinem siebzigsten Geburtstag," *Deutsche Presse*, II, No. 23. Quoted by Lessing, 8.

251. See note 232, above.

252. See Chap. I, p. 63.

253. See note 239, above.

254. *Prose Works 1892* (Stovall, ed.), II, 482.

255. Lessing, 14. Lessing first published his essay "Walt Whitman and the German Critics" in the *Journal of English and Germanic Philology*, IX, 85-98 (1910), but to avoid confusion references are given here only to the *American Collector* version.

256. Lessing, 14-15.

257. *Ibid.*, 15.

258. Quoted by Law-Robertson, 69, from *Wege nach Weimar*, Bd. I, S. 279 (1906).

259. *Ibid.*

260. Anna Jacobson, "Walt Whitman in Germany since 1914," *Germanic Review*, I, 133 (April 1926).

261. Quoted *Ibid.*, from "Ein Beispiel Kriegsdichtung," *Die Neue Zeit*. Dez. 1914, pp. 373-82.

262. Jacobson, 136.

263. The same charge had previously been made in France. See note 193, above.

264. Law-Robertson, 71.

265. "Whitman der Dichter der Demokratische, zu seinem 100. Geburtstag, 31 Mai 1919," *Der Kampf, Sozialdemokratische Wochenschrift*, May 31, 1919, pp. 342-44.

266. According to Associated Press dispatches in the *New York Times*, Jan. 1 and March 11, 1922.

267. Jacobson, 134.

268. *Ibid.*

269. *Ibid.*

270. "Drei Lieder Whitmans," übertragen von Gustav Landauer, *Menschliche Gedichte im Kriege*, Herausgegeben von René Schickele (Zürich, 1918).

271. Gustav Landauer. See Law-Robertson, 78.

272. *Walt Whitmans Werk*, Ausgewählt, übertragen und eingeleitet von Hans Reisiger (Berlin: S. Fischer, 1922), 2 vols.

273. Quoted by Law-Robertson, 30, from *Vossische Zeitung*, Nov. 17, 1919 (review of first edition in one volume).

274. Reisiger, I, xiii.

275. *Ibid.*, xix.

276. Quoted by Theodore Stanton, in a review of Reisiger's work, "Walt Whitman in Germany," *The Literary Review*, formerly the Literary Supplement of the *New York Evening Post*, September 30, 1922, p. 68. Most of this article is devoted to printing valuable letters from Reisiger and Thomas Mann.

277. Quoted *Ibid.* Same letter also quoted by Law-Robertson, 73-74, from *Frankfurter Zeitung*, V, April 16, 1922.

278. Republished in *Bemühungen, Neue Folge Gesammelten Abhandlungen und kleinen Aufsätse* (Berlin: Fischer, 1925), 141-90.

279. Stefan Zweig himself, in his biography, *Emile Verhaeren* (Boston: Houghton Mifflin, 1914), is often Whitmanesque in style.

280. Cf. Law-Robertson, 78. Actual influence of Whitman on Werfel is debatable. See also Detlev W. Schumann, "Enumerative Style and Its Significance in Whitman, Rilke, Werfel," *Modern Language Quarterly*, III, 171-204 (June 1942).

281. See especially the article by Thomas Mann's son, Klaus Mann, "The Present Greatness of Whitman," *Decision*, I, 14-30 (April 1941). Klaus Mann's *André Gide and the Modern Spirit* (New York: Creative Age Press, 1944) shows great admiration for Whitman.

282. *Grashalme*, Auswahl von Georg Goyert ins Deutsche übertragen (Berlin: Lothar Blansvalet Verlag, 1948). 106 pp.

283. *Walt Whitman, Ein Amerikaner* (Berlin: Lothar Blansvalet Verlag, 1948).

284. *Walt Whitman in Selbstzeugnissen und Bilddokumenten*, Darstellt von Gay Wilson Allen, Herausgegeben von Kurt Kusenberg ([Hamburg]: Rowohlt, 1961).

285. *Walt Whitman in Europe Today* (see note 215, above), 15.

286. Schyberg (trans.), 220.

287. "Walt Whitman, det Amerikanske Democratis Digter," *Ide og Virkelighed*, I, 152-216 (1872); "Walt Whitman," *Buster og Masker*, 1882, pp. 123-92.

288. Schyberg (trans.), 308.

289. *Ibid.*

290. A translation of Hamsun's satirical speech, "The Primitive Poet, Walt Whitman," by Evie Allison Allen is in *Walt Whitman Abroad*, ed. Gay Wilson Allen (Syracuse: Syracuse University Press, 1955), 112-23.

291. Schyberg (trans.), 312. Whitman's influence on Jensen himself is found mainly in his series of novels called (in translation) *The Long Journey*. See G. W. Allen, "Walt Whitman's 'Long Journey' Motif," *Journal of English and Germanic Philology*, XXXVIII, 76-95 (January 1939); reprinted in *Walt*

Whitman as Man, Poet, and Legend, ed. G. W. Allen (Carbondale: Southern Illinois University Press, 1961), 62-82.

292. *Walt Whitman, Digte* (Copenhagen: Gyldendal, 1933). 126 pp.

293. Schyberg (trans.), 311.

294. *Walt Whitman in Europe Today*, 28.

295. Gay Wilson Allen, "Walt Whitman's Reception in Scandinavia," *Papers of the Bibliographical Society of America*, XL, 259-75, Fourth Quarter 1946. The visit of an American university professor to Bjørnson is quoted from R. B. Anderson, *Life Story* (Madison, Wisconsin: privately printed, 1915. See also Arne Kildal, *Amerikas Stemme* (Voice of America) (Oslo: Steenske, 1939), "Walt Whitman," 69-86.

296. Kristofer Janson, *Amerikanske Forhold: fem foredrag* (Copenhagen: Gyldendal, 1881). "The most original poetic mind America has at present is undeniably Walt Whitman," p. 63.

297. *Walt Whitman Abroad* (see note 291, above), 112.

298. *Walt Whitman: Sangen om Meg Selv av Leaves of Grass*, Oversettelse og Innledning ved Per Arneberg, Tegninger [illustrations] av Kai Fjell (Oslo: H Aschehoug & Co., 1947). 123 pp.

299. See Gay Wilson Allen, "The Problem of Metaphor in Translating Walt Whitman's "Leaves of Grass," *English Studies Today* (Bern, Switzerland: Francke Verlag, 1961), 269-80.

300. Kjell Krogvig, "Til Whitman Gjennem Wergeland," *Samtiden*, 57 Aarg., Heft 3, 196-202 (1948). Translated by Sigrid Moe, *Walt Whitman Abroad*, 137-43.

301. *Walt Whitman in Europe Today*, 29.

302. Translation by Evie Allison Allen in *Walt Whitman Abroad*, 127-36.

303. *Strån av Gräss* av Walt Whitman, Ett Urval Översättning och med Inledning av K. A. Svensson (Stockholm: A. B. Seelig & Co., 1935). 207 pp.

304. *Walt Whitman in Europe Today*, 30.

305. *Ibid.*, 31-32.

306. *The Sunday Star*, Washington, D. C., January 1, 1956.

307. Stephen Stepanchev, in *Walt Whitman Abroad*, 144.

308. *Ibid.*, 145.

309. *Ibid.*

310. First published in 1856 *Leaves of Grass* as "Liberty Poem for Asia, Africa, Europe, America, Australia, Cuba, and The Archipelagoes of the Sea." The same edition contained "Poem of the Dead Young Men of Europe. . . ," first published as "Resurgemus" in the New York *Daily Tribune*, June 21, 1850.

311. Kornei Chukovsky, "A Poet of Wrath and Sorrow [Nikolai Nekrasov]," *Soviet Life*, Dec. 1971, pp. 46-47.

312. See p. 252, above.

313. I. Chistova, "Turgenev and Whitman," *Russkay Literatura*, No. 2, 1966, pp. 196-99. Kornei Chukovsky, "Turgenev and Whitman" [in Russian], *Literaturnaya Rossiya*, July 28, 1967.

314. *Walt Whitman Abroad*, 145.

315. *Ibid.*, 146.

316. *Ibid.*, 147.

317. From Chukovsky's own translation of an extract from *Moi Uitmen*, "My Whitman," *Sputnik*, June, 1967, p. 86.

318. *Ibid.*

319. *Walt Whitman Abroad*, 149.

320. *Sputnik* [editor's introductory note], June 1967, pp. 84-85.

321. *Walt Whitman in Europe*, 35.

322. D. Mirsky, "Poet of American Democracy," translated by Samuel Putnam, *Walt Whitman Abroad*, 169.

323. *Ibid.*, 170, 172.

324. *Ibid.*, 185.

325. *Walt Whitman Abroad*, 185.

326. Leonard Spier, "Walt Whitman," *International Literature*, No. 9, September 1935, p. 89.

327. *Walt Whitman in Europe Today*, 34.

328. *Walt Whitman Abroad*, 156; also Juliusz Zuławski's introduction, "Słowo Wstepne," to his edition of *Źdźbla Trawy* (Warszawa: Institut Wydawniczy, 1966), 5-17.

329. Juliusz Zuławski, *Wielka Podróz Walta Whitmana* (Warszwa: Państwowy Instytut Wydawniczy, 1971). 375 pp.

330. *Walt Whitman: Költeményei*, Keszthelyi Zoltán Fordïtásában (Budapest: Magyar-Amerikai Társaság Kiadása, 1947). 93 pp.

331. *Walt Whitman: Füszálak* (Budapest: Új Magyar Könyvkiadó 1955). 419 pp.

332. *Walt Whitman: Füszálak*, Osszes Költemények (Budapest: Magyar Helikon, 1964). 772 pp.

333. *Walt Whitman in Europe Today*, 23-24.

334. Sonja Basić, "Walt Whitman in Yugoslavia," *Walt Whitman in Europe Today*, 24-26.

335. *Walt Whitman: Opere Alese*, Traducere si prezentare de Mihnea Gheorghiu (Bucuresti: Editura de Stat Pentru Literatura si Arta, 1956). 590 pp.

336. Ph. D. dissertation at New York University, unpublished.

337. *Foglie di erba*, translated by Luigi Camberale (Palermo: Remo Sandron, 1907; rev. 1923). 2 vols.

338. *Foglie d'erba e Prose di Walt Whitman*, traduzione di Enzo Giachino (Einaudi, 1950). 958 pp.

339. Mariolina Meliadò Freeth, "Walt Whitman in Italy," *Walt Whitman in Europe Today*, 20.

340. *Walt Whitman, Giorni rappresentativi e altre prose*, ed. Mariolina Meliadò Freeth (Vicenza: Neri Pozza, 1968).

341. *Walt Whitman in Europe Today*, 22, n. 11.

342. "Walt Whitman," *Fanfulla della domenica*, Dec. 7, 1879, p. 1.

343. "Walt Whitman," *Ritratti straniere: 1908-1921*, Firenze, 1932. Trans. by Roger Asselineau, *Walt Whitman Abroad*, 189.

344. Grippi, 61.

345. *Ibid.*, 62. Giacomo Leopardi (1798-1837), Alessandro Manzoni (1785-1873).

346. Letter to Nencioni, August 26, 1881, in Carducci, *Lettere* (Bologna, 1951), XIII, 172-73. (Quoted by Grippi, 63.)

347. Quoted by Grippi, 99.

348. Pasquale Jannaccone, *La Poesia di Walt Whitman e l'Evoluzione delle Forme Ritmiche* (Torino: Roux, 1898). Translated by Peter Mitilineos, *Walt Whitman's Poetry and the Evolution of Rhythmic Forms* (Washington, D. C.: Microcard Edition, 1973), esp. pp. 104, 137-38.

349. Cf. W. S. Kennedy, *Reminiscences of Walt Whitman* (London: Alexander Gardener, 1896), 151.

350. Grippi, 137. Meliadò, *Walt Whitman nella cultura italiana, 1872–1903* (unpublished thesis, University of Rome, 1961).

351. "Whitman—Poetry of Poetry Writing," trans. by Roger Asselineau, *Walt Whitman Abroad*, 193; from *La Letteratura Americana e Altri Saggi* (Turin: Einaudi, 1951).

352. Reader's Ed. *L. G.*, 721; "reality and the soul," 714.

353. "Whitman" in "Four American Symbolists," 16-26, *Symbolism and American Literature* (University of Chicago Press, 1953).

354. *Walt Whitman Abroad*, 188.

355. Cambon, "Walt Whitman in Italy," *Aut-Aut*, n. 39 (July 1957), 244. Quoted, Grippi, 258.

356. *Walt Whitman in Europe Today*, 21.

357. Whitman used the phrase in *American Primer*, and F. O. Matthiessen, in *American Renaissance: Art and Expression in the Age of Emerson and Whitman* (New York: Oxford University Press, 1941), uses this as a text for analysing the language of *Leaves of Grass*.

358. Mario Praz, "Whitman e Proust," *Mondo*, (March 24, 1951), p. 8. Quoted by Grippi, 276.

359. See p. 293, above.

360. Mario Alicata, "Note su Whitman," *Rinascita* [Communist monthly], anno V, no. 8 (1943), 310. Quoted by Grippi, 268.

361. *Walt Whitman: Obras Escogidas*: Ensayo, Biográficocrítico, Versión, Notas y Bibliografía de Concha Zardoya (Madrid: M. Aguilar, 1946); *Hojas de Hierba*, Version Directa e Integra, Conforme al Texto de la Edicion Definitiva de 1891-2, por Francisco Alexander (Quito, Ecuador: Casa de la Cultura Ecuatoriana, 1953).

362. See *Walt Whitman Abroad*, 279; and Concha Zardoya, "Walt Whitman in Spain," *Walt Whitman in Europe Today*, 9-12.

363. Zardoya, *Obras Escogidas*, 703-811; *Perspectivas Democráticas*, estudio preliminar por Dardo Cuneo, traducción de Luis Azua (Buenos Aires: Ed. Americalee, 1944).

364. See p. 317, above.

365. From unpublished manuscript supplied the author while writing the first edition of this *Handbook* (see p. 334, 1946 ed.).

366. Zardoya, *Walt Whitman in Europe Today*, 10.

367. Translation in *Walt Whitman Abroad*, 220-23.

368. Zardoya, *Walt Whitman in Europe Today*, 11; quoted from *Obras completas* (Buenos Aires: Losada, 1944), 197.

369. Zardoya, 11; *Obras completas*, 225.

370. Translated by Edwin Honig in *García Lorca* (Norfolk, Conn.: New Directions, 1944), 90.

371. *Walt Whitman in Europe Today*, 11.

372. *Ibid.*, 12.

373. Fernando Alegría, *Walt Whitman en Hispanoamerica* (Mexico: Ediciones Studium, 1954).

374. See note 365, above.

375. Pablo Neruda, "We Live in a Whitmanesque Age," *New York Times*, April 14, 1972; reprinted in *Walt Whitman in Europe Today*, 41-42.

376. "Toward an Impure Poetry," *Pablo Neruda: Five Decades: Poems 1925-1970*, a bilingual edition edited and translated from the Spanish by Ben Belitt (New York: Grove Press, 1974), xxi-ii.

377. Quoted by Belitt, xvii, from "El siglo muere."

378. *Five Decades*, 389.

379. *Walt Whitman Abroad*, 232.

380. *Selected Poems by Fernando Pessoa*, translated by Edwin Honig (Chicago: Swallow Press, 1971), 56-71.

381. *Ibid.*, 59.

382. *Ibid.*, 71.

383. *Ibid.*, 12.

384. Complete version unseen; selections: *Phylla Chloes (Leaves of Grass)*, Greek rendition by Nick Proestopoulos (Athens: M. Pechlibanides [1936]. Reviewed by Peter Mitilineos *The Long-Islander*, Huntington, L. I., September 27, 1972 (annual Walt Whitman page, Section One, p. 11).

385. Iwao Matsuhara, "Walt Whitman in Japan," *Thought Currents in English Literature* (Tokyo), XXIX (Jan. 1957); reprinted in *Norton Critical Edition of* Leaves of Grass (New York: Norton, 1973), 912-18. Shigenobu Sadoya, *Walt Whitman in Japan* (Fukuoka: Bulletin No. 9, Research Institute, Seinan Gakuin University, 1969). Abstract in English, pp. 1-7; Bibliography, 9-20.

386. *Walt Whitman in Europe Today*, 38.

387. See note 385, above.

388. Kinnosuke (Sōseki) Natsume, "On Walt Whitman's Poetry—a Democratic Poet in the Literary World," *Tetsugaku Zasshi* (The Journal of Philosophy), Oct. 1892.

389. Letter from Naganuma in the *Long-Islander* (annual Whitman page [See note 384 above], May 29, 1969, p. 2, Whitman Section.

390. *Complete: Leaves of Grass*, vol. I, II, Trans. completely by Shigetaka Naganuma (Tokyo: Mikasa-shobō, 1950; revised edition, 1954.

391. Mentioned in Naganuma's letter. See note 389, above.

392. Sadoya, 2.

393. *Ibid.*

394. *Ibid.*, 4.

395. *Ibid.*, 6.

396. Matsuhara, 917, names: Leon Howard, 1954; Robert A. Jelliffe, 1955; Gay Wilson Allen, 1955.

397. Tokyo: Taibundo, 1966.

398. *Alei Esev (Leaves of Grass) by Walt Whitman*, being a selection and translation into Hebrew (with notes and an essay on the poet's life and work) by Simon Halkin (Merhavia: Sifriat Poalim [Workers' Book Guild], 1952).

399. Sholom Kahn contributed "Whitman's Sense of Evil: Criticisms," to *Walt Whitman Abroad*, 236-53.

400. *New York Herald Tribune Book Review*, March 26, 1950.

401. *Hasifrut*: Quarterly for the Study of Literature, Tel-Aviv University, Vol. I, No. 1 (Spring, 1968), 176-205. Summary in English, xiv.

402. "Whitman in Israel, 1969," *The Long-Islander*, May 29, 1969. See note 389 above.

403. Schyberg (trans.), 251.

404. See note 402, above.

405. Letter to author [G. W. A.].

406. *Selections from Whitman's "Leaves of Grass,"* Translated and Selected by T'u-nan Ch'u (Peking: People's Literary Publishing Society, 1955). 324 pp. Review by Angela Chih-ying Jung Palandri in *Walt Whitman Review*, IV, 94-97 [should be pp. 110-13] (Sept., 1958).

407. Quoted from Palandri's translation in her review. See note 406 above.

Note: for SELECTED BIBLIOGRAPHY 1975–1985 see pp. xvii-xxi.

SELECTED BIBLIOGRAPHY
Chapter I: Growth of Biography

BOOKS

ALLEN, GAY WILSON. *The Solitary Singer: A Critical Biography of Walt Whitman.* New York: Macmillan. 1955. 616 pp. Grove Press, 1959. Rev. ed.: New York University Press. 1967.
(The Fullest biography.)

ARVIN, NEWTON. *Whitman.* New York: The Macmillan Co. 1938. 320 pp.
[Whitman as social thinker.]

ASSELINEAU, ROGER. *L'Evolution de Walt Whitman: Après la première édition des Feuilles d'herbe.* Paris: Didier. 1954. 567 pp. *The Evolution of Walt Whitman: The Creation of a Poet.* Harvard University Press. 1960. 376 pp. *The Evolution of Walt Whitman: The Creation of a Book.* Harvard University Press. 1962. 392 pp.
[A major biography and critical interpretation.]

BAILEY, JOHN. *Walt Whitman.* London and New York: The Macmillan Co. 1926. 220 pp.
[Unoriginal life in the English Men of Letters Series.]

BARRUS, CLARA. *Whitman and Burroughs: Comrades.* Boston: Houghton Mifflin and Co. 1931. 392 pp.
[Contains valuable correspondence of Burroughs, Whitman and their friends—also reliable criticism.]

BAZALGETTE, LÉON. *Walt Whitman, L'Homme et son oeuvre.* Paris: Mercure de France. 1908. 2 vols.
[A romantic biography.]

369

————. *Walt Whitman, the Man and His Work*. Translated by Ellen FitzGerald. Garden City: Doubleday. 1920. xviii, 355 pp.
[The translation is expurgated and slightly edited.]

BERTZ, EDUARD. *Der Yankee-Heiland*. Dresden: Carl Reissner. 1906. 253 pp.
[An attack on Whitman's claim as a prophet and thinker; analysis of sex pathology.]

BINNS, HENRY BRYAN. *A Life of Walt Whitman*. London: Methuen and Co. 1905. 369 pp.
[First exhaustive life—very sympathetic. Binns started the theory of the New Orleans romance.]

BLODGETT, HAROLD. *Walt Whitman in England*. Ithaca, N.Y.: Cornell University Press, 1934. 244 pp.
[Not a biography but discusses the English biographies.]

BORN, HELENA. *Whitman's Ideal Democracy*. Boston: Everett Press, 1902. 88 pp.
[Impassioned defense of Whitman by a devoted socialist friend.]

BUCKE, RICHARD MAURICE, M.D. *Walt Whitman*. Philadelphia: David McKay. 1883. 236 pp.
[An "official portrait," edited and partly written by Whitman himself. Contains also: "Appendix: *The Good Gray Poet* reprinted from the pamphlet of 1866, with an Introductory Letter (1883), written for this volume by William D. O'Connor."]

BUCKE, RICHARD MAURICE; HARNED, THOMAS B.; and TRAUBEL, HORACE L. "Introduction" [biographical] to *The Complete Writings of Walt Whitman*. New York: G. P. Putnam's Sons. 1902. Vol. I, pp. xiii-xcvi.
[Last official biography by Whitman's literary executors.]

BULLETT, GERALD. *Walt Whitman, a Study and a Selection*. London: Grant Richards. 1924. Philadelphia: J. B. Lippincott. 1925. 166 pp.
[Discriminating biographical essay, pp. 3-24.]

BURROUGHS, JOHN. *Notes on Walt Whitman as Poet and Person*. New York: American News Co. 1867. 108 pp. Sec. Ed., New York: J. S. Redfield. 1871.
[Whitman wrote some of this first book on his life.]

————. "The Flight of the Eagle." *Birds and Poets*. Boston: Houghton Mifflin and Co. 1877, 1895. Pp. 185-235.

————. *Whitman, A Study*. Boston: Houghton Mifflin and Co. 1896. 268 pp.
[Mainly critical rather than biographical.]

CANBY, HENRY SEIDEL. *Walt Whitman, An American*. Boston: Houghton Mifflin and Co. 1943. 381 pp.
[Reassertion of Whitman's importance as national poet and critic of democracy. A valuable contribution to Whitman interpretation rather than of biographical fact.]

CARPENTER, EDWARD. *Days with Walt Whitman: with Some Notes on His Life and Works*. London: George Allen; New York: The Macmillan Co. 1906. 187 pp.
[Friendly but critical—first publication of Whitman's letter to Symonds claiming the paternity of six children. An important book in the growth of Whitman biography.]

CATEL, JEAN. *Walt Whitman: la Naissance du Poète*. Paris: Les Éditions Rieder. 1929. 483 pp.
[Psychological study of the origin of *Leaves of Grass*. Oversimplifies the problem, but illuminating.]

CHASE, RICHARD. *Walt Whitman Reconsidered*. New York: Sloane Associates. 1955. 191 pp.
[Whitman's "sensibility of annihilation" enabled him to give meaning to "chaos and death" in his best poems; "Song of Myself" is a comic "drama of identity."]

CLARKE, WILLIAM. *Walt Whitman*. London: Swan Sonnenschein and Co.; New York: Macmillan and Co. 1892. 132 pp.
[Of little value to the modern student; good at time of publication.]

DE SELINCOURT, BASIL. *Walt Whitman: A Critical Study*. London: Martin Secker. 1914. 250 pp.
[Another romantic life, like Bazalgette's, though more critical. New Orleans romance still flourishes.]

DEUTSCH, BABETTE. *Walt Whitman, Builder for America*. New York: Messner. 1941. 278 pp.
[A competent biography for juveniles.]

DONALDSON, THOMAS. *Walt Whitman, the Man*. New York: Francis P. Harper. 1896. 278 pp.
[By an intimate friend of the Camden period; adds little to Bucke and Burroughs, but somewhat more critical.]

DOWDEN, EDWARD. "The Poetry of Democracy: Walt Whitman." *Studies in Literature: 1789-1877*. London: C. Kegan Paul and Co. 1878. Pp. 468-523.
[Interprets Whitman as product and representative of American environment, life, and unstabilized culture.]

ELLIOT, CHARLES N. *Walt Whitman, as Man, Poet and Friend*.

Boston: Badger. 1915. 257 pp.

[Autograph tributes of friends and admirers; a curiosity, but of little biographical value.]

FAUSSETT, HUGH I'ANSON. *Walt Whitman: Poet of Democracy.* New Haven: Yale University Press. 1942. 320 pp.

[Presents Whitman as a divided personality.]

GLICKSBERG, CHARLES I. *Walt Whitman and the Civil War: A Collection of Original Articles and Manuscripts.* Philadelphia: University of Pennsylvania Press. 1933. 201 pp.

[New source of material for the Civil War period.]

HAYES, WILL. *Walt Whitman: the Prophet of the New Era.* London: C. W. Daniel. n.d. [1921]. 194 pp.

[Continuation of the literal interpretation of Whitman's prophetic rôle.]

HOLLOWAY, EMORY. *Whitman: an Interpretation in Narrative.* New York: Knopf. 1926. 330 pp.

[Still one of the major biographies.]

———. *Free and Lonesome Heart: The Secret of Walt Whitman.* New York: Vantage Press. 1960. 232 pp.

[The "secret" is Whitman's illegitimate children; Holloway identified a John Whitman Wilder said to be Walt Whitman's son.]

KELLER, ELIZABETH LEAVITT. *Walt Whitman in Mickle Street.* New York: Mitchell Kennerley. 1921. 227 pp.

[Details of Whitman's domestic life in Camden, N. J.]

KENNEDY, WILLIAM SLOANE. *Reminiscences of Walt Whitman,* with extracts from his letters and remarks on his writings. London: Alexander Gardner. 1896. 190 pp.

[First-hand account by a friend of the Camden period—very sympathetic. Excellent discussion of the poet's "organic" theory of style.]

LAWRENCE, D. H. "Whitman." *Studies in Classic American Literature.* New York: Albert Boni. 1923. Pp. 241-264.

[A condemnation of Whitman's sentimental Christianity.]

LONG, HANIEL. *Walt Whitman and the Springs of Courage.* Santa Fe: Writers Editions, Inc. 1938. 144 pp.

[On the origins of the poet's self-confidence and intellectual history.]

LOVING, JEROME (Editor). *Civil War Letters of George Washington Whitman.* Introduction by Gay Wilson Allen. Durham: Duke University Press. 1975. 173 pp.

MASTERS, EDGAR LEE. *Whitman*. New York: Charles Scribner's Sons. 1937. 342 pp.
[A mediocre biography, but frank treatment of the "Calamus" problem.]

MILLER, EDWIN H. *Walt Whitman's Poetry: A Psychological Journey*. Boston: Houghton Mifflin Co. 1968. 245 pp. Reprinted by New York University Press. 1969.
[This critical study of Whitman's poetry includes considerable psychoanalytical interpretation of his life.]

MOLINOFF, KATHERINE. *Some Notes on Whitman's Family:* Mary Elizabeth Whitman, Edward Whitman, Andrew and Jesse Whitman, Hannah Louisa Whitman. Introduction by Oscar Cargill. Brooklyn: privately printed by the author. 1941. 43 pp.
[New and important information.]

MORRIS, HARRISON S. *Walt Whitman, a Brief Biography with Reminiscences*. Cambridge, Mass.: Harvard University Press. 1929. 122 pp.
[Interesting for the reminiscences; otherwise of slight value.]

O'CONNOR, WILLIAM DOUGLAS. *The Good Gray Poet, A Vindication*. New York: Bunce and Huntington. 1866. Pamphlet.
[Reprinted in Bucke's *Walt Whitman*, 1883, q.v.]
[A defense of Whitman's life and character after his dismissal by Harlan. The first biography and the beginning of the "Modern Christ" legend.]

PERRY, BLISS. *Walt Whitman, His Life and Work*. London: Archibald Constable and Co.; Boston: Houghton Mifflin and Co. 1906. 318 pp.
[The first scholarly biography.]

REISIGER, HANS. *Walt Whitman* [in German]. Berlin: Suhrkamp Verlag. 1946. 104 pp.
[A brief biography by one of Whitman's friendly critics and translators in Germany.]

RIVERS, W. C. *Walt Whitman's Anomaly*. London: George Allen. 1913. 70 pp.
[Study in sex pathology—circulation limited to the medical profession.]

ROGERS, CAMERON. *The Magnificent Idler: The Story of Walt Whitman*. Garden City: Doubleday, Page and Co. 1926. 312 pp.
[Fictionized and romanticized, but faintly anticipates Catel and Schyberg.]

RUBIN, JOSEPH JAY. *The Historic Whitman*. University Park: The

Pennsylvania State University Press. 1973. 406 pp.

[Excellent history of Whitman as journalist to 1855.]

SCHYBERG, FREDERIK. *Walt Whitman*. København: Gyldendalske Boghandel. 1933. 349 pp.

[Continues the interpretation of Catel by searching through all the editions of *Leaves of Grass* for autobiographical revelations.]

——. *Walt Whitman*. Translated by Evie Allison Allen. New York: Columbia University Press. 1951. 387 pp.

SHEPHARD, ESTHER. *Walt Whitman's Pose*. New York: Harcourt, Brace and Co. 1938. 453 pp.

[A source study affecting biographical interpretation.]

SMITH, LOGAN P. "Walt Whitman." *Unforgotten Years*. Boston: Little, Brown and Co. 1939. Pp. 79-108.

[Charming reminiscences of the poet's visits in the Smith home.]

SMUTS, JAN CHRISTIAN. *Walt Whitman: A Study of the Evolution of a Personality*. Edited by Alan L. McLeod. Detroit: Wayne State University Press. 1973. 205 pp.

[Written in 1895, and out of date as biography, but valuable as criticism and history of Whitman's reputation.]

STOUTENBURG, ADRIEN, and BAKER, LAURA NELSON. *Listen America: A Life of Walt Whitman*. New York: Charles Scribner's and Sons. 1968. 182 pp.

[A biography for young readers.]

SYMONDS, JOHN ADDINGTON. *Walt Whitman, A Study*. London: George Routledge; New York: E. P. Dutton. 1893. 160 pp.

[Critical study by a friend and admirer—still valuable.]

THOMSON, JAMES. *Walt Whitman, the Man and the Poet*. With an introduction by Bertram Dobell. London: Bertram Dobell. 1910. 106 pp.

[Biographical details mainly from Burroughs and Bucke, but some critical comments give the work value.]

TRAUBEL, HORACE. *With Walt Whitman in Camden, March 28–July 14, 1888*. Boston: Small Maynard and Co. 1906. Second Volume, *July 16–October 31, 1888*. New York: D. Appleton and Co. 1908. Third Volume, *November 1, 1888–January 20, 1889*. New York: Mitchell Kennerly, 1914. Fourth Volume, *January 21–April 7, 1889*. Carbondale: Southern Illinois University Press. 1959. Fifth Volume, *April 8–September 14, 1889*. Carbondale . . . 1964. Sixth Volume, *September 15, 1889–July 6, 1890*. Carbondale . . . 1982.

Sixth Volume, 15 September 1889 to 6 July 1890. Carbondale . . . 1982. [Daily conversations with Whitman.]

TRAUBEL, HORACE; BUCKE, RICHARD MAURICE; and HAR-NED, THOMAS B. *In Re Walt Whitman.* Edited by his Literary Executors. Philadelphia: David McKay, 1893. 452 pp.
[Along with much worthless praise by the "disciples," some valuable new testimony from Doyle, George Whitman, etc., and translations of critical essays from French, German, and Danish.]

TRIMBLE, W. H. *Walt Whitman and Leaves of Grass, an Intro-duction.* London: Watts and Co. 1905. 100 pp.
[Of slight biographical importance but interesting because com-piled from lectures given in Dunedin, New Zealand, 1904.]

TROWBRIDGE, JOHN TOWNSEND. *My Own Story: with Recollec-tions of Noted Persons.* Boston: Houghton Mifflin and Co., 1903. Pp. 360-401.
[Valuable for poet's own testimony to Trowbridge of Emerson's influence.]

WINWAR, FRANCES. *American Giant: Walt Whitman and His Times.* New York: Harper and Brothers. 1941. 341 pp.
[Journalistic and sentimental narrative—unreliable.]

ARTICLES OF BIOGRAPHICAL VALUE

BRADLEY, SCULLEY. "Walt Whitman on Timber Creek." *Ameri-can Literature*, V, 235-246 (November, 1933).
[Based on visits to the place.]

BYCHOWSKI, GUSTAV. "Walt Whitman—A Study in Sublima-tion," *Psychoanalysis and the Social Sciences*, III (1950), 223-61.

CARPENTER, F. I. "Walt Whitman's Eidólon." *College English*, III, 534-545 (March, 1942).
[Refutation of O'Higgins and Shephard; Whitman achieved his ideal in his poetry if not in his own life—anticipation of Canby's "Symbolical Whitman."]

CHUPACK, HENRY. "Walt Whitman and the Camden Circle," *Pro-ceedings of the New Jersey Historical Society*, LXXII (1955), 274-99.

FURNESS, CLIFTON JOSEPH. Review of Winwar's *American Giant: Walt Whitman and His Times. American Literature*, XIII,

423-432 (January, 1942).
[Although ostensibly a book review, this essay contains new and startling information about Whitman's family and the motives of some of his poems.]

HOLLOWAY, EMORY. "Walt Whitman's Love Affairs." *The Dial*, LXIX, 473-483 (November, 1920).
[The discovery that in the original manuscript "Once I Pass'd Through a Populous City" was a "Calamus" poem led Holloway to reject the New Orleans romance.]

O'HIGGINS, HARVEY. "Alias Walt Whitman." *Harper's Magazine*, CLVIII, 698-707 (May, 1929).
[Anticipates Esther Shephard's interpretation of Whitman's "pose"; a relentless attempt to expose the poet as a fraud.]

NOTE: See also "Anthologies of Criticism," pp. 399-400.

NOTES ON ILLUSTRATIONS

The dauguerrotype, taken in Brooklyn in 1854, is reproduced from a negative presented to the author by the late Oscar Lion. The original daguerrotype is now in the Lion Collection of the New York Public Library.***The drawing by "Carybé" is reproduced from *Poemas*, Versión de Armando Vasseur (Buenos Aires, 1943?) with the permission of the artist in Brazil, Hector Júlio Páride Bernabó. ***Whitman meeting Lafayette is from a page of a comic book in color distributed to the Armed Forces by the U. S. Government during World War II.***The photograph of the 1855 *Leaves of Grass* is from the collection of the late Clifton Furness, though the author also owns this volume.***"I am ashamed. . . ," from a woodcut by Franz Masereel, in *Calamus: Poèmes*, vérsion nouvelle de Léon Bazalgette, Geneva, 1919.***Editions in Russian, French, Oriya, Spanish, photographed by R. J. Mason, Westwood, N. J. ***Russian exhibition, courtesy of Library of Congress, from photographs supplied by Russian Embassy.

SELECTED BIBLIOGRAPHY
Chapter II: Growth of Leaves of Grass

BIBLIOGRAPHY

[There is no definitive bibliography for Whitman.]

ALLEN, EVIE ALLISON. "A Checklist of Whitman Publications 1945-1960." In *Walt Whitman as Man, Poet, and Legend*. By Gay Wilson Allen. Carbondale: Southern Illinois University Press. 1961. Pp. 179-260.
[See Allen, Gay Wilson, below, and Tanner, below.]

ALLEN, GAY W. *Twenty-Five Years of Walt Whitman Bibliography: 1918-1942*. Boston: The F. W. Faxon Co., 1943. 57 pp.
[Supplements Holloway and Saunders. See below.]

HOLLOWAY, EMORY, and SAUNDERS, HENRY S. "[Bibliography of Walt] Whitman." *Cambridge History of American Literature*. New York: G. P. Putnam's Sons. 1918. Vol. II, pp. 551-581.
[Best up to 1918.]

LIBRARY OF CONGRESS. *Walt Whitman, a Catalog Based Upon the Collections of the Library of Congress With Notes*. Washington, D. C.: Government Printing Office. 1955. 147 pp.

SHAY, FRANK. *The Bibliography of Walt Whitman*. New York: Friedmans'. 1920. 46 pp.
[Editions.]

TANNER, JAMES T. *Walt Whitman, a Supplementary Bibliography 1961-67*. Kent State University Press. 1968. 59 pp.

[Supplements Allen, E. A., and G. W., above.]

TRIGGS, OSCAR LOVELL. "Bibliography of Walt Whitman." *Complete Writings of Walt Whitman*. New York and London: G. P. Putnam's Sons. 1902. Vol. X, pp. 139-233.
[Useful description of editions with extended list of biographical and critical material before 1902.]

WELLS, CAROYLN, and GOLDSMITH, ALFRED F. *A Concise Bibliography of the Works of Walt Whitman*. Boston: Houghton Mifflin and Co. 1922. 107 pp.
[A descriptive checklist of editions with a selection of fifty books about Whitman.]

WHITE, WILLIAM. "Walt Whitman's Journalism: A Bibliography." *Walt Whitman Review*, Vol. 14, No. 3 (Sept., 1968), 67-141.
[Whitman's journalistic writings are also discussed in considerable detail by Thomas L. Brasher in *Whitman as Editor of the Brooklyn Daily Eagle* (Detroit: Wayne State University, 1970), 264 pp.; and Joseph Jay Rubin in *The Historic Whitman* (The Pennsylvania State University Press, 1973), xv, 406 pp.]

EDITIONS AND ISSUES

Note: The first publication of all of Whitman's books and pamphlets, 1855–1892, is listed here, but not all reprints or special issues of the major editions.

Leaves of Grass. Brooklyn: [Printed by Rome Brothers]. 1855. (xii, 95 pp. 29cm.)
[First edition. About 1000 copies printed, bound in batches at different times, with slight variations in binding, which was blind-stamped green cloth with gilt letters. Frontispiece steel engraving by Samuel Hollyer from daguerrotype by Gabriel Harrison. Author's name only in copyright notice and in poem ("Song of Myself") on p. 29.]

——. Facsimile of 1855 edition. With an Introduction by Clifton Joseph Furness. Facsimile Text Society, Publication No. 47. New York: Columbia University Press. 1939 [Out of print.]

——. A Facsimile of the First Edition 1855 As Issued by Whitman and Received by Emerson. New York: The Eakins Press. 1966.
[Original cover reproduced with high fidelity; deluxe.]

———. A Facsimile of the First Edition. With an Introduction, a note on the text, and a bibliography prepared by Richard Bridgman. San Francisco: Chandler Publishing Company. 1968. [Inexpensive paperback, fair print, good Introduction.]

Walt Whitman's Leaves of Grass: The First (1855) Edition. Edited, with an Introduction, by Malcolm Cowley. New York: The Viking Press. 1959. [Not a true facsimile, but accurate text in new typesetting, with valuable Introduction.]

Leaves of Grass. Brooklyn: [Fowler & Wells]. 1856. (iv, 384 pp. 16cm.) [Second edition. Frontispiece same as first edition. Bound in green cloth; stamped on backstrip in gold: "I greet You at the/ Beginning of a Great Career/ R. W. Emerson." An Appendix called "Leaves-Droppings" contains Emerson's "Greeting" letter, dated July 21, 1855, and Whitman's open-letter reply to his "Master." Appendix also contains reviews of the first edition. The 1855 preface omitted; poems numbered and titled, the original twelve now being, after much revision, Nos. 1, 4, 32, 26, 7, 27, 19, 16, 22, 25, 29, and 6.]

Leaves of Grass. Boston: Thayer and Eldridge. Year 85 of the States, 1860-61. (iv, 456 pp. front. port. 19½cm.)
[Third edition. Two printings (possibly a third) of 1000 copies each, several color bindings, first orange cloth, second green, third plum. Frontispiece portrait from painting by Charles Hine. 146 new poems; total of 152 grouped in "clusters." Later many pirated copies were printed from these plates, which lack this inscription on copyright page: Electrotyped at the Boston Stereotype Foundry. Printed by George C. Rand & Avery.]

———. Facsimile Edition of the 1860 Text. With an Introduction by Roy Harvey Pearce. Ithaca: Cornell University Press. 1961. [Paper cover, good print, valuable Introduction.]

Walt Whitman's Drum-Taps. New York: [Printed by Peter Eckler]. 1865. (iv, 72 pp. 19 cm.)
[After President Lincoln's death Whitman withdrew this edition until he could add his elegy—in all three elegies, but the "great hymn" was "When Lilacs Last in the Dooryard Bloom'd," which he published in the autumn of 1865 in a *Sequel to Drum-Taps*.]

Walt Whitman's Drum-Taps. New York: [Printed by Peter Eckler]. 1865. (72, 24 pp. 19 cm.)
[Second issue of *Drum-Taps* with *Sequel* appended, pp. 1-24. Title-page: *Sequel to Drum-Taps/* (Since the Preceding Came

From the Press.)/ WHEN LILACS LAST IN THE DOOR-YARD BLOOM'D./ And Other Pieces./ Washington./ 1865-6. Seventeen poems besides "Lilacs," including "O Captain! My Captain!"]

Leaves of Grass. New York: [Printed by William E. Chapin]. 1867. (338, 72, 24, 36 pp. 20 cm.)
[Fourth edition. Separate title page and pagination for *Drum-Taps* (72 pp.), *Sequel . . .* (24 pp.), and *Songs Before Parting* (36 pp.)]

After All, Not to Create Only. Recited by Walt Whitman on Invitation of Managers of the American Institute on Opening their 40th Annual Exhibition, New York, noon, September 7th, 1871. Boston: Roberts Brothers. 1871. (24 [4] pp. 20 cm.)

Democratic Vistas. Washington, D. C. 1871. [New York: J. S. Redfield, publisher.] (84 pp. 21 cm.) [Light green paper cover.]

Leaves of Grass. Washington, D. C. [J. S. Redfield] 1871. (384 pp. 21 cm.)
[Fifth edition. Second issue in 1872 includes *Passage to India*, with 120 added pages. Thirteen new poems exclusive of the annexes in the later printings. In the fifth edition the groupings and revisions approach the final arrangement.]

Memoranda During the War. Camden, N. J.: Author's Publication. 1875-76 [c. 1875] ([2] 68 [3] pp. 20½ cm.)
[On cover: "Walt Whitman's Memoranda of the War written on the spot 1863-1865."]

Leaves of Grass. Camden, N. J.: Author's edition, with portraits from life. 1876. (384[3] pp. 2 ports. 20½ cm.)
[Reprinted from 1871-72 plates. Backstrip: Centennial edition. Bound in half-leather, marble boards, uniform with *Two Rivulets*, the two volumes to constitute *Whitman's Complete Works*.]

Two Rivulets, Including Democratic Vistas, Centennial Songs, and Passage to India. Camden, N.J.: Author's edition. 1876. (32, 84, 18, x, 16, 68, 120 pp. 20 cm.)
[Centennial edition. Poetry and prose. New setting of type for *Two Rivulets*; other parts reprinted from plates on hand. Sold as Vol. II of Author's Edition of the *Complete Works*.]

Leaves of Grass. Boston: James R. Osgood & Co. 1881-82 [c 1881]. (382 pp. 21 cm.)
[Sixth edition (formerly called seventh). Poems arranged in final order, later additions made in annexes without disturbing the

1881 text. Reprinted in Philadelphia by Rees Welsh and Co. in 1882 (also later issues) and by David McKay in 1888.]

Specimen Days and Collect. Philadelphia: Rees Welsh & Co. 1882-83. (374 pp. port. 20 cm.)

[Reprinted by David McKay, 1882-83.]

November Boughs. Philadelphia: David McKay. 1888. (140 pp. 23½ cm.)

[Prose includes "A Backward Glance O'er Travel'd Roads" and miscellaneous notes which were reprinted in the 1892 *Prose Works*, pp. 375-476. Poems in cluster "Sands at Seventy," which became the First Annex to the 1892 *Leaves of Grass.*]

Complete Poems and Prose of Walt Whitman 1855 ... 1888. Authenticated & Personal Book (Handled by W. W.) Portraits from Life ... Autograph. Philadelphia: [Printed by Ferguson Brothers & Co.]. 1888. (900 pp. 27 cm.)

[Reprint of 1882 *Leaves of Grass and Specimen Days*, with poems from *November Boughs* and "A Backward Glance ..." annexed.]

Good-Bye My Fancy: 2d Annex to Leaves of Grass. Philadelphia: David McKay. 1891. (66 pp. 23½ cm.)

[Uniform with *November Boughs*; prose and poems.]

Leaves of Grass. Philadelphia: David McKay. 1891-92. (438 pp. 21½ cm.)

[Often called the "ninth edition" but actually a reprint of the sixth (1881-82) edition, with poems from *November Boughs* added as First Annex and poems from *Good-Bye My Fancy* as Second Annex. Whitman "authorized" this text for all future reprints.]

Leaves of Grass. Boston: Small, Maynard and Co. 1897. (455 pp. 21½ cm.)

[This has been called the "tenth edition" because it contains the posthumous cluster, "Old Age Echoes"; however, except for the posthumous poems it is a reprint of the 1891-92 issue.]

Complete Prose Works. Philadelphia: David McKay. 1892. (522 pp. 21½ cm.)

[Contains all the prose of *Specimen Days and Collect, November Boughs*, and *Good-Bye My Fancy*. This was also sold as Vol. II of *Complete Works.*]

The Complete Writings of Walt Whitman. Issued under the editorial Supervision of the Literary Executors, Richard Maurice Bucke,

Thomas B. Harned, and Horace L. Traubel, with additional bibliographical and critical material by Oscar Lovell Triggs, Ph.D. New York and London: Putnam's Sons. 1902. 10 vols.
[Although this became the standard edition of Whitman for half a century, it was not "complete," as claimed, and it was edited by amateurs. It is now being superseded by *The Collected Writings of Walt Whitman* published by the New York University Press under the general editorship of Gay Wilson Allen and Sculley Bradley. The Putnam edition was sold in a variety of issues, with different paper and bindings. It contained all the poetry and prose which up to 1902 had been collected, with a biographical essay by the literary executors, letters of the poet to his mother, *Notes and Fragments* previously edited by Dr. Bucke, and other miscellanies.]

The Collected Writings of Walt Whitman. General Editors Gay Wilson Allen and Sculley Bradley. New York University Press. Volumes published 1963–75:

Prose Works 1892. Edited by Floyd Stovall. Volume I, *Specimen Days.* 1963. (xx[2], 358 pp.) Volume II, *Collect and Other Prose.* 1964. (xvi, 359-803[2]pp.) New York: New York University Press.

The Early Poems and the Fiction. Edited by Thomas L. Brasher. 1963. (xx, 352 pp.)

Leaves of Grass. Reader's Edition, Including the Annexes, The Prefaces, "A Backward Glance O'er Travel'd Roads," "Old Age Echoes," the Excluded Poems and Fragments, and the Uncollected Poems and Fragments. Edited by Harold W. Blodgett and Sculley Bradley. 1965. (lviii[2], 768 pp.)

The Correspondence. Edited by Edwin Haviland Miller. Volume I: 1842-1867. 1961. (x[1], 394 pp.) Volume II: 1868-1875. (viii[1], 387 pp. 1961. Volume III: 1876-1885. (ix[1], 473 pp.) 1964. Volume IV: 1886-1889. (viii[1], 458 pp.) 1969. Volume V: 1890-1892. (ix[1], 365 pp.) 1969.

Day-Books and Notebooks. Edited by William White. 3 Vols. 1978. See also p. xvii.

UNCOLLECTED WRITINGS
(In order of publication)

Calamus: A Series of Letters Written during the Years 1868–1880. By Walt Whitman to a Young Friend (Peter Doyle). Edited with an Introduction by Richard Maurice Bucke, M.D. Boston: Laurens Maynard. 1897. (viii, 172 pp.)

The Wound-Dresser: A Series of Letters Written from the Hospitals in Washington during the War of Rebellion By Walt Whitman. Edited by Richard Maurice Bucke, M.D. Boston: Small, Maynard and Co. 1898. viii, 201 pp.

Notes and Fragments. Edited by Dr. Richard Maurice Bucke. (Printed for Private Distribution Only.) London, Ontario, Canada. 1899. 211 pp.

[Manuscript fragments of both poetry and prose, including some early notebooks and a list of magazine and newspaper clippings kept by the poet (now in the Trent Collection, Duke University Library). *Notes and Fragments* also included in *The Complete Writings of Walt Whitman,* Vol. IX. Most of this material is being re-edited by Edward F. Grier for the new edition of *Collected Writings* . . .]

Letters Written by Walt Whitman to His Mother from 1866 *To* 1872. Together with Certain Papers Prepared from Material now First Utilized. Edited by Thomas B. Harned. New York and London: G. P. Putnam's Sons. 1902.

[Excerpted from *Complete Writings,* Vol. VIII, 169-243. Reprinted by Alfred F. Goldsmith, with an Introductory Note by Rollo G. Silver. New York. 1936. 71 pp. Now included in Edwin H. Miller's *Correspondence.*]

Walt Whitman's Diary in Canada. With Extracts from other of his Diaries and Literary Note-Books. Edited by William Sloane Kennedy. Boston: Small, Maynard and Co. 1904. 73 pp.

[*Diary in Canada* is included in William White's edition of *Walt Whitman's Day-Books and Notebooks* in *Collected Writings.*]

An American Primer. With Facsimiles of the Original Manuscript. Edited by Horace Traubel. Boston: Small, Maynard and Co. 1904. 35 pp.

[Also included by White in *Day-Books and Notebooks.* See above.]

The Letters of Anne Gilchrist and Walt Whitman. Edited by Thomas B. Harned. New York: Doubleday, Doran and Co. 1918. 241 pp.

The Gathering of the Forces. Editorials, Essays, Literary and Dramatic Reviews and other Material Written by Walt Whitman as

Editor of the Brooklyn *Daily Eagle* in 1846 and 1847. Edited by Cleveland Rodgers and John Black. With a foreword and a sketch of Whitman's Life and Work During Two Unknown Years. New York and London: G. P. Putnam's Sons. 1920. 2 Vols.

The Uncollected Poetry and Prose of Walt Whitman. Much of Which Has Been But Recently Discovered with Various Early Manuscripts Now First Published. Collected and Edited by Emory Holloway. New York: Doubleday, Doran and Co. 1921. 2 Vols. Reprinted by Peter Smith, New York, 1932.

[These manuscripts are being re-edited by Edwin F. Grier and the fiction has been edited by Thomas L. Brasher. See *Collected Writings*, New York University Press.]

Pictures. An Unpublished Poem by Walt Whitman. With an Introduction and Notes by Emory Holloway. New York: The June House. 1927. London: Faber and Gwyer. 1927. 37 pp.

[Included by Blodgett and Bradley in Comprehensive Reader's Edition of *Leaves of Grass*, 642-49.]

The Half-Breed and Other Stories. Edited by Thomas Ollive Mabbott. New York: Columbia University Press. 1927. 129 p.

Walt Whitman's Workshop. Edited by Clifton Joseph Furness. Cambridge: Harvard University Press. 1928. x, 265 pp.

[Speeches and unpublished prefaces; these are being included in the *Collected Writings*, New York University Press, but Furness's notes (181-265) still have useful information.]

I Sit and Look Out. Editorials from the Brooklyn *Daily Times*. Selected and Edited by Emory Holloway and Vernolian Schwarz. New York: Columbia University Press. 1932. xii, 248 pp.

New York Dissected. A Sheaf of Recently Discovered Newspaper Articles by the author of *Leaves of Grass*. Introduction and Notes by Emory Holloway and Ralph Adimari. New York: Rufus Rockwell Wilson. 1936. 257 pp.

Whitman's Manuscripts: Leaves of Grass (1860): A Parallel Text. Edited with Notes and Introduction by Fredson Bowers. Chicago: University of Chicago Press. 1955. lxxiv, 264 pp.

The Eighteenth Presidency! A Critical Text Edited by Edward F. Grier. Lawrence: University of Kansas Press. 1956. 47 pp.

An 1855-56 Notebook Toward the Second Edition of Leaves of

Grass. Introduction and Notes by Harold W. Blodgett. With a Foreword by Charles E. Feinberg. Additional Notes by William White. Carbondale: Southern Illinois University Press. 1959. x, 41[1] pp.

Walt Whitman's Blue Book: The 1860-61 *Leaves of Grass* Containing His Manuscript Additions and Revisions. Vol. I: Facsimile of the unique copy in the Oscar Lion Collection of the New York Public Library. Vol. II: Textual analysis by Arthur Golden. New York: The New York Public Library. 1968. Vol. I, 456 pp. (third edition of *LG*); Vol. II, lxv, 428 pp.

Walt Whitman's Autograph Revision of the Analysis of Leaves of Grass (For Dr. R. M. Bucke s Walt Whitman). Introductory Essay by Quentin Anderson. Text Notes by Stephen Railton. With thirty-five facsimile pages of t ie manuscript. New York: New York University Press. 1974. 191 pp.

SPECIAL EDITIONS

Walt Whitman's Poems: Selections with Critical Notes. Edited by Gay Wilson Allen and Charles T. Davis. New York: New York University Press. 1955. (x, 280 pp.) Paper cover, 1968, 1972.

Walt Whitman: Complete Poetry and Selected Prose. Edited by James E. Miller, Jr. Boston: Houghton Mifflin Co. (Riverside Editions.) 1959. (liii, 516 pp.)

Leaves of Grass: A Norton Critical Edition. Edited by Sculley Bradley and Harold W. Blodgett. New York: W. W. Norton & Co. 1973. (lx, 1008 pp.)
[Reprint of the contents of The Reader's Edition of *Leaves of Grass*, plus "Whitman on His Art" and essays by thirty critics. Inexpensive paper cover edition.]

The Portable Walt Whitman. Revised and enlarged edition. Edited by Mark Van Doren [revised by Malcolm Cowley]. Introduction by Mark Van Doren. "A Note on the New Edition" by Malcolm Cowley. Chronology and Bibliographical Check List by Gay Wilson Allen. New York: The Viking Press. 1974. (xxxi, 648 pp.)
[Seven poems and the 1855 Preface reprinted from the 1855 edition; other poems from the 1891-92 text; complete text of *Specimen Days*.]

TEXTUAL STUDIES
(*Alphabetical order*)

ALLEN, GAY WILSON. *The Solitary Singer: A Critical Biography of Walt Whitman*. New York: The Macmillan Company. 1955. New York University Press. 1968. (xii, 616 pp.) [Discussion of first edition, 149-176; second, 177-190; third, 221-259.]

ASSELINEAU, ROGER. *The Evolution of Walt Whitman*: The Creation of a Book. Cambridge: Harvard University Press. 1962. (392 pp.)

BLODGETT, HAROLD W., and BRADLEY, SCULLEY, editors. "Introduction: The Growth of 'Leaves of Grass,'" *Leaves of Grass*: Comprehensive Reader's Edition. New York: New York Universtiy Press. 1965. (Pp. [xxvi]-liii.)

BOWERS, FREDSON. "The Walt Whitman Manuscripts of 'Leaves of Grass' (1860)." *Textual and Literary Criticism*. Cambridge: Cambridge University Press. 1959. (Pp. 35-65.)
[See also Bowers' edition of these MSS, above, "Uncollected Writings."]

CAMPBELL, KILLIS. "The Evolution of Whitman as Artist." *American Literature*, VI, 254-263 (November, 1934).
[Traces the poet's growth by means of his textual improvements.]

CATEL, JEAN. *Walt Whitman: La Naissance due Poète*. Paris: Les Editions Rieder. 1929. (483 pp.)
[Whitman's "naissance" in 1855.]

COWLEY, MALCOLM. "Editor's Introduction." *Walt Whitman's Leaves of Grass: The First (1855) Edition*. New York: The Viking Press. 1959. (Pp. [vii]-xxxvii.)

CRAWLEY, THOMAS EDWARD. *The Structure of* Leaves of Grass. Austin & London: University of Texas Press. 1970. (xii, 256 pp.)
[More on themes than bibliography.]

DE SELINCOURT, BASIL. *Walt Whitman: A Study*. New York: Mitchell Kennerley. 1914. London: Martin Secker. 1914. (Chap. VI, "Plan," traces the "skeleton design" of *Leaves of Grass*.)

GOLDEN, ARTHUR. See Vol. II of *Walt Whitman's Blue Book*, above, "Uncollected Writings."

KENNEDY, WILLIAM SLOANE. "The Growth of 'Leaves of Grass' as a Work of Art (Excisions, Additions, Verbal Changes)." *The Fight of a Book for the World*. West Yarmouth, Mass.: Stone-

croft Press. 1926. (304 pp.)
[Much valuable information but erratic criticism.]

SCHYBERG, FREDERIK. *Walt Whitman.* Translated from the Danish by Evie Allison Allen. Introduction by Gay Wilson Allen. New York: Columbia University Press. 1951. (xv, 387 pp.) [Schyberg's biographical interpretations are based on textual studies of the editions of *Leaves of Grass.*]

STOVALL, FLOYD. "Main Drifts in Whitman's Poetry." *American Literature,* IV, 3-21 (March 1932).

STRAUCH, CARL F. "The Structure of Walt Whitman's 'Song of Myself,'" *English Journal* (College Edition), XXVII, 597-607 (September 1938).

WEATHERS, WILLIE T. "Whitman's Poetic Translations of His 1855 Preface," *American Literature,* XIX, 21-40 (March 1947).

SELECTED BIBLIOGRAPHY
Chapter III: Whitman's Ideas

BACKGROUND

CARGILL, OSCAR. *Intellectual America: Ideas on the March*. New York: Macmillan. 1941.
[Discussion of fecundity especially pertinent, 538 ff.]

CARPENTER, FREDERIC I. *Emerson and Asia*. Cambridge: Harvard University Press 1930.

CHRISTY, ARTHUR. *The Orient in American Transcendentalism*. New York: Columbia University Press. 1932.

EMERSON, RALPH WALDO. *Nature* (1836), *Collected Works*, I, 7-45. Edited by Robert E. Spiller and Alfred R. Ferguson. Cambridge: Harvard University Press. 1971.

HARROLD, CHARLES F. *Carlyle and German Thought, 1819–1834*. New Haven: Yale University Press. 1934.

JAMES, WILLIAM. "Mysticism," *Varieties of Religious Experience*, pp. 379-420. London: Longmans, Green. 1902. Facsimile reprint: New Hyde Park: University Books. 1963.

KNUDSON, ALBERT C. *The Philosophy of Personalism*. New York: Abingdon Press. 1927.

KOESTLER, ARTHUR. *The Ghost in the Machine*. New York: Macmillan. 1967.

OTTO, RUDOLF. *Mysticism East and West: A Comparative Analysis of the Nature of Mysticism*. New York: Macmillan. 1932.

RILEY, WOODBRIDGE. *The Meaning of Mysticism*. New York: Harper and Brothers. 1930.
[Compares "the pantheism of the Rhine region . . . with the poetic pantheism of Walt Whitman . . ."]

RUSSELL, BERTRAND. *Mysticism and Logic and Other Essays*. London: Longmans, Green. 1921.

TEILHARD DE CHARDIN, PIERRE. *Man's Place in Nature: The Human Zoological Group*. Translated by René Hague. New York: Harper & Row. 1966. *The Phenomenon of Man*. Translated by Bernard Wall. New York: Harper & Row. 1961. *The Divine Milieu*. New York: Harper & Row. 1960. *Building the Earth*. Translated by Noël Lindsay. Wilkes-Barre, Pa.: Dimensions Books 1965.

TOMPKINS, PETER, and BIRD, CHRISTOPHER. *The Secret Life of Plants*. New York: Harper & Row. 1972.

UNDERHILL, EVELYN. Mysticism: *A Study in the Nature and Development of Man's Spiritual Consciousness*. New York: E. P. Dutton. 11th Ed. 1926.

VOLNEY, COUNT C. F. *The Ruins; or Meditation on the Revolution of Empires* . . . To Which is Added *The Law of Nature*. New York: Calvin Blanchard, n. d. [*c*.1800.]

WALZEL, OSKAR. *German Romanticism*. Translated by Alma Elise Lussky, from *Deutsche Romantik* (Berlin, 1923). New York: Putnam. 1932.

CRITICAL STUDIES

ALLEN, GAY WILSON. "Walt Whitman's 'Long Journey' Motif," *Journal of English and Germanic Philology*. XXXVIII, 76-95 (January 1939).
[The "Long Journey" is the evolution of the human race.]

ARVIN, NEWTON. *Whitman*. New York: Macmillan. 1938.
[Discusses social and political ideas, and relations of Whitman's ideas to French rationalism and German romanticism.]

BEAVER, JOSEPH. *Walt Whitman, Poet of Science*. New York: King's Crown Press. 1951.
[Strongest on astronomy—demonstrates Whitman's knowledge.]

BECK, MAXIMILIAN. "Walt Whitman's Intuition of Reality." *Ethics*, LIII, 14-24 (October 1942).

BENOIT, RAY. "The Mind's Return: Whitman, Teilhard, and Jung," *Walt Whitman Review*, XIII, 31-28 (March 1958).

BERTZ, EDUARD. *Der Yankee-Heiland*. Dresden: Reissner. 1906.
[Debunks Whitman as a thinker; compares him unfavorably with
Novalis and Nietzsche.]

BOATRIGHT, MODY C. "Whitman and Hegel." *Studies in English
(The University of Texas Bulletin)*, IX, 134-50 (July 8, 1929).

BUCKE, RICHARD MAURICE. *Cosmic Consciousness*. New York:
E. P. Dutton. 1923.
[Gives examples of Whitman's mystical experiences.]

CARPENTER, EDWARD. *Days with Walt Whitman*. London:
George Allen. 1906.
[In chapter on "Whitman as Prophet" cites parallels between
Upanishads and *Leaves of Grass*; also Emerson and Whitman.]

CARPENTER, FREDERIC I. "Walt Whitman's Eidólon." *College
English*, III, 534-45 (March 1942).
[On Whitman's "idealism."]

COLUM, MARY M. "The Ideas that Have Made Modern Literature,"
From These Roots, pp. 260-311. New York: Charles Scribner &
Sons. 1937.

COOKE, ALICE LOVELACE. "Whitman's Background in the Industrial Movements of His Time." *Studies in English (The University of Texas Bulletin:*, XV, 89-115 (July 8, 1935).

COWLEY, MALCOLM. Introduction to *Walt Whitman's Leaves of
Grass: His Original (1855) Edition*. New York: Viking Press.
1959.

FALK, ROBERT P. "Walt Whitman and German Thought." *Journal
of English and Germanic Philology*, XL, 315-30 (July 1941).

FULGHUM, W. B., JR. "Whitman's Debt to Joseph Gostwick."
American Literature, XII, 491-96 (January 1941).

GIRGUS, SAM B. "Culture and Post-Culture in Walt Whitman." *The
Centennial Review*, XVIII, 392-410 (Fall 1974).

GODHES, CLARENCE. "Whitman and Emerson." *Sewanee Review*,
XXXVII, 79-93 (January 1929).

GOODALE, DAVID. "Some of Walt Whitman's Borrowings." *American Literature*, X, 202-13 (May 1938).
[Borrowings from Volney, Frances Wright, and others.]

HOWARD, LEON. "For a Critique of Whitman's Transcendentalism."
Modern Language Notes, XLVII, 79-85 (February 1932).

HUNGERFORD, EDWARD. "Walt Whitman and His Chart of
Bumps." *American Literature*, II, 350-84 (January 1931).
[Phrenology as an important source.]

JENSEN, MILLIE. "Whitman and Hegel: The Curious Triplicate Process." *Walt Whitman Review*, X, 27-34 (June 1964).

LONG, HANIEL. *Walt Whitman and the Springs of Courage*. Santa Fe, N. M.: Writers' Editions. 1938.

MATTHIESSEN, F. O. "Whitman," *American Renaissance*: Art and Expression in the Age of Emerson and Whitman, pp. 517-625. New York: Oxford University Press. 1941.

MAXWELL, WILLIAM. "Some Personalist Elements in the Poetry of Whitman." *Personalist*, XII, 190-99 (July 1931).

MOORE, JOHN B. "The Master of Whitman." *Studies in Philology*, XXIII, 77-89 (January 1926).

MYERS, HENRY ALONZO. "Whitman's Conception of the Spiritual Democracy, 1855–56." *American Literature*, VI, 239-53 (November 1934).
  [Whitman's basic metaphysical assumptions.]

——. "Whitman's Consistency." *American Literature*, VIII, 243-57 (November 1936).
  [Consistency of his "idealism."]

PAINE, GREGORY. "The Literary Relations of Whitman and Carlyle with Especial Reference to their Contrasting views of Democracy." *Studies in Philology*, XXXVI, 550-63 (July 1939).

PARSONS, OLIVE W. "Whitman the Non-Hegelian." *PMLA*, 1073-93 (December 1943).

REED, H. B. "The Heraclitan Obsession of Whitman." *Personalist*, XV, 125-38 (Spring 1934).

REISS, EDMUND. "Whitman's Debt to Animal Magnetism." *PMLA*, LXXVIII, 80-88 (March 1963).

SARRAZIN, GABRIEL. "Walt Whitman," translated by Harrison S. Morris, *In Re Walt Whitman*, pp. 159-94. Philadelphia: David McKay. 1893.
  [First critical interpretation of Whitman's "pantheism."]

SHIPLEY, M. "Democracy as a Religion: The Religion of Walt Whitman." *Open Court*, XXXIII, 385-93 (July 1919).
  [Study of Whitman's ideas for a "new religion."]

SMITH, FRED M. "Whitman's Debt to *Sartor Resartus*." *Modern Language Quarterly*, III, 51-65 (March 1942).

——. "Whitman's Poet-Prophet and Carlyle's Hero." *PMLA*, LV, 1146-64 (December 1940).
  [Important study of Carlyle's influence on Whitman.]

STOVALL, FLOYD. "Main Drifts in Whitman's Poetry." *American*

Literature, IV, 3-21 (March 1932).

[Shift in attitudes and thought as Whitman matured.]

———. *The Foreground of Leaves of Grass*. Charlottesville: University of Virginia Press. 1974.

[Exhaustive study of sources.]

SYMONDS, JOHN ADDINGTON. *Walt Whitman: A Study*. London: George Routledge. 1893.

TANNER, JAMES. "The Lamarckian Theory of Progress in 'Leaves of Grass.' " *Walt Whitman Review*, IX, 3-11 (March 1963).

WROBEL, ARTHUR. "Whitman and the Phrenologists: The Divine Body and the Sensuous Soul." *PMLA*, LXXXIX, 17-23 (January 1974).

SELECTED BIBLIOGRAPHY
Chapter IV: Literary Technique

BACKGROUND—STYLE AND STRUCTURE

COOK, A. S. "The 'Authorized Version' and Its Influence." *Cambridge History of English Literature*, IV, 29-58. New York and London: G. P. Putnam's Sons. 1910.

DAHLSTROM, C. W. W. L. *Strindberg's Dramatic Expressionism*, pp. 3-82. Ann Arbor: University of Michigan. 1930.
[Definitions and history of "Expressionism."]

DRIVER, S. R. *Introduction to the Literature of the Old Testament.* New York: Charles Scribner & Sons. 1910.

GARDINER, J. H. *The Bible as English Literature.* New York: Charles Scribner & Sons. 1906.

GROSS, HARVEY. *Sound and Form in Modern Poetry: A Study of Prosody from Thomas Hardy to Robert Lowell.* Ann Arbor: University of Michigan Press. 1964. (See index for Whitman.)

KAUTZSCH, EMIL FRIEDRICH. *Die Poesie und die Poetischen Bücher der Alten Testaments.* Tübingen: Mohr. 1902.
[Based on Bishop Lowth's discovery of parallelism as the prosodic principle of Biblical verse: *De sacra poesi Hebraeorum praelectiones academiae oxonii habitae*, 1753.]

KRUSHOVSKI, BENJAMIN. "The Theory and Practice of Rhythm in the Expressionist Poetry of U. Z. Grinberg." *Hasifrut*: Quarterly for the Study of Literature, Tel-Aviv University, I, 176-205 (Spring, 1968).

[Compares rhythms of Mayakovsky and Whitman in relation to Grinberg's two levels of rhythm. Written in Hebrew.]

MOULTON, R. G. *The Literary Study of the Bible*. Boston: D. C. Heath. 1895.

[Parallelism. *Moulton's Modern Reader's Bible* (New York: Macmillan, 1922) arranges the Biblical poetry in accordance with the principles of "thought-rhythm."]

SMITH, C. ALPHONSO. *Repetition and Parallelism in English Verse*. New York: University Publishing Co. 1894.

SUTCLIFFE, EMERSON GRANT. "Emerson's Theories of Literary Expression." *University of Illinois Studies in Language and Literature*, VIII, 9-143 (1943).

[Background for influence of Transcendentalism on Whitman's theory and practice.]

WAGGONER, HYATT, H. *American Poets: From the Puritans to the Present*. Boston: Houghton Mifflin Co. 1968.

[Argues that Emerson's influence on Whitman has not been sufficiently appreciated.]

TEXTS OF SPECIAL IMPORTANCE

AN AMERICAN PRIMER. Edited by Horace Traubel. Boston: Small, Maynard and Co. 1904. Re-edited by William White in *Walt Whitman's Day-Books and Notebooks*. New York: New York University Press. 1978.

NOTES AND FRAGMENTS. Edited by Richard Maurice Bucke. London, Ontario: printed for the editor. 1899. Reprinted: Folcroft, Pa.: Folcroft Library Editions. 1972.

PICTURES. Edited by Emory Holloway, from unpublished manuscript. London: Faber and Gwyer. 1927. Reprinted: *Leaves of Grass: Comprehensive Reader's Edition*, pp. 642-649. Edited by Harold W. Blodgett and Sculley Bradley. New York: New York University Press. 1965.

PREFACES. Reprinted in *Reader's Edition*; see above.

CRITICAL STUDIES

ALLEN, GAY WILSON. "Biblical Analogies for Walt Whitman's Prosody." *Revue Anglo-Américaine*, X, 490-507 (August 1933).

———. "Walt Whitman," *American Prosody*, pp. 217-42. New York: American Book Co. 1935.
[Parallelism as Whitman's basic rhythmical principle.]

———. "Form and Structure," *A Reader's Guide to Walt Whitman*, pp. 156-212. New York: Farrar, Straus & Giroux. 1970.
[Adds "expressive form" to previous analyses of Whitman's prosody.]

ASSELINEAU, ROGER. *The Evolution of Walt Whitman: The Creation of a Book*. Cambridge: Harvard University Press. 1962.
[Part Two discusses Style, Language, and Prosody.]

BAHR, HERMANN. Introduction to Max Hayek's translation, *Ich Singe das Leben*. Leipzig, Wien, Zürich: E. P. Tall and Co. 1921.

BRADLEY, SCULLEY. "The Fundamental Metrical Principles in Whitman's Poetry." *American Literature*, X, 437-59 (January 1939).
[Tries to prove that Whitman's "organic rhythms" are fundamentally metrical.]

CATEL, JEAN. *Rythme et langage dans la 1er édition des "Leaves of Grass," 1855*. Paris: Les Editions Rieder. [1930]
[Stresses oratory as great influence in formation of Whitman's poetic style.]

CHRISTADLER, MARTIN. "Walt Whitman: Sprachtheorie und Dichtung," *Jahrbuch für Amerikanstudien*, 13 (1968), 84-97.

COFFMAN, STANLEY K. " 'Crossing Brooklyn Ferry': A Note on the Catalogue Technique in Whitman's Poetry." *Modern Philology*, LI, 225-32 (May 1954).

CORY, ROBERT E. "The Prosody of Walt Whitman." *North Dakota Quarterly*, XXVIII (1960), 74-79.

COY, REBECCA. "A Study of Whitman's Diction." *University of Texas Studies in English*, XVI, 115-124 (July 1936).

DE SELINCOURT, BASIL. *Walt Whitman: A Critical Study*. London: Martin Secker. 1914.
[Especially good on analogies with music.]

ERSKINE, JOHN. "A note on Whitman's Prosody." *Studies in Philology*, XX, 336-44 (July 1923).

FANER, ROBERT D. *Walt Whitman & Opera*. Philadelphia: University of Pennsylvania Press. 1951.
[Weak on actual influence of opera on Whitman's versification, but provides information for such a study.]

FEIDELSON, CHARLES, JR. *Symbolism and American Literature*.

Chicago: University of Chicago Press. 1953.
[On Symbolist esthetics.]

FURNESS, CLIFTON JOSEPH. *Walt Whitman's Workshop*. Cambridge: Harvard University Press. 1928.
[Notes contain many observations on style and technique.]

GRIFFIN, ROBERT J. "Notes on Structural Devices in Whitman's Poetry." *Tennessee Studies in Literature*, VI (1961), 15-24.

HINDUS, MILTON. "Notes Toward the Definition of a Typical Poetic Line in Whitman." *Walt Whitman Review*, IX (1963), 75-81.

HOLLIS, C. CARROLL. "Whitman and the American Idiom." *Quarterly Journal of Speech*, LXIII (1957), 408-20.

HOPKINS, GERARD MANLEY. *Letters of Gerard Manley Hopkins*, 154-58. Edited by Claude Colleer Abbott. (London, 1935). Reprinted by Edwin H. Miller in *A Century of Whitman Criticism* (Bloomington: Indiana University Press. 1969), pp. 77-80.
[Letter to Robert Bridges regarding Whitman's influence on Hopkins's "sprung rhythm"—which Hopkins denies.]

HOSBAUM, PHILIP. "Eliot, Whitman and the American Tradition." *Journal of American Studies*, III, 239-64 (1969).

JANNACCONE, P. *La Poesia di Walt Whitman e l'Evoluzione delle Forme Ritmiche*. Torino. 1898. Translated by Peter Mitilineos. Washington, D. C.: Microcard Editions. 1973.
[Demonstrates Whitman's primitive techniques but also discovers metrical patterns in his rhythms.]

KALLSEN, T. J. " 'Song of Myself': Logical Unity through Analogy." *West Virginia University Bulletin*, IX (1953), 33-40.

KENNEDY, W. S. "The Style of Leaves of Grass." *Reminiscences of Walt Whitman*, pp. 149-90. London: Alexander Gardner. 1896.
[Defends the "organic" style.]

McELDERRY, BRUCE, JR. "Personae in Whitman (1855–1860)." *American Transcendental Quarterly*, No. 12 (Fall 1971), 26-28. (1971), 26-28.

MATTHIESSEN, F. O. "Only a Language Experiment." *American Renaissance*, pp. 517-625. New York: Oxford University Press. 1941.
[A major critical contribution.]

MITCHELL, ROGER. "A Prosody for Whitman?" *PMLA*, LXXXIV (1969), 1606-12.

MORE, PAUL ELMER. "Walt Whitman." *Shelburne Essays*, 4th Ed., New Ser., pp. 180-211. Boston: Houghton Mifflin. 1922.

PEARCE, ROY HARVEY. *The Continuity of American Poetry*, Chap. IV. Princeton: Princeton University Press. 1961.

POLLAK, GEORGIANA. "The Relationship of Music to 'Leaves of Grass,' " *College English*, XV, 384-94 (April 1954).

REED, HARRY B. "The Heraclitan Obsession of Walt Whitman." *The Personalist*, XV, 125-38 (April 1934).
[On flux and progression in Whitman's literary style.]

ROBBINS, J. ALBERT. "The Narrative Form of 'Song of Myself,' " *American Transcendental Quarterly*, No. 12 (Fall 1971), 17-20.

ROSS, E. C. "Whitman's Verse." *Modern Language Notes*, XLV, 363-364 (June 1930).
[Importance of punctuation and end-stopped lines.]

SCHUMANN, DETLEV W. "Enumerative Style and Its Significance in Whitman, Rilke, Werfel." *Modern Language Quarterly*, III, 171-204 (June 1942).

SCHYBERG, FREDERIK. *Walt Whitman*. Translated by Evie Allison Allen. New York: Columbia University Press. 1951.

SCOTT, FRED NEWTON. "A Note on Whitman's Prosody." *Journal of English and Germanic Philology*, VII, 134-53 (1908).

TANNENBAUM, KARL. "Pattern in Whitman's 'Song of Myself.' " *CLA Journal*, VI, 44-49 (September 1962).

TEMPLEMAN, W. D. "Hopkins and Whitman: Evidence of Influence and Echoes." *Philological Quarterly*, XXXIII, 48-65 (1954).

WARE, LOIS. "Poetic Conventions in Leaves of Grass." *Studies in Philology*, XXVI, 47-57 (January 1929).

WASKOW, HOWARD. *Whitman: Exploration in Form*. Chicago: University of Chicago Press. 1966.

WEATHERS, WILLIE T. "Whitman's Poetic Translations of His 1855 Preface." *American Literature*, XIX, 21-40 (March 1947).

WEEKS, RUTH M. "Phrasal Prosody" [with special reference to Whitman]. *English Journal*, X 11-19 (January 1921).

WILEY, AUTREY NELL. "Reiterative Devices in 'Leaves of Grass.' " *American Literature*, I, 161-70 (May 1929).
[Rhetorical devices of epanaphora and epanalepsis.]

WILLIAMS, WILLIAM CARLOS. "An Essay on *Leaves of Grass*," pp. 22-31. *Leaves of Grass One Hundred Years After*. Edited by Milton Hindus. Palo Alto: Stanford University Press. 1955.

ANTHOLOGIES OF CRITICISM

Leaves of Grass: One Hundred Years After. Edited with Introduction by Milton Hindus. Stanford: Stanford University Press. 1955.

Whitman: A Collection of Critical Essays. Edited by Roy Harvey Pearce. Englewood Cliffs, N.J.: Prentice-Hall Inc. 1962.

A Century of Whitman Criticism. Edited by Edwin H. Miller. Bloomington: University of Indiana Press. 1969.

Walt Whitman: The Critical Heritage. Edited by Milton Hindus. London: Routledge & Kegan Paul. (Critical Heritage series.) 1971.

Studies in Leaves of Grass. Compiled by Gay Wilson Allen. Columbus, Ohio: Charles E. Merrill Publishing Co. 1972.

Walt Whitman in Europe Today. Edited by Roger Asselineau and William White. Detroit: Wayne State University Press. 1972.

Walt Whitman: A Collection of Criticism. Edited by Arthur Golden. New York: McGraw-Hill, Inc. 1974.

Walt Whitman Quarterly Review, edited by William White and Ed Folsom, publishes essays, reviews, and a "Current Bibliography." Address: 308 EPB, The University of Iowa, Iowa City, Iowa 52242.

SELECTED BIBLIOGRAPHY
Chapter V: World Literature

GENERAL

Walt Whitman Abroad: Critical Essays from Germany, France, Scandinavia, Russia, Italy, Spain and Latin America, Israel, Japan, and India. Edited by Gay Wilson Allen. Syracuse University Press. 1955.
Contents: *Germany*: Introduction by editor; translations of Freiligrath, Hans Reisiger, Thomas Mann, Hermann Pongs. *France*: Introduction by editor; translations of Valéry Larbaud, Jean Catel, Roger Asselineau. *Scandinavia*: Introduction by editor; translations of Knut Hamsun, Johannes V. Jensen, Roland Fridholm, Kjell Krogvig; *Russia and other Slavic Countries*: Introductions by Stephen Stepanchev; translations of Anon. reviewer of Chukovsky, D. Mirsky. *Italy*: Introduction by editor; translations from Giovanni Papini, Cesare Pavese. *Spain and Latin America*: Introduction by editor; translations of José Martí, Cebrïa Montoliu, Miguel de Unamuno, Gilberto Freyre. *Israel*: Introduction by editor; essay by Sholom Kahn. *Japan*: Introduction by editor. *India*: Introduction by editor; essay by V. K. Chari. *Note*: below, this work will be abbreviated WWA.
Walt Whitman in Europe Today: A Collection of Essays. Edited by Roger Asselineau and William White. Detroit: Wayne State University Press. 1972.

Contents: Walt Whitman in *Spain*, by Concha Zardoya; *Germany*, Hans-Joachim Lang; *Belgium*, Guillaume Toebosch; *France*, Marcel Martinet, Jules Romains, Jean Guehenno, Jean Marie Le Clezio; *Italy*, Mariolina Meliadò Freeth; *Czechoslovakia*, Ján Boor; *Jugoslavia*, Sonja Bašić; *Denmark*, Jørgen Erik Nielsen; *Sweden*, Frederic Fleisher; *Iceland*, Leedice Kissane; contributions by Jorge Guillén (*Spain*), Léopold Sédar Senghor (*Senegal*), Chukovsky (*Russia*), Asselineau (*France*), and Pablo Neruda (*Chile*). *Note*: below, this work will be abbreviated WWET.

ENGLAND AND AMERICAN TRANSCENDENTALISM

BLODGETT, HAROLD W. *Walt Whitman in England*, Ithaca: Cornell University Press. 1934.

FROTHINGHAM, O. B. *Transcendentalism in New England*. New York: G. P. Putnam's Sons. 1876.

GODDARD, H. C. *Studies in New England Transcendentalism*. New York: Columbia University Press. 1908.

MUSGROVE, S. *T. S. Eliot and Whitman*. Wellington: New Zealand University Press. 1952.

INDIA

CARPENTER, EDWARD. [The Upanishads and *Leaves of Grass*] *Days With Walt Whitman*, pp. 94-102. London: George Allen. 1906.

CARPENTER, F. I. *Emerson and Asia*. Cambridge: Harvard University Press. 1930.

CHARI, V. K. *Whitman in the Light of Vedantic Mysticism: An Interpretation*. Lincoln: University of Nebraska Press. 1965.

CHRISTY, ARTHUR. *The Orient in American Transcendentalism*. New York: Columbia University Press. 1932.

GUTHRIE, WILLIAM N. *Walt Whitman, Camden Sage*. Cincinnati: Robert Clarke Co. 1897.

MERCER, DOROTHY FREDERICA. *Leaves of Grass* and the *Bhagavad Gita*. Doctoral Dissertation, unpublished. 1933 (See note 52 to Chap. V.)

RAJASEKHARAIAH, T. R. *The Roots of Leaves of Grass: Eastern Sources of Walt Whitman's Poetry*. Rutherford, N. J.: Fairleigh Dickinson University Press. 1970.

GERMANY

CLARK, GRACE DELANO. "Walt Whitman in Germany." *Texas Review*, VI, 123-37 (Jan., 1921).

FALK, ROBERT P. "Walt Whitman and German Thought." *Journal of English and Germanic Philology*, XL, 315-30 (July 1941).

JACOBSON, ANNA. "Walt Whitman in Germany since 1914."*Germanic Review*, I, 132-41 (April 1926).

LAW-ROBERTSON, HARRY. *Walt Whitman in Deutschland.* Giessen: Münchowsche Universitäts. 1935.

LANG, HANS-JOACHIM. See WWET.

LESSING, OTTO EDUARD. "Walt Whitman and His German Critics prior to 1910." *American Collector*, III, 7-15 (October 1926).

POCHMANN, HENRY. "Walt Whitman," *German Culture in America: 1600–1900,* pp. 416-70. Madison: University of Wisconsin Press. 1957.

RIETHMUELLER, RICHARD. "Walt Whitman and the Germans." *The German American Annals*, n. s. IV, nos. 1-3 (January-March, 1906).

THORNSTENBERG, EDWARD. "The Walt Whitman Cult in Germany." *Sewanee Review*, XIX, 71-86 (January 1911).

VON ENDE, AMELIA. "Walt Whitman and Arno Holtz." *Poet Lore*, XVI, 61-65 (Summer 1905).

ZAREK, OTTO. "Walt Whitman and German Poetry." *Living Age*, CCXVI (Vol. XXIX in 8th ser.), 334-37 (February 10, 1923).

FRANCE

BALDENSPERGER, F. "Walt Whitman in France." *Columbia University Quarterly*, XXI, 298-309 (October 1919).

JONES, P. M. "On the Track of an Influence in 1913." *Comparative Literature Studies*, VI-VII, 20-21 (1942).
[Notes on Whitman's influence in France before World War I.]
———. "Whitman and Verhaeren." *Aberystwyth Studies* (University College, Wales), II, 71-106 (1914).
[A very important comparative study.]

LANUX, PIERRE DE. *Young France and New America.* New York: Macmillan. 1917.
[Whitman frequently mentioned.]

PUCCIANI, O. F. *French Criticism of Walt Whitman.* (Doctoral dissertation Harvard University, unpublished, 1943.)

SARRAZIN, GABRIEL. *La Renaissance de la Poésie Anglasie, 1798-1889.* Paris: Perrin, 1889. (Translation, *In Re Walt Whitman*, 159-94).

SCANDINAVIA

ALLEN, GAY WILSON. "Walt Whitman's Reception in Scandinavia." *Papers of the Bibliographical Society of America*, XL, 259-75 (Fourth Quarter 1946).

FLEISHER See WWET.

KISSANE See WWET.

NEILSEN See WWET.

SCHYBERG, FREDERIK. *Walt Whitman.* Translated by Evie Allison Allen. New York: Columbia University Press. 1951.

RUSSIA

CHUKOVSKY See WWET.

MIRSKY See WWA.

STEPANCHEV See WWA, for Russia and Other Slavic Countries.

ITALY

FREETH See WWET.

GRIPPI, CHARLES S. *The Literary Reputation of Walt Whitman in Italy.* (Doctoral dissertation, unpublished, New York University, 1971.

McCAIN, REA. "Walt Whitman in Italy." *Italica*, XX, 4-16 (March 1943).

SPAIN AND LATIN AMERICA

ALEGRÍA, FERNANDO. *Walt Whitman en Hispanoamerica.* Mexico: Ediciones Studium. 1954.

DE MOSHINSKI, ELENA AIZÉN. *Walt Whitman y La America Latina.* Mexico City: Universidad Nacional Autonoma de Mexico. 1950.

DONOSO, ARMANDO. "The Free Spirit of Walt Whitman." *Inter-America*, III, 340-46 (August 1920).

ZARDOYA See WWET.

JAPAN

MATSUHARA, IWAO. "W. Whitman in Japan." *Thought Currents in English Literature* (Aoyama Gakuin University). 1957. (Reprinted in *Norton Critical Edition of* Leaves of Grass, ed. Harold Blodgett and Sculley Bradley, New York: W. W. Norton, 1973, pp. 912-18.)

SADOYA, SHIGENOBU. *Walt Whitman in Japan: His Influence in Modern Japan*. Fukuoka: Bulletin No. 9, Reserach Institute, Seinan Gakuin University. 1969.
[Mostly in Japanese, but in English: "Walt Whitman in Japan (Abstract)," 1-7; Bibliography: Selected Literary Essays and Studies, 9-16; Translations, 16-20 [translations listed.]

TRANSLATIONS

(Selected)

CHINESE

Selections from Whitman's "Leaves of Grass" [title in Chinese]. Translated and Selected by Ch'u T'u-nan. Peking: People's Literary Publishing Society, 1955. 324 pp.

Song of the Open Road and Other Poems [title in Chinese]. Translated by Kao Han. Shanghai: Tu-shu cheu-pan she, 1947. 273 pp.

Whitman: Selections [title in Chinese]. Translated by Chow Tao-Naa. Peking: People's Literary Publishing Society, 1957. 324 pp.

CZECH

Walt Whitman: Demokracie, Zeno Ma! [Democracy, Ma Femme!]. Translated and edited by Pavel Eisner. Prague: Jaroslav Podrouzek, 1945. 181 pp.

Walt Whitman: Pozdrav Svety [Selected Poetry—poetry, prose, and letters]. Translated by Ján Boor. Bratislava: SVKL, 1956, 224 pp.

Pozdrav Svety: Výber z diela. [*Leaves of Grass*, selections, translated by Ján Boor, *Democratic Vistas* by Magda Seppová.] Bratislava: Slovenské Vydavatel'stvo, Krásnej Literatúry. 1956. 224 pp.

DANISH

Walt Whitman: Digte [Poetry—selected]. Translated by Frederik Schyberg. Kφbenhavn: Gyldendal, 1949 (2nd rev. ed.). 133 pp.

Walt Whitman: Fuldkomne Dage [Specimen Days—selections]. Translated by P. E. Seeberg. Kφbenhavn: Steen Hasselbachs Forlag (Hasselbachs Kultur-Bibliotek, Bind XCV), 1950. 55 pp.

DUTCH

Grashalmen [*Leaves of Grass*]. Translated by Maurits Wagenvoort. Amsterdam: Wereld-Biblioteek, 1956 (3rd ed.).

FINNISH

Walt Whitman: Ruohonlehtiá [Selections.]. Translated by Viljo Laitinet. Turku: Suomentajan Kustantama, 1954. 114 pp.

FRENCH

Walt Whitman: Choix de Poèmes. Traduction et préface de Pierre Messiaen. Paris: Aubier [1951]. 354 pp.

Walt Whitman: Feuilles d'herbe (Choix). Introduction et traduction de Roger Asselineau, Paris: Société d'Édition "Les Belles Lettres," 1956. 358 pp.

"Walt Whitman: Fragments politiques inédits en français" [extracts from "The Eighteenth Presidency!", *Democratic Vistas*, and a letter to a would-be Russian translator], *La Nouvelle Critique,* VII (juillet-août 1955), 239-56.

"Walt Whitman, Perspectives Democratiques" [selections from *Democratic Vistas*] in *L'Énigme du Nouveau-Monde.* [Introductory note and translation by Ch. Neveu.] Paris: Flammarion [1946], pp. 41-72.

Walt Whitman: Une Étude, un choix de poèmes. Par Paul Jamati. Paris: Pierre Seghers, 1948. 238 pp.

Whitman [biographical-critical study with translation of selected poetry and prose]. Par Alain Bosquet. Paris: Gallimard (La Bibliothèque Idéale), 1959. 270 pp.

GERMAN

Tagebuch: 1862-1864, 1876-1882 [selections from *Specimen Days*]. Deutsch von Hans Reisiger. Berlin: Suhrkamp Verlag, 1946. 84 pp.

Grashalme [*Leaves of Grass*]. Auswahl von Georg Goyert ins Deutsche übertragen. Berlin: Lothar Blanvalet Verlag, 1948. 106 pp.

Grashalme. In Auswahl neu übertragen von Elisabeth Serelman-Küchler und Walther Küchler. Stuttgart: Dipax Verlag, 1947. 331 pp.

Walt Whitmans Werk [complete *Leaves of Grass*]. Übertragen und eingeleitet von Hans Reisiger. Hamburg: Rowohlt Verlag, 1956. 502 pp.

GREEK

Ἐκλογή ἀπό τά Φύλλα Χλόης. Ἑλληνική Ἀπόδοση Νίκου Προεστόπουλου. "Ἐκλεκτά,,. Βιβλία τῆs Τσέπηs Ἀθῆναι. [n.d.β 1936?] 153 pp.
[Selections from *Leaves of Grass* translated by Nick Proestopoulos]

Φύλλα Χλόηs. Ἑλληνική Ἀπόδοση Νίκου Προεστόπουλου. Προλογικό Σημείωμα Ἀγγέλου Σικελιανοῦ. Βιβλιοπωλεῖον τῆs " Ἑστίαs,,. [Athens, n.d.]
[Complete *Leaves of Grass*, translated by Nick Proestopoulos, Home Bookshop, Athens, undated.]

HEBREW

Aleyesev . . . [*Leaves of Grass being a selection and translation into Hebrew with notes and an essay on the poet's life and work*]. By Simon Halkin. Jerusalem: Workers Book Guild, *1952. 550 pp.*

HUNGARIAN

Fuszálak, Osszes Koltemények. . [Translations by 21 people, edited by Országh László.] [Budapest:] Magyar Helikon. 1964.

INDIAN

Durbadala. [*Leaves of Grass* in the Oriya language.] Orissa, India: Prafulla Chandra Das. 1957. 74 pp.

Hullina Dalagalu. [101 selections from *Leaves of Grass.*] Translated into Kannada by M. Gopalakrishna Adiga. [New Delhi:] Sahitya Akademi. 1966. 222 pp.

Ghah Diyan Pattiyan: Selections from Whitman's *Leaves of Grass.* Translation into Punjabi by Gurbakhsh Singh. [New Delhi:] Sahitya Akademi. 1968. 260 pp.

ITALIAN

Walt Whitman: Foglie d'erba e Prose [*Leaves of Grass* and (selected) Prose]. Traduzione di Enzo Giachino. Torino: Giulio Einaudi, 1950. 958 pp.

Giorni Rappresentativi e Altre Prose [selected prose]. Traduzione di Mariolina Meliadò Freeth. Vicenza: Neri Pozza. 1968.

JAPANESE

Kusa no Ha [*Leaves of Grass*]. Translation and introduction by Shigetaka Naganuma. Tokyo: (vol. I) Nippon Dokusho Kumiai, 1946; (vol. II) Mikasa Shobo, 1950. 354 and 345 pp. (Complete *Leaves of Grass* in 2 vols., based on 1892 text.)

Kusa no Ha. Translated by Saika Tomita. Tokyo: Asahi Shimbun-sha, 1950. 502 pp.

Wago Kuso yo Saraba [*Good Bye My Fancy*]. Translated by Izumi Yanagida. Tokyo: Nippon Dokusho Kumiai, 1947. 295 pp.

[*Whitman's Letters to His Mother and to Jeff*]. Translated by Shigetaka Naganuma. Tokyo: Arechi Shuppan-sha, 1958. 270 pp.

Whitman Shisen [Selected Poems of Whitman]. Translated by Koju Kiguchi and Masao Yahisa. Tokyo: Azuma-shobo, 1949. 279 pp.

Whitman Shishū [Poems—selected]. Translated by Makoto Asano. Tokyo: Sojin-sha. 1953. 294 pp.

Whitman Shishū. Translated by Akira Asano. Tokyo: Kanto-sha (229 pp.) and Sojin-sha (294 pp.), 1950.

Whitman Shishū. Translated by Shogo Shiratori. Nara: Yotoku-sha, Tambashi-machi, 1947, 128 pp.; Tokyo: Oizumi Shoten, 1949, 285 pp.; Tokyo: Shincho-sha (Bunko Series), 1954, 171 pp.

JUGOSLAVIAN (*Serbo-Croatian*)

Vlati Trave [*Leaves of Grass*—selections]. Translated by Tin Ujević; Preface by Gustave Krklec. Zagreb: Zora, 1951. 140 pp.

NORWEGIAN

Walt Whitman: Sangen om Meg Selv ["Song of Myself"] *av Leaves of Grass*. Oversettelse og Innledning ved Per Arneberg. Tegninger [illustrations] av Kai Fjell. Oslo: Forlagt av H. Aschehoug & Co., 1947. 123 pp.

POLISH

Żdżbla Trawy, Poezje Wybrane [*Leaves of Grass*, Selections] Słowe wstepne wybór i opracowanie Juliusz Zuławski. Warsawa: Panstwowy Instytut Wydawniczy. 1966. 233 pp.

Walt Whitman, Poezje Wybrane [selected poetry]. Wyboro dokanałi wstepem opatrzył Hieronim Michalski. Warsawa: Ludowa Społdzielnia Wydawnicza. 1970. 183 pp.

PORTUGUESE

Canção da Estrada Larga. Traducão de Luis Cardim. Lisbon: Cadernos da "Seara Nova" Secção de Textos Literários, 1947. 26 pp.

Cantos de Walt Whitman. Traducão de Oswaldino Marques; introducão de Anibal Machado. Rio de Janeiro: Editora José Olympio, 1946. 88 pp.

Videntes e Sonâmbulos: Coletâneo de Poemas Norte-Americanos [Collection of North American Poems]. [Edited and translated by] Oswaldino Marques. Dio de Janeiro: Ministério do Educacio e Cultura, 1955. Whitman, pp. 36-79.

RUMANIAN

Poeme, Talmaciri. Commenta si Vignete de Margareta Sterian. Bucuresti: Pro Pace, 1945. 38 pp.

Walt Whitman: Opere Alese [Selections]. Traducere si presentare de Mihnea Gheorghiu. Bucureşti: Editură de Stăt Pentru Literatură si Artă, 1956. 592 pp.

RUSSIAN

Uolt Uitmen: List'ya Travy [Walt Whitman: *Leaves of Grass—* selected]. (Introductions by Kornei Chukovsky and M. Mendelson; several translators, including Chukovsky.) Mosco: OGIZ [Government Publishing Office for Belles Lettres], 1955. 355 pp.

SPANISH

Hojas de Hierba [*Leaves of Grass*]. Version directa e integra conforme al texto de la edicion definitiva de 1891-2. Por Francisco Alexander. Quito [Ecuador]: Casa de la Cultura Ecuatoriana, 1953. 603 pp. (Complete *Leaves of Grass*.)

La ultima vez que florecieron las lilas en el patio ["When Lilacs Last in the Dooryard Bloom'd"]. Traducción de Arturo Torres-Rioseco. Mexico City: Coleccion Literaria de la Revista Iberioamericana, 1946. 13 pp.

Saludo al Mundo ["Salut au Monde!"]. Traducción de Gregorio Gasman. Santiago, Chile: Libreria Negra, 1949. 44 pp.

Walt Whitman, Cantor de la Democracia: Ensayo biográfico y breve antologia [Walt Whitman, Poet of Democracy: Biographical Essay and brief Anthology]. Por Miguel R. Mendoza. Mexico City: Secretaría de Educación Pública, 1946. 76 pp.

Walt Whitman: Obras Escogidas: Ensayo Biográficocrítico [selections with a biographical-critical essay]. Versión, notas, y bibliografía de Concha Zardoya; prólogo de John Van Horne. Madrid: M. Aguilar, 1946. 851 pp.

Whitman y Otras Cronicas [Whitman and Other Chronicles]. Selección prólogo y notas de Emilio Abreu Gomez. Washington, D. C.: Unión Panamericana, 1950. "Yo Canto al cuerpo eléctrico de Walt Whitman" ["I Sing the Body Electric"], introducción, traducción y notas por Fernando Alegría, *ARS*, No. 1 (October-December 1951), pp. 47-54.

SWEDISH

Strån av Gräss [*Leaves of Grass*]. Ett urval i översätting och med inledning av K. A. Svensson. Stockholm: A. -B. Seelig & C:o. 1935. 207 pp.

INDEX

Note: "n" after the number indicates "Notes;" "b," "Bibliography;" "q," quoted. For "Bibliography" (pp.378-385) only editions and editors are indexed.